Fostering Inclusive Education With AI and Emerging Technologies

Mageswaran Sanmugam
Centre for Instructional Technology and Multimedia, Universiti Sains Malaysia, Malaysia

Bosede Iyiade Edwards
Universiti Sains Malaysia, Malaysia

Nurul Maziah Mohd Barkhaya
Universiti Sains Malaysia, Malaysia

Zuheir Khlaif
An-Najah National University, Palestine

IGI Global
Publishing Tomorrow's Research Today

Vice President of Editorial	Melissa Wagner
Managing Editor of Acquisitions	Mikaela Felty
Managing Editor of Book Development	Jocelynn Hessler
Production Manager	Mike Brehm
Cover Design	Phillip Shickler

Published in the United States of America by
IGI Global Scientific Publishing
701 East Chocolate Avenue
Hershey, PA, 17033, USA
Tel: 717-533-8845
Fax: 717-533-8661
E-mail: cust@igi-global.com
Website: https://www.igi-global.com

Library of Congress Cataloging-in-Publication Data

Names: Sanmugam, Mageswaran, 1982- editor. | Edwards, Bosede, 1971- editor. | Barkhaya, Nurul Maziah Mohd, 1988- editor. | Khlaif, Zuheir, 1971- editor.
Title: Fostering inclusive education with AI and emerging technologies / Edited by Mageswaran Sanmugam, Bosede Edwards, Nurul Maziah Mohd Barkhaya, Zuheir N Khlaif.
Other titles: Fostering inclusive education with artificial intelligence and emerging technologies
Description: Hershey, PA : IGI Global Scientific Publishing, [2025] | Includes bibliographical references and index. | Summary: ". This book explores how these technologies can be leveraged to foster inclusive education, ensuring equitable learning opportunities for all students, regardless of their physical, cognitive, or socio-economic status"-- Provided by publisher.
Identifiers: LCCN 2024050237 (print) | LCCN 2024050238 (ebook) | ISBN 9798369372555 (hardcover) | ISBN 9798369372593 (paperback) | ISBN 9798369372562 (ebook)
Subjects: LCSH: Inclusive education. | Artificial intelligence--Educational applications. | Youth with disabilities--Education. | Educational equalization. | Education--Effect of technological innovations on.
Classification: LCC LC1200 .F67 2025 (print) | LCC LC1200 (ebook) | DDC 371.9/046--dc23/eng/20241101
LC record available at https://lccn.loc.gov/2024050237
LC ebook record available at https://lccn.loc.gov/2024050238

Vice President of Editorial: Melissa Wagner
Managing Editor of Acquisitions: Mikaela Felty
Managing Editor of Book Development: Jocelynn Hessler
Production Manager: Mike Brehm
Cover Design: Phillip Shickler

British Cataloguing in Publication Data
A Cataloguing in Publication record for this book is available from the British Library.

Table of Contents

Detailed Table of Contents

This chapter delves into the influence of Artificial Intelligence (AI) on inclusive education. This chapter explores how AI might support inclusive education. Moreover, it delves into challenges of this support. To achieve this, a phenomenological qualitative approach is adopted. Experiences with qualitative approach was used. Engaging 45 college instructors from diverse academic specialties, qualifications, and experiences. This study conducted three focus group sessions and 15 semi structured interviews. Thematic analysis was used to analyze data. For opportunities, three themes emerged: AI tailored experience with five subthemes, improved accessibility, and insights into Students' Needs. Three themes also emerged for challenges: algorithm bias, data privacy, and professional development. More empirical studies should be conducted with different groups.

Artificial intelligence (AI) is profoundly transforming the way we live and work, raising ethical, legal, and social questions. This chapter examines the technical and ethical implications of AI in education. Technical challenges are categorized into three key areas: infrastructure and implementation, data collection and management, and the development of tailored algorithms. A contextualized approach and customized training are essential to avoid inappropriate pedagogical decisions. Critical ethical issues include privacy protection, equity, and transparency of AI systems. Three strategic axes for the ethical adoption of AI are presented: establishing appropriate regulatory and policy frameworks, training and raising awareness among relevant stakeholders, and the ethical design of AI systems. The chapter concludes with perspectives on integrating AI into immersive learning environments, requiring a systemic redesign of pedagogical approaches, teacher training programs, and educational curricula.

Artificial intelligence (AI) in education has significantly transformed the methodology of imparting knowledge in classrooms. AI-based education has revolutionized teaching and learning, transitioning from traditional classroom teaching to personalized learning. AI has provided many learning possibilities for students and instructors to discover and implement innovative teaching techniques using technology. The limitations of the conventional educational system will become outdated as AI-generated learning will make classroom instruction easily accessible with just a click. Each time a new technology emerges, there is a concern about its potential for abuse. The advent of AI has brought about a rise in issues that have led to doubts and the gradual decline of the conventional schooling system. The chapter explores the techniques and procedures for incorporating AI into the conventional educational system, promoting a more advanced and improved learning environment. Artificial intelligence has the potential to enhance the online education system significantly.

Students often require personalized attention, yet teachers face challenges with large classes and limited time. Tutoring offers tailored guidance and promotes effective learning. An Intelligent Tutoring System (ITS) serves as an excellent alternative to traditional tutoring. This software simulates a real tutor by presenting problems, offering support, correcting mistakes, and providing encouragement. ITS operates as an intelligent, computer-assisted instructional program and it customized environments for education works most when complemented with a teacher-centric methodology. Teachers play a crucial role in assisting children to learn, helping them navigate new AI-powered platforms, and encouraging creativity and critical thinking. The chapter focuses on the relevance of teacher preparedness and the shifting function of academics in AI-augmented classrooms as it studies the opportunities of ITS and adaptive learning environments to improve the quality of education.

The rise of generative AI in education presents both opportunities and challenges, particularly in the realm of student assessment. This paper examines the transformative impact of generative AI on educational assessment practices, drawing insights from recent training workshops conducted for educators in the Global South. The paper explores how AI can enhance traditional assessment methods by promoting critical thinking, creativity, and collaboration. It introduces innovative frameworks such as AI-resistant assessments and the Process-Product Assessment Model, which focus on evaluating the final output and the student's engagement with AI tools throughout the learning process. The paper also highlights practical strategies for integrating AI into assessment practices, emphasizing the need for ethical AI use and preserving academic integrity.

Artificial intelligence is the ability to design intelligent methods or develop self-learning software suggestions that mimic human traits. This study will reveal pre-service teachers' attitudes toward employing artificial intelligence applications in special educational settings. The descriptive approach was used to achieve the research objectives. The closed questionnaire was applied as a study tool on a random sample of 138 pre-service teachers from Al Qasimi Academy College. The study raises the following questions: What are the attitudes of pre-service teachers towards employing artificial intelligence applications in special educational settings? Do pre-service teachers' attitudes towards employing artificial intelligence applications in special education environments change depending on the type of school, the gender of the pre-service teachers, their ages, and the year of study? The study showed that pre-service teachers' attitudes are neutral in employing artificial intelligence in special education settings. .

This chapter explores the use of the digital divide in inclusive education through multisensory learning and emerging technologies to bridge the digital divide. The researcher examines the concepts, manifestations, and types of the digital divide in Inclusive Education and proposes the content of indicators to evaluate the digital divide. This chapter uses multi-sensory learning and emerging technologies to improve the digital skills of different groups as an important hand in bridging the technological divide, aiming to address the realities of educational inequity, insufficient depth of participation in Education, and digital exclusion due to the technological divide. The paper also explores the implementation of multisensory learning. The thesis also explores the ethical considerations and challenges of implementing multisensory learning and emerging technologies to bridge the technological divide in Inclusive Education. This chapter is useful in further developing the value implications of digital transformation in Education for Inclusive Education.

In rural Nigeria, access to quality education is still a challenge that needs attention, as there are numerous hindrances to the attainment of knowledge. This chapter suggests a transformative paradigm shift that leverages the confluence between artificial intelligence (AI) and mobile technologies in democratizing education and promoting inclusive learning environments. This chapter imagines a future where the gap between digital technology haves and have-nots, will have been closed, by discussing AI powered mobile applications that transcend borders of both geography and economics. The chapter proposes taking advantage of existing telecommunication infrastructure to deliver educational content and facilitate virtual classrooms as mobile devices have become ubiquitous even in remote areas. We imagine a future that sees the removal of barriers such as geography, language and socio-economic status, enabling every Nigerian child access quality education.

In order to provide readers with an overview of, and to summarize, the content of the chapter, the purpose of the research discussed is stated as to gain an understanding of technology integration in an inquiry-based learning (IBL) classroom, concerning how South African Grade 12 Life Sciences teachers use relevant technologies to accommodate their learners' needs, difficulties, and cognitive capabilities. Against the background of the power of persuasive educational technologies in enhancing learning, the chapter will discuss e.g., games and gamification, higher education, early childhood education and Artificial Intelligence (AI).

The inclusion of digital technology into the study of languages has revolutionised approaches to education, especially in multicultural environments, at a period that has witnessed swift progress in technology. The study examines the impact of technological innovations on improving the learning of the English language for a wide range of learners, including individuals with challenges and different levels of fluency. This study investigates a range of technology tools and platforms, including language learning apps, versatile software, and augmented reality (AR), that are designed to meet the diverse learning styles and educational requirements of individuals. The study examines scenarios and current research to demonstrate that technological advances may improve mobility, offer personalised learning experiences, and facilitate inclusive educational opportunities. The results emphasise the capacity of technology to address disparities in language acquisition, encourage active participation, and advance equal access to education.

With the rapid advancement in educational technology, the integration of artificial intelligence has transformed language learning environments. However, the impact of these technologies on learning among multilingual young learners remains underexplored. This study investigates the effectiveness of integrating AI technologies in enhancing learning among multilingual young learners. Qualitative data were collected from 17 primary school students in Istanbul, Turkiye, through observations and semi-structured interviews following interactive gameplay sessions with Duolingo. Findings revealed that AI-driven language tools improve comprehension, engagement, sentence formation, pronunciation, vocabulary acquisition, and writing skills, particularly when instructions are provided in learners' native languages.

Preface

As the world rapidly advances into the era of artificial intelligence (AI) and emerging technologies, education faces a pivotal transformation. This shift presents both opportunities and challenges, especially when it comes to fostering inclusivity in learning environments. *Fostering Inclusive Education With AI and Emerging Technologies* explores the dynamic intersection of AI, technology, and education, aiming to reimagine how we can create equitable, accessible, and adaptive learning spaces for all students, regardless of their backgrounds or abilities.

In this book, educators, researchers, and practitioners will find a comprehensive examination of how AI can reshape inclusive education. From personalizing learning experiences to addressing digital divides, each chapter delves into critical aspects of using technology to enhance learning outcomes while maintaining ethical and pedagogical integrity.

Chapter 1 begins by exploring the opportunities AI offers in fostering inclusivity, such as tailored learning and improved accessibility, while also addressing significant challenges like algorithmic bias, data privacy concerns, and the professional development needs of educators.

Chapter 2 expands on these themes by focusing on the technical challenges and ethical considerations of AI in education, offering solutions to navigate the complexities of AI integration in schools, including infrastructure and regulatory frameworks.

Chapter 3 redefines the role of teaching in the age of AI, illustrating how generative AI can revolutionize the classroom, enhance personalized learning, and potentially lead to the gradual decline of traditional educational systems if not approached thoughtfully.

Chapter 4 explores Intelligent Tutoring Systems (ITS) and adaptive learning environments, emphasizing the importance of a teacher-centric approach to fully harness AI's potential in classrooms, where human guidance remains essential.

The focus shifts in **Chapter 5** to how AI is reshaping educational assessment, promoting creativity and critical thinking through innovative models such as AI-resistant assessments and the Process-Product Assessment Model, which focus on both the learning journey and outcomes.

Chapter 6 highlights the use of AI to enhance learning in primary education, presenting a systematic review of how AI innovations can foster inclusive learning experiences and make education more accessible to all learners.

In **Chapter 7**, young learners are introduced to AI and coding, providing an engaging and practical guide to creating basic AI applications using platforms like Scratch and Blockly, inspiring early interest in technology and lifelong learning.

Chapter 8 investigates pre-service teachers' attitudes toward using AI in special education, revealing neutral perspectives and identifying key factors influencing their views. This chapter offers insights into the future role of AI in supporting special education environments.

Chapter 9 tackles the digital divide, offering strategies for using multisensory learning and emerging technologies to bridge gaps in digital access and participation, particularly for underrepresented and disadvantaged groups.

Chapter 10 turns to rural Nigeria, proposing transformative ways to democratize education using AI and mobile technologies to overcome barriers of geography and socioeconomic status, envisioning a future where every child has access to quality education.

Chapter 11 examines the use of AI in technology-integrated, inquiry-based learning in South African classrooms, focusing on how educators use digital tools to meet the diverse needs of Grade 12 learners in Life Sciences.

Chapter 12 explores how technological innovations, including language learning apps and augmented reality, are improving English language learning in multicultural and inclusive settings, making education more accessible for all students.

Chapter 13 closes the book by examining the impact of AI-driven tools in enhancing learning for multilingual young learners, particularly in English as a Foreign Language (EFL) settings, highlighting how AI fosters improved comprehension and engagement.

Together, these chapters offer a holistic view of how AI and emerging technologies can be leveraged to build more inclusive, adaptive, and equitable education systems. The contributions in this book not only highlight the current state of AI in education but also provide a roadmap for future innovations and challenges. By embracing these technologies thoughtfully and ethically, we can pave the way for a future where every learner has the opportunity to thrive in an inclusive educational landscape.

Mageswaran Sanmugam

Universiti Sains Malaysia

Acknowledgment

The editor would like to extend their deepest gratitude to all those who contributed to the successful completion of this book, Fostering Inclusive Education With AI and Emerging Technologies. First and foremost, sincere thanks go to the authors for their groundbreaking research, dedication, and perseverance. Their valuable insights and innovative contributions have been instrumental in shaping this volume and advancing our understanding of how AI and emerging technologies can transform inclusive education.

The editor is also profoundly grateful to the editorial team for their unwavering support and guidance throughout the publication process. Their professionalism, attention to detail, and commitment to excellence have been invaluable in bringing this project to life.

A special note of appreciation is extended to the reviewers, whose meticulous feedback and constructive evaluations were essential in ensuring the quality, depth, and rigor of the content. Their thoughtful insights have greatly enhanced the scholarly value of this work.

The editor wishes to acknowledge the educators, researchers, and practitioners who generously shared their experiences and knowledge. Their contributions enriched the discussions presented in this book and provided real-world perspectives on the challenges and opportunities that come with integrating AI into inclusive education.

This collaborative effort would not have been possible without the collective support, dedication, and expertise of each and every one of you. Your contributions have made this project a success, and for that, the editor is deeply thankful.

Chapter 1
Inclusive Education in the Artificial Intelligence Era:
Opportunities and Challenges

Reham Ahmed Salhab
https://orcid.org/0000-0002-3457-389X
Palestine Technical University – Kadoorie, Palestine

ABSTRACT

This chapter delves into the influence of Artificial Intelligence (AI) on inclusive education. This chapter explores how AI might support inclusive education. Moreover, it delves into challenges of this support. To achieve this, a phenomenological qualitative approach is adopted. Experiences with qualitative approach was used. Engaging 45 college instructors from diverse academic specialties, qualifications, and experiences. This study conducted three focus group sessions and 15 semi structured interviews. Thematic analysis was used to analyze data. For opportunities, three themes emerged: AI tailored experience with five subthemes, improved accessibility, and insights into Students' Needs. Three themes also emerged for challenges: algorithm bias, data privacy, and professional development. More empirical studies should be conducted with different groups.

INTRODUCTION

Education ought to be impartial and equitable, ensuring that it is accessible to all individuals regardless of their identity or social standing. There's been a heightened global interest in inclusive education spurred by the United Nations' 2030 Sustainable Development Goals (SDGs), notably SDG 4, which underscores quality education as a fundamental human right. This principle prioritizes equal value of all students,

DOI: 10.4018/979-8-3693-7255-5.ch001

acknowledges education as a catalyst for other rights, and aims to dismantle barriers to education access. Inclusive educational approaches nurture the confidence, skills, and potentials of every child while respecting their dignity (Salhab, 2023). Recent educational policies emphasize accommodating the diverse needs of all students, fostering learning within the same community (Joubert & Harrington, 2020). Inclusive education rejects discrimination, ensuring that every student has equal access to education without preconditions. The "Education for All" movement aims to support marginalized individuals who have been denied their right to education or are at risk of marginalization. Consequently, there' should be a focus on addressing opportunities and challenges hindering the fulfillment of this goal.

This interest in addressing this challenge stems from the shortcomings observed in traditional classroom environment. In many educational institutions, teachers face problems during delivery of information to a large number of students within a limited timeframe, aiming for successful outcomes in assessments. However, achieving this is often hindered by various factors, including differences in learning styles, prior knowledge levels, cognitive abilities, emotional dispositions, and individual learning needs among students. The fields of Artificial Intelligence in Education (AIED) have emerged to tackle this issue head-on since their formal inception in the late 1980s (Mohammed & Nell Watson, 2019). Both areas of research strive to develop intelligent software tutors tailored to promote inclusive learning requirements of every student.

In today's critical pursuit of achieving educational fairness, there's a growing emphasis on harnessing the advancing AI capabilities to foster inclusive education. It's widely acknowledged that establishing fair and accessible educational systems is crucial for building equitable and progressive societies. Therefore, strategically leveraging AI tools has the potential to significantly promote accessibility and quality of education, paving the way for more inclusive learning opportunities, especially for marginalized or underprivileged communities. For example, AI's adaptive learning systems with their predictive analytics offer a considerable opportunity to revolutionize the delivery and reception of education, creating environments that cater to the diverse needs and abilities of students globally. Moreover, integrating AI into educational platforms holds the promise of improving personalization and accessibility, potentially overcoming barriers that have impeded educational advancement for various groups (Aguilar et al., 2021). It's envisaged that with AI's capabilities, we could witness a transformation in educational settings where personalized learning plans become standard, facilitating a tailored approach to teaching that acknowledges and embraces the diverse spectrum of learners in our societies.

The Rationale of the Study

It is imperative to offer quality education for all students. Since AI as new technologies possesses the potential to transform the way things are done, it is important to understand how they can be used to support inclusive education. Many students with diverse interests should be offered the chance to learn differently by utilizing AI. Hence, the objective of this chapter to is explore potentials and challenges of integrating AI in inclusive education.

Significance of the Study

This chapter aims to encourage the integration of AI into inclusive education within higher education institutions. It will assist decision-makers within these institutions in understanding the challenges faced by college instructors when implementing AI in inclusive education. By identifying these challenges, opportunities for success can be pinpointed, highlighting the importance of offering college instructors opportunities to enhance their understanding and expertise in this area.

As such, in this chapter, our objectives are to investigate opportunities and challenges of AI integration in inclusion education discuss future research directions. The rest of the chapter is structured as follows: The next section gives an overview of AI in inclusive education.

Theoretical Framework

The core concern is how AI platforms reinforce specific notions of "learning" by incorporating particular concepts into their design and operation. These data-driven educational platforms often rely on radical behaviorist ideas of learning, reflecting the influence of psychologist B.F (Knox et al., 2024). Skinner's theories, which have seen a resurgence. Historically, Skinner's radical behaviorism fell out of favor in education due to its view of the human mind as a blank slate and education as a means of environmental control to shape desired behaviors. Skinner argued that education's role in the "struggle for freedom" was not to eliminate control but to analyze and alter the types of control people experience.

This emphasis on external control and lack of interest in the mind's inner workings became outdated in educational theory, especially with the rise of cognitivism and constructivism in the early 1990s. Most modern educators view learning as an ongoing social and relational process, drawing on the work of scholars like Illeris and Lave and Wenger. However, as Watters (2017) notes, "behavior design" seems to be re-emerging, now through AI-driven educational technologies that aim to customize digital environments to "nudge" and guide students toward specific learning objectives or performance metrics. This approach is evident in "adaptive" and "personalizing" platforms offered by companies many AI.

LITERATURE REVIEW

Inclusive Education

Due to the NCLB act, there's been increased recognition of the importance of enacting human rights protocols by the Palestinian National Authority to ensure that all children and individuals with disabilities are afforded their rights, notably inclusive and fair education. Nonetheless, the Israeli occupation has severely damaged Palestine's infrastructure, causing economic turmoil and leaving certain areas with minimal government assistance. This has led to ineffective regulations and laws, hindering the implementation of inclusive education in schools. The educational system and overall development in Palestine have suffered greatly from more than 70 years of military control, with violence escalating notably since October 2015 (UNRWA, 2021). Studies on the effects of violent conflicts indicate that violence negatively impacts various educational metrics such as enrollment, attendance, and achievement (Assefa et al., 2022; Budianti et al., 2023; Kotamena et al., 2024). Consequently, the economic situation in Palestinian territories remains bleak, with projected growth insufficient to enhance living standards (World Bank, 2024). Amidst this backdrop, widespread ignorance, stigma, shame, and bias towards disability pose significant obstacles to inclusive education efforts. A study conducted by Chitiyo et al. (2024) necessitated to reconsider the curriculum and practicum for upskilling special and general educators to focus on inclusive practices and strategies to prepare teachers to excel in inclusive education settings and to influence school-based strategies to advance inclusionary practices.

Meanwhile, Uthus and Qvortrup (2024) explained the primary difficulty in increasing inclusive education which lies in finding a middle ground between recognizing and addressing the individual distinctions among students while promoting equality and uniform treatment, However, they mentioned achieving inclusivity demands substantial financial investment from society and must be sustainable over the long haul. Additionally, they mentioned that insufficient customization heightens the risk of student exclusion and attrition, potentially leading to enduring societal costs. Indeed, the task of integrating a diverse student body into regular classrooms also demands considerable resources. Similarly, Zabeli and Gjelaj (2020) and Nazaretsky et al (2023) added that some challenges that face teachers to build inclusive environments that they have no proper and sufficient skills and knowledge of the learning method for teaching students with special needs.

AI in Inclusive Education

Artificial intelligence involves creating computer systems that can carry out tasks typically requiring human intelligence (Gibellini et al., 2023) There are three categories of AI: narrow AI, general AI, and artificial superintelligence. Narrow AI is the most prevalent and developed form so far. It is highly focused and employs machine learning to accomplish a single specific task, such as image and facial recognition or virtual assistants like Siri and Alexa. General AI, also known as deep AI, is considered to be on par with human intelligence, capable of understanding the needs and emotions of other intelligent beings. Lastly, artificial superintelligence surpasses human capabilities in all aspects (Marrone et al., 2022).

In the educational context, the development of artificial intelligence is likely to stay focused on narrow AI. Current educational technologies encompass speech semantic recognition, image recognition, Augmented Reality/Virtual Reality, machine learning, brain neuroscience, quantum computing, blockchain, and more. These technologies are quickly being incorporated into classrooms. A growing number of artificial intelligence education products are being utilized in higher education settings (Yufeia et al., 2020). These tasks encompass learning from experience, recognizing patterns, making decisions, and adapting to new information (Helem, 2020). There is a transformative shift due to AI integration into education with significant implications for its role in fostering a more inclusive and equitable education system. The swift and significant changes in the workforce due to AI advancements highlight the crucial need for AI literacy as a fundamental skill for future citizens (Ng et al., 2021). Recognizing that today's students will become tomorrow's workforce emphasizes the importance of making AI education more inclusive and accessible in educational institutions (Long & Magerko, 2020). This is vital for increasing participation in AI careers, fostering diversity, and driving economic progress in related sectors (Fidalgo & Thorrmann, 2024; Gibellini et al., 2023; Henriksen et al., 2024). Research suggests that diverse groups, including individuals of various genders, races, and cultural backgrounds, excel in conflict resolution within organizations and are more inclined to consider diverse perspectives in decision-making, thereby avoiding groupthink. Given these findings, there is a growing societal demand for greater equity and inclusion in educational institutions (Gaither et al., 2018; Vought, 2018).

Previous studies (Roshanaei et al., 2023; Searson, 2024) in AI era showed how it has the capacity to enhance personalized learning, thereby potentially enhancing educational outcomes among varied student demographics. Additionally, adaptive learning environments powered by AI hold promise in significantly enhancing individual learning achievements through tailored content and learning trajectories that cater to a range of learning styles and speeds. A similar study of Mallory

(2024) who mentioned that AI empowers educators to design dynamic, engaging, and personalized learning experiences that connect with every student, regardless of their unique circumstances or special needs. These tools, from automating lesson plans to producing customized educational content, are transforming what can be achieved in classrooms and tutoring sessions. They explained how AI, with its adaptability and personalization features, offers a promising solution for special education students to develop individualized, student-centered content and provides valuable lessons applicable to all learners. Many advantages were reported by previous studies (ElNaggar et al., 2024; Khazanchi, & Khazanchi, 2024; Salsa-Pilco et al., 2024) such as enhancing academic performance for minority students, offering personalized feedback, enhancing self-efficacy. Similarly, Kazimzade et al. [72] highlighted that technology could be advantageous in inclusive education by boosting students' performance and competence. Similarly, Zhang and Zang (2024) reported that AI can positively influence inclusive teaching by supporting classroom management that enhances inclusive learning environments and enriches digital skills by personalizing teaching strategies, and strengthening social relationship between teachers and students.

On the other hand, Salsa-Pilco identified how AI offer pedagogical and technological that satisfy the needs of minority student by offering contextualized technologies that are customized to minorities' diverse contexts and sociocultural solutions to facilitate the inclusion of minority groups. Focusing on the advantages of AI for inclusive education. more efforts in terms of dynamic paths and flexibility are needed. For example, a study conducted by Bulathwela et al. (2024) suggested a collaborative culture that involves a networked community of educators, trainers, lifelong learners, and community that integrate Open Educational Resources (OERs) which offers pedagogical opportunities to enhance teaching and learning environments. This is will enable learners to co-create learning material and access knowledge which will foster a culture of openness and democratize inclusive education.

Additionally, study conducted by Kakish et al., (2022) showed that predictive analytics for customized interventions utilizing AI, can lead to enhance educational equity for students at risk. Also, a study Gligorea et al., 2023 who conducted a systematic review investigating AI and adaptive learning and found that the integration of AI in e-learning platforms significantly contributes to effective personalization of learning process which improves engagement and motivation through interactive learning experiences, potentially decreasing dropout rates. By incorporating features such as gamification and customized information, they can boost student motivation and determination, resulting in better learning outcomes.

Moreover, the emergence of AI has substantially reshaped the educational realm, providing greater accessibility, especially for students facing disabilities. Many studies Khazanchi and Khazanchi, (2024) and Marino et al. (2023) have emphasized the significance of AI in the creation of tools such as screen readers and Braille translators, which have notably improved educational accessibility for visually impaired students. Speech-to-Text Technologies Studies have demonstrated that AI-powered speech-to-text technologies have played a crucial role in aiding students with hearing impairments, granting them enhanced access to learning materials and classroom discussions. AI-integrated Learning Management Systems (LMS) can be customized to address the varied needs of students with disabilities, facilitating an inclusive learning environment.

After examining the relevant literature concerning the topic of this chapter, it became evident that there is a scarcity of studies conducted in this area. Consequently, it is believed that this chapter will enrich the literature by employing a qualitative approach and gathering data to evaluate the challenges encountered by Palestinian college instructors regarding inclusive education in higher education institutions. The current chapter aims to achieve the following objective: identifying opportunities and challenges that faces inclusive education in Palestinian colleges from the point of view of their instructors.

Research Questions

What are the opportunities and challenges of integrating AI for college students in inclusive education from college instructors?

Methodology

A qualitative research method was conducted as it aligns well with the study objectives in studying the perspectives of inclusive education among college instructors. Furthermore, phenomenology was chosen for the qualitative method because it reflects on a lived experience with a specific group or object to arrive at a more profound and deep understanding of the phenomenon which is AI in this chapter (Patten & Newhart, 2017).

Additionally, a phenomenological approach is used in this chapter to investigate the lived experience of a group of PTUK college instructors AI in their teaching. As a result, the researcher is digging deeper into the meaning of college instructors' lived experiences with the phenomenon of AI; the phenomenological approach was the best choice for this particular study.

Participants

The researcher recruited a diverse sample of college instructors by sending inquiries to different colleges at a Palestinian university. Two focus groups and a semi structured interview with 15 participants will be conducted. This chapter aims to explore the lived experiences of college instructors' students who use AI in their teaching practices at Palestine Technical University Kadoorie (PTUK). These college instructors are the only group at the university with firsthand experience using AI applications in education. Participants were selected for based on their experiences with AI. Specifically, small groups of 8, 8, and 9 college instructors were chosen forming three focus groups. The sampling strategy was purposeful, selecting participants with at least five years of university teaching experience, and with prior experience using AI in their courses. Purposive sampling was used to ensure participants provided relevant data for the study (Merriam & Tisdell, 2015). According to Creswell and Poth (2016), a phenomenological study should have 5-25 participants, with a sample size of 6 to 20 being considered adequate. In line with Creswell's guidelines, 25 participants were selected for this phenomenological investigation. This number of participants was deemed sufficient to achieve both code saturation and meaning saturation (Hennink et al., 2017). Some variables are held constant like experience with AI and technical skills to increase credibility of the findings.

Data Collection

Data was collected by using two tools. The first tool is the three focus group sessions.

The second tool is 15 semi structured interviews. The focus group sessions and interview transcripts will be carefully examined to identify and categorize themes from these texts. Initially, the focus groups with teachers will be analyzed to extract primary codes. These codes will then be transformed into themes.

Credibility and Trustworthiness

Member checking and peer debriefing were used to enhance the credibility of the findings. Feedback from participants during member checking sessions helped confirm the accuracy of the interpretations of their experiences, ensuring the analysis reflected their perspectives. Peer debriefing involved discussions with colleagues to critically review the research process and findings, providing diverse viewpoints and insights that strengthened the study's rigor. Additionally, triangulating data sources, such as semi-structured interviews and focus groups, provided multiple perspectives on the phenomena under investigation, further enhancing the study's credibility. Transparent and systematic data analysis procedures, including thorough coding and thematic analysis, were followed to ensure consistency and rigor in interpreting the findings. These methodological strategies collectively contributed to the study's robustness and increased its credibility and trustworthiness.

Data Analysis

This chapter utilizes phenomenological approach to better understand how AI could be used to support inclusive education. The information was gathered using verbatim transcriptions of focus group discussions and individual interviews. Information was gathered through focus group discussions and interviews, was used to identify major themes and categories of potentials and challenges of using AI in inclusive education.

Content analysis of semi-structured interviews and focus group transcripts using inductive method. The content analysis includes an abstraction process and material grouping in order for the researchers to use inductive reasoning to respond to the research questions (Kyngäs, 2020). Inductive analysis is used to generate the categories that emerge from participant responses. The constant comparison analysis method was used to analyze data and identify recurring themes and actions, as well as to aid in the explanation of aspects of how AI is used in inclusive education. This enables the researcher to assess both across-group saturation and saturation in general. To code the data, the researcher used Creswell's (2013) six-step approach First, data from focus group discussions and interviews were transcribed and organized. Second, data was analyzed to determine the tone and get a general sense of the ideas. Third, code statements by inserting segment and text data into them and categorizing and labeling them. Fourth, discuss themes. Fifth, data representation, and finally, data interpretation.

Results

AI and Inclusive Education: Opportunities

AI presents a multitude of opportunities for bolstering inclusive education by customizing learning experiences, improving accessibility, and offering insights into students' individual needs.

1. Tailored Learning Experiences

One of AI's most significant advantages in inclusive education is its capacity to personalize learning experiences. AI-driven platforms can analyze student data, encompassing their learning preferences, capabilities, and progress, to devise customized learning paths. This empowers educators to furnish each student with learning experiences tailored to their specific needs and preferences.

For instance, an AI-powered platform could identify a student grappling with reading comprehension and recommend targeted interventions like supplementary reading materials or structured support. Similarly, AI could identify a mathematically adept student and propose stimulating activities to sustain their engagement and motivation.

Personalized Learning

Instructor 2 suggested "the use of AI to tailor learning experiences to individuals, sparking a shift in my perspective. I envisaged AI fostering connections among learners globally, learners collaborating on shared topics regardless of geographical boundaries which is facilitated by AI, I do believe that AI has the potential in making learning more inclusive."

Adaptive Learning:

AI facilitates adaptive learning, which involves customizing instruction content, pace, and feedback to align with each learner's capabilities, objectives, and preferences. Adaptive learning systems utilize data and algorithms to track learners' progress, identify their strengths and weaknesses, and offer personalized support and guidance. This approach assists learners in addressing knowledge gaps, mastering skills at their own speed, and attaining improved educational outcomes. Additionally, adaptive learning supports individuals with special needs, including those with disabilities, learning challenges, or language barriers, by delivering accessible and suitable content and feedback.

Instructor 8 acknowledged the diversity in learning styles and underscores AI's potential to enhance educational fairness. She envisioned AI-driven adaptive learning "as a means to efficiently generate multiple course versions and automate grading, emphasizing practical application as a key indicator of expertise."

Instructor highlighted the significant impact of AI-driven adaptive learning on enriching educational experiences. He emphasizes the transformative nature of tailored content, pace, and feedback in teaching methods, particularly in addressing individual learning gaps and supporting students with special needs.

Instructor 10 suggested "utilizing free generative AI platforms as personalized tutors, outlining parameters for setting up AI-driven tutoring sessions. He emphasizes AI's potential to effectively cater to individual learning requirements."

Collaborative Learning

AI also supports collaborative learning, which entails learning with and from others through social interaction and cooperation. Collaborative learning boosts motivation, engagement, and social skills while fostering community. AI facilitates collaborative learning by creating virtual or augmented reality environments for interactive engagement and providing intelligent mentors or peers for feedback and guidance.

Instructor 11 reported: "through my teaching experience, I've noted how AI significantly enhances collaborative learning dynamics among my students. Collaborative learning, with its emphasis on social interaction and cooperation, emerges as a potent catalyst for boosting motivation, engagement, and social aptitude, thereby fostering a cohesive classroom community"

Creative Learning

AI fosters creative learning, encouraging the generation of novel ideas through exploration and experimentation. Creative learning stimulates curiosity, imagination, and problem-solving skills. AI provides tools and platforms for creating and sharing digital artifacts, offering feedback and suggestions to enhance creativity.

Instructor 10 said "As a college instructor, I've observed how AI profoundly fosters creative learning among my students. Creative learning, which encourages the exploration of novel ideas through experimentation and expression, has the capacity to spark curiosity, imagination, and innovation while refining critical thinking and problem-solving skills."

AI acts as a potent driver for creative learning by equipping students with tools and platforms to create and distribute their digital creations, whether in the realm of gaming, storytelling, or artistic expression. These avenues for self-expression empower students not just to absorb knowledge but to actively participate in its creation, instilling a sense of ownership over their learning journey.

Ethical Learning

AI helps learners understand the ethical implications of AI usage itself and its societal and environmental impact.

Instructor 3 commented “I’ve learned to appreciate the crucial impact AI can have on fostering ethical learning among students. Ethical learning, centered on cultivating values, principles, and responsibilities guiding interactions with oneself, others, and society, is fundamental for nurturing moral awareness, reasoning, and empathy. When utilized with care, AI emerges as a potent instrument for promoting ethical learning through diverse means.

Primarily, AI can broaden learners' horizons by introducing them to a wide spectrum of perspectives, cultures, and contexts.

Lifelong Learning

AI supports lifelong learning by offering personalized learning pathways, guiding learners through relevant experiences, and validating their achievements. Lifelong learning fosters personal and professional growth, adaptability, and resilience

Instructor 9 “As an educator, I've seen firsthand how AI has revolutionized lifelong learning, a crucial concept in our rapidly changing world. Lifelong learning, the ongoing process of acquiring new skills and knowledge throughout life, is essential for personal and professional development. AI plays a pivotal role in this endeavor by offering tailored learning paths and adaptable approaches, empowering individuals to navigate a dynamic landscape marked by innovation and evolution.”

AI provides quality learning experiences tailored to the diverse needs of all students, regardless of their backgrounds, abilities, or requirements. In this discourse, we'll delve into the opportunities and challenges presented by the integration of AI in supporting inclusive education.

2. Improved Accessibility

AI can also enhance the accessibility of educational content for students with diverse needs.

Instructor 2 said: “ AI-driven speech recognition and text-to-speech technologies aid students with hearing impairments in accessing audio content. Likewise, AI-driven image recognition and description tools assist visually impaired students in comprehending visual materials.”

Moreover, AI can facilitate the creation of personalized learning environments for students with cognitive or learning disabilities, such as dyslexia or autism. Adaptive learning platforms powered by AI can present content in varied formats, colors, or layouts to cater to each student's preferences and needs, thereby enhancing accessibility and engagement with learning materials.

3. Insights into Students' Needs

Another advantage of AI in inclusive education is its ability to offer insights into students' needs. AI algorithms can analyze extensive data generated by students during their learning journey, encompassing their interactions with learning materials, responses to assessments, and engagement patterns. This analysis unveils patterns and trends that can inform educators about students' strengths, weaknesses, and areas requiring attention.

For instance, instructor 5 stated " AI can help educators identify students at risk of falling behind or disengaging, enabling early intervention and targeted support. Additionally, AI can aid educators in monitoring the progress of students with special needs, ensuring they receive the requisite accommodations and support to thrive."

AI and inclusive education: Challenges

Despite the vast opportunities AI presents for inclusive education, it also poses several challenges, including concerns regarding data privacy, algorithmic bias, and the necessity for professional development.

1. Data Privacy

Privacy of student data is a major concern surrounding AI in education.

Instructor 3 "AI systems rely on substantial amounts of student data to operate effectively, often containing sensitive information about students' abilities, backgrounds, and requirements. Safeguarding student privacy is imperative to prevent misuse or compromise of this information."

To address this challenge, educational institutions must implement robust data security measures like data encryption and secure storage solutions. Additionally, clear policies and guidelines should be established for the collection, storage, and utilization of student data, ensuring compliance from all stakeholders.

2. Algorithmic Bias

Another challenge in leveraging AI for inclusive education is the potential for algorithmic bias. AI algorithms are trained on extensive datasets, and if these datasets harbor biases, the AI systems may inadvertently perpetuate or exacerbate existing inequalities. For example, instructor 7 said " Unfortunately, an AI-powered platform using biased data to devise personalized learning paths could disadvantage certain student demographics, such as those from underrepresented backgrounds or with specific disabilities."

To mitigate algorithmic bias, it's crucial to ensure that datasets used to train AI systems are diverse and representative of all students. Moreover, AI systems should undergo regular auditing and evaluation to ensure fairness, transparency, and accountability.

3. Professional Development

Effective implementation of AI in inclusive education necessitates adequate professional development for educators. Educators need to comprehend how to utilize AI tools effectively, interpret their outputs accurately, and integrate them into teaching practices to support inclusive education.

Instructor 8 said "professional development initiatives should concentrate on enhancing educators' understanding of AI and its potential applications in inclusive education. Additionally, they should offer educators hands-on experience with AI tools, enabling them to explore their benefits and limitations and gain proficiency in their effective use."

Discussion

To answer the first question which is related to opportunities of AI integration in inclusive education, three themes emerged with a main theme of tailored learning experiences. It appears from the results that one of AI's most significant advantages in inclusive education is its capacity to personalize, adapt learning experiences. AI provides quality learning experiences tailored to the diverse needs of all students, regardless of their backgrounds, abilities, or requirements. This is in line with several studies of Morris (2020) and Roshanaei et al. (2023) who highlighted the influence of AI based learning systems in promoting personalized learning and showed that AI algorithms have the ability to analyze data of students. Hence, AI based learning systems can customize content delivery by addressing various learners; needs and styles effectively. It seems that AI not only creates a more individualized learning experience, but also fosters an environment where students can progress at their own pace, avoiding feelings of being left behind. Additionally, Gligorea et al. (2023) suggest that AI-facilitated personalized learning systems improve student engagement and academic learning outcomes. As AI continues to develop, it holds the promise of further promoting equity in education by offering inclusive learning experiences for students from diverse backgrounds and with varying needs. It seems that AI technologies can transform education by encouraging creativity, providing personalized learning experiences, and enabling collaborative problem-solving.

However, to achieve this potential, educators, policymakers, and technology developers must work together to address the challenges discussed in this paper and create frameworks that ensure the responsible and equitable use of generative AI in educational settings (Searson, 2024).

Moreover, this conquers with Kakish et al. (2022) found that AI hold promise in adaptive learning by enhancing individual learning achievements through tailored content and learning trajectories that cater to a range of learning styles and speed. More specifically, LMS that is integrated with AI, was found supportive for special needs student in this study. AI integrated LMS systems can be adapted to meet the diverse needs of students with disabilities, facilitating an inclusive learning environment. Other subthemes of tailoring learning experiences like AI makes learning more collaborative, creative, ethical, and life -long.

It seems that AI assumes a central role in facilitating collaborative learning by generating immersive virtual or augmented reality settings, enabling learners to interact with each other and lifelike simulations of real-life situations. These interactive encounters offer students more than just a platform for gaining knowledge; they provide a dynamic arena where they can actively collaborate, and solve problems. This is in line with Kim et al. (2022) anticipated that AI has a role in collaborative learning that has been positioned mainly three-fold: learning with AI, learning about AI, and learning together. This in turn will foster inclusive education since collaborative learning was found potentially effective means of promoting the academic and social development of students in inclusive education (Vollinger & Supnac, 2020).

Participants also mentioned the role of AI tools in fostering inclusive education by supporting creative learning. Essentially, the abilities of AI tools, such as natural language processing, predictive analytics, and pattern recognition, are relevant as technological affordances that can foster creative and sustainable learning environments (Henriksen et al., 2024).

Ethical learning was found as a subtheme of tailored learning while using AI. AI promotes ethical learning by exposing learners to diverse perspectives and challenging them to reflect on their beliefs and actions. Ethical learning cultivates moral awareness, reasoning, and empathy. A study conducted by Railton (2020) investigating artificial intelligence and highlighted the potential of AI to develop autonomous human-level skills. Students might similarly develop independent social and ethical abilities through comparable processes. Rather than encoding ethics directly into robots, this chapter suggests that artificial systems could achieve ethical competence through general-purpose learning, akin to how infants partially learn human ethics by observing adult behavior.

Interestingly, many participants also reported that AI promoting tailored learning is life-long learning. Different learners with diverse views experience the AI influence differently in unique ways, according to their specific interests, goals, and motivations within the field. These perspectives are shaped by varying social, political, and economic contexts, leading to distinct interpretations of AI unique to each social group of learners. These diverse viewpoints and related practices in AI development and application significantly impact the design and experiences within lifelong learning. However, engaging diverse groups of learners in AI and lifelong learning holds the potential for inclusive education.

The last subtheme of tailoring learning while using AI is supporting creative learning. Using AI, you can create innovative and varied outputs like music, art, or stories that can ignite your imagination and boost your creativity. This finding is supported by L Markauskaite et al. (2022) and Morren et al. (2020). These authors highlighted that AI can execute routine cognitive tasks much faster than humans. Consequently, humans will need to advance their cognitive work to areas where AI is less proficient. Knowledge practices like sense-making and meaning-making will become increasingly significant. Additionally, creative activities such as brainstorming and divergent thinking will become more crucial skills. By exposing students to AI technologies with its various applications, instructors can better satisfy students' needs and equip them with diverse tools they need to thrive in a data-driven environment.

Another theme that was found is improved accessibility for special needs students. It seems that participants reported that AI-enabled applications can facilitate hands-free internet navigation for individuals with mobility challenges. Voice command technology, for instance, allows users to browse websites, type, and perform various tasks without the need for a keyboard or mouse (Khan, 2024). AI can play a crucial role in making websites and applications accessible to individuals with various disabilities. By simulating the use of a website or application with screen readers and other assistive technologies, AI can identify potential barriers that could hinder people with disabilities from effectively using the software.

For the second question in this chapter that related to challenges of fostering Ai in inclusive education. Three themes emerged: algorithm bias, data privacy, and professional development. While AI offers numerous opportunities to promote inclusive education, its integration comes with significant challenges.

Many participants mentioned that these critiques present according to their experiences. One of the most significant concerns regarding the integration of AI in inclusive education is data privacy. AI systems require the collection and analysis of large volumes of data to function effectively, which can lead to misuse and privacy breaches. Previous literature (Roshanaei et al., 2023) highlighted increasing apprehension about how personal information is handled, stored, and potentially exploited. Moreover, integrating AI technologies in education involves collecting sensitive information, including students' behavioral patterns, learning styles, and academic progress.

This raises concerns about potential surveillance and the commodification of personal data. Additionally, the risk of data leaks and unauthorized access adds complexity, necessitating robust data protection frameworks to safeguard students' privacy and prevent misuse. Beyond data privacy concerns, other challenges exist as well like algorithm bias. For example Bozkurt et al.(2021) reported that some issues in AI is that data can be susceptible to bias. Moreover, AI algorithms are created by programmers and developed by organizations or governments, which may introduce their own agendas or biases during the development process.

Professional development is another challenge that face fostering AI in inclusive education. Educating employees about data protection best practices and potential risks associated with AI plays a critical role in ensuring data protection. Regular training sessions should be provided to employees that introduce them to data privacy best practices, explain potential threats, and how to act and respond to security incidents.

Nazaretsky et al. (2022)in their study explained that professional development helps enhance the culture of security within the organization and makes every individual aware of their responsibility to protect data and handle it carefully and consciously. In addition, continuous communication between employees, information security management and data administrators can be enhanced for continuous knowledge sharing and providing necessary guidance in the event of security challenges or data breaches.

The examination of the challenges and opportunities presented by integrating generative AI into inclusive education highlights the necessity of a comprehensive and cooperative approach to leverage AI's transformative potential in inclusive teaching and learning. By addressing ethical issues, ensuring accessibility and equity, overcoming technical barriers, and embracing AI's innovative possibilities, educators can foster more engaging, personalized, and inclusive learning environments. This will help empower students to thrive in a rapidly changing world.

CONCLUSIONS

Artificial intelligence holds immense promise for bolstering inclusive education by personalizing learning experiences, enhancing accessibility, and providing insights into students' individual needs. This paper thoroughly explores the role of AI in education, highlighting its potential advantages and challenges. On the positive side, AI introduces promising innovations such as personalized learning experiences, adaptive learning, collaborative learning, creative learning, and enhanced accessibility for students with special needs. However, the integration of AI also presents challenges, including concerns about data privacy, the risk of exacerbating existing educational inequalities, and technical hurdles.

However, as we integrate AI into inclusive education, we must navigate challenges surrounding data privacy, algorithmic bias, and professional development, ensuring ethical, responsible, and effective utilization of AI. With meticulous planning and thoughtful implementation, AI can emerge as a potent tool for advancing inclusive education, paving the way for a more equitable and inclusive future for all students. In essence, the introduction of AI into education marks the beginning of a new era that will require educators to not only innovate and adapt, but also to reshape teaching and learning approaches. The potential for a more dynamic, responsive, and accessible learning environment is held by the synergistic link between AI and inclusive education, which will eventually pave the way for a more inclusive and equitable digital future.

Implications

The results of this study emphasize the significance of incorporating AI to enhance inclusive education. Policymakers and educators should take into account the implications of adopting AI in inclusive education and devise strategies to overcome challenges while optimizing the benefits of AI technologies in teaching and learning.

Limitations

This study has several limitations. Firstly, it was confined to higher education college instructors. Some confounding variables like gender, years of experience, and technical skills since they interfere with college instructors' views of AI. Secondly, while the focus groups and interviews offered rich and detailed insights, additional empirical studied could have provided even deeper insights.

Conflict of Interest: The authors declare no conflict of interest.

ACKNOWLEDGMENT

Thanks to Palestine Technical University-Kadoorie for the granted financial support and funding this paper. We really appreciate PTUK support for the scientific research.

REFERENCES

Aguilar, J., Garces-Jimenez, A., R-moreno, M., García, R. J. R., & Reviews, S. E. (2021). A systematic literature review on the use of artificial intelligence in energy self-management in smart buildings. *151*, 111530. DOI: DOI: 10.1016/j.rser.2021.111530

Assefa, Y., Tilwani, S. A., Moges, B. T., & Shah, M. A. (2022). The impact of armed violence on students' educational attainment and the role of parents in resilience schooling and the education process. *Heliyon*, 8(12), e12192. DOI: 10.1016/j.heliyon.2022.e12192 PMID: 36536914

Bozkurt, A., Karadeniz, A., Baneres, D., Guerrero-Roldán, A. E., & Rodríguez, M. E. (2021). Artificial intelligence and reflections from educational landscape: A review of AI Studies in half a century. *Sustainability (Basel)*, 13(2), 800. DOI: 10.3390/su13020800

Budianti, Y., Ruwaidah, R., & Megawati, B. (2023). Violence in Education: A Bibliometric Analysis from Scopus Database. *Jurnal Basicedu*, 7(3), 1637–1648. DOI: 10.31004/basicedu.v7i3.4844

Bulathwela, S., Pérez-Ortiz, M., Holloway, C., Cukurova, M., & Shawe-Taylor, J. (2024). Artificial intelligence alone will not democratise education: On educational inequality, techno-solutionism and inclusive tools. *Sustainability (Basel)*, 16(2), 781. DOI: 10.3390/su16020781

Chitiyo, J., Brobbey, G., & Asare, K. B. (2024). Teacher Attitudes and Perceptions of Inclusive Education: A Case of Ghana. *Journal of International Special Needs Education*, 27(1), 23–35. DOI: 10.9782/JISNE-D-23-00008

Cresswell, J. (2012). Educational research: Planning, conducting, and evaluating quantitative and qualitative research.

Creswell, J. W., & Clark, V. L. P. (2017). *Designing and conducting mixed methods research*. Sage publications.

El Naggar, A., Gaad, E., & Shannaiah, A. M. I. (2024). Enhancing inclusive education in the UAE: Integrating AI for diverse learning needs. *Research in Developmental Disabilities*, 147, 104685. DOI: 10.1016/j.ridd.2024.104685 PMID: 38330845

Fidalgo, P., & Thormann, J. (2024). The Future of Lifelong Learning: The Role of Artificial Intelligence and Distance Education. DOI: DOI: 10.5772/intechopen.114120

Gaither, S. E., Apfelbaum, E. P., Birnbaum, H. J., Babbitt, L. G., & Sommers, S. R. (2018). Mere membership in racially diverse groups reduces conformity. *Social Psychological & Personality Science*, 9(4), 402–410. DOI: 10.1177/1948550617708013

Gibellini, G., Fabretti, V., & Schiavo, G. (2023). Ai education from the educator's perspective: Best practices for an inclusive ai curriculum for middle school. In Extended abstracts of the 2023 CHI conference on human factors in computing systems (pp. 1–6).

Gligorea, I., Cioca, M., Oancea, R., Gorski, A.-T., Gorski, H., & Tudorache, P. (2023). Adaptive Learning Using Artificial Intelligence in e-Learning: A Literature Review. *Education Sciences*, 13(12), 1216. DOI: 10.3390/educsci13121216

Helm, J., Swiergosz, A. M., Haeberle, H. S., Karnuta, J. M., Schaffer, J. L., Krebs, V. E., Spitzer, A. I., & Ramkumar, P. N. (2020). Matthew, Swiergosz Andrew M., Haeberle Heather S., Karnuta Jaret M., Schaffer Jonathan L., Krebs Viktor E., Spitzer Andrew I., Ramkumar Prem N. Machine learning and artificial intelligence: Definitions, applications, and future directions. *Current Reviews in Musculoskeletal Medicine*, 13(1), 69–76. DOI: 10.1007/s12178-020-09600-8 PMID: 31983042

Hennink, M. M., Kaiser, B. N., & Marconi, V. C. J. Q. h. r. (2017). Code saturation versus meaning saturation: how many interviews are enough?, *27*(4), 591-608

Henriksen, D., Mishra, P., & Stern, R. (2024). Creative Learning for Sustainability in a World of AI: Action, Mindset, Values. *Sustainability (Basel)*, 16(11), 4451. DOI: 10.3390/su16114451

Joubert, R., & Harrington, I. (2020). Inclusive Education: Origins,'Defectology', and Kosovo's Experiences of Inclusive Education. *International Journal of Higher Education*, 9(1), 52–59. DOI: 10.5430/ijhe.v9n1p52

Khan, M. R. (2024). Role of AI in Enhancing Accessibility for People with Disabilities. *Journal of Artificial Intelligence General science (JAIGS) ISSN: 3006-4023, 3*(1), 281-291. DOI: DOI: 10.60087/jaigs.vol03.issue01.p142

Khazanchi, R., & Khazanchi, P. (2024). Generative AI to improve special education teacher preparation for inclusive classrooms. *Exploring New Horizons: Generative Artificial Intelligence and Teacher Education, 159.*

Kim, J., Lee, H., & Cho, H. (2022). Learning design to support student-AI collaboration: Perspectives of leading teachers for AI in education. *Education and Information Technologies*, 27(5), 6069–6104. DOI: 10.1007/s10639-021-10831-6

Knox, J., Wang, Y., & Gallagher, M. (2019). Introduction: AI, inclusion, and 'everyone learning everything'. *Artificial intelligence and inclusive education: Speculative futures and emerging practices*, 1-13.

Kotamena, F., Sinaga, P., Sudibjo, N., & Hidayat, D. (2024). Student use behavior in determining majors: Is it determined by self-congruity, social influence, information usefulness, through mediating information adoption, and behavioral intention. *Computers in Human Behavior Reports*, 14, 100383. DOI: 10.1016/j.chbr.2024.100383

Kyngäs, H. (2020). Inductive content analysis. In *The application of content analysis in nursing science research* (pp. 13–21). Springer. DOI: 10.1007/978-3-030-30199-6_2

Leifler, E. (2020). Teachers' capacity to create inclusive learning environments. *International Journal for Lesson & Learning Studies.*

Lina, M., Rebecca, M., Oleksandra, P., Simon, K., Roberto, M.-M., Sarah, H., Jo, T., Maarten, D. L., Buckingham, S. S., & Dragan, G.. (2022). Rethinking the entwinement between artificial intelligence and human learning: What capabilities do learners need for a world with AI? *Computers and Education: Artificial Intelligence.*, 3, 100056. DOI: 10.1016/j.caeai.2022.100056

Liu, Y., Salmiza, S., Huang, J., & Mohamad, S. S. (2020). Review of the Application of Artificial Intelligence in Education. *International Journal of Innovation. Creativity and Change.*, 12, 548–562. DOI: 10.53333/IJICC2013/12850

Long, D., & Magerko, B. (2020). What is ai literacy? Competencies and design considerations. In *Proceedings of the 2020 CHI conference on human factors in computing systems* (pp. 1–16). DOI: 10.1145/3313831.3376727

Mallory, J. (2024, March). Empowering Special Needs STEM Students Through Unique Generative AI Tools: A Path to Inclusive Learning. In *Society for Information Technology & Teacher Education International Conference* (pp. 2156-2161). Association for the Advancement of Computing in Education (AACE).

Marino, M. T., Vasquez, E., Dieker, L., Basham, J., & Blackorby, J. (2023). The future of artificial intelligence in special education technology. *Journal of Special Education Technology*, 38(3), 404–416. DOI: 10.1177/01626434231165977

Marrone, R., Taddeo, V., & Hill, G. (2022). Creativity and artificial intelligence—A student perspective. *Journal of Intelligence*, 10(3), 65. DOI: 10.3390/jintelligence10030065 PMID: 36135606

Merriam, S. B., & Tisdell, E. J. (2015). *Qualitative research: A guide to design and implementation*. John Wiley & Sons.

Mohammed, P. S., & 'Nell' Watson, E. (2019). Towards inclusive education in the age of artificial intelligence: Perspectives, challenges, and opportunities. *Artificial Intelligence and Inclusive Education: Speculative futures and emerging practices*, 17-37.

Morris, M. R. (2020). AI and accessibility. *Communications of the ACM*, 63(6), 35–37. DOI: 10.1145/3356727

Nazaretsky, T., Ariely, M., Cukurova, M., & Alexandron, G. (2022). Teachers' Trust in AI-Powered Educational Technology and a Professional Development Program to Improve It. *British Journal of Educational Technology*, 53(4), 914–931. DOI: 10.1111/bjet.13232

Ng, D. T. K., Leung, J. K. L., Chu, K. W. S., & Qiao, M. S. (2021a). Ai literacy: Definition, teaching, evaluation and ethical issues. *Proceedings of the Association for Information Science and Technology*, 58(1), 504–509. DOI: 10.1002/pra2.487

Patten, M. L., & Newhart, M. (2017). *Understanding research methods: An overview of the essentials*. Routledge. DOI: 10.4324/9781315213033

Roshanaei, M., Olivares, H., & Lopez, R. R. (2023). Harnessing AI to Foster Equity in Education: Opportunities, Challenges, and Emerging Strategies. *Journal of Intelligent Learning Systems and Applications*, 15(04), 123–143. DOI: 10.4236/jilsa.2023.154009

Salas-Pilco, S. Z., Xiao, K., & Oshima, J. (2022). Artificial intelligence and new technologies in inclusive education for minority students: A systematic review. *Sustainability (Basel)*, 14(20), 13572. DOI: 10.3390/su142013572

Searson (2024). Generative AI to improve special education teacher preparation for inclusive classrooms. *Exploring New Horizons: Generative Artificial Intelligence and Teacher Education, 159.*

United Nation Relief and Work Agency for Palestine Refugees in the Near East(UNRWA). 2021.Schools on the front line the impact of armed conflict and violence on UNRWA schools and education services. Accessed 25 May 2024 https://www.unrwa.org/sites/default/files/content/resources/gazawb_flashappeal-eng-final.pdf

Uthus, M., & Qvortrup, A. (2024). Lessons learned from Norway: A values-based formulation of inclusive education. *European Journal of Special Needs Education*, •••, 1–15. DOI: 10.1080/08856257.2024.2354603

Völlinger, V. A., & Supanc, M. (2020). Student teachers' attitudes towards cooperative learning in inclusive education. *European Journal of Psychology of Education*, 35(3), 727–749. DOI: 10.1007/s10212-019-00435-7

Vought, R. T. (2018). Charting a course for success: America's strategy for stem education. Wang, P. (2019). On defining artificial intelligence. *Journal of Artificial General Intelligence*, 10, 1–37.

Watters, A. (2017). Education Technology and the New Behaviourism. Hack Education, July 29. Available: https://hackeducation.com/2017/12/23/top-ed-tech-trends-social-emotional-learning

World Bank. 2024. Delivering Education in the Midst of Fragility, Conflict, and Violence (FCV). Accessed May 2024. https://www.worldbank.org/en/topic/education/brief/education-in-fragile-conflict-violence-contexts

Zhang, J., & Zhang, Z. (2024). AI in teacher education: Unlocking new dimensions in teaching support, inclusive learning, and digital literacy. *Journal of Computer Assisted Learning*, 40(4), 1871–1885. DOI: 10.1111/jcal.12988

Chapter 2
Adopting AI in Education: Technical Challenges and Ethical Constraints

Mehdi Kaddouri
https://orcid.org/0000-0001-7696-0276
Mohamed First University, Morocco

Meriem Marhraoui
https://orcid.org/0009-0004-5994-5794
Mohammed First University, Morocco

Khalid Mhamdi
https://orcid.org/0009-0007-3994-7743
Mohammed First University, Morocco

Mohamed Khaldi
https://orcid.org/0000-0002-1593-1073
Mohammed First University, Morocco

Ilham Chniete
https://orcid.org/0000-0003-1126-3028
Mohammed First University, Morocco

Sabrine Jmad
https://orcid.org/0009-0008-1400-1457
Mohammed First University, Morocco

ABSTRACT

Artificial intelligence (AI) is profoundly transforming the way we live and work, raising ethical, legal, and social questions. This chapter examines the technical and ethical implications of AI in education. Technical challenges are categorized into three key areas: infrastructure and implementation, data collection and management, and the development of tailored algorithms. A contextualized approach and customized training are essential to avoid inappropriate pedagogical decisions. Critical ethical issues include privacy protection, equity, and transparency of AI systems. Three strategic axes for the ethical adoption of AI are presented: establishing appropriate regulatory and policy frameworks, training and raising awareness among relevant stakeholders, and the ethical design of AI systems. The chapter concludes with perspectives on integrating AI into immersive learning environments, requiring

DOI: 10.4018/979-8-3693-7255-5.ch002

a systemic redesign of pedagogical approaches, teacher training programs, and educational curricula.

INTRODUCTION

Artificial intelligence (AI), which traces its origins back to the 1950s, is undergoing a remarkable expansion across various sectors of society. This groundbreaking technology has become pervasive in nearly every aspect of our daily lives, influencing fields as diverse as healthcare, education, transportation, and entertainment. Its impact is reshaping our world and redefining the possibilities of human achievement. To fully grasp the significance of AI, it is crucial to understand its fundamental components and underlying principles.

Attempts at an Expanded Definition of AI

AI is a branch of computer science that develops systems capable of performing tasks typically requiring human intelligence. It extends beyond imitating human cognitive functions to include various techniques and technologies. These systems encompass:

- Machine learning is available as "supervised, unsupervised, and reinforcement learning". Machines learn from data, without being explicitly programmed.
- Computer vision translates into object recognition, object detection and tracking, image segmentation, and 3D reconstruction, giving machines the ability to interpret and analyze the visual components of the environment (Szeliski, 2022).
- Advanced robotics designs machines that can interact seamlessly with humans and their environment.
- Deep learning uses artificial neural networks to learn and extract complex, high-level features from raw data. This data is often unstructured or semi-structured.
- Predictive analytics is deployed through data mining and distributed learning, to anticipate trends and future behaviors.
- Intelligent agents can perceive their environment, and enable decision-making and action autonomously in various contexts (Russell & Norvig, 2021).

These artificial intelligence systems can perceive and interpret environmental elements, process collected information and data, learn and adapt based on experiences, and make independent decisions to perform specified tasks. This comprehensive definition of AI highlights its transformative influence across various facets of society, reshaping how we live, work, and interact. As a catalyst for innovation and advancement, AI is creating new opportunities in diverse fields such as healthcare, education, transportation, and industry. Its potential appears boundless, and its impact on everyday life is expanding rapidly. Nonetheless, the rise of AI introduces complex ethical, legal, and social challenges. It is crucial to consider the implications for employment, including job automation and the creation of new career paths. Additionally, safeguarding user privacy and personal data, as well as ensuring the ethical and equitable use of AI, are pressing concerns that require careful consideration.

Figure 1. History of Artificial Intelligence in Education (Class Point, 2023)

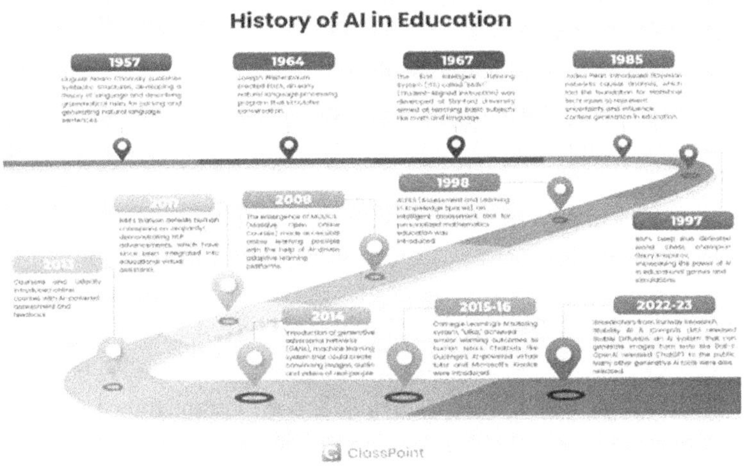

To tackle these challenges, it is crucial that AI development proceeds in a manner that is both responsible and beneficial for all of humanity. This involves establishing robust regulatory frameworks and ethical guidelines to ensure fair and inclusive use, developed through international and interdisciplinary cooperation. The adaptability and versatility of AI contribute to its expanding presence across numerous sectors and its significant transformation of our daily lives and interactions.

Overview of Technical and Ethical Issues Related to AI in Education

The accuracy and robustness of AI algorithms are fundamental for delivering reliable and relevant results in educational contexts. Ensuring data security is paramount to protect sensitive user information and maintain trust. The interoperability of AI systems is crucial for seamless integration with other educational and technological platforms, which facilitates a consistent and smooth user experience. Scalability is essential for AI systems to handle increasing numbers of users and larger volumes of data effectively. By addressing these technical aspects, the educational sector can fully harness the potential of AI to enhance learning experiences and outcomes.

In addition to these considerations, there are ethical concerns raised by various actors directly or indirectly involved in the use of AI in education and other sectors involving human interactions. These concerns relate to fundamental issues such as:

- Respect for the privacy and protection of learners' personal data;
- Fairness and inclusion in access to AI-based educational technologies;
- Transparency, explainability, and interpretability of algorithms used in decision-making processes;
- The potential impact on learners' autonomy and cognitive development;
- The risks of bias and discrimination inherent in AI systems;
- Responsibility and accountability in case of errors or questionable decisions made by AI;
- The long-term impact on human skills and the job market.

TECHNICAL CHALLENGES OF AI IN EDUCATION

The technical challenges addressed in this section focus on three key areas relevant to the educational field: infrastructure and implementation, data collection and management, and the development of algorithms tailored to education. We will explore the hardware and software requirements necessary to effectively integrate AI into learning environments, taking into account the specific constraints of educational institutions. Additionally, we will analyze the challenges related to the secure acquisition, storage, and processing of educational data, with an emphasis on privacy and regulatory compliance. Finally, we will examine the design and optimization of AI algorithms specifically crafted to meet educational needs, ensuring their relevance, effectiveness, and adaptability to diverse educational contexts.

Infrastructure and Implementation

The successful integration of AI in education rests on three essential infrastructural pillars, each presenting its challenges and opportunities: adequate computer equipment, reliable high-speed Internet access, and dedicated AI software and educational platforms (Peng et al., 2022). This triadic infrastructure forms the foundation upon which educational AI innovations can be effectively built and deployed while taking into account ethical considerations and accessibility for all learners.

Computer Equipment Required

To successfully integrate AI into education (Díaz and al. 2024), it is essential to have adequate computing equipment. This includes high-performance computers and dedicated servers with high-performance processing capabilities to handle AI applications. Servers should be equipped with high-performance multi-core processors, with a minimum of 16 cores, and a generous amount of RAM, at least 128 GB. To optimize AI-related computations, it is highly recommended to incorporate cutting-edge graphics cards (GPUs). Storage devices such as SSDs for frequently accessed data and NAS for long-term storage are essential to manage the data flows generated by AI applications. It is also vital to ensure system compatibility and provide robust solutions for data backup and recovery, including automated backup systems, to maintain data integrity and availability (Peng, 2022).

For increased flexibility and adaptability to evolving project needs, cloud solutions specialized in artificial intelligence, offering dedicated and scalable resources, could be the optimal choice. Moreover, it is crucial to consider the ergonomics and accessibility of the equipment for all learners, including those with specific needs, to guarantee inclusive learning experiences. Peripherals such as cameras and microphones are necessary for data capture and interaction (Holmes et al., 2022).

Internet Access

A reliable and stable high-speed Internet connection, ideally through fiber optics or equivalent advanced technology, is essential for the optimal use of AI tools in education. Educational institutions, in collaboration with governing authorities, can set up appropriate network infrastructures (high-performance switches and routers) capable of handling the significant data flow generated by AI. The recent White House executive order emphasizes the importance of this requirement by calling for substantial investments in AI-related infrastructure for education (The White House, 2023).

The installation of a high-performance and secure Wi-Fi network with complete coverage, using Wi-Fi 6 access points or higher, greatly benefits educational stakeholders. These systems, combined with next-generation firewalls and intrusion detection and prevention systems (IDS/IPS), contribute to securing access to AI resources.

Ensuring equitable access to the Internet remains a major challenge. A collaborative approach between educational institutions, local authorities, and service providers can help ensure adequate connectivity, including in rural or disadvantaged areas, for all potential users. The report by the Task Force on an AI Research Resource (NAIRR) also highlights the importance of democratizing access to AI resources to stimulate innovation in education (National Artificial Intelligence Research Resource Task Force, 2023).

This perspective is reinforced by the NSF's call for proposals for AI Research Institutes, which emphasizes the need for a robust infrastructure to support AI research and education (National Science Foundation, 2023).

AI Software and Platforms

To effectively meet the needs of educators and learners, it is crucial to make appropriate choices of AI software and platforms for educational use. Compatibility with existing computer systems and regular updates of digital tools are essential to optimize their use and benefit from the latest technological advances (Holmes et al., 2022). Upfront evaluation of this compatibility promotes the successful adoption of new technologies, optimizes performance, and prevents potential problems. Note that a rigorous selection of these tools helps identify solutions best suited to different educational contexts, covering various levels of education and different disciplinary fields.

Educational institutions should conduct thorough and systematic evaluations to confirm the compatibility of the AI software with their existing IT infrastructure (Holmes et al., 2022). This proactive approach facilitates the successful adoption of new technologies, optimizes performance, and avoids potential issues related to technical incompatibilities, unforeseen additional costs, and disruptions to the institution's operations. Notable examples of AI platforms include Carnegie Learning for mathematics, Duolingo for language learning, and Century Tech for personalized learning. Ensuring these tools align with institutional needs and technical capabilities is vital for maximizing their educational impact.

Several AI platforms stand out in the educational landscape. Carnegie Learning continues to innovate in mathematics education with the integration of generative AI. Duolingo has evolved considerably, offering increasingly personalized language learning paths. Century Tech has expanded its capabilities to a wider range of subjects, analyzing individual learning styles in depth.

Aligning these tools with institutional needs and technical capabilities maximizes their educational impact, often leading to significant improvements in learner engagement, learning outcomes, and pedagogical effectiveness.

The current trend shows an evolution towards more open and interoperable AI platforms, allowing institutions to customize and adapt tools to their specific needs. This increased flexibility facilitates the integration of AI into various aspects of the educational experience, from administrative management to classroom teaching and online learning, thus opening new perspectives for pedagogical innovation and continuous improvement of educational processes.

Maintenance and Technical Support

The optimal utilization of AI infrastructures in education necessitates continuous support, regular technical maintenance, and monitoring. This requires a dedicated technical team composed of system administrators, data security experts, and user support specialists to ensure appropriate technical assistance for both learners and educators. This team is tasked with the regular updating of digital tools, such as adaptive learning platforms, Learning Management Systems (LMS), AI-driven tutoring systems, and virtual reality applications, to maintain their relevance and efficacy amid rapid technological advancements. They also intervene to promptly and effectively resolve technical issues, ensuring uninterrupted service delivery. Furthermore, the technical team, in collaboration with educators, administrators, and IT departments, ensures constant performance optimization for a fluid and engaging user experience. They manage proactive security measures and data protection, addressing the particularly sensitive nature of these issues in the educational context. As Zalavra (2022) emphasizes, the effective management of these AI infrastructures is crucial not only to guarantee the quality of the learning experience but also to maintain user confidence in these advanced educational systems. By minimizing downtime and enhancing the personalization of learning experiences, these efforts significantly contribute to improved learning outcomes.

This proactive strategy involves continuous monitoring of systems, anticipating potential problems, and preventive intervention before difficulties arise or worsen. For example, predictive analytics can be used to identify potential misuse of the system and predict risks of technical infrastructure failure before they affect users. The principles of proactive management are directly linked to quality factors that influence learner satisfaction in an online learning environment, such as system quality, information quality, and service quality. Continuous monitoring and timely system updates can significantly enhance system quality by ensuring smooth operation and minimizing downtime.

These improvements contribute to ensuring system quality, information reliability, and service efficiency, which in turn promote learner satisfaction and their intention to continue using online learning tools adaptively. Consequently, this reinforces the argument that proactive management of AI infrastructures is essential to ensure a satisfactory and sustainable online learning experience. By anticipating and addressing potential issues before they impact users, proactive management creates a more stable, reliable, and effective learning environment, ultimately enhancing the overall educational experience.

Moreover, investing in continuous training for technical and pedagogical staff ensures optimal use of AI tools and rapid adaptation to new features. Zawacki-Richter et al. (2019) highlight the urgent need for educator training in the field of AI in education. The comprehensive and collaborative approach to maintenance and technical support not only contributes to system reliability but also to their sustainable adoption and effective integration into educational practices. Consequently, it greatly enhances student engagement and optimizes learning outcomes.

Data Collection and Management

To optimize the use of AI infrastructures in education, educational institutions are encouraged to implement effective processes for the ethical and secure collection, storage, and analysis of learning data. This begins with establishing a robust technical infrastructure, including reliable servers and advanced analytical tools, to efficiently manage large data volumes (Larini & Barthes, 2019). Concurrently, institutions should define clear and transparent policies for data collection and use, prioritizing learner privacy and informed consent (Organization for Economic Cooperation and Development, 2016).

Staff training plays a crucial role in this process. Personnel benefit from education in data management best practices, security protocols, and ethical considerations to ensure responsible data use (Fernández & al., 2023). Adhering to data protection regulations such as the GDPR (European Commission, 2023) is equally important, requiring the implementation of vigorous security measures to safeguard sensitive information.

Interoperability is another key consideration. The adoption of recognized standards like xAPI or SCORM (Advanced Distributed Learning Initiative, 2022) facilitates seamless data exchange between different educational systems and platforms, creating a more integrated and efficient learning ecosystem. To oversee these various aspects, institutions could establish an educational data governance committee at the institutional level. This committee would be responsible for overseeing management practices, ensuring compliance with regulations and standards, and promoting a culture of responsible data use throughout the organization.

By focusing on these aspects, institutions can create a solid foundation for leveraging learning data to improve educational outcomes while maintaining ethical standards and data security. This approach enables the effective integration of AI in education, harnessing the power of Big Data to revolutionize the educational landscape (Lis, 2023).

Big Data in Education

The educational sector is presented as a particularly fertile field for Big Data technologies (Shen et al., 2023). This new digital reality is characterized by three important aspects, often referred to as the "3Vs" in the context of education (Daniel, 2015): volume, which refers to the massive amount of data accumulated; variety, which encompasses the multiplicity of types and origins of information; and velocity, which describes the sustained pace at which these data are produced and analyzed.

Educational institutions, across all levels, generate significant amounts of data on their management, learner activities, and the activities of academic, technical, and administrative staff. Intelligent exploitation of this data allows for a nuanced understanding of learning mechanisms and continuous improvement of pedagogical practices. However, the use of Big Data also raises crucial questions regarding the quality, relevance, and ethics of data collection and utilization.

Collection and exploitation of big data from learners and the educational process. The use of digital technologies in education generates a considerable amount of data on learners and their interactions with their educational environments. This data can be categorized as follows:

Demographic and contextual data. Learners' demographics and contextual data play a crucial role in profiling target audiences and in explaining their educational pathways. This piece of information refers to age, gender and educational level. These can influence learners' learning styles and pedagogical needs. The socio-economic background of the latter can determine their access to educational resources and their academic success. Indicators on the geographical location of learners can highlight regional disparities in terms of accessibility and educational inclusion.

Digital Traces. Digital traces are a crucial component of learning analytics, which aims to measure, collect, analyze and report data about learners and their contexts, for purposes of understanding and optimizing learning and the environments in which it occurs (Siemens & Long, 2011). The digital traces are produced voluntarily or involuntarily by a user during their activity on the Internet and digital devices. Voluntary traces include social media posts, comments on forums, or online purchases, while unintentional traces are generated automatically by computer devices. In a highly digitalized educational context that integrates the technological advances of AI, these digital traces are of paramount importance. The digital traces of learners on educational platforms are indeed a rich source of information to observe and analyse their learning behaviours in digital environments. This data includes traces of their browsing within the platforms. Examining these traces helps to identify the learning paths and resources accessed by each learner. Indicators relating to the time spent by the learner on each activity or educational resource provide information on his or her level of commitment and the difficulties encountered. The number of attempts required to complete an activity sheds light on the level of perseverance of learners as well as the knowledge that requires more attention. An appropriate analysis of digital traces allows a better understanding of learners' behaviours and attitudes, and can contribute significantly to the improvement of pedagogical practices and the personalisation of learning (Viberg et al., 2018).

Assessment Results. In the digital age, the assessment of learning is significantly enhanced by the collection and analysis of learners' academic results. Data from assessments, quizzes, assignments, and other evaluation methods provide a robust quantitative database that precisely measures learners' academic performance. This analysis extends beyond mere scores, offering a comprehensive view of learners' difficulties. By identifying common errors and patterns, it allows for a more nuanced understanding of where students struggle, enabling educators to adjust their teaching strategies to better address the actual needs of their audience. Tracking learners' performance sheds light on their individual learning journeys, highlighting phases of progression or stagnation in relation to established educational standards. This detailed monitoring supports targeted interventions and personalized learning experiences, ultimately fostering better educational outcomes. Adaptive learning systems, which use this data to tailor instruction to individual learners, have shown promising results in improving learning outcomes (VanLehn, 2011)

Participation in online activities. The active online presence of learners is a key indicator of their involvement in the delivery of digital learning activities. This presence takes several forms: the connection to the digital work environment (ENT), and the duration of connection to the ENT, which are signs of learners' attendance and commitment. However, interactions on discussion forums, synchronous discussion spaces and online collaboration are the richest indicators capable of providing information on the level of involvement of learners, the degree of mastery of teamwork skills in a virtual environment and on their overall engagement in scripted learning activities at the ENT level. The question is to what extent does data on learners' participation and online activities offer many opportunities to analyse and optimise pedagogical practices? This concept of digital engagement is crucial in understanding how learners interact with technology-mediated learning environments (Henrie et al., 2015).

Opportunities for analysis and optimization of pedagogical practices. Once processed and analyzed following ethical and legal standards, the vast amount of data collected during online teaching and learning activities can significantly enhance our understanding of educational processes from both the learner's and the teacher's perspectives. This data can help identify recurring difficulties faced by learners, define various learning profiles to personalize their educational paths, and assess the effectiveness of the pedagogical strategies implemented. By leveraging this usage, educators can tailor their approaches to meet individual needs and improve overall educational outcomes.

Issues of data quality, relevance and representativeness. The reliability and representativeness of the collected and processed educational data present significant challenges in improving pedagogical practices. Ensuring the objectivity of data collection is crucial, particularly when accounting for the socio-economic contexts of learners during analysis. The quality of the algorithms used for data processing is equally important to prevent biased or potentially discriminatory interpretations. Alongside concerns about data quality, relevance, and representativeness, it is vital to address issues related to data security and storage in the context of AI in education. Ensuring strong security measures and effective storage solutions is essential to protect sensitive information and maintain the integrity of educational data. The AI for the Oceans activity by Code.org for example aimed to raise awareness among students about how biases influence machine learning and encourage them to think about the importance of diverse and equitable data. Code.org introduced students (grades 3-12) to the concepts of AI, algorithms, and machine learning (with an emphasis on biases) by classifying objects such as "fish" or "not fish" to clean up the ocean and modifying their model based on feedback and errors. Students explored how human biases affect the quality of AI models, adjusting training data to include various sea creatures (AI for Oceans - Code.org, 2024).

Security and Data Storage

This section explores key issues related to data security and storage within the realm of AI in education. According to a 2021 OECD study titled 'OECD Digital Education Outlook 2021: Pushing the Frontiers with Artificial Intelligence, Blockchain and Robots', 58% of member countries expressed significant concerns about the protection of learners' data in digital learning environments (OECD, 2021). Ensuring the security and confidentiality of both learners' and teachers' personal information is crucial for maintaining trust and safeguarding all stakeholders involved. To achieve this, it is imperative to implement robust security measures and adhere to stringent privacy protocols, such as the General Data Protection Regulation (GDPR) or the Family Educational Rights and Privacy Act (FERPA), thereby protecting sensitive data and ensuring its integrity in educational contexts.

Ensuring robust security measures and effective storage solutions is essential to protect sensitive information and maintain the integrity of educational data. However, this also raises important ethical considerations regarding the use of learner data and the obligation of institutions to act on the insights gained from this data (Prinsloo & Slade, 2017). These ethical considerations go beyond mere data protection and touch upon issues of privacy, consent, and the responsible use of data-driven insights in educational decision-making processes.

One major concern in this regard is the risk of data poisoning attacks, where malicious actors manipulate training data to introduce biases or vulnerabilities into AI models. These attacks can compromise the integrity and reliability of AI systems in educational contexts, leading to erroneous or dangerous behaviors that negatively impact students' learning outcomes (Jagielski et al., 2018).

To counter these threats, educational institutions must implement a multi-faceted defense strategy (Steingartner et al., 2021). This includes deploying AI-based anomaly detection systems to continuously monitor data streams and identify suspicious behavior, utilizing federated learning techniques and differential privacy to protect data confidentiality and reduce the risk of poisoning. Federated learning allows AI models to be trained on decentralized data, minimizing the need for data sharing and reducing the attack surface. Differential privacy techniques add noise to the data, making it difficult for attackers to identify specific individuals or manipulate the data without detection. Additionally, adopting rigorous data governance practices, such as regular audits and source validation processes, is essential.

Protection of Learners' and Teachers' Personal Data

Protection of learners' and teachers' personal data. The security of personal data for educational stakeholders is crucial, encompassing not just the information of learners and teachers, but also sensitive institutional data, creating a complex data ecosystem. As highlighted by Williamson and Piattoeva (2019), the effectiveness of data protection systems is intricately linked to the perceived legitimacy of educational institutions in the digital era. This complexity is further emphasized by Prinsloo and Slade (2016), who explore the vulnerability of students in the context of learning analytics and data collection.

Transparency is a fundamental principle in managing the security of educational data. This involves establishing clear procedures that allow users to exercise their fundamental rights, including access to their data, understanding how it is collected and used, and the ability to rectify or delete incorrect information. Rubel and Jones (2016) underscore the importance of these rights in their examination of student privacy in learning analytics from an information ethics perspective. By fostering awareness of these procedures, educational institutions can enhance stakeholder trust and engagement in digital systems.

However, transparency alone is insufficient. Ensuring data security requires a continuous process of evaluation and updates to address evolving technologies and emerging threats. Slade and Prinsloo (2013) discuss this ongoing challenge in their analysis of ethical issues and dilemmas in learning analytics. This ongoing vigilance also necessitates regular training for educational actors on data security challenges, enabling them to actively contribute to protecting their personal information. West et al. (2016) emphasize the importance of putting an ethical lens on these practices, particularly in the context of learning analytics.

The complexity of balancing data utilization for educational improvement with privacy protection is further explored by Pardo and Siemens (2014), who propose a set of ethical and privacy principles for learning analytics. These principles provide a framework for educational institutions to navigate the intricate landscape of data protection while harnessing the potential of data-driven educational technologies.

Implementing Security Protocols

Protecting this data necessitates the use of end-to-end encryption, multi-factor authentication, and adherence to international security standards such as ISO/IEC 27001 for information security management. Additionally, the principles of privacy by design should be integral to the development process, ensuring that security measures are embedded from the outset in the design and architecture of information systems, rather than being implemented retroactively. These security measures should be guided by the following protective principles:

- Data minimization to collect only the data strictly necessary for processing;
- Anonymization or pseudonymization of data before processing;
- Strict and granular access control, based on the principle of least privilege and using vigorous authentication mechanisms;
- Encryption of data, both in transit and at rest, using robust and regularly updated encryption algorithms;
- Implementation of logging and auditing systems to monitor and detect unauthorized access or suspicious behavior;
- Adoption of security incident management protocols, including data breach notifications following Article 33 of the General Data Protection Regulation (GDPR).

A study by the European Data Protection Board (2022) revealed that 72% of European educational institutions have aligned their data collection and processing practices with the EU GDPR standards, leading to notable improvements in the security of educational data management. However, Baker and Hawn (2021) highlight a critical concern: AI algorithms designed to predict student performance can inadvertently reinforce socioeconomic biases if the training data is not meticulously curated. To address this, it is essential to implement robust mechanisms that empower users with rights to access, rectify, and delete their personal data, ensuring greater control and transparency in data management.

Recent systematic reviews of AI in education have further emphasized the importance of these security and ethical considerations. Wang et al. (2024) underscored the need for a holistic approach to AI implementation in educational systems, taking into account not only technological aspects but also ethical considerations and data security. Similarly, Zhai et al. (2021) identified data privacy and security as key challenges in the integration of AI in education, highlighting the need for ongoing research and development in these areas.

Data Access Management and Permissions

Protecting sensitive data requires strict and transparent access and authorization rules. These rules must clearly define who has the right to access the data, the reasons for which and how to access it. A dynamic authorization management system should be deployed, with regular checks and updates. It is equally essential to limit access to data to the people concerned.

To fully harness the potential of AI systems in education, ensuring their interoperability is crucial. This involves enabling seamless data exchange and collaboration between various AI tools and platforms. Interoperability is vital for establishing a cohesive and effective digital educational ecosystem. Achieving this requires the adoption of standardized protocols and frameworks. Key standards, such as xAPI for tracking learning activities and SCORM for transferring educational content, are essential for ensuring compatibility and data portability across AI systems. Additionally, standards like IMS Global Learning Tools Interoperability (LTI) and Common Cartridge are instrumental in enhancing interoperability among diverse systems. According to the IMS Global Learning Consortium (2021), the use of LTI in higher education surged by 35% from 2019 to 2021 (IMS Global Consortium, 2021). The broad implementation of these standards promotes innovation and collaboration by addressing technical challenges, thereby fostering a dynamic and collaborative environment that supports adaptive AI solutions tailored to the specific needs of learners and educators. Despite its advantages, interoperability presents notable challenges. The EDUCAUSE 2021 Horizon Report highlights that 64% of higher education institutions consider interoperability a barrier to adopting new digital tools, citing concerns over data protection and technical compatibility (Pelletier et al., 2021).

Open Data Formats and Interoperability Mechanisms

The adoption of open data formats and interoperability mechanisms has the potential to stimulate innovation and the development of artificial intelligence (AI) solutions in education. This strategy encourages the creation of cutting-edge applications and services, cultivating a dynamic and collaborative ecosystem. Ensuring compatibility, interoperability, and effective communication among various educational AI tools and platforms is vital for fully harnessing their potential and facilitating seamless navigation for both educators and learners. A 2020 case study by the IMS Global Learning Consortium revealed that implementing standardized protocols like LTI (Learning Tools Interoperability) led to a 40% reduction in tool integration time and a 30% increase in user satisfaction (IMS Global Learning Consortium, 2021). For instance, the seamless integration of intelligent tutoring systems with Learning Management Systems (LMS) (Kaddouri et al., 2023) through such standardized protocols enhances the user experience and maximizes the educational impact of AI technologies. Promoting the adoption of open data formats and interoperability can serve as a catalyst for AI innovation in education, resulting in the development of more effective solutions tailored to the specific needs of learners. According to 78% of EdTech developers, open standards are essential for driving innovation (Cohen & Popof, 2022). These practices not only facilitate the creation of innovative applications and services but also contribute to a vibrant and collaborative ecosystem. Furthermore, they enable the sharing of data and resources across different institutions, thereby amplifying the collective impact of AI solutions in education. This synergy among technological tools empowers teachers and learners to thrive within a cohesive and efficient digital learning environment.

Development of Adapted Algorithms

The effective deployment of AI algorithms in education requires careful consideration of several key factors. Firstly, the integration of AI necessitates the design of algorithms specifically tailored to the educational context. Among the approaches considered are artificial neural networks for predicting student performance and decision trees for diagnosing learning difficulties (Alyahyan & Düştegör, 2020; Hussain et al., 2018).

Neural networks excel at analyzing large datasets to identify subtle patterns in learning behaviors, potentially offering insights into complex learning processes that might not be immediately apparent through traditional analysis methods (Alyahyan & Düştegör, 2020). Decision trees, on the other hand, provide a clear visualization of the decision-making process, aiding in the identification of key factors influencing performance (Hussain et al., 2018). This transparency can be particularly valuable in educational settings, where understanding the reasoning behind predictions or recommendations is crucial for both educators and learners.

Secondly, algorithms should be designed with a modular architecture to ensure they can be seamlessly integrated and adapted to diverse learning contexts. The development of modular and adaptive AI architectures is essential for creating systems that can evolve with changing educational needs and contexts (Essa, 2016). These architectures allow for the integration of new data sources and the updating of algorithms as new research findings emerge, ensuring that the AI system remains relevant and effective over time. Their inherent flexibility and dynamic adaptability are crucial for meeting the evolving needs of individual learners, allowing for the delivery of varied and personalized content and activities.

Thirdly, the granularity of information is vital, enabling algorithms to provide detailed and accurate analyses and recommendations. This level of detail supports the creation of personalized learning experiences, targeted pedagogical interventions, and tailored learning pathways.

However, developing AI algorithms for education comes with its own set of challenges, particularly in terms of explainability. The interpretability of AI models in education is a critical aspect that needs to be addressed (Conati et al., 2018). The decisions and recommendations generated by AI must be understandable and justifiable. To address this challenge, model interpretation techniques such as LIME (Local Interpretable Model-agnostic Explanations) or SHAP (SHapley Additive exPlanations) have been developed to provide insights into the decision-making processes of complex AI models (Adadi & Berrada, 2018). These approaches allow complex predictions to be broken down into individual contributions of each variable, thereby offering greater transparency on how the models function and facilitating their adoption by end-users in the educational field.

By designing AI algorithms tailored to the educational context, ensuring their modularity, flexibility, and granularity, and incorporating model interpretation techniques, we can create transparent and justifiable AI systems that effectively support teaching and learning processes. This approach enhances the potential of AI to improve educational outcomes through personalized learning, automated assessment, and predictions of academic performance.

Current Limitations

Despite significant advancements, AI in education still faces important limitations. One of the most pressing challenges is the difficulty of accurately evaluating complex cognitive skills such as creativity and critical thinking (Zawacki-Richter et al., 2019). While AI can efficiently process and analyze structured data, it needs to tackle the nuanced and context-dependent nature of creative expression and critical reasoning. This limitation can lead to incomplete or potentially biased assessments of students' higher-order thinking skills (Luckin et al., 2016). Additionally, there is a risk of overestimating AI's capabilities, which can lead to unrealistic expectations among educators, students, and policymakers (Holmes et al., 2019). It is crucial to address clearly and honestly the actual capacities and limitations of AI systems to all stakeholders, acknowledging that AI, while powerful in many domains, is not a panacea for all educational challenges and should be seen as a complementary tool rather than a replacement for human expertise and judgment.

Furthermore, challenges such as the accessibility of AI technologies in underfunded educational environments and the integration of AI into curricula need to be addressed (Reich & Ito, 2017). Concrete examples, such as cases where AI has failed to accurately assess creativity or critical thinking, can illustrate these points more vividly. For instance, a study by Zhai et al. (2020) found that current AI systems find it difficult to evaluate the originality and relevance of ideas in open-ended problem-solving tasks, highlighting the limitations in assessing creative thinking.

To address these limitations and the ethical implications of AI in education, such as data privacy concerns and the potential for algorithmic bias, ongoing research and development efforts are focusing on enhancing AI's ability to understand and evaluate complex cognitive processes (Tuomi, 2018). This includes the development of more sophisticated natural language processing techniques, the integration of multidisciplinary approaches that combine insights from education, psychology, and computer science, and creating AI systems that can provide more detailed and constructive feedback on students' creative and critical thinking processes (Luckin & Cukurova, 2019). As the field progresses, it is essential to maintain a balanced perspective on AI's role in education, leveraging its strengths while being mindful of its current limitations.

This approach will help ensure that AI is used effectively and ethically to enhance, rather than replace, the crucial human elements of teaching and learning. It also emphasizes the need for transparent and accountable AI decision-making processes, especially when these systems influence important educational outcomes (Williamson & Eynon, 2020). Collaboration among educators, AI researchers, and policymakers will be key to maximizing the benefits of AI while minimizing its risks (Selwyn, 2019).

System Integration

Integrating artificial intelligence into existing digital educational environments requires a strategy to address the specific challenges associated with this integration. The challenges include developing standardized APIs to connect AI to current learning management systems (LMS), ensuring seamless communication, security, and confidentiality of student data, as well as extensibility to integrate future AI features. For example, the Advanced Distributed Learning (ADL) Initiative has developed the Total Learning Architecture (TLA), which provides a framework for integrating AI and other advanced technologies into learning ecosystems (Folsom-Kovarik & Raybourn, 2020).

To successfully achieve this integration, it is essential to adopt a progressive transition strategy from existing systems to AI-compatible architectures. This strategy includes evaluating existing systems, planning by phases, developing interfaces, conducting iterative testing, and providing training and support for educational and technical staff. A study by Xu et al. (2024) on the integration of AI-powered chatbots in an information technology curriculum demonstrated the positive impact on students' academic performance and higher-order thinking skills, highlighting the importance of careful implementation and ongoing support.

By adopting this progressive integration strategy, educational institutions can modernize their systems while ensuring the continuity of educational services. This will enable them to benefit from the advantages of AI in education, such as improving the learning experience, personalizing teaching, and increasing the efficiency of educational processes. For instance, a study by Hwang et al. (2020) found that AI-enhanced adaptive learning systems can significantly improve student engagement and learning outcomes in STEM subjects.

Looking towards the future, the integration of AI in education is expected to evolve rapidly. Emerging trends include the use of AI for more sophisticated learning analytics, the development of AI-powered virtual reality learning environments, and the integration of emotion recognition technologies to enhance personalized learning experiences (Zhai et al., 2021). As these technologies advance, the challenges of system integration will likely become more complex, requiring ongoing adaptation and innovation in educational technology infrastructure.

Personalized Learning

Personalized learning is a cornerstone of artificial intelligence (AI) applications in education. This approach tailors content and learning pathways to meet each learner's unique needs, considering their diverse learning styles and paces (Holmes et al., 2022). The principles of flexibility, modularity, and granularity are crucial to this process. Flexibility allows for content and methods to be adjusted based on individual preferences and goals, while modularity and granularity enable the creation of customized learning paths by integrating various units or modules according to specific learner needs (Zawacki-Richter et al., 2019).

In a case study, Zhiyenbayeva (2022) explored the use of AI to create personalized learning paths in psychological disciplines such as zoopsychology and speech therapy, as well as in practical training for children with disorders. The sample included 184 second-year students from Abay Kazakh National Pedagogical University and Kuban State Technological University. The training, conducted remotely over three months, allowed students to test adapted educational tools. The results demonstrated the significant benefits of AI in higher education teaching. The following graph illustrates the influence of AI technologies in education (AIED) on personalized learning.

Figure 2. The influence of AI technologies in education (AIED) on personalized learning (Zhiyenbayeva, 2022).

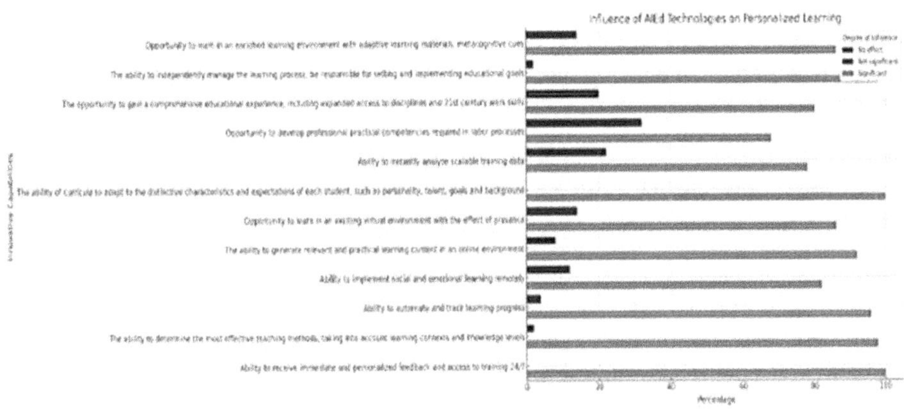

For instance, Carnegie Learning, an AI system for mathematics education, utilizes adaptive algorithms to make real-time adjustments to content and exercise difficulty based on the learner's performance (Pane et al., 2014). Carnegie Learning evaluates learners' performance to identify their strengths and weaknesses, providing tailored exercises and explanations to address their specific needs. This innovative use of AI in personalized learning significantly enhances skill acquisition and knowledge retention.

Recent studies have shown the effectiveness of AI-driven personalized learning systems. For example, a study by Kulik and Fletcher (2016) found that intelligent tutoring systems produced significant learning gains across various subjects and educational levels. Furthermore, research by Hwang et al. (2020) demonstrated that

AI-enhanced adaptive learning environments can improve student engagement and academic performance in STEM subjects.

As a result, personalized learning is increasingly becoming the standard in higher education, transforming the educational experience and creating new opportunities for future generations (Luckin & Cukurova, 2019). The integration of AI in personalized learning continues to evolve, with emerging trends such as the use of natural language processing for more nuanced learner-AI interactions and the incorporation of multimodal data for more comprehensive learner profiling (Renz & Hilbig, 2020).

Adaptation of Content and Learning Paths to Individual Needs

AI can analyze learners' data such as academic performance and interactions with educational platforms—to pinpoint their strengths, weaknesses, and learning styles. This analysis enables the customization of content and learning pathways, providing exercises, tutorials, and activities specifically tailored to each individual (Hwang et al., 2020). For instance, an AI system can offer targeted exercises and tutorials to a learner struggling with a particular subject, aligning the difficulty level with their needs. Conversely, advanced learners receive more complex content and challenging problems to further enhance their skills. This personalized approach ensures that each learner receives the appropriate level of support or challenge, optimizing their educational experience (Holmes et al., 2022).

Learning Styles, Preferences and Learner Rhythms

The development of adapted algorithms enables the consideration of learners' diverse learning styles and paces. AI can effectively identify these characteristics and provide personalized content and activities accordingly (Zawacki-Richter et al., 2019). For instance, a visually-oriented learner may benefit from videos and images, while an auditory learner would have access to audio recordings. The Knewton system, which leverages AI, has analyzed data from millions of learners to adapt content to their individual preferences and learning speeds (Essa, 2016).

While the specific study at Arizona State University mentioned in the original text could not be verified, recent research has demonstrated the effectiveness of AI-driven adaptive learning systems. For example, a study by Xu et al. (2024) found that integrating AI chatbots in an information technology curriculum led to important improvements in students' academic performance and higher-order thinking skills. Additionally, research by Chen et al. (2020) showed that AI-enhanced adaptive learning environments in STEM education resulted in improved learning outcomes and student engagement. These findings underscore the potential of AI-driven personalization to enhance educational outcomes.

Flexibility, Modularity and Granularity of AI Algorithms

To enable effective personalized learning, AI algorithms must address three key challenges: flexibility, modularity, and granularity (Khosravi et al., 2022). Algorithms need to exhibit cognitive plasticity to adapt to the individual and evolving needs of each learner, offering a range of content and activities that cater to diverse cognitive styles and learning preferences. For example, a flexible algorithm might alternate between visual, auditory, and kinesthetic content based on the learner's profile. Additionally, algorithms should be designed with a modular approach to ensure they can be easily combined and adapted to various educational contexts, whether formal or informal, synchronous or asynchronous. Lastly, information granularity allows algorithms to pinpoint not only broad areas where learners struggle but also specific concepts or problem types that are most challenging. This facilitates detailed analyses and precise recommendations, enabling targeted interventions and the creation of customized learning pathways. This triad of algorithmic competencies—adaptability, modularity, and granularity—forms the foundation for a robust and effective personalized learning ecosystem.

Khosravi et al. (2022) highlight the importance of these principles in their study on the development and adoption of an adaptive learning system. They emphasize that flexibility in algorithm design allows for better accommodation of diverse learning styles, while modularity enables easier integration and adaptation of the system across different educational contexts. The authors also stress the significance of granularity in providing precise and targeted interventions based on detailed learner data analysis.

Automated Assessment

Assessment, a cornerstone of any educational process, aims to measure learning outcomes, guide educational activities, and adapt teaching methods. However, it presents a complex challenge and a source of difficulties for all educational stakeholders. The field of automated assessment is a rich area for AI, with the potential to enhance the efficiency, reliability, and personalization of learning. Artificial Intelligence (AI) emerges as a promising tool, optimizing existing assessment processes and fostering the development of new, personalized evaluation forms that align with learners' needs in a rapidly evolving educational landscape. This section explores the advancements and challenges of automated assessment, focusing on three key aspects: automatic grading and scoring, reliability, and human oversight.

Automated Grading and Scoring of Learner Work

AI offers numerous possibilities for automating the evaluation of learners' work through various types of exercises. Exercises that can be automated include multiple-choice questions (MCQs) and short-answer questions, which focus on assessing understanding. A recent systematic review by Gao et al. (2024) explored the automatic assessment of text-based responses in post-secondary education, highlighting the significant progress made in this area. The study found that AI-based systems can effectively evaluate complex written work, offering potential time-saving benefits for educators and more consistent feedback for students.

AI has opened up new avenues in educational assessment, enabling the analysis of learners' online behaviors, interactions, and collaborations. It can now also evaluate oral presentations, concept maps, practical skills, and even make judgments on artistic work. Zheng et al. (2024) compared automated and peer assessment in English public speaking, demonstrating AI's capability to assess oral communication skills effectively. This research indicates that AI's capabilities extend beyond the lower levels of Bloom's revised taxonomy (recognition, comprehension, application) to include higher levels, such as analysis, evaluation, and creation. Automating these diverse assessment tasks not only enhances the efficiency and depth of evaluations but also frees up teachers' time, allowing them to focus on more critical activities, such as personalized student support.

Reliability, Validity, and Fairness of Automated Assessments

While automated assessments offer advantages in managing time and data related to educational processes and provide a comprehensive view of the evaluated activity, it is crucial to acknowledge their limitations concerning reliability, validity, and fairness. AI algorithms can be biased and may not account for all aspects of a learner's performance (Holmes et al., 2022). For instance, when evaluating an essay, AI may focus on quantifiable aspects such as length, structure, and vocabulary, but may overlook the subtle nuances of argumentation or creativity that require human intervention (Zawacki-Richter et al., 2019).

Gao et al. (2024) addressed these concerns in their review, noting that while AI systems have made significant strides in assessing text-based responses, challenges remain in ensuring fairness across diverse student populations and in evaluating highly subjective or creative elements of writing. Additionally, AI systems may fail to consider disparities among learners and the socio-economic difficulties some face, potentially perpetuating existing inequalities. To address these issues, it is essential to combine AI-based methods with other evaluation techniques and subject them to human expertise to ensure fair and inclusive assessments.

Human Supervision and Appeals

As previously discussed, human supervision remains essential to validate automated assessments. Educators must have the ability to review the results from automated evaluations to ensure their accuracy and fairness. Simultaneously, learners should have access to an appeals process that allows them to challenge the outcomes of automated assessments with human intervention. This process balances the efficiency of automation with the nuance and contextual understanding that human educators provide.

The study by Zheng et al. (2024) on English public speaking assessment provides an interesting perspective on this balance. While their research showed that automated assessment could be effective, it also highlighted the value of peer assessment, suggesting that a combination of automated and human-driven evaluation might yield the best results. This underscores the importance of maintaining a "human-in-the-loop" approach in AI-driven educational assessment to ensure ethical and effective implementation.

Prediction of Academic Success or Failure

A compelling example of AI's potential in predicting and improving student outcomes comes from Ivy Tech Community College in Indiana. The college implemented an AI-driven pilot program designed to identify students at risk of failing within the first two weeks of the semester. This AI system analyzed data from various course sections to predict which students were likely to face difficulties. The program then facilitated targeted interventions to support these students, addressing both academic and non-academic barriers to success. By the end of the semester, the program had significantly reduced failure rates among targeted students, with approximately 98% of identified students improving their performance to at least a C grade. This case highlights the importance of early intervention in educational settings and demonstrates AI's potential to manage large-scale data and provide actionable insights that can drastically improve educational outcomes (Google for Education, 2023).

Figure 3. Ivy Tech's AI-Infused Intervention (Verge Ai, 2024)

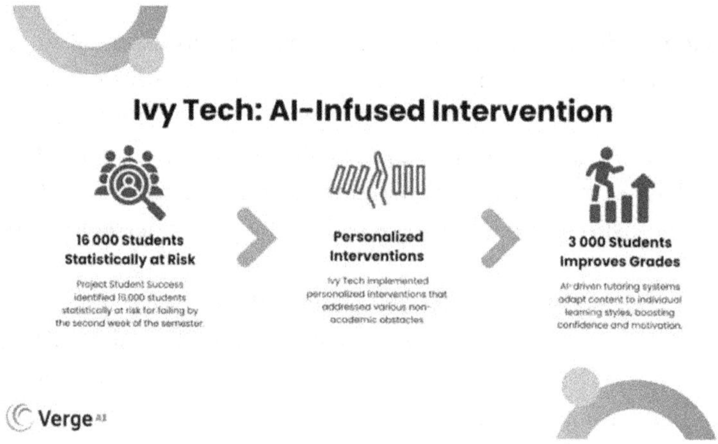

Predicting Academic Success or Failure is one of the most promising applications of AI in education. This approach leverages advanced algorithms to proactively manage learners' academic performance, enabling early and personalized interventions. The key aspects of these AI applications include analyzing data to identify success or failure factors, developing predictive models for anticipation and intervention, and incorporating contextual elements into predictions. Specifically, AI can be applied to: • Identify critical factors influencing success or failure; • Create predictive models; • Integrate socio-educational context into predictions.

These analyses encompass past performance, attendance, engagement in online learning activities, and socio-economic factors to generate nuanced and accurate predictions. Recent research by Alhazmi & Sheneamer (2023) demonstrates the effectiveness of early prediction models in higher education, highlighting the potential for timely interventions.

The effectiveness of these predictions depends heavily on the quality and diversity of the data used by AI systems. Arizmendi et al. (2023) provide a comprehensive review of using digital logs of learning behaviors to predict student outcomes, emphasizing the importance of standardized approaches and ethical considerations in data collection and analysis.

To maximize the positive impact of these predictive tools, it is advisable to integrate them into a comprehensive educational strategy that combines technological solutions with human intervention. This approach would not only help identify at-risk learners but also provide tailored and effective support strategies. Saidani et al. (2024) showcase the potential of ensemble learning approaches in predicting student academic success within multimedia-supported virtual learning environments, illustrating the evolving sophistication of these predictive models.

Data Analysis: Identifying Success Factors and Risk of Failure

AI systems analyze a wide range of data, including learners' demographic information, previous academic performance, learning habits, attendance, behaviors, and social interactions. These analyses help identify success indicators and signs of difficulties, as well as potential failure symptoms. By processing extensive data, AI systems highlight factors that contribute to success and those that indicate the risk of failure among learners. This data includes demographic information (such as age, gender, and socio-economic background) and previous academic performance (exam scores, continuous assessment grades), among others.

AI systems also examine learning habits, attendance, and learner behaviors. For instance, they can measure and track time spent on online learning platforms, frequency of participation in discussions, and submission timings for assignments. These indicators reveal the level of engagement and motivation of learners, which are crucial factors in academic success. Additionally, AI systems analyze learners' social interactions both online and in person. This analysis includes various aspects of learner exchanges with peers and teachers, participation in collaborative activities, and teacher follow-up on learners.

Gambini et al. (2022) conducted an explorative study on predictive tools for university performance, highlighting the potential of these technologies in identifying early indicators of academic success or struggle. Their work underscores the importance of considering multiple factors in predictive models to enhance accuracy and applicability across diverse educational contexts.

Identifying these success indicators and potential difficulties enables early and targeted interventions for learners at risk of failure. By fully leveraging these technologies, educational stakeholders could advance towards highly personalized and proactive teaching models that address the diverse needs of learners more effectively.

Predictive Models for Anticipation and Targeted Interventions

The results from these multidimensional analyses form the basis for developing predictive models that anticipate learners' academic trajectories. These predictions enable educators to implement personalized and preventive interventions for at-risk learners (Martinez Lunde, 2022). Sophisticated predictive models in education utilize a wide range of data, including academic performance and socio-economic factors, sourced from various platforms such as Learning Management Systems (LMS), academic records, and even Internet of Things (IoT) sensors.

Kurni et al. (2023) highlight that these models not only identify students at risk but also pinpoint specific factors contributing to their situations. They generate risk classifications of learners, allowing educators to prioritize interventions based on the severity of the difficulties. With continuous updates and iterative learning, these predictive models can adapt to changes in the learning environment and the needs of learners, enhancing their effectiveness in addressing potential issues proactively.

Interpretation, Transparency, and Contextual Factors in Predictions

While predictive models play a crucial role in transforming the educational experience, interpreting their predictions requires a nuanced and contextualized approach. Pacheco-Mendoza et al. (2023) emphasize the importance of carefully interpreting these predictions within the specific context of each learner, including their learning environment and history. This contextualization ensures a comprehensive and accurate understanding of predictions, thus mitigating the risk of reductive or potentially harmful interpretations.

Predictive algorithms in artificial intelligence are instrumental in reshaping educational experiences. However, the interpretation of their predictions must be approached with nuance and contextual awareness. It is vital to analyze these predictions in light of individual learner data, such as their learning context, environment, and educational background. This contextualization helps prevent reductive interpretations that could lead to stigmatization or inappropriate labeling of learners.

Aithal et al. (2024) argue that a decontextualized interpretation might result in unsuitable pedagogical decisions, hindering the delivery of tailored and effective support for learners. Thus, a reasoned and pragmatic approach is necessary for interpreting AI model predictions to ensure they contribute positively to educational outcomes.

Training of Teaching and Administrative Staff

The Harris Federation, one of the largest academy trusts in the UK, provides an excellent example of how AI can support teaching staff and enhance curriculum accessibility. The Federation implemented AI tools like ChatGPT and Microsoft Live to address challenges in managing teacher workloads and ensuring curriculum accessibility for students from diverse linguistic backgrounds. ChatGPT was used to adapt text for different age groups, making the curriculum more accessible, while Microsoft Live helped translate classroom instructions in real time, providing subtitles in students' native languages directly on their devices. These AI tools significantly reduced the time teachers spent on administrative tasks and adapted materials for diverse classroom needs, allowing them to focus more on direct teaching and student interaction. This case demonstrates the potential of AI to handle linguistic diversity in classrooms and support educational staff in creating more inclusive learning environments (Schools Week, 2023).

Integrating artificial intelligence (AI) into the field of education involves more than just acquiring and implementing computer equipment. An equally crucial aspect is the upgrading of human resources and the ongoing training of academic, technical, and administrative staff. This training is essential to ensure the effective and ethical use of AI technologies within the educational context. According to Martinez Lunde (2022), adequate preparation of personnel is a key factor in the successful implementation of AI in education. To address these needs, it is important to focus on several key areas.

Deployment and Adoption Challenges

The integration of AI in education faces several significant hurdles. Nagy et al. (2024) highlight that many educators and administrators may be hesitant to adopt AI technologies due to fear of job displacement, lack of understanding, or concerns about the impact on traditional teaching methods. There is often a significant disparity between the technical skills required to effectively implement and use AI systems and the current skill set of educational staff. Some institutions may lack the necessary technological infrastructure to support advanced AI systems. Issues surrounding data privacy, algorithmic bias, and the potential for AI to exacerbate existing educational inequalities can hinder adoption. The initial investment required for AI implementation can be substantial, which may be prohibitive for many educational institutions.

To address these challenges, several solutions and strategies can be implemented. Tyagi et al. (2024) suggest establishing mentorship initiatives where tech-savvy educators guide their colleagues, help bridge the knowledge gap and increase comfort with AI technologies. Fostering communities where educators can share experiences, best practices, and solutions can accelerate learning and adoption. Introducing AI technologies in phases allows for a smoother transition and gives staff time to adapt. Developing tailored training programs that address both technical skills and ethical considerations can boost confidence and competence. Highlighting successful AI implementations in education can help overcome skepticism and demonstrate tangible benefits. Forming partnerships between educational institutions, AI developers, and industry experts can provide valuable resources and expertise. Creating clear policies on AI use, data protection, and ethical guidelines can address concerns and provide a framework for responsible implementation. By addressing these challenges proactively and implementing targeted solutions, educational institutions can smooth the path for successful AI adoption and maximize its potential benefits for teaching and learning.

Development of Digital Skills

Developing digital skills among educational stakeholders is a key component of training. The goal is to equip staff with both the knowledge and practical skills needed to effectively utilize AI tools in their professional and everyday activities. Kurni et al. (2023) emphasize that this training should encompass not only the technical aspects of using these tools but also their pedagogical applications to enhance student learning outcomes. Dandan et al. (2024) further highlight the importance of developing computer literacy among students, which can be facilitated by educators who are well-versed in digital skills.

Awareness of Ethical Issues

Raising awareness of ethical issues related to AI in education is another crucial aspect of the training. Pacheco-Mendoza et al. (2023) argue that it is essential for staff to grasp the potential implications of AI use, including concerns about data privacy, algorithmic biases, and equitable access to these technologies. Such awareness enables educators to adopt AI tools responsibly and ethically.

Support and Guidance for Educational Stakeholders

The third element of the training involves providing support and guidance to educational stakeholders in their process of integrating AI tools into educational practices. This includes employing a multifaceted approach and complementary strategies. Aithal et al. (2024) propose a Mentoring System, which involves experienced teachers providing guidance to their peers with less familiarity with AI technologies. This type of mentoring fosters individualized support and the sharing of practical experiences, combining technical skill development with increased confidence and motivation among educators. Additional support can be offered through the establishment of communities of practice, either in person or online. These communities facilitate the exchange of practices, resource sharing, and problem-solving related to AI implementation. Continuing education workshops also play a crucial role in this support system, offering ongoing updates on AI applications, best pedagogical practices, and ethical considerations.

Pilot Projects and Action Research

This approach involves teachers in the experimentation and evaluation of AI in a structured and reflective educational framework. Pilot projects make it possible to evaluate the effectiveness of AI tools, and identify potential challenges in adjusting pedagogical practices. As noted by Zawacki-Richter et al. (2019), these projects can provide valuable insights into the practical implications of AI integration in educational settings. Action research, on the other hand, involves teachers in an iterative process of planning, acting, observing and reflecting on their use of AI.

Effective infrastructure demands investment in equipment, reliable internet access, specialized software, and continuous technical support. Data collection and management pose challenges related to quality, security, and interoperability. Algorithm development must focus on flexibility, reliability, and equity to facilitate personalized learning, automated assessments, and predict academic success. Ultimately, ongoing staff training is essential for the ethical integration of AI. A comprehensive approach to these dimensions can enhance AI's benefits while mitigating associated risks, as argued by Holmes et al. (2022).

ETHICAL CONSIDERATIONS IN THE USE OF AI IN EDUCATION

As artificial intelligence profoundly transforms the educational landscape, its use raises many important questions about its ethical impact. Its use in education raises crucial ethical issues, particularly in terms of the protection of privacy and personal data, fairness, non-discrimination, and the transparency and explainability of AI systems (Fadel et al., 2019). Taking these ethical issues into consideration has become an urgent matter, requiring in-depth reflection, actions and appropriate measures by educational actors.

Protection of Privacy and Personal Data

The appropriate use of AI in education involves the collection and analysis of personal data relating to learners. To gain access, it is ethically imperative to obtain informed consent from learners and their guardians before collecting and using them. Learners and their guardians should be informed in advance of how their personal data will be used, the potential risks and benefits of such exploitation, and their rights.

To safeguard privacy, learners' personal data should be anonymized or replaced with pseudonyms. It is essential to implement reliable and up-to-date security protocols to protect this data from cyberattacks and unauthorized access (Williamson & Piattoeva, 2019). Personal data should be retained only as long as necessary to attain the purposes for which it was collected. By observing data protection laws, such as the GDPR (EU 2016/679), individuals have the right to request the deletion of their personal information at any time. Educational institutions must adhere to the principle of full transparency by providing regular, accessible reports detailing how data is collected, stored, and utilized.

Equity and Non-Discrimination

The use of artificial intelligence (AI) in education raises valid concerns about the potential risks of discrimination. AI algorithms can exhibit biases that might adversely affect educational decisions related to learner guidance and support. Furthermore, these algorithms may not fully capture the complexity of individual learners' performance, often focusing on quantifiable aspects while overlooking other crucial, qualitative dimensions of learning.

The case of a New Zealand student of Asian descent whose passport photo was wrongly rejected illustrates discrimination based on skin color in facial recognition technologies. The system, claiming that his eyes were closed when they were open, reflects a bias related to non-representative training datasets. These technologies, often trained on images mostly from the United States, tend to misinterpret the features of ethnic minorities. Similar cases have affected dark-skinned women in the United Kingdom, whose photos were unjustly judged to be of poor quality (Stahl et al., 2022).

To mitigate these risks, it is essential to develop and employ AI systems that are free from biases, ensuring equitable access to technology for all learners, regardless of their background, socio-economic status, or individual characteristics (UNESCO, 2021). Regular and independent audits of AI algorithms are necessary to detect and address potential biases, thereby maintaining fairness in educational decision-making (Hakimi et al., 2021). Additionally, the design and development of AI systems should consider the diverse needs of the learner population, including those with special needs and those from disadvantaged backgrounds or minority groups (Knox et al., 2019). The primary goal of this approach is to make AI a genuine tool for inclusion, embracing the diversity of learning profiles to promote equal opportunities within the educational environment (Selwyn, 2019).

Transparency and Explainability of ai Systems

Nguyen & DiPaola (2020) designed a series of "AI and Data Privacy" workshops by the MIT Media Lab with the goal of raising awareness among students (7-14 years old) about data privacy and the design of privacy features. Using the Mystery YouTube Viewer tool, by observing videos, the students predict information about characters and simulate how recommendation algorithms work, the students were also able to create advertisements while learning the notion of transparency. They have also developed solutions for online consent on social media platforms with COPPA (Children's Online Privacy Protection) in mind. These workshops have contributed significantly to a better understanding of the challenges of data privacy, while promoting discussions on digital rights and ethics online.

Understanding and interpretability of algorithmic decisions

For full user trust and buy-in, educational AI systems must be transparent and explainable. Learners, teachers, and tutors need to understand how algorithms make decisions that influence their learning paths. Decision-making processes must be clear and interpretable to enhance commitment, responsibility, and fairness among users, giving them the opportunity to question and improve these processes.

Liability and Correction of Errors

The actors responsible for AI systems used in education must take accountability for any errors and malfunctions that arise. They must ensure that errors are promptly corrected, appropriate measures are implemented to anticipate and prevent future issues, and that compensation is provided to those affected by AI system errors (Kizilcec & Lee, 2022). This vigilant approach is crucial to maintaining learners' continuous trust in educational technologies.

Right to Object and Human Review

Artificial intelligence systems used in education must allow learners, teachers, and tutors to question the decisions made by these AI systems. This ensures fairness, transparency, and accountability in the educational use of AI. Implementing procedures as part of an appeal process for decisions deemed unfair, discriminatory, or harmful is essential. These procedures should enable stakeholders to request a thorough human review of AI-generated decisions, allowing them to present their case and provide additional evidence to support their challenge. The implementation of mechanisms for challenging and reviewing AI decisions is crucial to address algorithmic biases, errors in judgment, and potential negative consequences of automated decisions. It also builds user trust in educational AI systems and fosters the ethical and responsible use of these technologies (Kizilcec & Lee, 2022).

Participatory and Ethical Approach

To truly add value to education, AI must be adopted with a critical mindset within an ethical framework, involving all stakeholders (designers, teachers, learners, tutors) in the design and evaluation process of AI tools geared towards education. This collaborative approach, characterized by transparency, explainability, and dialogue, is essential to ensure that deployed systems align with real-world needs, fostering trust and putting AI at the service of learners and teachers.

From an interaction perspective, learners need to engage with teachers and peers to learn and develop. AI has great potential to enrich these human interactions in the learning process and enhance the central role of teachers. It can support reflective work without replacing teachers' judgment and expertise. Consequently, exchanges between teachers and learners, as well as among peers, are crucial for the cognitive, social, and emotional development of learners. AI can improve the conditions and quality of these interactions while preserving the richness of human relationships in the educational context.

In summary, the successful use of AI in education opens up new perspectives by combining innovative technologies with the preservation of essential human aspects of learning. However, this use must be guided by strong ethical principles and a human-centered approach to maximize its benefits while minimizing potential risks (UNESCO, 2021).

STRATEGIES FOR THE ETHICAL APPROPRIATION OF AI IN EDUCATION

The use of AI in education within an ethical framework requires the implementation of concrete strategies and measures. To ensure these strategies are appropriate and account for educational contextual factors, they need to be developed collaboratively, involving various stakeholders in the education system, including technologists, educators, ethicists, policymakers, and representatives of civil society. These strategies should focus on three main areas: regulatory and policy frameworks, training and awareness-raising for relevant stakeholders, and the ethical design of AI systems.

The integration of AI in education raises significant questions regarding regulation, ethics, and governance. Implementing appropriate regulatory and policy frameworks is necessary for the responsible, equitable, and effective use of AI in education. These frameworks include legislation, ethical charters, and governance mechanisms. Establishing legislation to regulate the use of AI in education is a priority for all educational stakeholders. These laws aim to set clear criteria for the development and use of educational AI systems to protect rights and ensure fairness and justice in education for learners.

In this context, the European Union established the AI Act in 2021, a regulatory framework that defines general criteria for determining if an AI system is considered "high-risk," without explicitly mentioning AI systems used in education (LÉGISLATION SUR L'INTELLIGENCE ARTIFICIELLE, 2021). In the United States, the Department of Education published a document in January 2023 titled "Supporting Responsible Use of AI in Education," providing recommendations and resources to help educational institutions frame the use of AI (Office of Educational Technology, 2023).

Nguyen et al., 2022 analyzed the current policies and guidelines of international organizations1 and synthesized (Table 1) the set of ethical principles for IAED (Nguyen et al., 2022).

Table 1. Ethical principles for IAED synthesized by Nguyen et al. (2022)

Principle	Description	Examples and Recommendations
Governance and Management	Ensure a responsible governance structure and management practices for the use of AI in education. Consider interdisciplinary and multi-stakeholder perspectives and adhere to ethical standards.	Implement data management policies, ensure technology alignment with educational goals, and enhance transparency and accountability.
Transparency and Accountability	Ensure transparency in the processes of data collection, analysis, and usage, as well as in the algorithms. Provide access to data and explain the decisions made by AI systems.	Provide clear information on data origin and usage, enable stakeholders to understand algorithmic decisions, and ensure regulatory transparency.
Sustainability and Proportionality	Consider the environmental, economic, and societal impact of AI. Ensure that AI technologies are developed and used sustainably and in proportion to educational needs.	Optimize energy efficiency, minimize environmental footprint, ensure that AI does not negatively impact employment, and promote sustainable innovation in education.
Data and Algorithm Ethics Privacy	Protect individuals' rights regarding personal data. Ensure the security and integrity of collected data while guaranteeing its ethical use and respect for human rights. AI in Education (AIED) must ensure informed user consent and maintain the confidentiality of personal information.	Ensure informed consent, prioritize the security of students' data, develop inclusive and fair algorithms. Use learning data without consent, make predictions based on accumulated information. Transparency in data collection and usage, informed consent, explanation of potential ramifications on learning and career.

continued on following page

Table 1. Continued

Principle	Description	Examples and Recommendations
Security and Safety	AIED must be robust against threats and protect data from cyberattacks.	Data manipulation or corruption by third parties, security breaches by cybercriminals. Robust design, continuous evaluation, monitoring mechanisms, and user training for secure usage.
Inclusion	AIED must be accessible to all, regardless of demographics and socio-economic status.	Inequality in technology access, exclusion of students from disadvantaged backgrounds. Consideration of infrastructure, equipment, skills, and societal acceptance, non-discriminatory design of data and algorithms.
Human-Centered AIED	AIED should complement human capabilities while preserving human autonomy and control.	Reduction in learners' interaction with others, cognitive biases caused by automatic recommendations. Develop adaptive systems based on negotiation, focus on transversal skills and metacognition, adequate educator training.

Also, Mouta et al., (2023) mapped the potential ethical issues related to AI systems that emerged from their systematic review of the literature in the field of education (Mouta et al., 2023).

Figure 4. Potential ethical issues related to AI systems on IAED (Mouta et al., 2023).

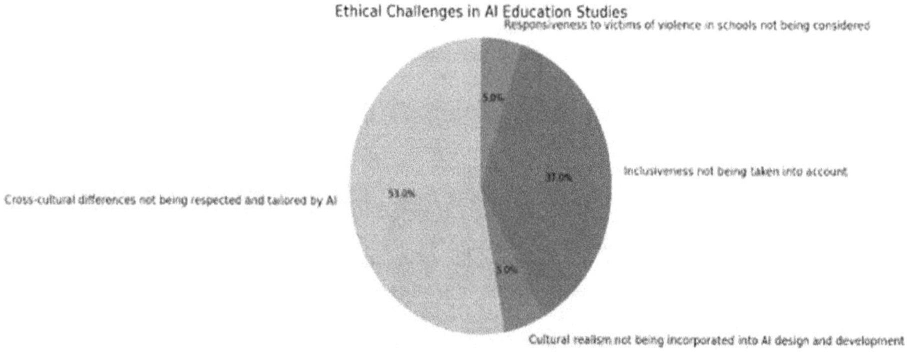

Ethical Charters Specific to AI in Education

The development of specific ethical charters for AI in education is crucial for guiding the decisions and practices of educational stakeholders. In this regard, several international initiatives have been launched. In 2021, UNESCO published the "Recommendation on the Ethics of Artificial Intelligence" (UNESCO, 2021), which provides a global framework for the ethical use of AI, with particular considerations for the education sector. This document serves as a key reference for countries in developing their own policies on the ethical use of AI in education.

Governance and Oversight Mechanisms

The governance and oversight of AI in education have become critical focus areas for educational institutions globally. Numerous significant initiatives have emerged to address these concerns. In 2021, UNESCO, in its report titled "AI in Education: Guidance for Policy-makers" (UNESCO, 2021), offered concrete recommendations for countries to establish governance mechanisms, including the formation of multisectoral oversight bodies. These recommendations aim to foster a comprehensive and inclusive approach to AI in education. Independent and transparent governance mechanisms are essential for ensuring compliance with regulations and ethical standards in the use of AI.

Several international initiatives have been introduced in this direction. Protecting personal data and respecting learners' privacy are major concerns in developing regulatory frameworks for AI in education. At the European level, the General Data Protection Regulation (GDPR) (European Data Protection Board, 2020), which took effect in 2018, plays a fundamental role in this area. This European regulatory framework governs the collection, processing, and storage of personal data, setting standards for the ethical and responsible use of learners' data. It ensures privacy while also highlighting the potential benefits of technological innovation in education.

In the United States, the protection of learners' data has been a concern of policymakers since the 1970s, concretized by the Family Educational Rights and Privacy Act (FERPA), which guarantees the confidentiality of educational records. In 2021, the Student Data Privacy Protection Act was reintroduced in Congress (Rep. Murphy, 2021), aiming to enhance the protection of learner data used by AI systems. This bill seeks to ensure that advances in educational technology do not compromise the privacy of learners and other educational stakeholders. These regulatory initiatives in Europe and the United States reflect a broader trend towards strengthening the protection of learners' data amid the growing use of AI in education. They underscore the need to balance technological innovation with the safeguarding of fundamental rights, setting standards that could influence practices globally.

Training and Awareness

The successful and ethical integration of AI in education extends beyond its technical and legal dimensions; it also encompasses the upgrading of human resources through a comprehensive approach to training and awareness. This involves equipping all educational stakeholders—from teachers and students to administrators and policymakers—with an understanding of both the opportunities and challenges associated with AI in education. The aim is not only to develop technical and legal skills but also to foster a critical awareness of the ethical, social, and pedagogical implications of AI in education.

This enhancement of educational human resources, through multidimensional training programs, is crucial for the effective and value-respecting use of AI. In this regard, UNESCO launched the "AI and Education" project in 2021, which aims to support countries in developing ethical policies and practices for the use of AI in education (UNESCO, 2021). This initiative emphasizes the need to train teachers and policymakers on AI-related issues, enabling them to integrate AI meaningfully into their pedagogical practices and educational policies. Additionally, the development of digital literacy and critical thinking among learners is crucial for the responsible use of AI in education. The Stanford CRAFT (Collaborative Research in Computational Thinking) initiative, offers online resources designed to help high school educators teach fundamental AI concepts to students. Launched in 2021, this project provides a wealth of adaptable materials co-designed with educators, enabling high school students to explore, understand, and critique artificial intelligence. The resources include readings, videos, podcasts, and guided explorations, all aimed at empowering students with the critical thinking skills necessary to navigate an AI-driven world.

The case study "AI and Ethics" Program for Middle School Students by the MIT Media Lab aimed to teach students the technical terminology of AI systems and the ethical and societal implications of AI. The students were introduced to using the different related concepts, to identify the predictions made, to create algorithms, and to reflect on the biases present in them. This approach has been successful in engaging students in discussions about bias, discrimination, surveillance, and autonomy related to AI systems (Payne, 2019).

In the same context, Celik's (2023) study aimed to fill a gap in understanding the use of artificial intelligence (AI) in education, based on the TPACK framework (Technological Pedagogical Content Knowledge). The researchers first created a tool to measure teachers' knowledge regarding the use of AI in a pedagogical context. This tool is based on the TPACK framework, which integrates the technological, pedagogical, and content knowledge necessary for effectively teaching with technology. By expanding the TPACK framework, the researchers added an ethical dimension that recognizes that understanding the ethical implications of AI is essential for teachers. The results suggest that an increase in teachers' knowledge about AI-based tools translates into a better understanding of the pedagogical benefits that AI can offer. Furthermore, a solid technological knowledge enables teachers to more effectively assess the decisions made by AI, which is crucial for ensuring the ethical and beneficial use of these technologies in the classroom.

Collaboration Between Technologists, Educators and Ethicists

Collaboration between technologists, educators, and ethicists is crucial to ensure the effective use of AI in education while upholding fundamental values. The "AI4K12" initiative, launched in the United States in 2018, is a prominent example of this collaborative approach. Bringing together experts in AI, education, and ethics, it develops guidelines for teaching AI from kindergarten through 12th grade (Touretzky et al., 2019). This initiative highlights the importance of a multidisciplinary approach to integrating AI responsibly into educational curricula.

The AI4K12 initiative is structured around five core concepts that serve as a general framework for AI education across different grade levels. The first concept, perception, focuses on understanding how learners interpret the world through machine sensors and data. The second concept, representation and reasoning, elucidates the mechanisms by which machines process and organize information. The third concept, representation, addresses how machines acquire knowledge from data. The fourth concept concerns human-machine interaction, emphasizing ways and methods for effective collaboration between humans and machines. The fifth and final concept involves critical reflection on the ethical, legal, and social implications of using AI in education. These five concepts are progressively implemented at various educational levels, allowing learners to engage with AI throughout their educational journey. This approach not only aims to master the technical components of AI but also fosters a critical attitude towards its applications among students.

Ethical and Responsible Design of AI Systems

The ethical and responsible design of educational AI systems has a fundamental role in ensuring that they serve the best interests of learners and educators, in alignment with the core values of education. This section of the chapter examines the fundamental principles and ethical considerations that should guide the design of AI systems in education, advocating for a:

Human-centric approach. From a human-centered perspective, the development of AI systems for educational purposes is based on a proactive approach that puts the needs and rights of educational actors at the heart of the design process, respecting fundamental values and ethical principles. To improve fairness and accuracy, designers are working to identify and mitigate potential biases present in training data and algorithms in educational AI systems.

Equity and Inclusion. AI systems designed to enhance human capabilities should be accessible to all learners, regardless of their individual characteristics or context. It is essential to consider the diversity of learners in terms of cognitive abilities, native language, culture, and level of access to technological resources, in order to design AI systems that are inclusive and equitable.

Transparency and Explainability. Transparency, explainability, and privacy protection are fundamental ethical principles governing AI systems in education. AI decision-making tools must be understandable and interpretable, utilizing explainable models or visualization interfaces. In designing education-focused AI systems, principles of data minimization and privacy—such as anonymization, encryption, and stringent access controls—are integrated from the early stages of development. Additionally, systems for logging and traceability are established to support audits. The roles and responsibilities of all stakeholders are clearly defined, in alignment with the principles of accountability, auditability, and sustainability.

Under the banner of a human-centered approach that upholds human values and fundamental rights (UNESCO, 2021), incorporating ethical requirements into the design of educational AI systems enhances users' trust in these systems within the educational context.

Privacy Protection and Data Security. From the outset of the development process, data minimization and privacy protection principles are proactively implemented. This involves limiting data collection and processing to what is necessary for achieving the educational goals and activities. This includes anonymization, encryption, and strict access controls to ensure the security of personal information belonging to learners and educators. Personal data of learners and educators must be systematically anonymized or pseudonymized to reduce the risks of direct identification. Additionally, robust encryption techniques are employed to protect data during storage and transmission, ensuring its confidentiality. Finally, strict access controls, based on the principle of least privilege, are applied to ensure that only authorized individuals can access personal information, and only to the extent necessary for their functions.

Responsibility and auditability. The roles and responsibilities of the various actors involved in the development and use of AI systems should be clearly defined, in line with the principles of accountability, auditability, and sustainability. To uphold these principles, logging and traceability systems should be integrated from the design phase to facilitate audits and ensure accountability and transparency throughout the lifecycle of the educational AI system.

Respect for human values and fundamental rights. In line with UNESCO's recommendations (2021), the design of educational AI systems must adhere to an approach that respects human values and fundamental rights. Incorporating ethical requirements from the design phase enhances user trust in these AI systems used in the educational field.

By adopting this comprehensive and ethical approach, designers of educational AI systems can create tools that not only enhance learning and teaching but also strengthen the trust and acceptance of these technologies within the educational environment.

CONCLUSION

In conclusion, artificial intelligence (AI) is initiating a paradigm shift in the educational sector, paving the way for unprecedented personalization and optimization of learning, yet posing complex ethical and socio-economic challenges. This technological revolution signals a profound and comprehensive redefinition of the roles of teachers, learners, and institutions. Such a disruptive scenario calls for a reflective and interdisciplinary approach to understand and preempt its implications.

This chapter has highlighted the multifaceted nature of this technological revolution, exploring its definition and ubiquity across various sectors, with a particular focus on its technical and ethical issues in education. We have presented the essential components of AI, such as machine learning, computer vision, and deep learning, and their transformative impact on sectors ranging from healthcare to industry, transportation, and commerce. In the educational context, AI offers unprecedented possibilities for personalization and adaptation, promising to radically transform modes of access and appropriation of knowledge.

However, integrating AI into education poses significant technical challenges, particularly in terms of the necessary infrastructure, management of massive data, and development of algorithms tailored to pedagogical needs. These technical aspects are closely linked to important ethical concerns, such as privacy protection, equity in access to educational technologies, and the transparency of the algorithms used. It is imperative to adopt a critical approach to the use of AI in education by conducting thorough research on its long-term impact, establishing appropriate regulatory frameworks, and ensuring continuous training for educational system stakeholders.

The ultimate goal remains to capitalize on the considerable advantages of AI to enhance the learning experience while respecting the fundamental values of education, equity, and inclusivity for all learners. Only by maintaining a balance between technological innovation and ethical considerations can we truly harness the transformative potential of AI in education, paving the way for a more adaptive, effective, and equitable educational future.

REFERENCES

Adadi, A., & Berrada, M. (2018). Peeking inside the black-box: A survey on Explainable Artificial Intelligence (XAI). *IEEE Access : Practical Innovations, Open Solutions*, 6, 52138–52160. DOI: 10.1109/ACCESS.2018.2870052

Advanced Distributed Learning (ADL) Initiative. (2022a). SCORM overview. https://adlnet.gov/projects/scorm/

Advanced Distributed Learning (ADL) Initiative. (2022b). The Total Learning Architecture (TLA) and the Experience API (xAPI). U.S. Department of Defense. https://adlnet.gov/projects/xapi/

AI for Oceans #1 - Code.org. (2024). Code.org. https://studio.code.org/s/oceans/lessons/1/levels/2

Aithal, P. S., Prabhu, S., & Aithal, S. (2024). Future of higher education through technology prediction and forecasting. [PIJMESS]. *SSRN*, 1(1), 1–50. DOI: 10.2139/ssrn.4901474

Alhazmi, E., & Sheneamer, A. (2023). Early predicting of students performance in higher education. *IEEE Access : Practical Innovations, Open Solutions*, 11, 27579–27589. DOI: 10.1109/ACCESS.2023.3250702

Alyahyan, E., & Düştegör, D. (2020). Predicting academic success in higher education: Literature review and best practices. *International Journal of Educational Technology in Higher Education*, 17(1), 1–21. DOI: 10.1186/s41239-020-0177-7

Arizmendi, C. J., Bernacki, M. L., Raković, M., Plumley, R. D., Urban, C. J., Panter, A. T., Greene, J. A., & Gates, K. M. (2023). Predicting student outcomes using digital logs of learning behaviors: Review, current standards, and suggestions for future work. *Behav Res*, 55(6), 3026–3054. DOI: 10.3758/s13428-022-01939-9 PMID: 36018483

Baker, R. S., & Hawn, A. (2021). Algorithmic bias in education. *International Journal of Artificial Intelligence in Education*, 31(4), 1–41. DOI: 10.1007/s40593-021-00285-9

Celik, I. (2023). Towards Intelligent-TPACK: An empirical study on teachers' professional knowledge to ethically integrate artificial intelligence (AI)-based tools into education. *Computers in Human Behavior*, 138, 107468–107468. DOI: 10.1016/j.chb.2022.107468

Chen, L., Chen, P., & Lin, Z. (2020). Artificial Intelligence in Education: A Review. *IEEE Access : Practical Innovations, Open Solutions*, 8, 75264–75278. DOI: 10.1109/ACCESS.2020.2988510

Conati, C., Porayska-Pomsta, K., & Mavrikis, M. (2018). AI in Education needs interpretable machine learning: Lessons from Open Learner Modelling. arXiv. https://doi.org//arXiv.1807.00154DOI: 10.48550

Dandan, L., Stoika, O., Stefanyuk, N., Nefedchenko, O., & Drok, V. (2024). Study of methods of teaching digital skills and development of computer literacy among students. Brazilian Journal of Education, Technology and Society, 17(Special Edition 1), 114-124. https://doi.org/DOI: 10.14571/brajets.v17.nse1.114-124

Daniel, B. (2015). Big Data and analytics in higher education: Opportunities and challenges. *British Journal of Educational Technology*, 46(5), 904–920. DOI: 10.1111/bjet.12230

Díaz, B., Nussbaum, M., Greiff, S., & Santana, M. (2024). The role of technology in reading literacy: Is Sweden going back or moving forward by returning to paper-based reading? *Computers & Education*, 213, 105014. Advance online publication. DOI: 10.1016/j.compedu.2024.105014

Essa, A. (2016). A possible future for next generation adaptive learning systems. *Smart Learning Environments*, 3(1), 1–24. DOI: 10.1186/s40561-016-0038-y

European Commission. (2023). Data protection in the EU. https://commission.europa.eu/law/law-topic/data-protection/data-protection-eu_en

European Data Protection Board. (2022). Guidelines on the use of facial recognition technology in the area of law enforcement. Retrieved from https://edpb.europa.eu/our-work-tools/our-documents/guidelines/guidelines-042022-use-facial-recognition-technology-area_en

Fernández, A., Gómez, B., Binjaku, K., & Meçe, E. K. (2023). Digital transformation initiatives in higher education institutions: A multivocal literature review. *Education and Information Technologies*, 28(10), 12351–12382. DOI: 10.1007/s10639-022-11544-0 PMID: 37361743

Folsom-Kovarik, J. T., & Raybourn, E. M. (2016). Total Learning Architecture (TLA) enables next-generation learning via meta-adaptation. In Interservice/Industry Training, Simulation, and Education Conference (I/ITSEC) 2016 (Paper No. 16279, pp. 1-13). Sandia National Laboratories/ADL.

Gambini, A., Desimoni, M., & Ferretti, F. (2022). Predictive tools for university performance: An explorative study. *International Journal of Mathematical Education in Science and Technology*, 55(3), 691–717. DOI: 10.1080/0020739X.2021.2022794

Google for Education. (2023). Case Studies : Ivytech GCP. Google for Education. https://edu.google.com/why-google/customer-stories/ivytech-gcp/

Henrie, C. R., Halverson, L. R., & Graham, C. R. (2015). Measuring student engagement in technology-mediated learning: A review. *Computers & Education*, 90, 36–53. DOI: 10.1016/j.compedu.2015.09.005

Holmes, W., Bialik, M., & Fadel, C. (2019). *Artificial intelligence in education: Promises and implications for teaching and learning*. Center for Curriculum Redesign.

Hussain, M., Zhu, W., Zhang, W., & Abidi, S. M. R. (2018). Student engagement predictions in an e-learning system and their impact on student course assessment scores. *Computational Intelligence and Neuroscience*, 2018, 6347186. Advance online publication. DOI: 10.1155/2018/6347186 PMID: 30369946

Hwang, G.-J., Xie, H., Wah, B. W., & Gašević, D. (2020). Vision, challenges, roles and research issues of Artificial Intelligence in Education. *Computers and Education: Artificial Intelligence*, 1, 100001. DOI: 10.1016/j.caeai.2020.100001

Institut de statistique de l'UNESCO (2016), Making Education Count for Development: Data Collection and Availability in Six PISA for Development Countries, PISA, Éditions OCDE, Paris, .DOI: 10.1787/9789264255449-en

Jagielski, M., Oprea, A., Biggio, B., Liu, C., Nita-Rotaru, C., & Li, B. (2018). Manipulating machine learning: Poisoning attacks and countermeasures for regression learning. *2018 IEEE Symposium on Security and Privacy (SP)*, 19-35. DOI: 10.1109/SP.2018.00057

Khosravi, H., Sadiq, S., & Gasevic, D. (2022). Development and adoption of an adaptive learning system: Reflections and lessons learned. In *Proceedings of the 52nd ACM Technical Symposium on Computer Science Education* (pp. 58-64), DOI: 10.1145/3328778.3366900

Kulik, J. A., & Fletcher, J. D. (2016). Effectiveness of intelligent tutoring systems: A meta-analytic review. *Review of Educational Research*, 86(1), 42–78. DOI: 10.3102/0034654315581420

Larini, M., & Barthes, A. (2019). *Quantitative and statistical data in education: From data collection to data processing. John Wiley & Sons, Inc.* ISTE, Ltd., DOI: 10.1002/9781119451457

Li, Z., Lou, X., Chen, M., Li, S., Lv, C., Song, S., & Li, L. (2023). Students' online learning adaptability and their continuous usage intention across different disciplines. *Humanities & Social Sciences Communications*, 10(1), 838. DOI: 10.1057/s41599-023-02376-5

Luckin, R., & Cukurova, M. (2019). Designing educational technologies in the age of AI: A learning sciences-driven approach. *British Journal of Educational Technology*, 50(6), 2824–2838. DOI: 10.1111/bjet.12861

Mouta, A., Pinto-Llorente, A. M., & Torrecilla-Sánchez, E. M. (2023). Uncovering Blind Spots in Education Ethics: Insights from a Systematic Literature Review on Artificial Intelligence in Education. *International Journal of Artificial Intelligence in Education*. Advance online publication. DOI: 10.1007/s40593-023-00384-9

Nagy, A. S., Tumiwa, J. R., Arie, F. V., & Erdey, L. (2024). An exploratory study of artificial intelligence adoption in higher education. *Cogent Education*, 11(1), 2386892. Advance online publication. DOI: 10.1080/2331186X.2024.2386892

National Artificial Intelligence Research Resource Task Force. (2023, January 13). Strengthening and Democratizing the U.S. Artificial Intelligence Innovation Ecosystem. https://www.ai.gov/wp-content/uploads/2023/01/NAIRR-TF-Final-Report-2023.pdf

National Science Foundation. (2023, August 1). National Artificial Intelligence (AI) Research Institutes (NSF 23-610). https://new.nsf.gov/funding/opportunities/national-artificial-intelligence-research-institutes/nsf23-610/solicitation

National Science Foundation. (n.d.). Artificial Intelligence. Retrieved September 19, 2024, from https://new.nsf.gov/focus-areas/artificial-intelligence

Nguyen, A., Ngo, H. N., Hong, Y., Dang, B., & Nguyen, B.-P. T. (2022). Ethical principles for artificial intelligence in education. *Education and Information Technologies*, 28(4), 4221–4241. DOI: 10.1007/s10639-022-11316-w PMID: 36254344

Nguyen, S., & DiPaola, D. (2020). AI & data privacy activities for k-9 students.

OECD. (2021). *OECD Digital Education Outlook 2021: Pushing the Frontiers with Artificial Intelligence, Blockchain and Robots*. OECD Publishing., DOI: 10.1787/589b283f-

Pacheco-Mendoza, S., Guevara, C., Mayorga-Albán, A., & Fernández-Escobar, J. (2023). Artificial intelligence in higher education: A predictive model for academic performance. *Education Sciences*, 13(10), 990. Advance online publication. DOI: 10.3390/educsci13100990

Pane, J. F., Griffin, B. A., McCaffrey, D. F., & Karam, R. (2014). Effectiveness of Cognitive Tutor Algebra I at Scale. *Educational Evaluation and Policy Analysis*, 36(2), 127–144. DOI: 10.3102/0162373713507480

Pardo, A., & Siemens, G. (2014). Ethical and privacy principles for learning analytics. *British Journal of Educational Technology*, 45(3), 438–450. DOI: 10.1111/bjet.12152

Payne, B. (2019). An Ethics of Artificial Intelligence Curriculum for Middle School Students. https://thecenter.mit.edu/wp-content/uploads/2020/07/MIT-AI-Ethics-Education-Curriculum.pdf

Peng, T., Luo, Y., & Liu, Y. (2022). AI-Based Equipment Optimization of the Design on Intelligent Education Curriculum System. *Wireless Communications and Mobile Computing*, 2022(1), 1–13. Advance online publication. DOI: 10.1155/2022/3614883

Pesovski, I., Santos, R., Henriques, R., & Trajkovik, V. (2023). *Generative AI for Customizable Learning Experiences*. Journal Name., DOI: 10.3390/xxxxx

Prinsloo, P., & Slade, S. (2016). Student vulnerability, agency, and learning analytics: An exploration. *Journal of Learning Analytics*, 3(1), 159–182. DOI: 10.18608/jla.2016.31.10

Prinsloo, P., & Slade, S. (2017). An elephant in the learning analytics room: The obligation to act. In *Proceedings of the Seventh International Learning Analytics & Knowledge Conference* (pp. 46-55). ACM. DOI: 10.1145/3027385.3027406

Reich, J., & Ito, M. (2017). *From good intentions to real outcomes: Equity by design in learning technologies*. Digital Media and Learning Research Hub.

Renz, A., & Hilbig, R. (2020). Prerequisites for artificial intelligence in further education: Identification of drivers, barriers, and business models of educational technology companies. *International Journal of Educational Technology in Higher Education*, 17(1), 1–21. DOI: 10.1186/s41239-020-00193-3

Rubel, A., & Jones, K. M. (2016). Student privacy in learning analytics: An information ethics perspective. *The Information Society*, 32(2), 143–159. DOI: 10.1080/01972243.2016.1130502

Saidani, O., Umer, M., & Alshardan, A.. (2024). *Student academic success prediction in multimedia-supported virtual learning system using ensemble learning approach*. Multimed Tools Appl., DOI: 10.1007/s11042-024-18669-z

Schools Week. (2023, june 24). AI : How are schools using the technology in classrooms? https://schoolsweek.co.uk/ai-how-are-schools-using-the-technology-in-classrooms/

Selwyn, N. (2019). *Should robots replace teachers? AI and the future of education*. John Wiley & Sons.

Shen, C., Wang, H., Xie, H., Poon, L. K., & Huang, R. (2023). Artificial intelligence in education: A review of two decades of research. *Journal of Educational Technology & Society*, 26(1), 36–52. https://www.jstor.org/stable/48678066

Siemens, G., & Long, P. (2011). Penetrating the fog: Analytics in learning and education. *EDUCAUSE Review*, 46(5), 30–40. https://er.educause.edu/articles/2011/9/penetrating-the-fog-analytics-in-learning-and-education

Slade, S., & Prinsloo, P. (2013). Learning analytics: Ethical issues and dilemmas. *The American Behavioral Scientist*, 57(10), 1510–1529. DOI: 10.1177/0002764213479366

Stahl, B. C., Schroeder, D., & Rodrigues, R. (2022). Unfair and illegal discrimination. In *Ethics of artificial intelligence: Case studies and options for addressing ethical challenges* (pp. 9–23). Springer International Publishing.

Steingartner, W., Galinec, D., & Kozina, A. (2021). Threat defense: Cyber deception approach and education for resilience in hybrid threats model. *Symmetry*, 13(4), 597. DOI: 10.3390/sym13040597

The White House. (2023, October 30). Executive Order on the Safe, Secure, and Trustworthy Development and Use of Artificial Intelligence. https://www.whitehouse.gov/briefing-room/presidential-actions/2023/10/30/executive-order-on-the-safe-secure-and-trustworthy-development-and-use-of-artificial-intelligence/

Tuomi, I. (2018). *The impact of artificial intelligence on learning, teaching, and education*. Publications Office of the European Union.

Tyagi, S., Gupta, V., & Mehndiratta, V. (2024). Building Smart Campuses: Integrating AI in Higher Education. In Arya, R., Sharma, S. C., Verma, A. K., & Iyer, B. (Eds.), *Recent Trends in Artificial Intelligence Towards a Smart World. Frontiers of Artificial Intelligence, Ethics and Multidisciplinary Applications*. Springer., DOI: 10.1007/978-981-97-6790-8_15

VanLehn, K. (2011). The relative effectiveness of human tutoring, intelligent tutoring systems, and other tutoring systems. *Educational Psychologist*, 46(4), 197–221. DOI: 10.1080/00461520.2011.611369

Viberg, O., Hatakka, M., Bälter, O., & Mavroudi, A. (2018). The current landscape of learning analytics in higher education. *Computers in Human Behavior*, 89, 98–110. DOI: 10.1016/j.chb.2018.07.027

Wang, S., Wang, F., Zhu, Z., Wang, J., Tran, T., & Du, Z. (2024). Artificial intelligence in education: A systematic literature review. *Expert Systems with Applications*, 237, 124167. DOI: 10.1016/j.eswa.2024.124167

Williamson, B., & Piattoeva, N. (2019). Objectivity as standardization in data-scientific education policy, technology and governance. *Learning, Media and Technology*, 44(1), 64–76. DOI: 10.1080/17439884.2018.1556215

Zawacki-Richter, O., Kerres, M., Bedenlier, S., Bond, M., & Buntins, K. (Eds.). (2020). *Systematic Reviews in Educational Research: Methodology, Perspectives and Application*. Springer Fachmedien Wiesbaden., DOI: 10.1007/978-3-658-27602-7

Zawacki-Richter, O., Marín, V. I., Bond, M., & Gouverneur, F. (2019). Systematic review of research on artificial intelligence applications in higher education – where are the educators? *International Journal of Educational Technology in Higher Education*, 16(1), 39. DOI: 10.1186/s41239-019-0171-0

Endnotes

1 UNESCO Ethic AI 2020 (Draft), UNESCO Education & AI (2021), Beijing Consensus (2019), OECD (2021), European Commission (2019), European Parliament Report AI Education (2021).

Chapter 3
Redefining Teaching in the Era of Generative Artificial Intelligence: A 360-Degree Perspective

Rahul Joshi
https://orcid.org/0000-0002-5467-5105
Manav Rachna International Institute of Research and Studies, Haryana, India

Krishna Pandey
https://orcid.org/0000-0001-8290-3681
Manav Rachna International Institute of Research and Studies, Haryana, India

Suman Kumari
Manav Rachna International Institute of Research and Studies, Haryana, India

ABSTRACT

Artificial intelligence (AI) in education has significantly transformed the methodology of imparting knowledge in classrooms. AI-based education has revolutionized teaching and learning, transitioning from traditional classroom teaching to personalized learning. AI has provided many learning possibilities for students and instructors to discover and implement innovative teaching techniques using technology. The limitations of the conventional educational system will become outdated as AI-generated learning will make classroom instruction easily accessible with just a click. Each time a new technology emerges, there is a concern about its potential for abuse. The advent of AI has brought about a rise in issues that have led to doubts and the gradual decline of the conventional schooling system. The chapter explores the techniques and procedures for incorporating AI into the conventional educational system, promoting a more advanced and improved learning environment. Artificial

DOI: 10.4018/979-8-3693-7255-5.ch003

intelligence has the potential to enhance the online education system significantly.

INTRODUCTION

Technological progress in recent years has caused a rapid and significant change in higher learning. Generative artificial intelligence is a groundbreaking technical advancement with the ability. Generative AI uses algorithms and machine learning methods to create unique material in many formats, including text, graphics, and multimedia (Bandi et al., 2023). Today, Generative AI is a critical instrument in facilitating higher education through smooth dissemination of information between teachers and the learners. By transcending boundaries, it has diminished limitations of time and distance in the process of sharing among students and instructors from diverse backgrounds (Joshi et al., 2024). The emergence of Generative AI on the scene has brought a paradigm shift in the availability and processing of data in higher education institutions across the world. Generative AI acts as a catalyst in bringing widespread international cooperation in the domain of knowledge and prompts the experts, scholars, and students to discuss, deliberate and express views. Thus, developing a detailed and all-inclusive expression of knowledge (Horwitz and Santillan, 2012).

Worldwide there are hundreds of languages spoken and written. With so much diversity in culture, tradition and language, understanding culture, literature and collating information has been a tedious task for the experts. In fact, on the hindsight, it has been seen that language has acted as barrier in this endeavor. Now, this problem has been duly addressed by the Generative AI as it can provide linguistic support in the form of instant translation and research thereby expediting easy access to intercultural treasure troves of information and generate creativity (Ramzan et al., 2023). In this direction, AI algorithms are assisting the individuals in the process of studying the original and intricate sources of data base. Algorithms help the scholars in critical thinking and contribute towards developing new ideas and thoughts (Peters, 2023). More so, generative AI also helps in cultivating such experiences to suits the interests of the students and enhancing their efficiency. It is important that use of generative AI should be maximum for the purpose creating and assessing of information and students should be trained for a judicious use of artificial intelligence. Hence, it is necessary to continue to depend on specialists in different fields to assess the accuracy and effectiveness of outputs produced by AI systems.

For instance, an AI-generated curriculum is expected to undergo evaluation by experts in education and domain-specific expertise. Therefore, it must be ensured that students have the necessary tools to become proficient authorities in their respective domains, armed with the ability to analyze and assess the outcomes produced by

AI systems with sound reasoning and astute critical thinking. They are continuing with the emphasis on human interaction and interpersonal bonds. Students with the necessary socio-emotional abilities to traverse this realm likely have more favourable outcomes than those without such capabilities (Nicolaides et al., 2024). It must be guaranteed that our students can securely and proficiently operate and interact with AI systems. They must possess the ability to use AI, acknowledge its limitations, and determine the areas where it will need human enhancement. It is essential to guarantee that students have computational thinking abilities to create goods, services, and systems based on AI technologies. To successfully attain these aims, the interdisciplinary ties between AI and diverse disciplines should be set up from the outset. Integrating AI throughout our curriculum is essential to guarantee that students have the necessary skills and literacy to use AI in many disciplines rather than confining it to computer science courses.

Like educators, students will perpetually need skills to learn and develop throughout their educational journey. Furthermore, they must cultivate a growth mindset and acquire the necessary learning skills to effectively adjust to a dynamic and evolving environment. They need to acquire new talents, familiarize themselves with new technologies, and apply their fundamental skills and knowledge to other areas. They must persevere without succumbing to discouragement or disillusionment when an AI system supplants them (Abulibdeh et al., 2024).

Related Work

The recent advancements in AI in higher education have been shaped by two significant factors: the introduction of Open AI's ChatGPT and the surge in virtual learning, which the COVID-19 pandemic has accelerated (Bearman et al., 2024). This phenomenon was, and still is, more prevalent in underdeveloped countries (Al Dhaen et al., 2023). It is the duty of universities to provide their students with current, practical, and relevant learning resources. Universities are likewise obligated to adapt to the swiftly evolving technological environment, which encompasses AI as an increasingly significant element. In order to adequately prepare students for the workforce, which will eventually include artificial intelligence, it is necessary to make it mandatory for students to possess a fundamental understanding of AI ideas and vocabulary (Thurzo et al., 2023). Higher education institutions must provide fair and equal education to all students. Artificial intelligence can fulfil this requirement (McGrath et al., 2023). Universities must alter and update their curriculum material and pedagogical approaches in response to the current "AI paradigm shift."

University instructors sometimes need to work on embracing new technology, resulting in a delayed rate of adoption owing to their unwillingness to alter their teaching methods. University professors see AI as both a menace and a chance for advancement. One prevalent topic in discussions about AI in education is the concern that AI has the potential to replace teachers (AlDhaen, 2022). Bearman et al. (2023) characterize this as one facet of a "dystopia-is-now" viewpoint about AI in higher education. One significant issue related to AI in higher education is the possibility of students plagiarizing the work produced by AI systems (King and ChatGPT, 2023; Shoja et al., 2023), which has been coined as "AIgiarism" (Murugesan and Cherukuri, 2023). Additional dystopian forecasts include the subversion of scientific endeavours, apprehensions about privacy and ethics, the perpetuation of prejudices, and the dissemination of incorrect information (Bozkurt, 2023). Numerous instructors must learn about using AI as an instructional instrument or resist integrating it into their classrooms. A frequent factor is the need for more time to acquire the necessary skills to apply artificial intelligence proficiently (Crawford et al., 2023). Typically, educators prioritize external motivations such as recognition, promotion, and monetary rewards over internal motivations such as finding teaching and learning engaging, improving learning outcomes, and enhancing teaching quality. As a result, they often do not perceive any personal advantages in adopting AI-based learning and teaching methods.

In addition, some educators believe that AI technologies are still in the early stages of their development and need more accuracy in information retrieval and delivery to be used in learning and teaching settings. There are different divisions among user categories regarding the acceptance of AI solutions. For instance, ladies indicate they possess a lower level of understanding of AI than men. Non-native speakers and individuals with pronounced accents may need help with AI-powered voice recognition and dictation tools. These applications may need help accurately understanding accents and dialects, resulting in misunderstandings or miscommunications (Wang et al., 2023). Artificial intelligence disrupts the traditional concept of teaching and seeks to redefine the responsibilities of human educators. Teachers should modify their teaching methods and evaluation techniques to improve students' performance while preventing any unethical use of generative AI (Pearce and Chiavaroli, 2023). For this to happen, institutions must establish robust policies and ongoing research agendas that specifically tackle AI challenges, including ethical aspects. In the present and any subsequent eras of rapid technological advancements, it is essential to prioritize "future-proofing subjects and degrees consistently." Nevertheless, there are some positive aspects to consider. One of the conflicting utopian ideas is that AI can positively impact students' creativity and self-efficacy, provide an inclusive curriculum, and customize learning (Lodge et al., 2023). Research has shown that customized material improves the learning process and results in tremendous success for international students. Additionally, it has been discovered that it is a potent instrument for enhancing the professional knowledge of post-secondary instructors. ChatGPT has been shown to aid medical teaching by bringing out new and unconventional concepts that learners may not be aware of.

Exploring Generative AI: Understanding its Functioning

By 2022, the central area of artificial intelligence that had greatly influenced the general population was discriminative AI, which is this style of artificial intelligence, particularly in classifying and retrieving information. Nevertheless, there was a notable transformation in public communication with the widespread use of generative AI after the general availability of models such as ChatGPT. Although generative and discriminative AI share some basic principles and technology, their ultimate objectives differ dramatically. Discriminative AI aims to categorize and distinguish data by learning the distinctions between various data categories (Dhoni, 2023). In contrast, generative AI is specifically designed to produce novel material or outputs by leveraging the input it gets and its acquired comprehension of the data fed into its models. Training generative AI models often entails unsupervised learning, which allows the model to process and comprehend vast quantities of text, pictures, or videos. The objective is to discern regularities in the organization or generation of the data, enabling the AI to imitate and reproduce it. Two commonly used methods are autoencoding and Generative Adversarial Networks (GANs).

An autoencoder is a neural network designed to replicate its input as accurately as possible in its output. The intrinsic architecture of the system enables it to condense the input into a latent-space representation and then rebuild the output from it (Wang et al., 2014). The model takes the input and reduces it to its simplest form, then reconstructs it using the reduced version it has generated. Acquiring condensed representations, which are reduced versions, is advantageous for reducing noise and detecting anomalies. This is because the model reaches knowledge about which aspects of the input are crucial for preservation and which are insignificant. Autoencoders, when applied in the context of generative AI, can produce new data with similar characteristics to the training data. This is achieved by effectively understanding the distribution of the original data and then replicating the same process to generate new content that resembles the training set.

GANs are a distinct kind of generative artificial intelligence. The process entails training two neural networks, a generator, and a discriminator, in a competitive framework. The generator's function is to produce legitimate samples while the discriminator assesses the genuineness of these samples. This rivalry between the two networks enables the model to train itself successfully, improving its capacity to create persuasive data (Megahed and Mohammed, 2024; Sharma et al., 2024). This approach is prevalent in the development of image-generative AI models. Generative AI is distinguished by its ability to generate unique information, designs, and solutions not found in the original training data. The possibilities of generative AI are extensive and constantly expanding with the development of increasingly advanced models. These models can produce many types of content, such as high-resolution photographs, music compositions, articles, 3D models, and even computer code, in addition to introductory text and image production.

Implications for Education

The significant possibilities of AI in education are becoming evident, and the book's subsequent sections will further examine the consequences of generative AI in more tangible and pragmatic ways (Darvishi et al., 2024). Nevertheless, it is crucial to start by categorizing the results into a limited number of critical domains.

1. ***Goal-oriented:*** A significant portion of the skills that schools impart to learners are generative, such as writing papers, creating presentations, refining writing abilities, conducting research, and summarizing authoritative sources. Suppose AI systems can perform these tasks for students in the future. In that case, it raises the question of how the content and methodology of our current teaching practices can be justified to students and ourselves.
2. ***Personalized learning:*** Generative AI can provide customized educational materials and resources by adjusting to each student's unique requirements and preferred learning methods based on the information provided to them. One way to do this is by modifying a news story to cater to various levels of reading proficiency. Furthermore, Generative AI can enhance the accessibility of educational materials by automatically translating, summarizing, or modifying information to cater to a wide range of student demographics (Zhang et al., 2020).
3. ***Ethical concerns:*** It arises when using generative AI in education since it can perpetuate biases in defective data sets or generate improper material. There are further difficulties in the establishment and implementation of academic integrity rules, as well as the interpretation of what constitutes the creation of authentic work (Remian, 2019). The following are some primary ethical concerns in AI and education.
   a) The ethical implications of *algorithmic bias and discrimination* are the most extensively researched in the reviewed studies. AI models have shown prejudice and discrimination due to the training data, reinforcing existing preconceptions. The current body of research primarily examines the prejudice contained in databases and algorithms of AI models against certain groups of students, particularly those who are underrepresented minorities. This bias encompasses several factors, including gender, race or ethnicity,

socioeconomic status, and cultural background. More precisely, gender discrimination stands out as one of the most evident manifestations of this problem. Akgun and Greenhow exposed the gender biases inherent in using AI models in language learning courses. When students acquire the ability to interpret words using generative language models, such as those about physicians and soldiers, they often translate them with a male bias, hence intensifying certain societal biases and gender stereotypes (Akgun and Greenhow, 2022).

b) *Data privacy breaches* are a significant ethical concern when discussing using AI models in the classroom. AI models examine, evaluate, and forecast students' learning performance by aggregating extensive and varied data, including personal background information, academic achievements, facial expressions, and voice recordings (Reiss, 2021). Although these models may enhance the educational experience in the classroom, they also raise ethical concerns about data privacy, such as the potential disclosure of personal information, surveillance and monitoring of students, the lack of informed consent, and the right to erode personal data.

c) The research identified a *lack of openness* as the third most significant ethical problem. Transparency, often referred to as explainability in certain studies such as Jang et al.'s (2022) and Farrow's study (2023, pertains to thorough explanations of algorithmic judgments or the gathering and use of data. The use of AI models is seeing a widespread decrease in transparency. Kooli observed that the present use of AI models in the classroom needs more explanation. Specifically, most instructors and students must understand the AI decision-making process and the appropriate circumstances for using this data (Kooli, 2023). The potential hazards and practical disadvantages of deploying AI models in the classroom must be explained in depth (Larsson and Heintz, 2020).

d) *Decreased autonomy* is a significant ethical concern discussed in the evaluated research. It is crucial to mention that autonomy is also called agency in some research, such as Tuomi (2023) and Holmes et al. (2022). It pertains to individuals having the freedom to pursue objectives and values that they consider significant. Schiff proposed that using AI models in the classroom might lead to a reduction in appropriate decision-making authority, compromising the autonomy of instructors, students, and parents. He further highlighted that these issues have already emerged.

e) *Academic dishonesty* is the least ethically concerning issue in the reviewed studies. Nevertheless, the improper use of AI technology has resulted in several instances of academic dishonesty. The use of AI models, such as

ChatGPT, for cheating and plagiarizing in academic assignments and examinations undermines the efforts of others and creates an unfair environment.

4. ***Content generation:*** Educators may use generative AI to produce tailored learning materials, evaluations, presentations, or even whole curricula, reducing the time and effort required to prepare their classes. In addition, educators may use AI systems to facilitate student engagement in project creation, assist in the initial drafting of papers, and even autonomously evaluate tasks while providing tailored comments (Diwan et al., 2023).

Equipping Students for the Workforce Fueled by AI

If you have recently entered a National Highway in India, you may have seen a rise in the prevalence of automatic checkout lanes. Due to the increased use of automated procedures and less human involvement in checkout, the NHAI can employ a much smaller workforce than before. These improvements are not exclusive to NHAI and are expected to extend beyond supermarkets in the coming years. With the ongoing advancement of AI and robots, the employment landscape will inevitably undergo more changes, leading to the obsolescence of many roles and necessitating the need for people to acquire new skills. The advent of generative AI has expanded the range of activities that AI can do and augmented the number of occupations that machines instead of humans will soon execute (Aoun, 2017).

These are Some Significant Employment Markets That Will Transform:

1. ***Retail industry:*** Self-service kiosks and e-commerce platforms are diminishing the need for human cashiers and salespeople.
2. ***Means of conveyance:*** Autonomous vehicles are currently being developed with the potential to replace human drivers someday.
3. ***Production Industry:*** Robotics are used to mechanize several functions in manufacturing, including welding, painting, and assembling. These automated machines with more sophisticated artificial intelligence systems will further diminish human involvement and quality assurance requirements.
4. ***Financial management:*** AI-driven software may automate numerous duties currently handled by accountants, such as compiling financial assertions and auditing economic data. They possess the ability to classify information and operations, as well as elucidate financial data.

5. ***Judicial:*** AI-driven solutions can automate several operations that attorneys carry out, including legal research and document review. They might draft legal papers, file paperwork, and review work before it is filed.
6. ***Customer services:*** Artificial intelligence-driven chatbots will respond to client inquiries and effectively address any problems. AI services like Intercom can use corporate documents and information to answer inquiries.
7. ***Medical:*** AI-driven systems can identify ailments accurately, provide therapy suggestions, and even perform surgical procedures. In addition, they can immediately interact with patients to get fundamental data, compile medical records, and explain findings and diagnoses, even in various languages.

Although the examples provided are just a few, there are several more instances where employment is expected to be replaced or significantly altered shortly as various sectors and corporations investigate the use of AI and robots in their everyday operations. In general, most jobs that may be repetitive or synthesis-based (using much information to make choices or judgments) can be replaced by AI. New employment sectors will likely emerge as novel methods to use our time and skills are discovered. However, the current industries will also see a growing need for more workforce. To thrive in these marketplaces and advance their professional trajectories amidst the growing influence of AI, students must cultivate the necessary aptitudes. The AI-powered workforce will need a combination of technical and interpersonal abilities.

The Following are Many Crucial Abilities That Will be Indispensable:

1. ***Technical abilities & Creativity:*** A fundamental comprehension of AI and machine learning principles, programming languages, data analysis, and cybersecurity will be necessary regardless of the sector students pursue. Proficiency in creative thinking and the capacity to generate groundbreaking concepts will be greatly esteemed (Wang et al., 2023). The ability to make aesthetic evaluations, develop innovative and groundbreaking ideas and designs, and effectively address human requirements will distinguish creative individuals who depend primarily on artificial intelligence for production from those who use AI as a tool.
2. ***Problem Solving & Emotional Intelligence:*** With the increasing dominance of AI in handling repetitive jobs, the need for human workers will shift towards addressing intricate challenges that require critical thinking and inventive resolutions (Sood, 2008). Proficiency in understanding and managing human emotions will be crucial, particularly in education, healthcare, and social services.

3. ***Continual education:*** Ongoing learning and adjusting will be crucial as technology advances. Acquiring the ability to acquire new knowledge continuously is the fundamental talent that students must develop. Teachers may cultivate these talents in students by redirecting their attention in the classroom toward open-ended and innovative activities while ensuring that students obtain the fundamental skills required to navigate established and emerging markets.

Improving Analytical Thinking and Problem-Solving

Using project-based learning to deliver hands-on, real-world experiences that encourage students to think critically, collaborate, and create. Promoting the development of students' abilities to examine intricate scenarios, integrate data, and arrive at well-informed choices (Karenina et al., 2020).

Facilitating Collaboration and Adaptability

Establishing collaborative learning settings that foster student motivation, encourage idea sharing, and facilitate peer-to-peer learning. Improving communication and teamwork abilities, motivating students to work efficiently with varied teams, and using collective intelligence. Encouraging educators to investigate the relationships between different topics, promoting innovative problem-solving skills and flexibility. Recognizing the increasing speed of change, students need to be able to adjust to novel technology and methods of operation. Encouraging educators to see problems as chances for personal development, aiding them in cultivating resilience and a mindset conducive to continuous learning throughout their lives (Ramachandran et al., 2024). Emphasizing the cultivation of transferable abilities rather than specialized topic knowledge to equip students for many sectors and employment positions.

Improving Digital Literacy and Social Intelligence

By incorporating artificial intelligence and digital technologies into the curriculum, students are equipped with the essential skills and knowledge required to thrive in a profession heavily relying on AI. Instruct educators on proficiently using, navigating, and comprehending digital tools and technology, including AI systems. Since AI relies on data, students must gather, scrutinize, and decipher data proficiently. Promoting an awareness of one's emotions aids educators in efficiently regulating their sentiments. Encouraging empathy for others is an ability that remains distinctively human (Koravuna and Surepally, 2020). Enabling individuals to acquire knowledge from past events, accept and adapt to new circumstances, and successfully navigate unpredictability in a swiftly changing labour market.

Advancing Education in Artificial Intelligence and Computational Intelligence

Given the increasing prevalence of AI in our society, students need to understand this technology thoroughly to assess its consequences critically. Proficiency in comprehending the operation of AI and engaging in critical analysis of its repercussions are vital aptitudes that students will need in the AI era. By cultivating this understanding, students may be given the essential resources to traverse a progressively digital society, including their personal and professional domains. Equipped with the appropriate information and expertise, students can make well-informed choices about AI use's ethical, social, and technical consequences. This includes considering any biases, privacy concerns, and ethical ramifications. As indicated in the previous section, the fast job market transformation also needs students' active engagement in the constantly expanding, AI-driven work environment (Shin, 2019). It will be essential to adapt to future developments by prioritizing the development of basic AI knowledge and comfort in schools.

AI literacy requires proficiency in addressing the following inquiries:

- *Define AI & Machine learning? Explain existing tools in the market.*
- *Why does AI represent a major step forward for human civilization?*
- *How often will AI pop up in the workplace and personal life?*
- *How can we employ AI to address our issues?*
- *When should we utilize AI or a tool?*

For educational institutions to effectively address these inquiries, they will need to prioritize the following:

1. ***Essentials of AI & Data Literacy:*** It understands core ideas, principles, machine learning, and AI-associated technologies. The capacity to comprehend, analyze, and evaluate data, recognizing its function in AI-driven decision-making processes (Semeler et al., 2024).
2. ***Thinking computationally, critically and evaluating:*** An essential talent for comprehending AI algorithms is the ability to deconstruct complex issues into more digestible components systematically. The capacity to critically examine

AI systems and applications' strengths, limits, and possible biases needs to be developed.

3. ***Ethics and understanding of responsible behaviour in the digital realm:*** Comprehending the ethical ramifications and societal repercussions of AI use, including concerns about privacy, equity, and responsibility. Fostering conscientious and secure conduct on the internet while also cultivating an understanding of the influence of artificial intelligence on both society and people.

In order to guarantee comprehensive skill development in students, they must go beyond just instructing them on the concept of AI in a dedicated computer science course. Everyone needs to incorporate the following aspects in our classrooms.

1. ***Integration of many disciplines and learning via project-based methods:*** Integrate AI principles and abilities into many courses, demonstrating their significance and practicality in various situations. Allocate assignments that compel students to use their comprehension of AI ideas and principles (Baser et al., 2017).
2. ***AI-powered products and platforms, as well as ethical debates and case studies:*** Employ AI-powered educational tools, such as adaptive learning platforms and intelligent tutoring systems, to familiarize students with the practical applications of AI technology. Promote the development of analytical thinking and moral contemplation by examining case studies, ethical issues, and scenarios connected to artificial intelligence.

Incorporating AI literacy into conventional academic disciplines would guarantee that students can use their knowledge in any situation. For instance, in mathematics, students may acquire knowledge about artificial intelligence by delving into the mechanisms via which algorithms tackle issues and the underlying principles of machine learning. Within science, students may learn about artificial intelligence by delving into its applications in medical diagnostics or the advancement of pharmaceuticals. Within social studies, students can learn about artificial intelligence by delving into its applications in criminal justice and immigration, where it plays a pivotal role in decision-making processes.

Current and Needed Policies for AI in Education

A careful equilibrium between innovation and regulation is required to harness the benefits of integrating AI in education while minimizing possible hazards. Hence, many countries focus on critical areas like Data privacy legislation, such as the General Data Protection Regulation (GDPR) in Europe and the Family Educational Rights and Privacy Act (FERPA) in the United States for framing of regulatory policies. These are necessary for protecting and judicious use of students' data. Moreover, ethical norms set up by international bodies like UNESCO and OECD clearly give structured guidelines for the prudent use AI in education. The guidelines also mandate against the unethical use of AI by causing discrimination and discrepancies.

Although, governments and educational institutions world over have been concentrating on the inclusion of AI in their literacy programs with the objective to improve teaching learning efficiency by using AI-generated knowledge system in the school curricula. It is also fostering skill development as AI is fast becoming the part and parcel of day-to-day life and employment. The need for statutes for checking the unethical and rampant use of AI is of prime concern before the governments all over the world. It has to be seen that the use of AI in educational institutions should benefit all with no discrimination. Laws relating to AI guaranteeing free and fair access to data for all is the need of the hour. As the technology constantly evolves so is the greater need for regular change and up gradation of laws to meet the new challenges. Besides giving guidelines on the fair and judicious use of AI in education, laws should also help the teachers and instructors in their training and quality enhancement.

Only enactment of law will not do. The meticulous implementation of these laws is also necessary. Effective checks are required to prevent algorithmic bias, leading to transparency in decision-making processes driven by artificial intelligence, and thereby, protecting against the unethical use of AI, especially in domains such as student monitoring and automated grading. Research is one area where AI can be used maximum. Data collection, collation, assessment, and verification through AI results in data finesse and fund allocation for further research. Here, public –private partnership plays an important role in facilitating AI-driven research and its funding. Public- Private Partnership is also needed in supporting AI infrastructure for schools and institutions. These comprehensive regulations are essential to guarantee that the incorporation of AI into education is efficient, fair, and morally sound, maximizing its advantages while minimizing any hazards.

Promoting a Growth Perspective and Continuous Education Culture

An essential consequence of AI on our society is the accelerated rate at which change will persistently occur. Over the following decades, artificial intelligence will likely have a significant and far-reaching influence on all facets of society, including our professional endeavours and social interactions. As previously discussed in the first section, the employment market will undergo a significant and striking transformation, particularly in terms of the types of work that will continue to need human involvement. Additionally, the rise of new disciplines, increased opportunities for creative thinking and groundbreaking advancements, and the many consequences of delegating a significant portion of tasks to AI systems fostering an environment conducive to human growth and prosperity were explored. Historically, technological advancements have generally occurred gradually and incrementally, allowing us enough time to acclimatize to them (Woolf et al., 2013).

Nevertheless, AI is revolutionizing the globe at an exponential pace. Consequently, predicting future outcomes becomes difficult. Artificial intelligence will profoundly affect many aspects of society, necessitating proactive consideration of strategies to adapt to this transformation. Students must possess resilience and a development attitude to surmount the many hurdles from such quick adjustments. As the saying goes, "Change is Constant." Technology is constantly evolving. Humans must adjust and upgrade themselves to reap the benefits of this regularly changing landscape. However, technology has yet to conquer the human mind. With the ever-growing technology, students must be proactive about issues and challenges. AI promotes constant learning and requires relentless adeptness and adjustments to the AI milieu. Progressive AI also provides ample opportunities to enhance communication skills and leadership talents.

Furthermore, these possibilities facilitate perpetual personal development and acquisition of knowledge as students persistently enhance their interpersonal abilities and adeptly use them in diverse circumstances. Educators must exemplify these attitudes themselves. By demonstrating a commitment to staying updated with the most recent advancements and integrating them into your teaching methods, you are already serving as a role model for adapting and nurturing curiosity in educators. The projects and assignments in our classrooms must prioritize fostering curiosity, investigation, and inquiry rather than emphasizing specific information or isolated skills. Our school's incentive systems and communication style must consistently highlight students' work and development rather than focusing exclusively on their achievement to promote a growth-oriented mindset. AI solutions may enhance the manageability of these activities by offering instructors the ability to personalize and adapt to the unique learning experience of each student. Those students who believe in rigorous and personalized learning can take advantage of AI tools-based learning and have the capacity to grow beyond classroom learning. AI-driven tools cater to individual needs and requirements, thus offering them a very personalized experience. AI tools also assist the students in their overall personality growth and strengthen their learning curve. The process becomes lifelong.

Developing Innovative and Creative Abilities in the Age of AI

With the entry of Generative AI in the education sector, the role of educators has suddenly become important, especially in the context of innovation and creativity. Undoubtedly, AI can perform many such activities as humans initially did. However, AI cannot beat the human brain for its intelligence and intellectual understanding. Furthermore, the ability of AI to produce ideas and solutions beyond human imagination highlights the need to cultivate these skills in our teachers. Our educators must be able to implement, question, and refine the ideas produced by AI. By developing these abilities, students are prepared for a swiftly changing future, enabling them to make meaningful contributions to human advancement by recognizing possibilities and generating value in the age of artificial intelligence (Lim, 2018). As automation takes over more chores, individuals will have more free time for personal growth and interests. To live fulfilling lives, students must be able to express their creativity in meaningful ways. Cultivating a propensity for unconventional thinking will enable students to discover novel approaches to constructing significance and direction in their lives, fostering enhanced self-expression and personal development.

Educators must provide a conducive atmosphere that fosters students' inclination toward inventive thinking. They can provide a conducive educational environment encouraging risk-taking, experimenting, and learning from failures. Prioritizing the advancement and progress of teachers rather than their performance would instill confidence and encourage them to explore new opportunities without fearing negative consequences. Integrating activities that foster cooperation and collaboration will facilitate their acquisition of skills in idea sharing and leveraging diverse viewpoints. Granting students more autonomy in selecting projects and determining how they demonstrate mastery of a subject will allow them to apply their knowledge innovatively. Although these are objectives that most instructors currently strive for, discovering additional methods to prioritize these aims rather than just using them as a pathway to achieving content-area proficiency will assist teachers and students in reevaluating the purpose and objective of these activities in the era of artificial intelligence. Educators may use AI to cultivate a creative mentality and instill in teachers the practice of using technology as a tool in their creative endeavors. An essential element in fostering inventive and creative abilities in our kids will include moving away from the segmented framework of our existing educational systems. The future will be shaped by individuals who can think outside conventional fields of study. As educators, it is our responsibility to develop this attitude inside our classrooms. Promoting interdisciplinary linkages among our students enhances their capacity for inventive thinking in their personal and future professional endeavors.

Interdisciplinary learning enables educators to conceptualize the broader scope, investigate many viewpoints, and grasp the interrelatedness of our reality. Adopting a multidisciplinary curriculum will allow our students to navigate and make significant contributions in a world influenced by artificial intelligence. By acquiring the skill of establishing correlations across many fields of study, students may cultivate the capacity to tackle intricate, practical problems from several perspectives. Interdisciplinary learning fosters adaptation and facilitates flexible thinking skills, enabling students to navigate and respond to novel settings and circumstances effectively. Having a larger perspective will also allow educators to cultivate an understanding of the worldwide (both symbolic and real) consequences of their actions and choices. Artificial intelligence can facilitate the development of transdisciplinary thinking.

Transforming Classroom Experience Through Active Learning and AI

AI may significantly contribute to active learning, encouraging student participation and engagement. Artificial intelligence may enhance active learning, strengthen student autonomy and decision-making, and promote the growth of metacognitive abilities in dynamic learning settings. Active learning classrooms place students as the primary leaders in their education. They fully immerse themselves in the subject matter and actively participate in debates, collaborative projects, and practical exercises. The use of AI-powered systems enables the customization of learning to align with the individual objectives of each learner. Artificial intelligence can tailor classes to accommodate individual educators' strengths, limitations, interests, and learning styles. This customization enables every student to interact with the content most advantageously for their educational progress (Shreeve, 2008).

AI can also expedite active learning by providing immediate feedback on assignments and quizzes. For example, an AI-powered quiz platform could highlight a student's recurring mistake in solving a specific math problem. This immediate feedback enables students to learn from errors and promptly modify their strategies. AI can also support autonomy and decision-making by offering personalized recommendations based on a student's learning profile and progress. For example, imagine an AI system suggesting a visual learner student use a specific graphic-based resource to prepare for an upcoming biology test. AI can guide students in making more informed decisions by providing these personalized suggestions. AI can also help foster metacognitive skills so students can better decide their learning journeys. For example, AI can facilitate reflective activities like self-assessment quizzes or journal prompts. An example might be an AI-driven journaling app that offers immediate, personalized feedback based on students' reflections, prompting them with further thoughtful questions based on their entries.

Role of Bloom Taxonomy, Critical Thinking, and AI Enhanced Classroom

Bloom's Taxonomy is a framework used by educators to categorize educational objectives. It helps them consider the cognitive complexity of activities and ensures that they progressively increase the complexity of students' comprehension of the subject matter, ultimately reaching the highest levels. Although this strategy is generally acknowledged, it requires meticulous planning and preparation to provide appropriate support and guidance for each level of content (Krathwohl, 2002). AI may alleviate the effort by aiding students in transitioning from comprehending fundamental principles to implementing them in intricate problem-solving situations. Bloom's Taxonomy may provide a framework for students to use AI in educational settings effectively. In order to integrate Bloom's Taxonomy into our approach to AI integration, educators might contemplate the alignment of learning goals, the development of activities, the evaluation of learning, and the facilitation of reflection (Seddon, 1978).

With the continuous evolution of AI technology and the emergence of specialized educational technology solutions, Bloom's Taxonomy will probably likely be included in learning platforms. For instance, an educational platform might focus on various levels of Bloom's Taxonomy according to each student's specific requirements and advancement. This will enable educators to customize learning activities based on students' cognitive capacities and facilitate students' interaction with information and tasks at the appropriate degree of cognitive intricacy (Elkins et al., 2024; Rodgers, 2023). Furthermore, according to Bloom's Taxonomy, AI technologies can enhance conventional classroom instruction and alleviate the burden on teachers. Educators may use artificial intelligence technologies for several purposes, such as:

1. ***Modify Content:*** AI technologies can modify the difficulty of educational materials and mental requirements to match Bloom's Taxonomy's particular levels.
2. ***Resources for frameworks:*** AI chatbots can propose additional tasks that assist educators in advancing through various stages of Bloom's Taxonomy (Ramandanis and Xinogalos, 2023).
3. ***Generate formative feedback:*** AI systems can provide individualized feedback for educators, focusing on several Bloom's Taxonomy levels and offering suggestions for improvement and advancement (Lin and De Silva, 2023).
4. ***Evaluate the design:*** AI technologies may assist educators in creating tests that align with Bloom's Taxonomy based on the instructor's specific objectives.

5. ***Establish educational trajectories:*** AI-powered platforms can generate customized learning paths that direct students via more intricate cognitive activities that align with Bloom's Taxonomy.

Analyze Student Data Privacy and AI's Long-Term Effects on Education

The increasing use of artificial intelligence in education provides significant advantages, such as tailored learning experiences and efficient administrative procedures. Nevertheless, it raises substantial apprehensions, including over the privacy of student data and the enduring consequences of incorporating AI. It rely on extensive datasets that include sensitive information, including academic records, behavioral tendencies, and personal factors such as socio-economic status. This data is crucial for artificial intelligence to customize learning, forecast student outcomes, and provide focused interventions.

Despite data being pivotal, too much data availability may jeopardize privacy and breach confidence. Security protocols like encryption, stringent limits to access, and periodic audits are the need of the hour to protect crucial data. The students and their parents should be sensitized on the relevant data management issues. To instill confidence among the stakeholders, the regulatory bodies should ensure data ownership and data management are strictly controlled and checked. Free data opens up the possibility of data abuse. This underscores the need for explicit data retention, anonymization, and deletion directives.

The enduring consequences of AI on education are progressively becoming more evident, with several crucial domains where AI is expected to have a substantial influence. AI can provide highly customized learning experiences by evaluating individual student data to adapt material, speed, and teaching techniques to meet each student's specific requirements. While AI can enhance learning outcomes and increase engagement, over-dependence on AI may impede the cultivation of critical thinking and problem-solving abilities. In addition, artificial intelligence can address educational disparities by offering instructional materials to students who lack access to resources. However, if not handled fairly, it might exacerbate existing inequalities, leaving underprivileged schools behind. AI can change instructors' responsibilities by automating duties such as grading freeing their time to engage in more meaningful student interactions. However, this development also raises worries about teachers losing their jobs. Teachers must adapt by obtaining new abilities, particularly in data analysis and technology integration, which requires continuous professional development. The incorporation of AI also gives rise to ethical considerations since AI systems have the potential to perpetuate or magnify social prejudices. Hence, it is imperative to establish ethical frameworks to guarantee that AI fosters equity and inclusiveness. Ultimately, while AI can improve learning, there is a possibility of excessive dependence on technology, which might decrease the human aspects of education, such as empathy, creativity, and social interaction. Maintaining a balance between AI's capabilities and the maintenance of human-centred characteristics is crucial.

The Need for Collaboration and AI Literacy Among Educators and Students

Effective integration of AI into the classroom necessitates collaboration among educators, as it demands a comprehensive grasp of the complexities and nuances involved in using AI technologies. Through collaboration, educators may exchange knowledge, techniques, and exemplary methods, allowing them to evaluate the merits and drawbacks of different AI technologies and customize them to suit their students' requirements. Collaborative endeavors provide a nurturing atmosphere where instructors may gain knowledge from one another's experiences, diminishing the difficulty of acquiring proficiency in emerging AI technologies. Professional learning communities, workshops, and collaborative projects provide effective venues for teachers to collectively improve their skills in AI, eliminating the need for every teacher to tackle the complexity of AI on their own.

It is equally essential for educators to have a high level of understanding and knowledge of AI. To use and apply AI in a competent and morally responsible manner, teachers must possess a comprehensive understanding of AI, including an awareness of how AI algorithms formulate judgments, the possible biases that may arise, and the consequences of depending on AI for activities such as grading and assessment. By possessing AI literacy, educators can effectively assess AI technologies, guaranteeing their compatibility with educational objectives and avoiding unintended harm to pupils. In addition, when instructors gain more excellent expertise in AI, they are more capable of instructing students in comprehending and maneuvering AI technology, clarifying the complexities of AI, and promoting critical and innovative involvement.

Students must develop AI literacy as AI technologies become increasingly integral to daily life and future employment. Understanding AI empowers students to enhance their critical thinking skills, enabling them to analyze AI outcomes and avoid potential issues such as algorithmic bias and misinformation. With the pervasive influence of AI on industries, students who possess AI knowledge will have a competitive edge in the job market. Furthermore, they may be inspired to pursue AI-related careers, thereby contributing significantly to the development of ethical, inclusive, and efficient technologies in the future. The collaboration between educators and students in learning about AI enriches the educational experience. Collaborative projects and interactive classroom discussions foster mutual learning, creating a dynamic environment where teachers and students actively contribute to the learning process.

CONCLUSION

As we go further into the era of artificial intelligence, our society's environment, and therefore the field of education, will see a substantial metamorphosis. Although it may seem intimidating, it is evident that we must redefine the objective of education and adapt our methods to match the rapid advancement of artificial intelligence to adequately equip our kids for the future they will soon encounter. Our students should be able to assume the role of evaluators, demonstrating astute reasoning and critical thinking abilities and being prepared to scrutinize and use the outcomes of AI systems. It is essential to promote their socioemotional skills to effectively navigate a world abundant in human interaction and relationships despite the increasing presence of robots. Crucially, we must provide our students with the essential knowledge and abilities to effectively use AI systems, comprehend their constraints, and enhance them as needed. Proficiency in computational thinking will be crucial, enabling students to create and analyze products and systems that use artificial intelligence and comprehend the intricacies of systems developed by others.

Promoting a comprehensive understanding of AI in other fields is essential, rather than limiting it to computer science. Additionally, the boundaries across disciplines to represent the world intricately accurately should be eliminated. Students should be able to adjust, acquire new information, and use their fundamental understanding in other areas, demonstrating resilience in the face of AI systems' potential replacement of their roles. Furthermore, educators must cultivate in the students the ability to think creatively and generate novel ideas, empowering them to take full advantage of the possibilities presented by AI and expand the limits of human advancement. Our educational institutions' core ideas and ideals stay constant despite the fast changes in environment and learning instruments. The fundamental objective of education, which is to provide students with the necessary skills and knowledge for their lives beyond the confines of the classroom, remains unaltered. Nevertheless, the "existence" they will embark upon will be noticeably different. The magnitude of this obligation is significant; however, it is a task we must confront. As educators, our responsibility is to guarantee that the current generation of students is adequately prepared to assume leadership roles, drive innovation, and contribute as members of society in the future world dominated by artificial intelligence.

Reference

Abulibdeh, A., Zaidan, E., & Abulibdeh, R. (2024). Navigating the confluence of artificial intelligence and education for sustainable development in the era of industry 4.0: Challenges, opportunities, and ethical dimensions. *Journal of Cleaner Production*, 437, 140527. DOI: 10.1016/j.jclepro.2023.140527

Akgun, S., & Greenhow, C. (2022). Artificial intelligence in education: Addressing ethical challenges in K-12 settings. *AI and Ethics*, 2(3), 431–440. DOI: 10.1007/s43681-021-00096-7 PMID: 34790956

Al Dhaen, E., Stone, M. D., & Mahmood, M. (2022). Higher education institutional strategies to sustain quality education: COVID-19 practices and lessons. In *Assessing university governance and policies in relation to the COVID-19 pandemic* (pp. 37-48). IGI Global.

AlDhaen, F. (2022). The use of artificial intelligence in higher education–Systematic review. *COVID-19 Challenges to University Information Technology Governance*, 269-285.

Aoun, J. E. (2017). *Robot-proof: higher education in the age of artificial intelligence*. MIT press. DOI: 10.7551/mitpress/11456.001.0001

Bandi, A., Adapa, P. V. S. R., & Kuchi, Y. E. V. P. K. (2023). The power of generative ai: A review of requirements, models, input–output formats, evaluation metrics, and challenges. *Future Internet*, 15(8), 260. DOI: 10.3390/fi15080260

Baser, D., Ozden, M. Y., & Karaarslan, H. (2017). Collaborative project-based learning: An integrative science and technological education project. *Research in Science & Technological Education*, 35(2), 131–148. DOI: 10.1080/02635143.2016.1274723

Bearman, M., Ryan, J., & Ajjawi, R. (2023). Discourses of artificial intelligence in higher education: A critical literature review. *Higher Education*, 86(2), 369–385. DOI: 10.1007/s10734-022-00937-2

Bozkurt, A. (2023). Generative artificial intelligence (AI) powered conversational educational agents: The inevitable paradigm shift. *Asian Journal of Distance Education*, 18(1).

Crawford, J., Cowling, M., & Allen, K. A. (2023). Leadership is needed for ethical ChatGPT: Character, assessment, and learning using artificial intelligence (AI). *Journal of University Teaching & Learning Practice, 20*(3), 02.

Darvishi, A., Khosravi, H., Sadiq, S., Gašević, D., & Siemens, G. (2024). Impact of AI assistance on student agency. *Computers & Education*, 210, 104967. DOI: 10.1016/j.compedu.2023.104967

Dhoni, P. (2023). Exploring the synergy between generative AI, data and analytics in the modern age. *Authorea Preprints*.

Diwan, C., Srinivasa, S., Suri, G., Agarwal, S., & Ram, P. (2023). AI-based learning content generation and learning pathway augmentation to increase learner engagement. *Computers and Education: Artificial Intelligence*, 4, 100110. DOI: 10.1016/j.caeai.2022.100110

Elkins, S., Kochmar, E., Cheung, J. C., & Serban, I. (2024). How Teachers Can Use Large Language Models and Bloom's Taxonomy to Create Educational Quizzes. *arXiv preprint arXiv:2401.05914*.

Farrow, R. (2023). The possibilities and limits of XAI in education: A socio-technical perspective. *Learning, Media and Technology*, 48(2), 266–279. DOI: 10.1080/17439884.2023.2185630

Holmes, W., Porayska-Pomsta, K., Holstein, K., Sutherland, E., Baker, T., Shum, S. B., Santos, O. C., Rodrigo, M. T., Cukurova, M., Bittencourt, I. I., & Koedinger, K. R. (2022). Ethics of AI in education: Towards a community-wide framework. *International Journal of Artificial Intelligence in Education*, 32(3), 1–23. DOI: 10.1007/s40593-021-00239-1

Horwitz, S. K., & Santillan, C. (2012). Knowledge sharing in global virtual team collaboration: Applications of CE and thinkLets. *Knowledge Management Research and Practice*, 10(4), 342–353. DOI: 10.1057/kmrp.2012.39

Jang, Y., Choi, S., & Kim, H. (2022). Development and validation of an instrument to measure undergraduate students' attitudes toward the ethics of artificial intelligence (AT-EAI) and analysis of its difference by gender and experience of AI education. *Education and Information Technologies*, 27(8), 11635–11667. DOI: 10.1007/s10639-022-11086-5

Joshi, R., Pandey, K., & Kumari, S. (2024, February). A Metaverse: Significance and Dimensions in Various Sectors. In *2024 11th International Conference on Computing for Sustainable Global Development (INDIACom)* (pp. 1781-1786). IEEE.

Karenina, A., Widoretno, S., & Prayitno, B. A. (2020, April). Effectiveness of problem solving-based module to improve analytical thinking. [). IOP Publishing.]. *Journal of Physics: Conference Series*, 1511(1), 012093. DOI: 10.1088/1742-6596/1511/1/012093

King, M. R., & Chat, G. P. T. (2023). A conversation on artificial intelligence, chatbots, and plagiarism in higher education. *Cellular and Molecular Bioengineering*, 16(1), 1–2. DOI: 10.1007/s12195-022-00754-8 PMID: 36660590

Kooli, C. (2023). Chatbots in education and research: A critical examination of ethical implications and solutions. *Sustainability (Basel)*, 15(7), 5614. DOI: 10.3390/su15075614

Koravuna, S., & Surepally, U. K. (2020, September). Educational gamification and artificial intelligence for promoting digital literacy. In *Proceedings of the 2nd International Conference on Intelligent and Innovative Computing Applications* (pp. 1-6). DOI: 10.1145/3415088.3415107

Krathwohl, D. R. (2002). A revision of Bloom's taxonomy: An overview. *Theory into Practice*, 41(4), 212–218. DOI: 10.1207/s15430421tip4104_2

Larsson, S., & Heintz, F. (2020). Transparency in artificial intelligence. *Internet Policy Review*, 9(2). Advance online publication. DOI: 10.14763/2020.2.1469

Lim, D. (2018). AI & IP: Innovation & creativity in an age of accelerated change. *Akron Law Review*, 52, 813.

Lin, F., & De Silva, S. (2023, May). An Approach to Generating Adaptive Feedback for Online Formative Assessment. In *International Conference on Intelligent Tutoring Systems* (pp. 88-99). Cham: Springer Nature Switzerland. DOI: 10.1007/978-3-031-32883-1_8

Lodge, J. M., Thompson, K., & Corrin, L. (2023). Mapping out a research agenda for generative artificial intelligence in tertiary education. *Australasian Journal of Educational Technology*, 39(1), 1–8. DOI: 10.14742/ajet.8695

McGrath, C., Pargman, T. C., Juth, N., & Palmgren, P. J. (2023). University teachers' perceptions of responsibility and artificial intelligence in higher education-An experimental philosophical study. *Computers and Education: Artificial Intelligence*, 4, 100139. DOI: 10.1016/j.caeai.2023.100139

Megahed, M., & Mohammed, A. (2024). A comprehensive review of generative adversarial networks: Fundamentals, applications, and challenges. *Wiley Interdisciplinary Reviews: Computational Statistics*, 16(1), e1629. DOI: 10.1002/wics.1629

Murugesan, S., & Cherukuri, A. K. (2023). The rise of generative artificial intelligence and its impact on education: The promises and perils. *Computer*, 56(5), 116–121. DOI: 10.1109/MC.2023.3253292

Nicolaides, A., Lim, A., Herr, N., & Barefield, T. (Eds.). (2024). *Reimagining Adult Education as World Building: Creating Learning Ecologies for Transformation.* Taylor & Francis. DOI: 10.4324/9781003371359

Pearce, J., & Chiavaroli, N. (2023). Rethinking assessment in response to generative artificial intelligence. *Medical Education*, 57(10), 889–891. DOI: 10.1111/medu.15092 PMID: 37042389

Peters, U. (2023). Explainable AI lacks regulative reasons: Why AI and human decision-making are not equally opaque. *AI and Ethics*, 3(3), 963–974. DOI: 10.1007/s43681-022-00217-w

Ramachandran, A., Schwellnus, M., Gladwin, D., Derby-Talbot, R., & Ellis, N. (2024). Cultivating educational adaptability through collaborative transdisciplinary learning spaces. *Discover Education*, 3(1), 2. DOI: 10.1007/s44217-023-00084-5

Ramandanis, D., & Xinogalos, S. (2023). Investigating the Support Provided by Chatbots to Educational Institutions and Their Students: A Systematic Literature Review. *Multimodal Technologies and Interaction*, 7(11), 103. DOI: 10.3390/mti7110103

Ramzan, M., Javaid, Z. K., & Ali, A. A. (2023). Perception of Students about Collaborative Strategies Employed by Teachers for Enhancing English Vocabulary and Learning Motivation. *Pakistan JL Analysis & Wisdom*, 2, 146.

Reiss, M. J. (2021). The Use of Al in Education: Practicalities and Ethical Considerations. *London Review of Education*, 19(1), n1. DOI: 10.14324/LRE.19.1.05

Remian, D. (2019). Augmenting education: ethical considerations for incorporating artificial intelligence in education.

Rodgers, D. L. (2023). Beyond the Cognitive Domain: Including All of Bloom's Learning Domains in Objective Development. *Academic Medicine*, 98(3), 294–295. DOI: 10.1097/ACM.0000000000005108 PMID: 36811921

Seddon, G. M. (1978). The properties of Bloom's taxonomy of educational objectives for the cognitive domain. *Review of Educational Research*, 48(2), 303–323. DOI: 10.3102/00346543048002303

Semeler, A., Pinto, A., Koltay, T., Dias, T., Oliveira, A., González, J., & Rozados, H. B. F. (2024). ALGORITHMIC LITERACY: Generative Artificial Intelligence Technologies for Data Librarians. *EAI Endorsed Transactions on Scalable Information Systems, 11*(2).

Sharma, D. M., Ramana, K. V., Jothilakshmi, R., Verma, R., Maheswari, B. U., & Boopathi, S. (2024). Integrating Generative AI Into K-12 Curriculums and Pedagogies in India: Opportunities and Challenges. *Facilitating Global Collaboration and Knowledge Sharing in Higher Education With Generative AI*, 133-161.

Shin, S. (2019). Designing the instructional framework and cognitive learning environment for artificial intelligence education through computational thinking. *Journal of The Korean Association of Information Education*, 23(6), 639–653. DOI: 10.14352/jkaie.2019.23.6.639

Shoja, M. M., Van de Ridder, J. M., & Rajput, V. (2023). The emerging role of generative artificial intelligence in medical education, research, and practice. *Cureus*, 15(6). Advance online publication. DOI: 10.7759/cureus.40883 PMID: 37492829

Shreeve, M. W. (2008). Beyond the didactic classroom: Educational models to encourage active student involvement in learning. *The Journal of Chiropractic Education*, 22(1), 23–28. DOI: 10.7899/1042-5055-22.1.23 PMID: 18483586

Sood, S. O. (2008, December). Emotional computation in artificial intelligence education. In *AAAI Artificial Intelligence Education Colloquium* (pp. 74-78).

Thurzo, A., Strunga, M., Urban, R., Surovková, J., & Afrashtehfar, K. I. (2023). Impact of artificial intelligence on dental education: A review and guide for curriculum update. *Education Sciences*, 13(2), 150. DOI: 10.3390/educsci13020150

Tuomi, I. (2023). A framework for socio-developmental ethics in educational AI.

Wang, S., Sun, Z., & Chen, Y. (2023). Effects of higher education institutes' artificial intelligence capability on students' self-efficacy, creativity and learning performance. *Education and Information Technologies*, 28(5), 4919–4939. DOI: 10.1007/s10639-022-11338-4 PMID: 36373050

Wang, S., Sun, Z., & Chen, Y. (2023). Effects of higher education institutes' artificial intelligence capability on students' self-efficacy, creativity and learning performance. *Education and Information Technologies*, 28(5), 4919–4939. DOI: 10.1007/s10639-022-11338-4 PMID: 36373050

Wang, W., Huang, Y., Wang, Y., & Wang, L. (2014). Generalized autoencoder: A neural network framework for dimensionality reduction. In *Proceedings of the IEEE conference on computer vision and pattern recognition workshops* (pp. 490-497). DOI: 10.1109/CVPRW.2014.79

Woolf, B. P., Lane, H. C., Chaudhri, V. K., & Kolodner, J. L. (2013). AI grand challenges for education. *AI Magazine*, 34(4), 66–84. DOI: 10.1609/aimag.v34i4.2490

Zhang, L., Basham, J. D., & Yang, S. (2020). Understanding the implementation of personalized learning: A research synthesis. *Educational Research Review*, 31, 100339. DOI: 10.1016/j.edurev.2020.100339

Chapter 4

Enhancing AI-Augmented Classrooms:

Teacher-Centric Integration of Intelligent Tutoring Systems and Adaptive Learning Environments

Bhupinder Singh
https://orcid.org/0009-0006-4779-2553
Sharda University, India

Christian Kaunert
https://orcid.org/0000-0002-4493-2235
Dublin City University, Ireland

Sahil Lal
https://orcid.org/0000-0001-9827-3717
Sharda University, India

Manmeet Kaur Arora
https://orcid.org/0009-0002-5071-117X
Sharda University, India

ABSTRACT

Students often require personalized attention, yet teachers face challenges with large classes and limited time. Tutoring offers tailored guidance and promotes effective learning. An Intelligent Tutoring System (ITS) serves as an excellent alternative to traditional tutoring. This software simulates a real tutor by presenting problems, offering support, correcting mistakes, and providing encouragement. ITS operates as an intelligent, computer-assisted instructional program and it customized environments

DOI: 10.4018/979-8-3693-7255-5.ch004

for education works most when complemented with a teacher-centric methodology. Teachers play a crucial role in assisting children to learn, helping them navigate new AI-powered platforms, and encouraging creativity and critical thinking. The chapter focuses on the relevance of teacher preparedness and the shifting function of academics in AI-augmented classrooms as it studies the opportunities of ITS and adaptive learning environments to improve the quality of education.

INTRODUCTION

Intelligent Tutoring Systems (ITS) assume the role of a human tutor, supporting children at each stage of experiencing an issue and offering advice and comments when required (Zint et al., 2024). They assess student's learning in real time and alter their approach accordingly to their improvement and perception (Singh & Kaunert, 2024). While video game-based learning systems package knowledge into captivating stages that conform to the student's competence, exploratory instructional systems provide individuals the freedom to decide on customized learning avenues (Singh et al., 2024). Teachers may free up time for more individualized instruction, data-driven decision-making, and focused corrections by incorporating AI technologies. Along with addressing moral dilemmas and potential directions for AI integration, it looks at case studies and best practices (Singh & Kaunert, 2024).

Teachers may use AI to create more customized, effective, and captivating educational adventures for learners through employing a teacher-centric approach (Raaj, 2024). The positive and negative aspects of embedding AI into education, the ethical questions raised by this method of learning and the demand for academics to responsibly adopt AI technology is to keep up with the constantly changing world of education (Singh, 2024). This chapter attempts to emphasize the potential of AI to completely alter classroom procedures while emphasizing the important function of teachers in directing and encouraging students through AI-powered instructional settings by looking at the working partnership between professionals and artificial intelligence (AI) instruments in curriculum development and course management (Singh et al., 2024).

Figure 1. displays the Landscapes of Introduction Split Sections (Source- Original)

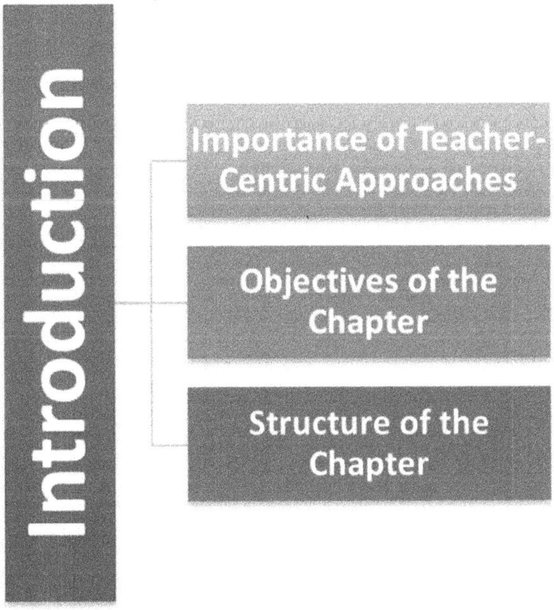

Importance of Teacher-Centric Approaches

The teaching strategies that instructors choose should be in line with the intended learning objectives. This alignment is critical to the efficacy of these techniques. Instructors should think about the requirements of their students, the learning environment, and the learning outcomes while making the best decision. Activities are the particular ways these approaches are put into practice, whilst teaching methods are the more general tactics utilized to assist students in meeting their learning objectives (Singh & Kaunert, 2024). Using efficient instructional strategies, students can recognize how to use the material in certain situations. Teacher-centered instruction primarily emphasizes the role of the educator, with classroom activities heavily dependent on the teacher's planning, design, and directions. In this setup, students are largely controlled by the teacher, which significantly reduces the chance of missing any essential content. Unlike student-centered classrooms, where students take an active role, those in teacher-centered environments are passive and react to external stimuli. The teacher holds the ultimate authority and is responsible for learning, limiting students' opportunities to develop critical thinking and problem-solving skills. This chapter explores the extent to which the teacher-centered approach is essential in the modern educational system (Garg & Singh, 2022).

Objectives of the Chapter

This Chapter has the following Objectives to:

- explore the ways in which AI technologies, particularly Intelligent Tutoring Systems (ITS) and Adaptive Learning Environments, might supplement and improve instruction in conventional classroom settings (Singh & Kaunert, 2024).

- look into ways to use AI technologies to empower teachers and enable them to continue playing a pivotal role in education while utilizing technology to enhance student results (Singh, 2024).

- ways that ITS and adaptive learning environments may be utilized to help students design personalized learning paths and get instruction that is catered to their specific requirements and learning preferences (Singh, 2023).

- determine and evaluate the best ways to use AI-augmented technologies in the classroom, taking into account case studies and actual data showing how these methods affect student accomplishment, comprehension, and engagement (Singh & Kaunert, 2024).

Figure 2. shows the Objectives of the Chapter (Source- Original)

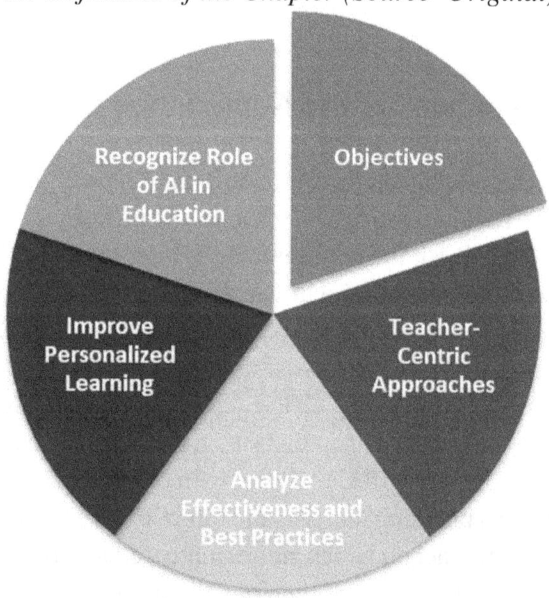

Structure of the Chapter

This chapter comprehensively explores the diverse aspects on Enhancing AI-Augmented Classrooms: Teacher-Centric Integration of Intelligent Tutoring Systems and Adaptive Learning Environments. Section 2 lays down the Intelligent Tutoring Systems (ITS): Enhancing AI-Augmented Classrooms. Section 3 elaborates the Adaptive Learning Environments (ALE). Section 4 specifies the Assimilation of ITS and Adaptive Learning Environments (ALE). Section 5 shares the Teacher-Centric Integration. Section 6 highlights the Benefits of AI-Augmented Classrooms. Section 7 Conclude the Chapter with Future Scope.

Figure 3. showcasing Flow of the Chapter (Source- Original)

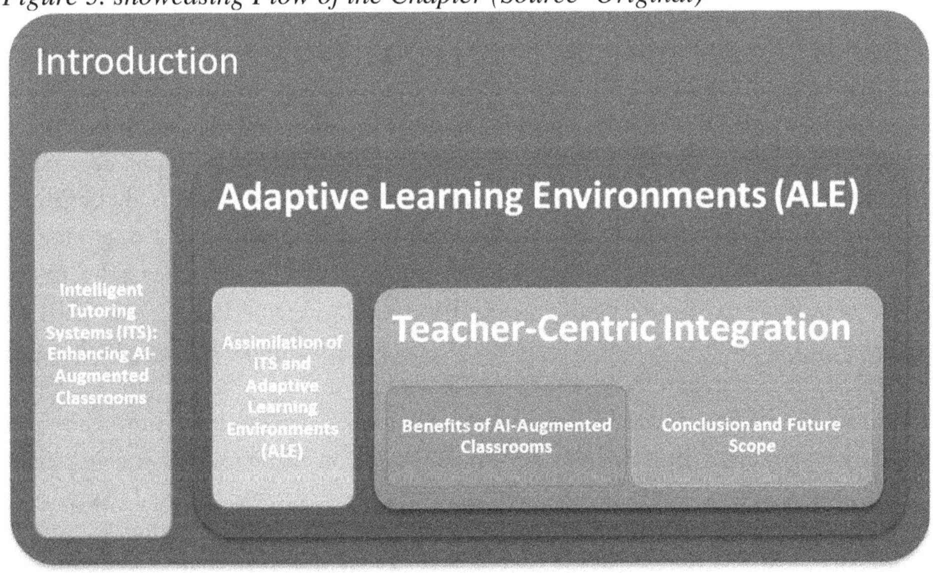

Intelligent Tutoring Systems (ITS): Enhancing AI-Augmented Classrooms

Intelligent Tutoring Systems (ITS) are computer based educational systems that try to emulate one-on-one instruction so that the learners benefit from the personal guidance that an expert human tutor would provide (Wang & Chao, 2022). These use artificial intelligence (AI) and cognitive science principles to make the student experience more personalized to meet the individual needs and abilities (Czerkawski, & Lyman, 2015). ITS is a model of the learner based on knowledge, skills, and cognitive processes. It is a model for diagnosing the current understandings of students; it identifies their strengths and weaknesses; and thus helps in content discrimination (i.e., what to teach), instruction, and teaching strategies (Romero et al., 2017). ITS focuses on continuous monitoring of a student's growth, provides personalized opportunities for learning by dynamically responding to her progress and process rather than being limited to using a generic one-size-fits-all teaching method. The feature of ITS that must be highly beneficial to students is their immediate and personalized feedback. The ITS runs in the background, and as the learner responds to its prompts, it uses those answers to identify any misconceptions or mistakes and then responds with targeted feedback and guidance to course-correct those errors. This quick feedback is absolutely necessary to reinforce learning and helps students to have a better grasp of the topic (Agbo et al., 2019). ITS are able to deliver the instructional content and manner of delivery that is most compatible with the individual's learning style and preferences (Apiola & Sutinen, 2021). Materials may include visual representations (which may suit some students) and more textual or auditory explanations or both. ITS is that it can adapt how it displays information so that it meets the specific demands of each student, making learning more interesting. ITS has been applied to many areas of education, including math, science, language, and programming, with successful outcomes. ITS can be used to help students develop a better understanding of mathematical concepts and improve problem-solving skills by providing step-by-step guidance and feedback on strategies for solving problems in the domain of mathematics. While ITS does offer many advantages, there exist some challenges and drawbacks as well (Pollock et al., 2019).

The third challenge is about the creation of a learner model that is both comprehensive and as accurate as possible, which becomes even harder since a lot of information for example load monitoring, sleep quality and content preference can only be obtained in a time consuming and resource consuming way. Learning in an Augmented RealityDespite of all the transformations, integration of ITSs within the reality of education and learning can be a paramount concern because it might change the way teaching potentially will be carried out as well as potential challenges in adapting to new tools (Lee et al., 2020). The ethical concerns about ITS are pervasive, regarding data privacy, algorithmic bias, and the effect that ITS can have on the teacher's role. It is essential to design and implement ITS in a manner that preserves the rights and welfare of both students and teachers in lieu of the rising sophistication of ITS. To sum up, it can be said that Intelligent Tutoring Systems are a hopeful direction in adaptive and personalized learning and they have been wildly successful in terms of educational results and excellence of the learning experience for students. Given the rapid pace of change within the field of AI, K-12 development and deployment of ITS are likely to remain an area of interest for educators, researchers, and policymakers alike (Psycharis et al., 2018).

Figure 4. specifies the Dimensions of Intelligent Tutoring Systems (ITS) (Source-Original)

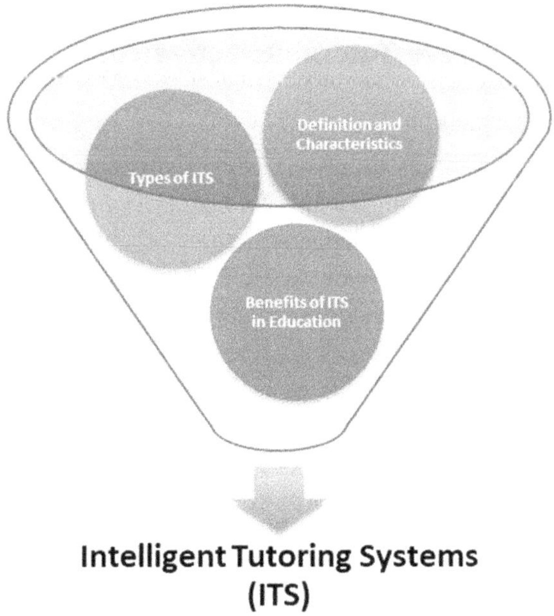

Definition and Characteristics

As the name suggests Intelligent Tutoring Systems (ITS) are computer-based educational systems created to deliver individualized instruction and feedback to learners. These systems use artificial intelligence (AI) to adjust to the needs of each student creating a personalized, one-on-one learning experience. ITS Basic Components An ITS comprises four core components: knowledge base, student model, pedagogical module, and user interface. In most case, the knowledge base has subject specific details and expertise, the student model reflect the state of the learner understanding about the domain (Pulimood et al., 2016). The pedagogical module personalizes the educational strategy according to the learning stages of the student, whereas the user interface allows correct communication between the system and the learner (Weintrop et al., 2016). ITSs can deliver instant, tailored replays, which distinguish them as a key form of computer-aided instruction. The designs are meant to simulate private tutoring that is especially effective in environments where students are likely to otherwise enjoy little or no private attention. ITSs have been successfully utilized in numerous educational settings (such as mathematics, language learning and professional training) and empirical studies have demonstrated its ED effects in enhancing learning and engagement of students (Montiel et al., 2021).

Types of ITS- Cognitive Tutors, Affective Tutors

Different forms of Intelligent Tutoring Systems (ITS) are formulated to target particular educational requirement and AI tactics. Two examples of ITS are Cognitive Tutors and Affective Tutors. Cognitive Tutors are ITSs centered on authenticating the cognitive processes and knowledge structures of students (Qin, 2009). These pillar systems are designed to interrogate the learner's knowledge, identify misconceptions, and intervene with targeted instruction and feedback to help the learner realise and overcome their challenges. Cognitive Tutors frequently use techniques from cognitive science, like knowledge tracing and model-tracing, in order to develop complex student models and then adjust the instructional experience accordingly (Barcelos et al., 2012).

Cognitive Tutors: Several successful examples of cognitive tutors include the Algebra Tutor and a Geometry Tutor, as well as the LISP Tutor which have shown dramatic increases in learning gains as a result of using the tutor Conversely, Affective Tutors represent ITSs, which take into consideration also the affective (i.e., emotional, motivational) factors of learning. Such systems share the basic assumption that learning is not a purely cognitive matter, but that there are many affective or emotional states associated with it, including moods, emotions and attitudes of learners v.

Affective Tutor - detects the student affect, offers empathy and adapts instructional strategies in order to keep the student engaged and motivated. That can include things like visual analytics, language processing and adaptations. Affective Tutors have been implemented on a variety of subjects such as math, language acquisition, and social skills training. So, contrary to the distinction made between Cognitive Tutors and Affective Tutors some of the more recent ITS merge aspects of the two (García-Peñalvo & Mendes, 2018).

Such hybrid systems understand the necessity of addressing the cognitive as well as the affective sides of learning for a more comprehensive and efficient learning process. Such advanced cognitive tutor-driven ITS can offer a powerful method of teaching and learning, using techniques from cognitive science, educational psychology, and artificial intelligence to personalize instruction, provide emotional support, and furnish adaptive feedback that helps students reach their learning goals. With ITS constantly maturing as the field advances, some yet unexplored directions in which current researchers and developers are moving may include integrating ITS with virtual reality (Shute et al., 2006), integrating social and collaborative learning (Dabbagh et al., 2009), and building on new technologies such as natural language processing (NLG) and deep-learning-based ITSs. These innovations bode well for even greater efficacy and acceptability of intelligent tutoring systems in many common learning and training situations (Psycharis, 2018).

Benefits of ITS in Education

Intelligent Tutoring System (ITS) by its nature has multiple advantages and it is worthwhile. Their personalized instruction can be tailored to each student's problem types and levels which is one of their greatest strengths. This individual approach can result in great success for the student due to the ability to cater to their own learning styles breaking the laying the foundation to difficult topics and enhancing a true understanding of the subject. They also enable more efficient and scalable instruction, as they are able to give instruction and feedback to many students all at once. This is especially useful in an educational set-up, which has a limitation of teacher resources leading to the problem of one single teacher providing attention to every single child (Bati et al., 2018). The other significant level of benefit in ITS is their potential to give immediate and targeted feedback to trainees so as to support them in recognising and rectifying their errors in near real-time. This support in the moment can be powerful in solidifying comprehension of difficult ideas and can greatly increase confidence among students in their abilities (Papadakis, 2020). ITS can also alleviate teacher load and improve teacher-student ratios, because they are able to automate many of the tasks related to traditional teaching (e.g. grading and feedback). Which can free up teachers to focus on higher order tasks, such as curriculum design and student mentoring, in turn making education at all levels more affordable and, we like to think, of higher quality (Yadav et al., 2014).

ADAPTIVE LEARNING ENVIRONMENTS (ALE)

An Adaptive Learning Environment (different series of computer-based systems) is a one which can facilitate accommodation of the specific needs, strengths, and weaknesses of an individual learner. Using sophisticated technology (e.g. AI, machine learning), these environments constantly analyze the student's habits, learning and recall rates to adapt the environment to the learner's performance/opinions, as well as to the specific style of learning. If the schools are applying for designation as ALEs, the overriding objective is to ensure that ALE instruction is personalized and effectively engages all students and achieves positive student outcomes (Pollak & Ebner, 2019). ALEs are also able to analyze and react positively to learner actions. It necessitates monitoring learner engagement, such as clicks, scrolling, and dwell times on certain content to discover strengths and weaknesses. This information is then used by the system to modify the content, speed and level of challenge to more closely fit the learner. An adaptive strategy, like rhetorical revision, lets determine who is ready for the challenge, does not get bored, decreases frustration, and increase motivation (Saritepeci, 2020).

These possibilities also give ALEs an ability to accommodate various ways of learning. This allows ALEs to be helpful for visual, auditory, and kinesthetic learning modalities by incorporating images, video, and audio. ALEs can also be interactive- using quizzes, games, and simulations to encourage active learning. ALEs leverage more sophisticated algorithmic and modeling techniques to anticipate learner behavior, enabling the platform and learning environment to adapt. Domain models, which provide a representation of the learning content and structure, and learner models that encapsulate what the user already knows, his competencies and preferences (Buitrago-Florez, 2021). The result is a way to mix these models so that ALEs can offer a learning experience that is more personalized and therefore effective, based on the needs of an individual learner. In addition, ALEs are able to be integrated with a variety of learning management systems (LMS) and educational platforms making interoperability exponentially easier and more effective. This allows educators to seamlessly administer and monitor learner progress, and incorporate ALEs within existing curricula and assessments (Gokçe & Yenmez, 2023). ALEs can also offer instantaneous feedback and assessment, which allows educators to keep track of how learners are doing and make any necessary adjustments in instruction. To sum up, Adaptive Learning Environments (ALEs) are modern learning solutions that take advantage of new technologies to offer personalized, efficient education. ALEs can dramatically increase learner engagement and performance by analyzing how learners behave, building on various learning styles and using complex algorithms and models. As education continues to change shape, ALEs are sure to continue to integrate themselves into the educational landscape of tomorrow (Lodi & Martini, 2021).

Mechanisms of Adaptation

Adaptive Learning Environments (ALEs) are characterized by having systems and agents that are capable of adapting to the particular features exhibited by each learner. These mechanisms help ALEs deliver highly individualized and efficient learning at scale to drive learner engagement and achievement. If you wonder what the mechanism of adaptation in ALE is all about, then here is the insight: Content Adaptation is one of the main adaptation mechanisms in ALE (Tsortanidou et al., 2019). This means that the content provided changes according to the performance, preferences, and learning style of the learner. For example, when a learner is facing difficulty with a specific concept the ALE can customize the content to show further explanations, examples, practice exercises to get a much clearer understanding. Similarly, if a learner shows evidence of understanding a concept, the ALE has the flexibility to provide higher level content that will keep the learner engaged. Most people create this type of adaptation by slowing the pace (Yilmaz Ince & Koc, 2021). It requires matching the pace and style of the learning experience to the learner. This means that, if a learner is moving at a fast pace (while still completing work with high levels of accuracy), the ALE can increase the pace at which the content is being delivered to maintain engagement. On the other hand, if a student is behind or needs more time to complete a task, the ALE will slow down and offer more support and guidance. ALEs are designed to be feedback and assessment-driven; they adapt to learner needs (Sırakaya et al., 2020).

This will involve not only the mechanisms driving real time targeted feedback to learners on their performance, but also assessing their comprehension and knowledge. It manipulates this feedback and assessment data to alter the content, pace and difficulty of the learning experience to better match the learner. ALE's can also use mechanisms of learner modeling and prediction (Hutchins et al., 2020). These mechanisms entail forms of informal metric making that includes detailed models concerning what the learners know, can do, or prefer, together with predictions of their future performance and learning needs. ALEs can achieve this by introducing such models to equip them to offer a personalised and effective learning experience, according to individual learners' personal requirements. ALEs can rebuild collaboration and social learning These instruments contains the collective work, sharing of voices, and learning from everyone, which help learners to foster from the area (Valovicova et al., 2020). These mechanisms allow ALEs to create a more immersive, interactive way of learning that supports community and social learning. Adaptive Learning Environments, in short, use different method to play a role in accommodating the unique requisites and capability of the learners. They will consist of a set of mechanisms for content adaptation, pace adjustment, feedback and assessment, learner modeling and prediction, and collaboration and social learning. Utilizing these mechanisms, ALEs are guaranteeing that each of their learners receives a personalized experience that best caters to each individual, essentially ensuring the maximum engagement and success of the learners (Lockwood & Mooney, 2017).

Advantages of ALE in Personalized Learning

Adaptive Learning Environments (ALEs): Represent an effective support alternative to improve learning conditions and results for learners. Among their merits are the capacity to deliver individualized instruction, there by customizing the content and speed to fit each learner's distinct needs and abilities. This individualized method keeps the students focused and driven as they are mobilized at a speed suitable for them and are given precise and to-the-point critique and support. ALEs aid in enhancing the learner outcomes by propagating real time feedback along with assessment, helping the learner to measure the progress and point out their area of improvement. An other advantage provided by ALES, is that they can alleviate the workload of the instructors by automating extensive number of tasks involved in the traditional teaching approaches such as grading, feedback, etc. What this means is that educators can spend more energy on more complex tasks such as curriculum design and one-to-one mentoring of students (Denning & Tedre, 2021). The other key benefit of ALEs to consider is how they can help develop learner autonomy and self-directed learning. ALEs give learners the autonomy to learn in a way that means something to them, to take control of their learning, and to develop much-needed soft skills, such as time and self-management. Finally, giving extra targeted support to students struggling is one way ALEs can help bridge the achievement gap. And by tailoring their supports to each learner, ALEs can ensure that all learners, regardless of background or ability, have access to relevant and rich learning resources and learning experiences (Hsu & Liang, 2021).

ASSIMILATION OF ITS AND ADAPTIVE LEARNING ENVIRONMENTS (ALE)

APA Learning Additions can be improved through the integration of Adaptive Learning Environments (ALEs) and Intelligent Tutoring Systems (ITS). While both ALEs and ITS are highly individual models that are meant to tailor learning exactly to the needs of the learner, the technologies work very differently and afford unique advantages. Adaptive learning environments (ALEs) are computer-based systems that adjust to the individual abilities and needs of a learner (Tedre & Denning, 2016). Such platforms employ advanced algorithms and machine learning mechanisms to study how learners interact with study material and adapt learning content, speed and complexity on the fly. And because ALEs offer real-time feedback and performance evaluation, it can help learners to monitor their own progress and locate their weaknesses. ITS, however, are software systems that replicate the human learner process and the human tutor process. Their program provides individualized coaching and feedback to learners using AI and cognitive science (Agbo et al., 2021).

An ITS can diagnose when learners have misconceptions, provide feedback tailored to the learner and adapt the learning experience to suit the needs of the learner. The homeostatic network contains two components which, when incorporated, can be used to facilitate a more complete and more authentic learning experience: ALE-s and ITS. ALEs, on which the learning process is built and provides content and pace customized for learners (Ulger, 2018). ITS can then take this foundation and use it to customize its instruction and feedback to help learners overcome obstacles and reach their goals. Personalization and Improved LeveragesAnother significant opportunity for connecting ALEs and ITS is being able to provide a far more personalized and targeted learning experience. In the same vein, the adaptive capabilities of ALEs can also be combined with the personalized instruction of ITS, providing a learner with a customized learning experience (Li et al., 2020).

The integration of ALEs and ITS also offers the benefit of higher revenues through increased learner outcomes. This can enable learners to achieve their goals and excel in their performance. In addition to these benefits, the relationship with ALEs and ITS will also reduce the intensity of workload of instructors. By automating several processes effectively aligned with traditional classroom instruction (i.e., assignement grading), ALE/ITS may enable instructors to focus on higher-value added areas of the instructorial praxis (i.e., curriculum development, student advising, etc.) A lastly, integrating ALEs and ITSs could contribute to enhancing the scalability and accessibility of education. As it seek to bring all learners to the same level in a personalized, meaningful way, ALEs and ITS offer one possible way to bridge the divide between two different learners and two different learning environments (Leonard et al., 2016). As a conclusion, we can say that the combinatory use of Adaptive Learning Environments with Intelligent Tutoring Systems has the power to change our meaning of education. The use of ALEs and ITS can be of value to create more effective and efficient learning environments given more personal and efficient learning, better performance in learning, relief of workload for an instructor and larger scale and increased pace in education (Hava & Koyunlu Unlu, 2021).

Framework for Integration

It is because the integration of an adaptive learning environment (ALE) along with intelligent tutoring systems (ITS) must have a particular interaction flow within these two platforms. This framework could allow the ALE to customize the learning experience to the needs of an individual learner, while the ITS offers individualized instruction and feedback (Gonzalez-Perez & Ramírez-Montoya, 2022). A Framework for ALE/ITS Integration The following is a framework to detail key aspects and steps required to integrate ALEs and ITS. The integration of ALEs and ITS require a robust technical infrastructure as e.g. high-speed internet, reliable servers and storage for data source. The development of an integration framework is necessary for co-working of Adaptive Learning Environments and Intelligent

Tutoring Systems. With these four steps, educators can implement a holistic and personalized learning experience for the learners (Iversen et al., 2018).

Modelling the Learner: The initial integration that could done between ALEs and ITS is by building learner model to represent learner's knowledge, skills and preferences. Those processing models should be also shared between the ALE and ITS to make the correctness.

Content Alignment: After a model is created, the content provided by the ALE must be aligned with the instructional strategies and feedback provided by the ITS. It helps provide a more coherent and efficient learning experience for the learner. The learning experience should be able to change and adapt to the needs of the learner, adaptively adjusting the content, pace, and difficulty level. Personalized instruction and feedback: Personalized instruction and feedback should be offered by the ITS based on the performance and progress of the individual learner.

Real-time Feedback: The ITS should be able to provide real-time feedback to the learner and this feedback should be in conjunction with the adaptive instruction of the ALE. This helps the learner get feedback and guidance on how they are performing, instantly.

Learner Engagement: ALEs that are integrated with ITS must ensure the priorite of enhancing learner engagement and motivation. For this, some companies use interactive assets: games, simulations, multimedia and other functionalities inside the leaning experience.

Support for Instructors: as well as students, the integration of ALE and ITS also needs to support instructors. This can range from monitoring progress of learners, tracking performance of learners to tweaking instructional strategies. The integration of ALEs and ITS should be scalable Scalability scaleXtoxin large population of learners/situations.

Evaluation and Assessment- ALEs with ITS integration should have the features of learner performance evaluation and progress tracking. So that performance of integrated system will be measurable and can be enhanced.

Continuous Improvement - ALE and ITS designer should facilitate ongoing collaboration And this can be done through feedback loops so that users and teachers can tell us how well the system is working.

Figure 5. specifies the Framework- Assimilation of ITS and Adaptive Learning Environments (ALE) (Source- Original)

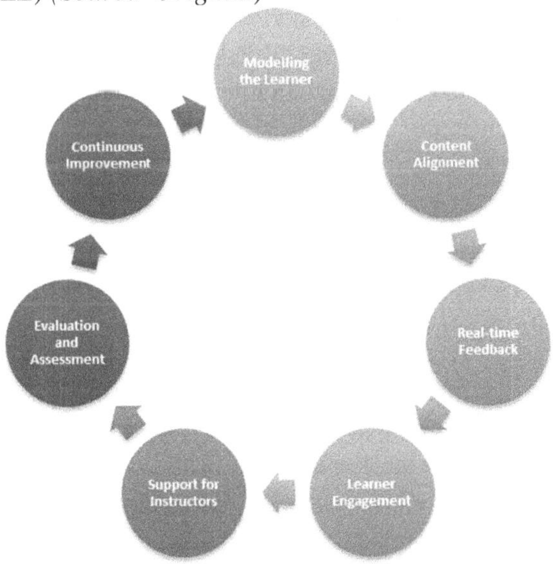

Role of AI in Facilitating Integration

Adaptive Learning Environments (ALEs) and Intelligent Tutoring Systems (ITS) can interact each other through Artificial Intelligence (AI). This is where AI technologies play an outsized role in making such a merger even more effective via enabling customization, flexibility, and intelligence in the unification of these two education systems. At the heart of this integration is the aptitude of AI to establish full-fledged learner models. ALEs and ITS make it possible to mine reuse learner performance, behavior, and preference data on a massive scale, in order to leave no stone unturned when profiling learner strengths, weaknesses and learning styles, and to that end ML algorithms come very handily into play (Miller et al., 2013).

These learner models are the basis for the adaptive, personalized instruction that is the hallmark of integrated ALE-ITS systems. This further allows AI to coordinate the adaptive capabilities of ALEs with the adaptive personalized tutoring from Implementational Support Tool (ITS). Built on advancements in AI like natural language processing, and computer vision, these systems read learner inputs to offer live feedback, even adapting content and instructional tactics to suit the changing requirements of the learner (Bocconi et al., 2022). AI-powered analytics and predictive modeling, for instance, enable integrated ALE-ITS systems to predict with increasing levels of confidence exactly where students are likely to struggle, as well as where they could improve, and offer them more immediate personally relevant assistance and additional guidance. This predictive power is fundamental in keeping the learning experience alive, relevant and specially catered to the unique learning course of every individual. Integrating ALEs and ITSs with AI helps to raise the level of personalization, adaptability and intelligent in educational technology, which ends up promoting a greater equality and democratization in the educational space, and better learning results for the students (Singh, 2023).

TEACHER-CENTRIC INTEGRATION

Teacher-centered collaboration between Adaptive Learning Environments (ALEs) and ITS: Collaboration involving participation from the teacher role in the process of design, implementation and evaluation of the integrated system. This approach acknowledges the crucial part that teachers play in how children learn and ensures that the system is responsive to their educational philosophy and pedagogical practices. In a teacher-centric integration, teachers collaborate closely with the developers of ALEs and ITS to configure the system to align with the needs of their students and curriculum (Singh, 2024). This collaboration in turn ensures the system is suited to the teacher's looking to teach a particular topic in a specific way & not generically, which ultimately increases learning quality and relevance. Finally, teachers provide essential evaluation of the overall system, in terms of ground truth feedback on the correctness and utility of learner models, feedback for refining the algorithm it employs, as well as design of instructional strategies. This long-term collaboration allows educators to iterate their instruction and system to accommodate changes in their students. The integration process is as such and by involving teachers as part of the working force that processes the system will better mirror the subtleties and complexities of actual teaching and learning resulting in a more efficient learning system, more personalized to individual needs (Singh, 2024).

Figure 6. convey the Teacher-Centric Integration (Source- Original)

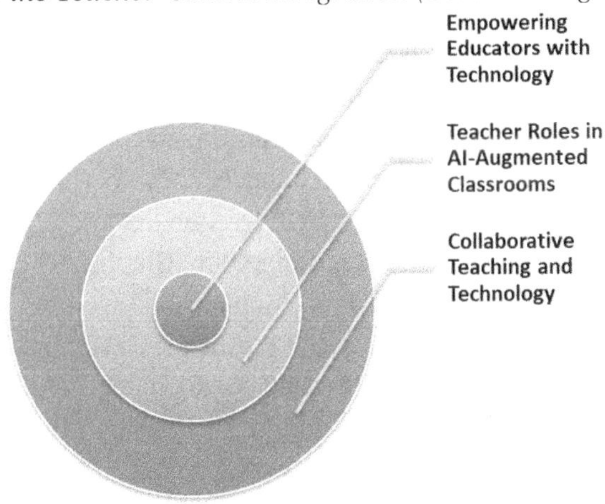

Empowering Educators with Technology

Enabling educators with technology is central to improving the quality of and access to education. Technology therefore offers instructors all sorts of tool and resources to better support students, improve teaching, and stay current in their content area. A significant way that technology can support and empower educators is by offering access to a broad range of educational resources and materials. These include online textbooks, instructional software, digital media, and a network of educators who can provide advice and guidance (Singh, 2024). Technology can offer more time and support as well - for instance, by taking over repetitive or administrative tasks, or by providing tools with which to follow up on student progress and provide feedback on student learning. Finally, technology allows teachers to take advantage of professional development opportunities available online, via courses and training, as well as to have access to extensive educational research and resources. Helping our educators do their work more efficiently provides them with the tools to make great things happen and the power to support students and their unique needs (Singh, 2024).

Teacher Roles in AI-Augmented Classrooms

The transformation of teachers in AI-augmented classrooms extends their tasks in a manner that utilizes artificial intelligence (AI) to improve the learning experience for students. Teachers do not get replaced by technology, they instead become mentors and facilitators working in tandem with AI systems to produce personalized learning which is much more effective. Expert teachers help teachers perform the subject matter expertise they already have in the curriculum and learning objectives in the design and implementation of AI-based tools in AI-augmented classrooms. With working directly with AI developers, teachers can ensure that the technology is standardized and catered to the specific requirements of their students. Teachers, in AI-augmented classrooms, on the other hand, become learning coaches and make use of discernments and data generated by AI systems to more precisely identify a student's strengths, weaknesses, and learning style (Singh, 2024). With this information, teachers are better equipped to provide personalized assistance, direction, and extensions to reach every student where they are. In addition, teachers continue to be essential for building relationships and for social and emotional learning in AI classrooms. Although AI can take some of the burden off of teachers when it comes to administrative and instructional work, teachers continue to be necessary to build a supportive, collaborative, and inclusive learning environment in which students can develop in a well-rounded manner. And now with AI, teachers can take advantage of the technology to improve their teaching techniques, save time to have more individual interactions and thus make the learning more active and effective for students (Singh, 2023).

Collaborative Teaching and Technology

In modern times, collaborative teaching and technology have made their room in education. Technology integration in the classroom provides interactive learning experiences tailored for different learning styles and needs to achieve this. Working with our colleagues to collaboratively plan technology enhanced lessons that are focused on student centered learning and critical thinking and problem solving. Peer-peer learning turned out to be another effective skill in the teaching/learning process, harnessing technology to bring students together, exchange their knowledge and ideas, as well as create community and collaboration (Singh, 2024). There are tools like the online forum to communicate, video conferencing, and collaboration of documents so that students and teacher can connect to each other and communicate their learning or any feedback. The co-instructing and technology may guide teacher professional development to more positive results by refining prospects for mentoring, coaching, and feedback. Teachers exchange ideas on best practices, resources, and expertise with colleagues or Apple Professional Learning Specialists as they learn how to more effectively incorporate technology into teaching and learning. Through collaborative teaching and technology, educators can build a more inclusive, student-centered and effective learning environment that equips students for the digital age (Singh, 2024).

BENEFITS OF AI-AUGMENTED CLASSROOMS

Such benefits of AI-augmented classrooms can revolutionize the way students learn. The second advantage this report shows is that aIs can be followed by the ability to personalise learning allowing reading the students and adjusting the course accordingly personalized (Singh, 2023). This customized method allows students to remain engaged and motivated, as they receive support and feedback that targets their individual areas of strengths and weaknesses. Aiding teachers in their day-to-day workloads, the AI augmentation of classrooms also frees teachers to concentrate on more pedagogic activities while automating significant administrative tasks. The automation of grading, data analysis and communication with parents can then free teachers to more devotedly craft lesson plans and provide the up close and personal attention every student needs (Singh, 2023). This way, AI-augmented classrooms, will provide in-time feedback and assessment which in turn can improve student outcomes by helping teachers to grop areas where students need more additional support. This feedback can also correlate to students' ability to use data that helps them identify and understand their weaknesses/needs in the learning process and apply it to encourage them to improve instead of leaving them in the vacuum of pass/fail mode. In all, classrooms that are strengthened by AI have the potential to transform the way we teach and learn - a faster, more efficient, more personal way of educating (Sharma & Singh, 2022).

Figure 7. highlights the Benefits of AI-Augmented Classrooms (Source- Original)

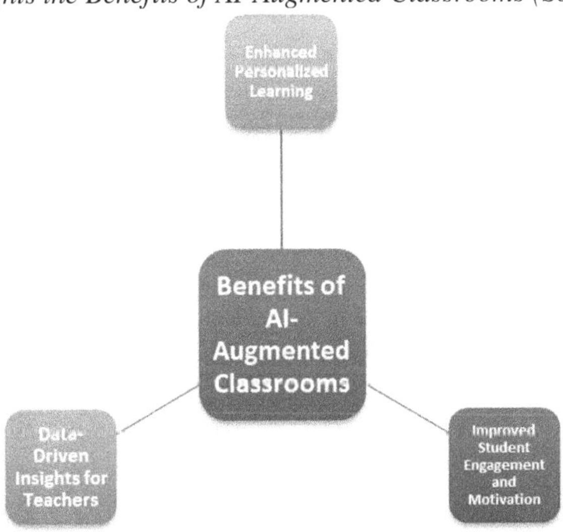

Enhanced Personalized Learning

AI-empowered classrooms are here to deliver optimized custom learning Using AI-powered systems, educators can design personalized learning experiences based on the individual needs, capabilities, and interests of a learner. AI systems can parse through mountains of data about student behaviors, learning styles and preferences in order to reveal areas where additional scaffolding or enrichment may be required. AI-augmented classrooms that are able to adapt to each student's needs allow students to learn more independently and delve into topics and concepts as deeply and quickly as they want. Not only will these AI systems be capable of in the moment feedback and assessment, but they will give student the ability to gauge their progress and adjust their learning accordingly (Díaz, 2024).

This personalized touch keeps students motivated and focused by receiving more tailored guidance and informal feedback based on individual strengths and areas for development. Not only can AI-augmented classrooms facilitate collaborative learning, it means students can work on projects together and share knowledge and ideas. With enabling peer-to-peer learning (Norman & Zoncita, 2024), AI systems can also help students learn from each other, honing their interpersonal skills, communication, teamwork and problem-solving skills. In utilising AI-enhanced classrooms, educators can design a learning environment for all students-taking into account the varying needs and abilities of students, to facilitate in a more inclusive and equitable way (Albuquerque et al., 2024).

Improved Student Engagement and Motivation

Better student engagement and motivation: Finally, AI-enhanced classrooms lead to higher student engagement and increased motivation as well. Using AI to power systems within the learning environment enables teachers in designing more interactive experiences to improve the engagement and keep the attention of the easily distracted generation. Multimedia: AI-based educational tools can also include images, sounds, videos, virtual reality experiences, interactive simulations, or even gamified learning activities (Zahra et al., 2024).

The essence of learning through engaging and immersive experiences can keep students hooked and inspired, encouraging them to be hands-on in the learning process. In addition, an AI-powered classroom can offer personalized feedback and support geared towards helping every individual student based on his/her specific requirements and style of learning (Singh, 2024). The benefit of this personalized touch, is that makes students feel a sense of ownership over their own education, which is particularly effective at guiding them over hurdles they face along the way toward their learning goals. AI-fueled systems also gather student behavior and performance data to find patterns and trends, thus allowing educators to adapt their teaching methods and provide more targeted and engaging content (Singh & Kaunert, 2024). This again is more of a tangible benefit, but having a data-driven approach to discovering why a certain target cohort of students is bored/not motivated can be huge in keeping the educational experience fresh and dynamic, tailored to said students. This in turn enhances the student engagement and motivation levels which contributes to the all-around bettered learning outcome for both the tutees and tutors in a more positive and enriching educational environment (Singh & Kaunert, 2024).

Data-Driven Insights for Teachers

While data-driven insights are essential for AI-augmented classrooms, the information gives the teachers valuable insight to help make better decisions based on the instruction (Singh, 2024). These AI-based systems analyse large volumes of data about a student's academic performance, learning style and preferences, such that teachers can get a full picture of strengths and weaknesses and how an individual student learns. Data-driven insights help teachers determine the right places to put students into small groups for additional support or enrichment, and help them adjust their teaching strategies accordingly (Singh & Kaunert, 2024). AI systems can give feedback and evaluation in real time to help teachers understand student performance and the adjustments teachers should make to their strategies. To compound this, insights into findings the data unveils can help hone-how teachers modify their instruction resulting in better student outcomes (Singh et al., 2024). While laser-focused individual attention is hardly scalable, AI-powered systems can at least suggest tailor-made ways for teachers to evolve and refine their education pathways for student learning, based on research-based indicators about strengths and weaknesses of those individual students. The information resulting from strategies used provides a solid learning environment and also one that adequately addresses the individual needs and abilities of all students (Nicolaides et al., 2024).

CONCLUSION AND FUTURE SCOPE

Through new AI-powered platforms, and fostering creativity and critical thinking, teachers play a crucial role in helping children learn. Intelligent Tutoring Systems (ITS) function like human tutors, assisting children at each stage of a problem and offering advice and feedback as needed (Singh, 2024). These systems evaluate students' learning in real-time, adapting their methods based on the students' progress and comprehension (Singh & Kaunert, 2024). Video game-based learning systems present knowledge in engaging stages that align with the student's skill level, while exploratory instructional systems allow individuals to choose personalized learning paths (Singh & Kaunert, 2024). ITS and customized educational environments are most effective when combined with a teacher-centered approach (Singh, 2024). Integrating AI in education brings both benefits and challenges, raising ethical questions and requiring educators to responsibly adopt AI technology to keep pace with the evolving educational landscape (Singh & Kaunert, 2024). With uniting AI technologies, teachers can save time for more personalized instruction, make data-driven decisions, and provide targeted interventions (Singh et al., 2024). The significance of teacher preparedness and the evolving role of educators in AI-enhanced classrooms is emphasized, examining the potential of ITS and adaptive learning environments to improve education quality, discussing ethical considerations, and presenting case studies and best practices for AI integration (Nicolaides et al., 2024).

References

Agbo, F. J., Oyelere, S. S., Suhonen, J., & Adewumi, S. (2019, November). A systematic review of computational thinking approach for programming education in higher education institutions. In *Proceedings of the 19th Koli Calling International Conference on Computing Education Research* (pp. 1-10). DOI: 10.1145/3364510.3364521

Agbo, F. J., Yigzaw, S. T., Sanusi, I. T., Oyelere, S. S., & Mare, A. H. (2021, October). Examining theoretical and pedagogical foundations of computational thinking in the context of higher education. In *2021 IEEE Frontiers in Education Conference (FIE)* (pp. 1-8). IEEE. DOI: 10.1109/FIE49875.2021.9637405

Albuquerque, U. P., Maroyi, A., Ladio, A. H., Pieroni, A., Abbasi, A. M., Toledo, B. A., Dahdouh-Guebas, F., Hallwass, G., Soldati, G. T., Odonne, G., Vandebroek, I., Vallès, J., Hurrell, J. A., Pardo de Santayana, M., La Torre-Cuadros, M. Á., Silva, M. T. P., Jacob, M. C. M., da Fonseca-Kruel, V. S., & Ferreira Júnior, W. S. (2024). Advancing ethnobiology for the ecological transition and a more inclusive and just world: A comprehensive framework for the next 20 years. *Journal of Ethnobiology and Ethnomedicine*, 20(1), 18. DOI: 10.1186/s13002-024-00661-4 PMID: 38360640

Apiola, M., & Sutinen, E. (2021). Design science research for learning software engineering and computational thinking: Four cases. *Computer Applications in Engineering Education*, 29(1), 83–101. DOI: 10.1002/cae.22291

Barcelos, T. S., & Silveira, I. F. (2012, October). Teaching computational thinking in initial series an analysis of the confluence among mathematics and computer sciences in elementary education and its implications for higher education. In *2012 XXXVIII Conferencia Latinoamericana En Informatica (CLEI)* (pp. 1-8). IEEE. DOI: 10.1109/CLEI.2012.6427135

Bati, K., Yetişir, M. I., Çalişkan, I., Güneş, G., & Gül Saçan, E. (2018). Teaching the concept of time: A steam-based program on computational thinking in science education. *Cogent Education*, 5(1), 1507306. DOI: 10.1080/2331186X.2018.1507306

Bocconi, S., Chioccariello, A., Kampylis, P., Dagienė, V., Wastiau, P., Engelhardt, K., ... & Stupurienė, G. (2022). Reviewing computational thinking in compulsory education: State of play and practices from computing education.

Buitrago-Flórez, F., Danies, G., Restrepo, S., & Hernández, C. (2021). Fostering 21st Century Competences through Computational Thinking and Active Learning: A Mixed Method Study. *International Journal of Instruction*, 14(3), 737–754. DOI: 10.29333/iji.2021.14343a

Czerkawski, B. C., & Lyman, E. W.III. (2015). Exploring issues about computational thinking in higher education. *TechTrends*, 59(2), 57–65. DOI: 10.1007/s11528-015-0840-3

Denning, P. J., & Tedre, M. (2021). Computational thinking: A disciplinary perspective. *Informatics in Education*, 20(3), 361.

Díaz, C. A. (2024). *From transdisciplinary concepts to undisciplined futures*. The Routledge International Handbook of Transdisciplinary Feminist Research and Methodological Praxis.

García-Peñalvo, F. J., & Mendes, A. J. (2018). Exploring the computational thinking effects in pre-university education. *Computers in Human Behavior*, 80, 407–411. DOI: 10.1016/j.chb.2017.12.005

Garg, N., & Singh, B. (2022). Sustainable Development-Adopting a Balanced Approach between Development and Development Induced Changes. *ECS Transactions*, 107(1), 15–31. DOI: 10.1149/10701.0015ecst

Gökçe, S., & Yenmez, A. A. (2023). Ingenuity of scratch programming on reflective thinking towards problem solving and computational thinking. *Education and Information Technologies*, 28(5), 5493–5517. DOI: 10.1007/s10639-022-11385-x

González-Pérez, L. I., & Ramírez-Montoya, M. S. (2022). Components of Education 4.0 in 21st century skills frameworks: Systematic review. *Sustainability (Basel)*, 14(3), 1493. DOI: 10.3390/su14031493

Gross, S., Kim, M., Schlosser, J., Mohtadi, C., Lluch, D., & Schneider, D. (2014, April). Fostering computational thinking in engineering education: Challenges, examples, and best practices. In *2014 IEEE Global Engineering Education Conference (EDUCON)* (pp. 450-459). IEEE. DOI: 10.1109/EDUCON.2014.6826132

Hava, K., & Koyunlu Ünlü, Z. (2021). Investigation of the relationship between middle school students' computational thinking skills and their STEM career interest and attitudes toward inquiry. *Journal of Science Education and Technology*, 30(4), 484–495. DOI: 10.1007/s10956-020-09892-y

Hsu, T. C., & Liang, Y. S. (2021). Simultaneously improving computational thinking and foreign language learning: Interdisciplinary media with plugged and unplugged approaches. *Journal of Educational Computing Research*, 59(6), 1184–1207. DOI: 10.1177/0735633121992480

Hutchins, N. M., Biswas, G., Maróti, M., Lédeczi, Á., Grover, S., Wolf, R., Blair, K. P., Chin, D., Conlin, L., Basu, S., & McElhaney, K. (2020). C2STEM: A system for synergistic learning of physics and computational thinking. *Journal of Science Education and Technology*, 29(1), 83–100. DOI: 10.1007/s10956-019-09804-9

Iversen, O. S., Smith, R. C., & Dindler, C. (2018, August). From computational thinking to computational empowerment: a 21st century PD agenda. In *Proceedings of the 15th participatory design conference: Full papers-Volume 1* (pp. 1-11).

Lee, I., Grover, S., Martin, F., Pillai, S., & Malyn-Smith, J. (2020). Computational thinking from a disciplinary perspective: Integrating computational thinking in K-12 science, technology, engineering, and mathematics education. *Journal of Science Education and Technology*, 29(1), 1–8. DOI: 10.1007/s10956-019-09803-w

Leonard, J., Buss, A., Gamboa, R., Mitchell, M., Fashola, O. S., Hubert, T., & Almughyirah, S. (2016). Using robotics and game design to enhance children's self-efficacy, STEM attitudes, and computational thinking skills. *Journal of Science Education and Technology*, 25(6), 860–876. DOI: 10.1007/s10956-016-9628-2

Li, Y., Schoenfeld, A. H., diSessa, A. A., Graesser, A. C., Benson, L. C., English, L. D., & Duschl, R. A. (2020). Computational thinking is more about thinking than computing. *Journal for STEM Education Research*, 3(1), 1–18. DOI: 10.1007/s41979-020-00030-2 PMID: 32838129

Liu, H. P., Perera, S. M., & Klein, J. W. (2017). Using model-based learning to promote computational thinking education. *Emerging research, practice, and policy on computational thinking*, 153-172.

Lockwood, J., & Mooney, A. (2017). Computational Thinking in Education: Where does it fit? A systematic literary review. *arXiv preprint arXiv:1703.07659.*

Lodi, M., & Martini, S. (2021). Computational thinking, between Papert and Wing. *Science & Education*, 30(4), 883–908. DOI: 10.1007/s11191-021-00202-5

Miller, L. D., Soh, L. K., Chiriacescu, V., Ingraham, E., Shell, D. F., Ramsay, S., & Hazley, M. P. (2013, October). *Improving learning of computational thinking using creative thinking exercises in CS-1 computer science courses. In 2013 ieee frontiers in education conference (fie).* IEEE.

Montiel, H., & Gomez-Zermeño, M. G. (2021). Educational challenges for computational thinking in k–12 education: A systematic literature review of "scratch" as an innovative programming tool. *Computers*, 10(6), 69. DOI: 10.3390/computers10060069

Nicolaides, A., Lim, A., Herr, N., & Barefield, T. (Eds.). (2024). *Reimagining Adult Education as World Building: Creating Learning Ecologies for Transformation*. Taylor & Francis. DOI: 10.4324/9781003371359

Norman, P. D., & Zoncita, D. (2024). Elaborating the Efficacy of Outdoor Arts-based Cooperative Learning Experiences on the Latino Immigrant Students' Engagement, and Academic & Social Success in ESL-STEAM Education. *Available atSSRN* 4757518.

Papadakis, S. (2020). Evaluating a teaching intervention for teaching STEM and programming concepts through the creation of a weather-forecast app for smart mobile devices. In *Handbook of research on tools for teaching computational thinking in P-12 education* (pp. 31–53). IGI Global. DOI: 10.4018/978-1-7998-4576-8.ch002

Pollak, M., & Ebner, M. (2019). The missing link to computational thinking. *Future Internet*, 11(12), 263. DOI: 10.3390/fi11120263

Pollock, L., Mouza, C., Guidry, K. R., & Pusecker, K. (2019, February). Infusing computational thinking across disciplines: Reflections & lessons learned. In *Proceedings of the 50th ACM Technical Symposium on Computer Science Education* (pp. 435-441). DOI: 10.1145/3287324.3287469

Psycharis, S. (2018). STEAM in education: A literature review on the role of computational thinking, engineering epistemology and computational science. computational steam pedagogy (CSP). *Scientific Culture*, 4(2), 51–72.

Psycharis, S., Kalovrektis, K., Sakellaridi, E., Korres, K., & Mastorodimos, D. (2018). Unfolding the curriculum: physical computing, computational thinking and computational experiment in STEM's transdisciplinary approach. *European Journal of Engineering and Technology Research*, 19-24.

Pulimood, S. M., Pearson, K., & Bates, D. C. (2016, February). A study on the impact of multidisciplinary collaboration on computational thinking. In *Proceedings of the 47th ACM technical symposium on computing science education* (pp. 30-35). DOI: 10.1145/2839509.2844636

Qin, H. (2009, March). Teaching computational thinking through bioinformatics to biology students. In *Proceedings of the 40th ACM technical symposium on Computer science education* (pp. 188-191). DOI: 10.1145/1508865.1508932

Raaj, S. (2024). EDUCATION, RESEARCH AND INNOVATION IN INDIA: THE SHIFTING PARADIGMS. *Journal of Higher Education Theory and Practice*, 24(1), 75.

Romero, M., Lepage, A., & Lille, B. (2017). Computational thinking development through creative programming in higher education. *International Journal of Educational Technology in Higher Education*, 14(1), 1–15. DOI: 10.1186/s41239-017-0080-z

Saritepeci, M. (2020). Developing computational thinking skills of high school students: Design-based learning activities and programming tasks. *The Asia-Pacific Education Researcher*, 29(1), 35–54. DOI: 10.1007/s40299-019-00480-2

Sharma, A., & Singh, B. (2022). Measuring Impact of E-commerce on Small Scale Business: A Systematic Review. *Journal of Corporate Governance and International Business Law*, 5(1).

Singh, B. (2023). Unleashing Alternative Dispute Resolution (ADR) in Resolving Complex Legal-Technical Issues Arising in Cyberspace Lensing E-Commerce and Intellectual Property: Proliferation of E-Commerce Digital Economy. *Revista Brasileira de Alternative Dispute Resolution-Brazilian Journal of Alternative Dispute Resolution-RBADR*, 5(10), 81–105. DOI: 10.52028/rbadr.v5i10.ART04.Ind

Singh, B. (2023). Blockchain Technology in Renovating Healthcare: Legal and Future Perspectives. In *Revolutionizing Healthcare Through Artificial Intelligence and Internet of Things Applications* (pp. 177-186). IGI Global.

Singh, B. (2023). Tele-Health Monitoring Lensing Deep Neural Learning Structure: Ambient Patient Wellness via Wearable Devices for Real-Time Alerts and Interventions. *Indian Journal of Health and Medical Law*, 6(2), 12–16.

Singh, B. (2023). Blockchain Technology in Renovating Healthcare: Legal and Future Perspectives. In *Revolutionizing Healthcare Through Artificial Intelligence and Internet of Things Applications* (pp. 177-186). IGI Global.

Singh, B. (2023). Federated Learning for Envision Future Trajectory Smart Transport System for Climate Preservation and Smart Green Planet: Insights into Global Governance and SDG-9 (Industry, Innovation and Infrastructure). *National Journal of Environmental Law*, 6(2), 6–17.

Singh, B. (2024). Evolutionary Global Neuroscience for Cognition and Brain Health: Strengthening Innovation in Brain Science. In *Biomedical Research Developments for Improved Healthcare* (pp. 246-272). IGI Global.

Singh, B. (2024). Featuring Consumer Choices of Consumable Products for Health Benefits: Evolving Issues from Tort and Product Liabilities. *Journal of Law of Torts and Consumer Protection Law*, 7(1).

Singh, B. (2024). Social Cognition of Incarcerated Women and Children: Addressing Exposure to Infectious Diseases and Legal Outcomes. In Reddy, K. (Ed.), *Principles and Clinical Interventions in Social Cognition* (pp. 236–251). IGI Global., DOI: 10.4018/979-8-3693-1265-0.ch014

Singh, B. (2024). Evolutionary Global Neuroscience for Cognition and Brain Health: Strengthening Innovation in Brain Science. In Prabhakar, P. (Ed.), *Biomedical Research Developments for Improved Healthcare* (pp. 246–272). IGI Global., DOI: 10.4018/979-8-3693-1922-2.ch012

Singh, B. (2024). Green Infrastructure in Real Estate Landscapes: Pillars of Sustainable Development and Vision for Tomorrow. *National Journal of Real Estate Law*, 7(1), 4–8.

Singh, B. (2024). Cherish Growth, Advancement and Tax Structure: Addressing Social and Economic Prospects. *Journal of Taxation and Regulatory Framework*, 7(1), 7–10.

Singh, B. (2024). Legal Dynamics Lensing Metaverse Crafted for Videogame Industry and E-Sports: Phenomenological Exploration Catalyst Complexity and Future. *Journal of Intellectual Property Rights Law*, 7(1), 8–14.

Singh, B. (2024). Evolutionary Global Neuroscience for Cognition and Brain Health: Strengthening Innovation in Brain Science. In *Biomedical Research Developments for Improved Healthcare* (pp. 246-272). IGI Global.

Singh, B. (2024). Social Cognition of Incarcerated Women and Children: Addressing Exposure to Infectious Diseases and Legal Outcomes. In Reddy, K. (Ed.), *Principles and Clinical Interventions in Social Cognition* (pp. 236–251). IGI Global., DOI: 10.4018/979-8-3693-1265-0.ch014

Singh, B. (2024). Lensing Legal Dynamics for Examining Responsibility and Deliberation of Generative AI-Tethered Technological Privacy Concerns: Infringements and Use of Personal Data by Nefarious Actors. In Ara, A., & Ara, A. (Eds.), *Exploring the Ethical Implications of Generative AI* (pp. 146–167). IGI Global., DOI: 10.4018/979-8-3693-1565-1.ch009

Singh, B., & Kaunert, C. (2024). Future of Digital Marketing: Hyper-Personalized Customer Dynamic Experience with AI-Based Predictive Models. *Revolutionizing the AI-Digital Landscape: A Guide to Sustainable Emerging Technologies for Marketing Professionals*, 189.

Singh, B., & Kaunert, C. (2024). Salvaging Responsible Consumption and Production of Food in the Hospitality Industry: Harnessing Machine Learning and Deep Learning for Zero Food Waste. In *Sustainable Disposal Methods of Food Wastes in Hospitality Operations* (pp. 176-192). IGI Global.

Singh, B., & Kaunert, C. (2024). Revealing Green Finance Mobilization: Harnessing FinTech and Blockchain Innovations to Surmount Barriers and Foster New Investment Avenues. In *Harnessing Blockchain-Digital Twin Fusion for Sustainable Investments* (pp. 265-286). IGI Global.

Singh, B., & Kaunert, C. (2024). Harnessing Sustainable Agriculture Through Climate-Smart Technologies: Artificial Intelligence for Climate Preservation and Futuristic Trends. In *Exploring Ethical Dimensions of Environmental Sustainability and Use of AI* (pp. 214-239). IGI Global.

Singh, B., & Kaunert, C. (2024). Integration of Cutting-Edge Technologies such as Internet of Things (IoT) and 5G in Health Monitoring Systems: A Comprehensive Legal Analysis and Futuristic Outcomes. *GLS Law Journal*, 6(1), 13–20. DOI: 10.69974/glslawjournal.v6i1.123

Singh, B., & Kaunert, C. (2024). Salvaging Responsible Consumption and Production of Food in the Hospitality Industry: Harnessing Machine Learning and Deep Learning for Zero Food Waste. In Singh, A., Tyagi, P., & Garg, A. (Eds.), *Sustainable Disposal Methods of Food Wastes in Hospitality Operations* (pp. 176–192). IGI Global., DOI: 10.4018/979-8-3693-2181-2.ch012

Singh, B., & Kaunert, C. (2024). Salvaging Responsible Consumption and Production of Food in the Hospitality Industry: Harnessing Machine Learning and Deep Learning for Zero Food Waste. In *Sustainable Disposal Methods of Food Wastes in Hospitality Operations* (pp. 176-192). IGI Global.

Singh, B., & Kaunert, C. (2024). Revealing Green Finance Mobilization: Harnessing FinTech and Blockchain Innovations to Surmount Barriers and Foster New Investment Avenues. In *Harnessing Blockchain-Digital Twin Fusion for Sustainable Investments* (pp. 265-286). IGI Global.

Singh, B., & Kaunert, C. (2024). Harnessing Sustainable Agriculture Through Climate-Smart Technologies: Artificial Intelligence for Climate Preservation and Futuristic Trends. In *Exploring Ethical Dimensions of Environmental Sustainability and Use of AI* (pp. 214-239). IGI Global.

Singh, B., & Kaunert, C. (2024). Salvaging Responsible Consumption and Production of Food in the Hospitality Industry: Harnessing Machine Learning and Deep Learning for Zero Food Waste. In Singh, A., Tyagi, P., & Garg, A. (Eds.), *Sustainable Disposal Methods of Food Wastes in Hospitality Operations* (pp. 176–192). IGI Global., DOI: 10.4018/979-8-3693-2181-2.ch012

Singh, B., Kaunert, C., & Vig, K. (2024). Reinventing Influence of Artificial Intelligence (AI) on Digital Consumer Lensing Transforming Consumer Recommendation Model: Exploring Stimulus Artificial Intelligence on Consumer Shopping Decisions. In Musiolik, T., Rodriguez, R., & Kannan, H. (Eds.), *AI Impacts in Digital Consumer Behavior* (pp. 141–169). IGI Global., DOI: 10.4018/979-8-3693-1918-5.ch006

Singh, B., Kaunert, C., & Vig, K. (2024). Reinventing Influence of Artificial Intelligence (AI) on Digital Consumer Lensing Transforming Consumer Recommendation Model: Exploring Stimulus Artificial Intelligence on Consumer Shopping Decisions. In *AI Impacts in Digital Consumer Behavior* (pp. 141-169). IGI Global.

Singh, B., Kaunert, C., & Vig, K. (2024). Reinventing Influence of Artificial Intelligence (AI) on Digital Consumer Lensing Transforming Consumer Recommendation Model: Exploring Stimulus Artificial Intelligence on Consumer Shopping Decisions. In Musiolik, T., Rodriguez, R., & Kannan, H. (Eds.), *AI Impacts in Digital Consumer Behavior* (pp. 141–169). IGI Global., DOI: 10.4018/979-8-3693-1918-5.ch006

Singh, B., Kaunert, C., & Vig, K. (2024). Reinventing Influence of Artificial Intelligence (AI) on Digital Consumer Lensing Transforming Consumer Recommendation Model: Exploring Stimulus Artificial Intelligence on Consumer Shopping Decisions. In *AI Impacts in Digital Consumer Behavior* (pp. 141-169). IGI Global.

Singh, B., Vig, K., & Kaunert, C. (2024). Modernizing Healthcare: Application of Augmented Reality and Virtual Reality in Clinical Practice and Medical Education. In Modern Technology in Healthcare and Medical Education: Blockchain, IoT, AR, and VR (pp. 1-21). IGI Global.

Sırakaya, M., Alsancak Sırakaya, D., & Korkmaz, Ö. (2020). The impact of STEM attitude and thinking style on computational thinking determined via structural equation modeling. *Journal of Science Education and Technology*, 29(4), 561–572. DOI: 10.1007/s10956-020-09836-6

Tedre, M., & Denning, P. J. (2016, November). The long quest for computational thinking. In *Proceedings of the 16th Koli Calling international conference on computing education research* (pp. 120-129).

Tsortanidou, X., Daradoumis, T., & Barberá, E. (2019). Connecting moments of creativity, computational thinking, collaboration and new media literacy skills. *Information and Learning Science*, 120(11/12), 704–722. DOI: 10.1108/ILS-05-2019-0042

Ulger, K. (2018). The effect of problem-based learning on the creative thinking and critical thinking disposition of students in visual arts education. *The Interdisciplinary Journal of Problem-Based Learning*, 12(1). Advance online publication. DOI: 10.7771/1541-5015.1649

Valovičová, Ľ., Ondruška, J., Zelenický, Ľ., Chytrý, V., & Medová, J. (2020). Enhancing computational thinking through interdisciplinary STEAM activities using tablets. *Mathematics*, 8(12), 2128. DOI: 10.3390/math8122128

Wang, C., Shen, J., & Chao, J. (2022). Integrating computational thinking in STEM education: A literature review. *International Journal of Science and Mathematics Education*, 20(8), 1949–1972. DOI: 10.1007/s10763-021-10227-5

Weintrop, D., Beheshti, E., Horn, M., Orton, K., Jona, K., Trouille, L., & Wilensky, U. (2016). Defining computational thinking for mathematics and science classrooms. *Journal of Science Education and Technology*, 25(1), 127–147. DOI: 10.1007/s10956-015-9581-5

Yadav, A., Mayfield, C., Zhou, N., Hambrusch, S., & Korb, J. T. (2014). Computational thinking in elementary and secondary teacher education. [TOCE]. *ACM Transactions on Computing Education*, 14(1), 1–16. DOI: 10.1145/2576872

Yilmaz Ince, E., & Koc, M. (2021). The consequences of robotics programming education on computational thinking skills: An intervention of the Young Engineer's Workshop (YEW). *Computer Applications in Engineering Education*, 29(1), 191–208. DOI: 10.1002/cae.22321

Zahra, A., Waheed, Z., Fatima, T., & Khong, K. W. (2024). Leveraging Technology for Environmental Awareness: Insights from Experimental Research with Middle School Students in Malaysia. *RMLE Online: Research in Middle Level Education*, 47(4), 1–17. DOI: 10.1080/19404476.2024.2322046

Zint, M., Michel, J. O., Valentine, T., & Collins, S. (2024). *Collaborating with Students to Advance Climate Change Education at the University of Michigan*. Insights and Recommendations.

Chapter 5 Rethinking Educational Assessment in the Age of Artificial Intelligence: Insights From Recent Training Workshops

Zuheir Khlaif
https://orcid.org/0000-0002-7354-7512
An-Najah National University, Palestine

ABSTRACT

The rise of generative AI in education presents both opportunities and challenges, particularly in the realm of student assessment. This paper examines the transformative impact of generative AI on educational assessment practices, drawing insights from recent training workshops conducted for educators in the Global South. The paper explores how AI can enhance traditional assessment methods by promoting critical thinking, creativity, and collaboration. It introduces innovative frameworks such as AI-resistant assessments and the Process-Product Assessment Model, which focus on evaluating the final output and the student's engagement with AI tools throughout the learning process. The paper also highlights practical strategies for integrating AI into assessment practices, emphasizing the need for ethical AI use and preserving academic integrity.

DOI: 10.4018/979-8-3693-7255-5.ch005

THE ROLE OF GENERATIVE AI IN EDUCATIONAL ASSESSMENT

Generative AI (Gen AI) has undergone significant advancements, transforming from simple text generation tools into highly sophisticated systems capable of producing human-like content across a broad spectrum of domains (Feuerriegel et al., 2024). With the emergence of advanced models like the GPT-40 and GPT-01 preview model, AI now has the ability to perform a range of complex tasks, including text analysis, natural language understanding, and even demonstrating creativity in writing and problem-solving (Shahriar et al., 2024). This leap in AI capabilities has opened up exciting new possibilities for its integration into education, particularly in the areas of providing feedback and enhancing assessment processes.

In the past year, the rapid development and increasing power of generative AI tools have sparked a revolution in education. These tools have enabled educators to devise innovative teaching strategies and redesign student tasks to better meet the demands of the AI era (Khlaif et al., 2023). As a result, there is a growing movement among decision-makers, educators, practitioners, and researchers to explore how generative AI can be integrated into higher and public education systems, creating opportunities for significant advancements across various educational contexts (Noroozi et al., 2024).

Within education, generative AI is proving to be much more than a tool for administrative efficiency. It is opening new doors for improving student engagement and transforming the way learning is assessed. Furthermore, generative AI is becoming a point of competition among higher education institutions, as these institutions strive to meet global goals such as the United Nations' Sustainable Development Goals (SDGs), particularly SDG 4 (quality education) and SDG 5 (gender equality) (George & Wooden, 2023; Pisica et al., 2023).

However, despite these promising advancements, significant challenges remain in the process of integrating AI into higher education. Based on the author's experience, supported by numerous studies, these challenges are not limited to financial costs. A critical issue lies in the attitudes and perspectives of the academic community, which are often accompanied by a lack of clear vision and strategy within higher education institutions, particularly in many countries of the Global South (Bozkurt et al., 2023; Jin et al., 2024). Even though UNESCO has published guidelines to assist decision-makers in these regions, progress in AI adoption remains slow. While individual initiatives, such as professional development workshops, attempt to address these gaps and integrate AI into educational practices, many countries continue to lag despite these efforts.

Thus, while generative AI offers tremendous potential for reshaping education and advancing institutional goals, its full integration will require overcoming technical and financial barriers and addressing the broader academic and structural challenges that persist, especially in less-resourced regions.

Assessment has always been a cornerstone of the educational process. It is a critical mechanism to measure learning outcomes, provide feedback, and ensure that educational goals are met (Botuzova et al., 2023). The development of traditional assessments, from standardized tests and exams to authentic assessments, as well as the emerging new flipped-assessment approaches, continue developing within the development of technology and emerging new teaching strategies (Aziz et al., 2020). The aim of this development was to align with 21st-century skills and to enhance the quality of education as one of the sustainability goals.

Addressing the Gaps in AI-Driven Assessment Research

While the use of AI in education has been explored extensively in areas such as personalized learning, instructional design, and administrative automation, there is a significant gap in understanding how generative AI can be integrated into assessment practices, particularly in higher education. Most current research focuses on the application of AI to automate grading or provide instant feedback, but there is limited research on how AI can transform the nature of assessments themselves. Additionally, much of the discourse around AI in education has been concentrated in the Global North, with insufficient attention paid to how these technologies can be adapted and implemented in Global South contexts, where resource constraints and educational challenges differ. This paper addresses these gaps by exploring how generative AI can be harnessed to rethink assessment methods, focusing on early adopters in the Global South and their diverse academic fields, such as medical education, humanities, and engineering.

Rethinking Assessment Strategies with AI

The purpose of this paper is to provide a comprehensive framework for rethinking assessment in the era of generative AI, drawing on both theoretical insights and practical experiences from workshops conducted with faculty members in higher education. By examining how generative AI can be integrated into assessment strategies, this paper aims to offer educators, particularly in the Global South, practical solutions for designing more meaningful, AI-enhanced assessments that align with modern educational needs. Furthermore, the paper will highlight how these assessments can promote the development of higher-order thinking skills, encourage creativity, and provide more equitable and scalable solutions to challenges faced by educators worldwide. Through this exploration, the paper seeks to contribute to the ongoing dialogue about the future of assessment in an AI-driven.

Key Insights from AI Assessment Workshops

During the last year, the author designed and delivered a series of comprehensive training workshops and public lectures aimed at rethinking educational assessment in the age of artificial intelligence (AI). These sessions were conducted both in-person and online, bringing together more than 300 Educators from countries such as Saudi Arabia, the UAE, Jordan, Palestine, Egypt, Iraq, South Africa, and others. The workshops were offered in both Arabic and English to accommodate the diverse linguistic backgrounds of the attendees. These sessions focused on equipping educators with theoretical insights and practical tools to redesign student assignments, fostering critical thinking, creativity, and ethical AI use in the classroom.

The workshops were structured into two key components: theoretical discussions and practical applications. In the theoretical part, we explored cutting-edge models and frameworks for assessing student work in the context of AI. One of the key models introduced was the AI Task Assessment Scale, a tool designed to help educators systematically evaluate student performance in assignments that incorporate AI tools. Another major framework discussed was the Process-Product Assessment Model, an emerging approach that not only assesses the final product of student work but also evaluates the quality of the steps students take during the process. This includes how they develop AI prompts and how they collaborate with AI tools throughout their learning journey. This shift in assessment philosophy places greater emphasis on human-AI interaction, which offers educators a richer and more comprehensive understanding of student learning and critical thinking processes.

In the practical component, educators engage in hands-on activities to design AI-resistant assignments. This approach aligns with the AI-Resistance Assessment Scale (AIAS), which I developed to guide educators in creating tasks that promote critical engagement and ethical AI use. Educators explored various ways to encourage students to use generative AI tools in a constructive manner, particularly during the brainstorming phase of assignments. This method of integrating AI into the learning process ensures that students remain responsible for the content generated by AI, fostering accountability and deepening their understanding of the material. By encouraging students to develop AI prompts carefully and strategically, educators can assess the cognitive processes involved in human-AI collaboration rather than just focusing on the output.

A central theme of the workshops was the Process-Product Approach, which we discussed extensively as a new and emerging method of assessment. Educators were trained to use this approach to evaluate both the quality of the final product and the process that led to it. This includes assessing the interactivity between students and AI, as well as the steps students take in developing effective prompts. The aim was to help educators design tasks that allow for a detailed evaluation of human-AI collaboration, ensuring that students engage critically with AI tools rather than using them passively. This focus on the process helps educators identify the depth of student understanding and decision-making during their assignments.

As the Educators engaged in these discussions, they reflected on ways to incorporate AI into student work while fostering critical thinking. One key suggestion was to allow students to use generative AI during the brainstorming and proofreading stages of their assignments. However, to ensure that students critically engage with the AI-generated content, educators recommended that students write a reflection paper about their experience using AI in course projects. This reflection would not only detail the student's interaction with AI but also include a critique of the ideas and content generated by the tools. The purpose of this approach is to equip students with critical thinking skills and foster the development of essential 21st-century skills such as problem-solving, ethical decision-making, and the ability to assess the credibility of AI-generated information.

Educators were particularly interested in designing a variety of AI-resistant tasks, which are assignments structured to minimize the risk of over-reliance on AI-generated content. These tasks require students to engage deeply with the subject matter, ensuring that they contribute their own insights and creativity while using AI as a supportive tool rather than a replacement for original thought. The emphasis was placed on designing assignments that challenge students to use AI ethically, critically, and responsibly. By requiring students to validate and reflect on AI outputs, educators can assess not only the final product but also how effectively students navigate the complexities of human-AI collaboration.

During the workshops, Educators raised concerns about the implications of generative AI on academic integrity. Many feared that AI might dilute the originality of student work or lead to plagiarism. To address these concerns, we discussed strategies for shifting the focus of assessment from the final product to the learning process itself. By assessing the quality of interaction between students and AI, educators can maintain academic integrity while still embracing the potential benefits of AI. Tasks that require problem-solving, critical thinking, and creativity were highlighted as particularly resistant to AI overreach, as they demand original input from students and cannot be fully automated.

One of the key insights that emerged from these discussions was the need for authentic assessment—assignments that reflect real-world challenges and require students to apply their knowledge in complex, context-rich situations. These tasks make it more difficult for students to rely entirely on AI-generated content, as they require critical thinking, collaboration, and ethical reasoning. This shift toward authentic and process-based assessments allows educators to better evaluate student learning in a way that safeguards academic integrity while fostering deeper engagement with course material.

Looking ahead, I plan to publish a detailed guide for teachers and academics on how to design AI-resistant assessments using the AI-Resistance Assessment Scale (AIAS). This guide will provide educators with practical strategies for creating tasks that enhance critical thinking, creativity, and ethical AI use. In the meantime, Educators can begin applying the concepts discussed in the workshops, using the AI Task Assessment Scale to navigate the integration of AI into their teaching while maintaining the integrity of student learning.

In conclusion, these training workshops offered more than just theoretical insights—they provided a platform for educators from diverse backgrounds to collaboratively rethink the future of educational assessment in the age of AI. By focusing on critical thinking, human-AI collaboration, and ethical responsibility, Educators are now better equipped to design assessments that are not only resistant to the misuse of AI but also promote deeper, more meaningful student learning. These workshops laid the foundation for educators to harness the potential of AI while safeguarding the essential values of creativity, originality, and academic integrity in education.

Open Discussions: Sharing Best Practices and Experiences

After each training session, Educators engaged in open discussions where they exchanged best practices for integrating AI into teaching and professional development. These conversations allowed faculty members to reflect on their individual experiences and learn from their colleagues' diverse approaches. The collaborative environment fostered an exchange of practical resources, including AI-based activities and assignments. By sharing these resources, educators were able to explore the broad potential of generative AI tools and consider how to implement them effectively within their own teaching contexts. This peer-to-peer learning was crucial in expanding their understanding of AI's applications in education.

Faculty Attitudes Toward AI: Enthusiasm vs. Concerns

Faculty attitudes towards using generative AI (Gen AI) in student tasks were divided. On one side, there was palpable enthusiasm for the technology. Many educators were excited about AI's potential to streamline administrative tasks, such as grading, thereby allowing them to focus more on fostering critical thinking and creativity in students. The time-saving aspect of AI tools, combined with the empowerment students felt using these advanced technologies, contributed to a positive outlook. Faculty also observed that students took pride in using AI, viewing it as a valuable tool that enhanced their learning experience and academic performance.

On the other side, some faculty members expressed significant concerns regarding academic integrity. The ease with which AI can generate content has raised fears of increased cheating and plagiarism. These concerns left many educators frustrated as they struggled to reconcile the potential benefits of AI with the possibility of compromising the authenticity of student work. For these educators, the integration of AI into teaching practices remained a source of uncertainty, and many expressed hesitancy toward adopting these tools without clear guidelines to mitigate these risks.

Redesigning Assessments for the AI Era

One of the most critical points of discussion during the workshops was the need to redesign student assessments to align with the realities of the AI era. Faculty explored strategies for adapting assessments that not only integrate AI tools but also ensure students are challenged in ways that AI cannot easily replicate. For instance, they emphasized context-specific solutions tailored to their disciplines and the unique challenges of their institutions. These discussions underscored the importance of designing assessments that encourage deeper engagement with the subject matter, creativity, and the development of critical thinking skills. The focus was on moving beyond rote learning and creating tasks that would require students to demonstrate higher-order thinking, problem-solving abilities, and ethical decision-making in their interactions with AI tools.

Institutional Policy and Vision: The Path Forward

A recurring theme throughout the workshops was the necessity of establishing a clear institutional vision and policy regarding the integration of AI into both teaching and research. Educators agreed that institutions must provide clear guidance on how AI should be used, with policies that encompass both the educational and research contexts. As noted by Pedro et al. (2019), such policies are essential for fostering positive attitudes toward AI, encouraging educators to adopt these tools in thoughtful and productive ways.

Moreover, institutions with well-defined AI policies can play a pivotal role in raising awareness about AI literacy and competencies. Faculty and students alike need a structured framework to navigate the ethical and practical implications of using AI in their academic work. As Spivakovsky et al. (2023) highlight, these policies can help build a more informed academic community capable of leveraging AI's benefits while being mindful of its challenges.

Policy Development for AI-Enhanced Courses: Addressing Assessment Challenges

Another key takeaway from the workshops was the importance of developing policies specifically for AI-enhanced courses, particularly in addressing assessment-related challenges. Such policies can provide students with clear guidelines on when and how to use AI tools in their coursework. By setting clear boundaries, these policies enhance students' understanding of the ethical implications of AI use, ensuring that the technology is applied responsibly.

Faculty members also discussed the importance of balancing AI's benefits with the need to preserve the authenticity of student work. A well-crafted policy framework would empower educators to manage AI's use effectively, reducing concerns about cheating and misuse. For example, a few educators reported creating GPT models for their courses, uploading lecture content, and using the tool to generate both closed and open-ended questions. While some colleagues appreciated this practice, others criticized it, noting that AI-generated questions were sometimes repetitive or not aligned with course material. These conversations highlighted the need for a thoughtful, well-monitored approach to integrating AI in assessments.

Human-AI Collaboration: Redefining Student Assignments

A recurring theme in the workshops was the importance of viewing AI as a collaborative tool that supports, rather than replaces, student learning. Some educators shared their experience using generative AI to help design assignments or generate initial ideas for tasks. These assignments were structured around the AI-Resistance Assessment Scale (Petihakis et al., 2023), which encourages students to engage critically with AI tools for brainstorming, idea generation, proofreading, and project development.

Educators suggested linking this AI assessment scale to Bloom's Taxonomy (Forehand, 2010) to ensure a deeper alignment with educational objectives. This integration encourages students to reflect on the ideas generated by AI, comparing them with their own thoughts and improving their critical thinking skills. By combining AI-supported tasks with a clear course policy, students are guided to use AI responsibly while deepening their understanding of the subject matter.

Product-Process Assessment: Emphasizing Critical Engagement with AI

During the workshop discussions, the facilitator introduced the concept of Product-Process Assessment, an emerging evaluation approach that shifts the focus from the final product to the process involved in completing a task. This approach is particularly relevant in the context of human-AI collaboration, where the interaction between the learner and AI tools becomes a vital component of the assessment.

The Product-Process Assessment method evaluates how students develop prompts to guide AI tools and how they collaborate with AI throughout the learning journey. This model encourages educators to assess not only the final output but also the decisions students make during the process. Faculty members were encouraged to involve students in the development of evaluation rubrics, creating a partnership in the assessment process. This collaborative approach allows students to critically engage with AI-generated content, refining their initial ideas based on comparison and critical reflection.

AI and Authentic Assessments: Real-World Applications in Education

Another significant topic covered during the workshops was the role of AI in fostering authentic assessments, which focus on real-world tasks and applications. Authentic assessments differ from traditional tests by requiring students to apply their knowledge in practical, context-rich scenarios, reflecting the complexities they will encounter in professional settings (Fatima et al., 2024; Thnh et al., 2023).

For example, instead of a traditional essay, educators might ask students to create podcasts, develop multimedia presentations, or solve real-world problems using AI tools. These assessments foster creativity, collaboration, and critical thinking, promoting higher-order skills that are essential in an AI-driven world.

Competency-Based Assessments: AI's Role in Real-World Learning

Educators working in medical education highlighted the growing importance of competency-based assessments in the AI era. Competency-based assessments go beyond knowledge recall, evaluating a student's ability to apply theoretical knowledge in practical, real-world situations. AI plays an instrumental role in this shift by providing tools for simulating complex environments where students can demonstrate skills in controlled yet dynamic settings (Waladi & Lamarti, 2024).

One medical educator shared how AI-enhanced virtual patients are used in her university's virtual lab to assess clinical decision-making and problem-solving skills in high-pressure scenarios. This example illustrates the potential of AI to transform assessments in ways that prepare students for real-world challenges, offering a dynamic and interactive learning experience.

AI-Resistant Assessments: A New Approach to Preserving Academic Integrity

AI-resistant assessments have emerged as a critical approach in the AI era, particularly as educators grapple with concerns about academic integrity. The rise of generative AI has made it easier for students to produce automated content, raising the risk of plagiarism and over-reliance on AI-generated outputs. To counter these challenges, educators and researchers have introduced AI-resistant assessments, which are designed to minimize the risk of students misusing AI tools while still leveraging AI for productive learning.

The central idea behind AI-resistant assessments is to create tasks that cannot be easily solved by AI, encouraging deeper engagement from students. This type of assessment typically requires higher-order thinking skills such as critical analysis, creativity, and problem-solving—areas where AI struggles to fully replicate human abilities. Additionally, AI-resistant assessments focus on the process of learning rather than just the final product. This means that students are evaluated based on their interaction with AI tools, including how they develop prompts, refine their ideas, and critically engage with AI-generated content.

One example of an AI-resistant assessment is reflective writing combined with AI use. In this assessment, students are encouraged to use AI tools to brainstorm ideas, generate drafts, or receive feedback on their work. However, rather than submitting the AI-generated content directly, students are required to write a reflection on how they used AI, detailing the specific prompts they used, their rationale for selecting certain AI-generated content, and how they modified or critiqued the AI's suggestions. This reflective component forces students to engage critically with AI, ensuring they remain responsible for the final product.

In addition to the reflection, educators can also ask students to identify inaccuracies or biases in the AI-generated material, fostering a deeper understanding of both the content and the limitations of AI tools. This approach ensures that students do not passively rely on AI but instead use it as a tool for enhancing their learning process.

Theoretical Implications

This paper offers several important theoretical implications for the field of education, particularly in the context of integrating AI into assessment practices. Traditionally, assessment methods in higher education have relied on standardized tests, essays, and projects. However, the introduction of AI shifts the focus towards more dynamic and complex forms of assessment, such as AI-resistant assessments and human-AI collaboration. The paper explores how AI can not only automate grading but also transform how educators assess higher-order thinking skills like critical analysis, creativity, and ethical reasoning. This challenges existing assessment paradigms by pushing the boundaries of what can be evaluated in educational settings.

One of the key theoretical contributions of the paper is the proposal of the AI Task Assessment Scale and the Process-Product Assessment Model, both of which offer frameworks for assessing student interaction with AI. These models provide a foundation for rethinking how students' learning processes, rather than just final outcomes, are evaluated. The paper also highlights the need for a shift from purely product-based assessments to assessments that evaluate both the process and the student's engagement with AI tools, which is a relatively unexplored area in educational theory. Additionally, the discussion on AI-resistant assessments introduces a new layer of complexity in how educators design tasks that mitigate the risks of over-reliance on AI, thus enriching the theoretical dialogue on the integrity of assessment.

Practical Implications

From a practical perspective, the paper provides educators and institutions with actionable strategies to integrate AI into their teaching and assessment practices. For faculty members, it outlines how to design assessments that encourage student engagement with AI while maintaining academic integrity. For example, the paper discusses the implementation of the AI-Resistance Assessment Scale (AIAS), which can be used to design tasks that promote critical thinking and responsible AI use. It also offers practical guidance on how educators can assess not only the final output but also the process students undergo when using AI tools, thus providing a more comprehensive understanding of student learning.

In addition to classroom practices, the paper underscores the importance of institutional policies in supporting the integration of AI into education. It recommends that institutions develop clear policies that guide both students and educators on how AI should be used ethically in educational settings. These policies can help mitigate risks such as academic dishonesty and ensure that AI is used as a tool to enhance, rather than replace, learning. Furthermore, the paper provides a roadmap for professional development, emphasizing the need for continuous training for educators to stay updated with AI advancements and their implications for assessment.

CONCLUSION

In conclusion, this paper demonstrates that the integration of generative AI into educational assessment offers both opportunities and challenges. While AI has the potential to enhance assessments by providing real-time feedback, automating grading, and fostering deeper engagement with learning, it also raises critical concerns about academic integrity and the role of human oversight in the educational process. The paper advocates for a balanced approach that leverages AI's capabilities while maintaining a focus on critical thinking, creativity, and ethical responsibility.

Through the introduction of innovative assessment models, such as the AI Task Assessment Scale and the Process-Product Assessment Model, this paper provides educators with practical tools to navigate the complexities of AI-enhanced learning environments. It also highlights the importance of clear institutional policies and continuous faculty development to ensure that AI is integrated into education in a way that is both ethical and effective. As AI continues to evolve, educators must remain vigilant in designing assessments that not only resist misuse but also encourage meaningful human-AI collaboration, fostering a new generation of learners equipped with the skills needed to succeed in an AI-driven world.

References

Aziz, M. N. A., Yusoff, N. M., & Yaakob, M. F. M. (2020). Challenges in Using Authentic Assessment in 21st Century ESL Classrooms. *International Journal of Evaluation and Research in Education*, 9(3), 759–768. DOI: 10.11591/ijere.v9i3.20546

Botuzova, Y., Iievliev, O., Okipniak, I., Yandola, K., & Charkina, T. (2023). Innovative Approaches to Assessment in Pedagogical Practice: New Technologies, Methods and Development of Objective Assessment Tools. *Cadernos de Educação Tecnologia e Sociedade*, 16(2), 386–398. DOI: 10.14571/brajets.v16.n2.386-398

Bozkurt, A., Junhong, X., Lambert, S., Pazurek, A., Crompton, H., Koseoglu, S., & Romero-Hall, E. (2023). Speculative futures on ChatGPT and generative artificial intelligence (AI): A collective reflection from the educational landscape. *Asian Journal of Distance Education*, 18(1), 53–130.

Fatima, S. S., Sheikh, N. A., & Osama, A. (2024). Authentic assessment in medical education: Exploring AI integration and student-as-partners collaboration. *Postgraduate Medical Journal*, •••, qgae088. DOI: 10.1093/postmj/qgae088 PMID: 39041454

Feuerriegel, S., Hartmann, J., Janiesch, C., & Zschech, P. (2024). Generative ai. *Business & Information Systems Engineering*, 66(1), 111–126. DOI: 10.1007/s12599-023-00834-7

Forehand, M. (2010). Bloom's taxonomy. Emerging perspectives on learning, teaching, and technology, 41(4), 47-56

George, B., & Wooden, O. (2023). Managing the strategic transformation of higher education through artificial intelligence. *Administrative Sciences*, 13(9), 196. DOI: 10.3390/admsci13090196

Grassini, S. (2023). Development and validation of the AI attitude scale (AIAS-4): A brief measure of general attitude toward artificial intelligence. *Frontiers in Psychology*, 14, 1191628. DOI: 10.3389/fpsyg.2023.1191628 PMID: 37554139

Jin, Y., Yan, L., Echeverria, V., Gašević, D., & Martinez-Maldonado, R. (2024). Generative AI in Higher Education: A Global Perspective of Institutional Adoption Policies and Guidelines. *arXiv preprint arXiv:2405.11800.*

Pedro, F., Subosa, M., Rivas, A., & Valverde, P. (2019). Artificial intelligence in education: Challenges and opportunities for sustainable development.

Petihakis, G., Farao, A., Bountakas, P., Sabazioti, A., Polley, J., & Xenakis, C. (2024, July). AIAS: AI-ASsisted cybersecurity platform to defend against adversarial AI attacks. In *Proceedings of the 19th International Conference on Availability, Reliability and Security* (pp. 1-7 DOI: 10.1145/3664476.3669920

Pisica, A. I., Edu, T., Zaharia, R. M., & Zaharia, R. (2023). Implementing artificial intelligence in higher education: Pros and cons from the perspectives of academics. *Societies (Basel, Switzerland)*, 13(5), 118. DOI: 10.3390/soc13050118

Shahriar, S., Lund, B. D., Mannuru, N. R., Arshad, M. A., Hayawi, K., Bevara, R. V. K., Mannuru, A., & Batool, L. (2024). Putting GPT-4o to the Sword: A Comprehensive Evaluation of Language, Vision, Speech, and Multimodal Proficiency. *Applied Sciences (Basel, Switzerland)*, 14(17), 7782. DOI: 10.3390/app14177782

Spivakovsky, O. V., Omelchuk, S. A., Kobets, V. V., Valko, N. V., & Malchykova, D. S. (2023). Institutional policies on artificial intelligence in university learning, teaching and research. *Information Technologies and Learning Tools*, 97(5), 181–202. DOI: 10.33407/itlt.v97i5.5395

Thanh, B. N., Vo, D. T. H., Nhat, M. N., Pham, T. T. T., Trung, H. T., & Xuan, S. H. (2023). Race with the machines: Assessing the capability of generative AI in solving authentic assessments. *Australasian Journal of Educational Technology*, 39(5), 59–81. DOI: 10.14742/ajet.8902

Waladi, C., & Lamarti, M. S. (2024). Adaptive AI-Driven Assessment for Competency-Based Learning Scenarios. In *Innovative Instructional Design Methods and Tools for Improved Teaching* (pp. 215–226). IGI Global.

Chapter 6
Innovations of AI in Primary School's Learning:
A Systematic Review

Arvin Cheong Kee Sin
https://orcid.org/0009-0008-3426-2339
Universiti Sains Malaysia, Malaysia

Nurul Maziah Mohd Barkhaya
https://orcid.org/0009-0002-2192-0706
Universiti Sains Malaysia, Malaysia

ABSTRACT

Inclusive education offers equitable learning opportunities for all students, regardless of their backgrounds or abilities. This paper explores the potential of artificial intelligence can be leveraged to overcome barriers in public school, focusing on primary level to ensuring inventive, invaluable and inclusive learning experiences. Through a systematic review, the study investigates how AI can foster accessible and inclusive learning in primary level. A structured systematic literature review approach was employed to analyze 20 studies from 2020 to 2024. Through detailed case studies and theoretical discussions, it examines various innovations of AI integral to inclusive education, such as AI-driven personalized learning, virtual classrooms, and technology-enhanced teacher training. These innovations contribute significantly to making education more accessible. By aligning with the goals of Sustainable Development Goal 4, this paper underscores the transformative potential of AI in fostering the accessibility of instructional tools and creating inclusive educational environments.

DOI: 10.4018/979-8-3693-7255-5.ch006

INTRODUCTION

Inclusive education is a cornerstone of equitable learning opportunities, aiming to ensure that all students, irrespective of their backgrounds or abilities, have access to quality education (Unesco, 2020; Ainscow, 2020). In recent years, the concept of inclusive education has evolved to address the diverse needs of students by integrating advanced technologies into the educational landscape. One such technological advancement is AI, which holds significant promise in transforming traditional educational paradigms (Luckin & Holmes, 2016; Holmes et al., 2019). AI's capabilities extend beyond simple automation and encompass personalized learning experiences, adaptive assessments, and enhanced teacher support systems. Innovations in AI, such as intelligent tutoring systems, real-time feedback mechanisms, and AI-driven educational analytics, further enhance these capabilities, offering dynamic and responsive solutions to educational challenges. These advancements present an opportunity to overcome the persistent barriers that impede inclusive education, particularly at the primary level (Zhai et al., 2021).

The potential of AI in fostering inclusivity in education has garnered considerable attention in recent academic discourse (Chen et al., 2020). Key areas of focus include AI-driven personalized learning, which tailors educational content to meet individual student needs; technology-enhanced teacher training, which equips educators with the skills necessary to effectively integrate AI tools into their teaching practices (Holmes et al., 2019; Miao et al., 2021). Additionally, innovative AI applications such as adaptive learning systems and intelligent tutoring have emerged, offering dynamic and responsive educational environments that further enhance inclusivity. These AI applications not only facilitate more inclusive learning experiences but also align with the broader goals of Sustainable Development Goal 4, which aims to ensure inclusive and equitable quality education for all (Seldon et al., 2020).

By systematically analyzing the existing literature, this paper seeks to provide a comprehensive understanding of the potential of AI in promoting inclusive education. The findings underscore the transformative role of AI in making education more accessible and equitable (Zawacki-Richter et al., 2019). Through detailed case studies and theoretical discussions, the paper illustrates how AI innovations, such as adaptive learning platforms, intelligent tutoring systems, and real-time educational analytics, can be harnessed to create an educational environment that accommodates the diverse needs of primary school students. This aligns with the global commitment to SDG4, emphasizing the importance of inclusive and equitable education in achieving sustainable development. As the educational landscape continues to evolve, the integration of these AI advancements presents a promising avenue for overcoming barriers and ensuring that all students have the opportunity to succeed (Zhai et al., 2021; Miao et al., 2021).

Background

Inclusive education aims to integrate all students, regardless of individual differences, into mainstream classrooms. This approach promotes the principle that every child, including those with disabilities or special needs, should have access to quality education alongside their peers (Team & Hunt, 2020). Historically, students with special needs were often segregated into separate institutions, but a shift towards inclusive practices has been driven by frameworks like the UNESCO Salamanca Statement and the UN Convention on the Rights of Persons with Disabilities (Unesco, 2020). Core principles of inclusive education include accessibility, equity, participation, and individualized support, which collectively aim to ensure that all students can thrive in an inclusive setting (Gottschalk & Weise, 2023). Despite challenges such as the need for specialized resources and teacher training, inclusive education fosters a more equitable learning environment, benefiting both students with and without disabilities (Smith, 2010).

Artificial Intelligence (AI) encompasses the development of systems capable of performing tasks that typically require human intelligence, such as learning, reasoning, and problem-solving. While the foundational concepts of AI can be traced back to early philosophical ideas about automata and cognition, modern AI research began in the 1950s with pioneering work by figures like Alan Turing. Turing (2009) proposed the idea of machines capable of simulating human intelligence and introduced the Turing Test as a measure of a machine's ability to exhibit intelligent behavior. The resurgence of AI in recent years has been fueled by advances in machine learning, particularly deep learning. These techniques utilize neural networks to analyze large datasets and improve their performance over time. Innovations such as neural architecture search, reinforcement learning, and generative adversarial networks (GANs) have further expanded AI's capabilities. Breakthroughs such as AlphaGo's victory over a world champion in the game of Go (Silver et al., 2016) and the development of sophisticated language models like GPT-4 have demonstrated AI's potential across various domains. AI is now integral to applications in healthcare, finance, automotive, and education, driving innovation and enhancing quality of life (Marr, 2020). The following diagram illustrates expectations of AI in various fields (Figure 1).

Figure 1. Subdisciplines differences between expectations and fields of AI

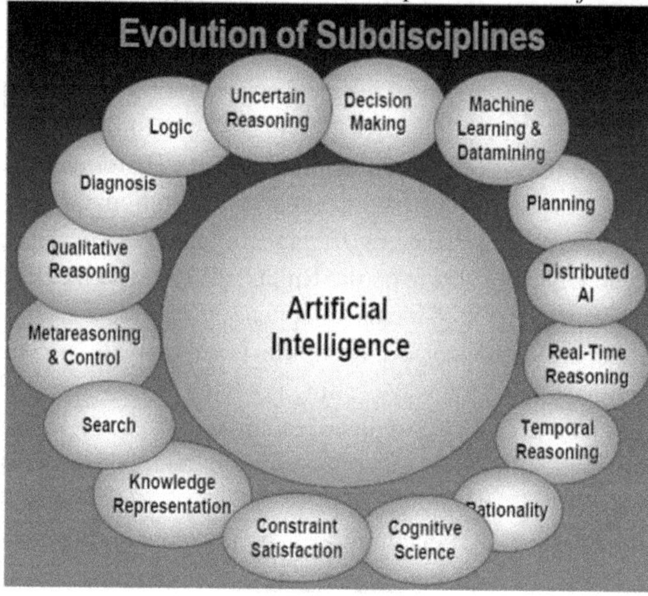

According to Shukla Shubhendu & Vijay (2013), the expectations of AI regarding the figure 1 could be derived into: (1) AI in daily life, (2) AI in science, (3) AI and Infrastructure, (4) AI and consumers. The following will further explain the expectations in different fields.

The integration of AI into our daily lives is transforming various aspects, from communication and time management to health and safety. In the realm of education, AI enhances learning experiences by supporting inclusive education, ensuring that all individuals, regardless of their abilities, learning styles, or backgrounds, have access to personalized learning opportunities. AI helps students achieve their goals by providing relevant information and resources tailored to their specific needs, fostering a more inclusive and supportive learning environment. Additionally, AI plays a role in recreational activities, such as games and hobbies, and influences consumer behavior through personalized marketing and product recommendations. Its contributions to opportunistic planning and cognitive augmentation make daily tasks more efficient and intelligent. AI's ability to perform real-time reasoning, search, and machine learning enables it to assist with decision-making and planning (Tien, 2017), ensuring timely and accurate support for everyday activities, including those that promote inclusive learning and equitable access to education. Xia et al. (2022) applied the Self-Determination Theory (SDT) design approach in AI education to enhance student engagement by inclusively addressing their needs in K-12 education. Similarly, a study by Garg & Sharma (2020) in the context of special education examined the impact of AI on education for students with special needs, highlighting its role in promoting inclusive education.

In the realm of science, AI is revolutionizing research through automated discovery and the design of experiments. It aids in triaging resources and interpreting complex data sets, allowing scientists to probe deeper into intricate phenomena. AI's applications span various scientific disciplines, including biology, chemistry, medicine, and climate science, leading to more profound and rapid advancements. The use of AI in science involves uncertain reasoning and rationality, facilitating complex decision-making and the exploration of new hypotheses (Marwala, 2015; Cohen, 1984). Machine learning and data mining uncover patterns within vast datasets, while knowledge representation and qualitative reasoning enhance the understanding of intricate scientific concepts. Holzinger et al. (2023) indicate that biotechnology companies are now utilizing AI and machine learning solutions to create autonomous robots capable of performing essential agricultural tasks like crop harvesting at speeds far surpassing those of human workers.

AI's impact on infrastructure is profound, affecting transportation systems, commerce decision-making, agriculture, and engineering and architecture. It plays a crucial role in power management and conservation, optimizing resources for better sustainability. The integration of AI in these sectors leads to smarter, more efficient, and resilient infrastructure. Distributed AI and real-time reasoning contribute to the management of large-scale systems, ensuring seamless and adaptive operations (Filip, 2008; Tien, 2017). Constraint satisfaction and planning algorithms optimize resource allocation and infrastructure development, while cognitive science and diagnosis logic improve maintenance and fault detection (Alvarez, 2020). In the United States, the incorporation of Artificial Intelligence (AI) into cybersecurity has become a key approach for strengthening the nation's defenses against cyber threats and safeguarding its critical infrastructure (de Azambuja et al., 2023; Abbas et al., 2019).

The evolving relationship between consumers and AI is characterized by the enhancement of computation through sensing, reasoning, and learning. Personalized smart applications cater to individual needs, while AI-driven products and services offer new levels of convenience and functionality. However, this evolution brings challenges and opportunities, particularly concerning data privacy and security, which need careful consideration and management. The ability of AI to perform temporal reasoning, search, and metareasoning & control allows for the development of intelligent consumer applications that adapt to changing needs and preferences (Jain et al., 2024). Decision-making supported by machine learning and cognitive science ensures that AI systems remain rational and user-centric (Wang et al., 2019). Baldauf et al. (2020) developed AI-driven self-diagnosis apps designed to scan consumer-facing medical data, using AI to detect potential issues such as malignant skin changes from photos or respiratory diseases from cough sounds.

Artificial Intelligence (AI) is increasingly shaping the landscape of primary education, offering innovative tools and methods to enhance teaching and learning experiences while promoting inclusivity. One significant application of AI in primary education is personalized learning (van der Vorst & Jelicic, 2019). AI-powered platforms, including adaptive learning systems and AI-driven content recommendation engines, analyze students' learning patterns, strengths, and areas needing improvement to tailor educational content and activities to individual needs. Ng et al. (2022) implemented AI literacy in K-16 classrooms to enhance students' future employability and learning potential while also equipping primary school students with the skills to solve real-world problems. These technologies not only cater to different learning styles but also ensure that students with diverse abilities, including those with special educational needs, receive the appropriate level of challenge and support. By continuously adjusting to each student's unique needs, AI helps create an inclusive learning environment that fosters effective learning outcomes for all students (Holmes et al., 2019).

AI is also used to support formative assessment through tools that provide real-time feedback to students and teachers. For example, AI-driven assessment tools with natural language processing capabilities can evaluate student responses and offer instant, nuanced feedback, helping teachers identify learning gaps and adjust instruction accordingly (Baker et al., 2016). Additionally, advancements like automated essay scoring and predictive analytics can enhance the learning process by providing deeper insights into student performance and learning trends. In addition to supporting personalized learning and assessment, AI can assist in automating administrative tasks, such as grading and scheduling, allowing teachers to focus more on instructional activities and student engagement. According to Woolf (2010), AI tools can also help with classroom management by analyzing student behavior patterns and suggesting strategies to improve classroom dynamics, leveraging innovations such as behavioral prediction models and sentiment analysis.

Methodology

Studies conducted between 2020 and 2024 indicate a growing interest in leveraging AI to create more inclusive and accessible learning environments. This paper conducts a systematic review of 20 studies, highlighting the diverse ways AI can be utilized to enhance primary education. Does AI foster inclusive learning in primary education? To answer this research question, we analyzed the available studies regarding this issue based on systematic review of the research. For the systematic review, we defined the search string and inclusion criteria as well as to decide, where to identically search for relevant studies (Newman & Gough, 2020). To search for relevant studies, databases that we used are SCOPUS and Web of Science (WoS). Through SCOPUS and WoS databases, there were many related references found with accurate criteria.

Data regarding to the string search was retrieved in Julai 2024. We specific the search topic throughout the recent five years which is from 2020-2024. We also included journal articles, book chapter and conference paper that were written in English language. The references also published or reporting empirical results as primary studies including both experimental and control group. Hence, we used the most common words suggested by *Thesaurus.com* and *Dictionary.com* in search string as shown in Table 1.

Table 1. Topic, search terms of SCOPUS and WoS

Topic	Search Terms
Artificial Intelligent	"AI" OR "artificial intelligence" OR "robotics" OR "expert system" OR "machine learning"
AND	
Primary School	"primary school" OR "primary level" OR "primary education" OR "k-12" OR "elementary school" OR "elementary level" OR "elementary education" OR "elementary grade" OR "lower grades"

After that data retrieved, we analyze the databases by following the steps and guidelines of the PRISMA statement by Moher et al. (2009). Figure 2 displayed the flow diagram of systematic literature review process throughout the whole screening process assist with *rayyan.ai* software to determine whether the inclusion and exclusion meet our research criteria.

Figure 2. Flow diagram of systematic literature review

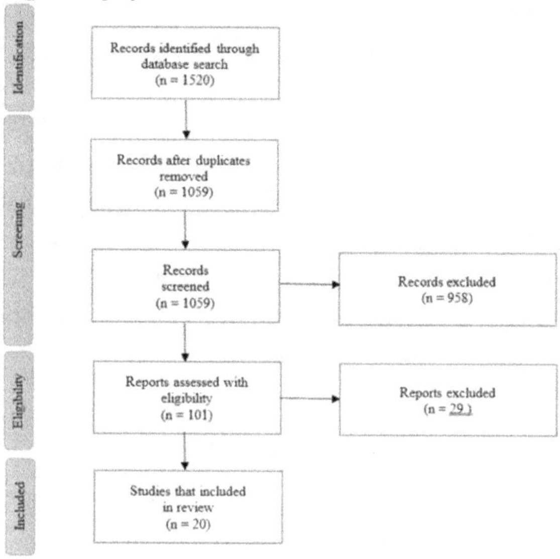

Initially there are 1520 documents were report in the 2 databases (781 in SCOPUS and 739 in WoS). Of these documents, 922 were duplicates and 461 was removed automatically by *rayyan.ai*. Hence, 1059 documents were screened after removed the duplicated documents. Of these records, 23 been excluded because it was secondary studies or wrong population. The main inclusion criteria were the AI and Primary School. The main screening included the reference to the educational context, as well as the studies involved in an empirical study, proposal, a systematic review, or theoretical contributions. In total, 985 documents did not meet the primary criteria and were exclude from the study. As a result, 101 documents were examined for eligibility. Of these documents, 2 were reports to excluded as several reasons such as not use AI as instructional tools, involved other groups than K-12, and no empirical research. Thus, 20 studies were chosen to analyzed in the review.

Results

In this section, we outline the 20 results from analyzed studies with AI and primary schools. The studies then classify into four categories: author, topic, type of AI, and objectives. A systematic literature review acquired from the analysis are presented in Table 2 below.

Table 2. Systematic literature review of AI in primary schools

Author	Topic	Type of AI	Objectives
Rumbelow & Coles (2024)	The Promise of AI Object-Recognition in Learning Mathematics: An Explorative Study of 6-Year-Old Children's Interactions with Cuisenaire Rods and the Blockplay. ai App	AI Object-Recognition Application (Blockplay.ai)	To identify the range of possible uses of object-recognition technology in the learning of mathematics
Kim et al. (2024)	Development and application of elementary school AI education program using the International Baccalaureate (IB) Primary Years Programme (PYP) approach	AI Education Program (Entry's AI blocks)	To enhance elementary school students' foundational understanding of artificial intelligence (AI) and to foster their Computational thinking
Butler & Starkey (2024)	OK Google, help me learn: an exploratory study of voice-activated artificial intelligence in the classroom	Voice-activated Intelligent Agent (Google Home)	To explore how two groups of New Zealand children aged 7–12 engaged with Google Home devices in their classroom
Tai & Chen (2024)	Improving elementary EFL speaking skills with generative AI chatbots: Exploring individual and paired interactions	GAI Chatbot (CoolE Bot)	To investigate the impact of GAI chatbots on elementary school English as a foreign language (EFL) learners' speaking skills
Kwon et al. (2023)	The application of chatbot as an L2 writing practice tool	Chatbot (Google's Diaogflow)	To investigate the effect of chatbot-based writing practices on second language learners' writing performance and user perceptions
Konijn et al. (2022)	Social robots for (second) language learning in (migrant) primary school children	Social Robot (SoftBank NAO robot)	To test the potential advantage of a social robot over a tablet in second language learning on performance, engagement, and enjoyment
Abdelghani et al. (2023)	GPT-3-driven pedagogical agents to train children's curious question-asking skills	Chatbot (GPT-3)	To investigate the efficiency of using a large language model (LLM) for automating the production within a curious question-asking (QA) training
Bulut & Yildirim-Erbasli (2022)	Automatic story and item generation for reading comprehension assessments with transformers	Story Generation Model (GPT-2 Model & T5 Model)	To create new, authentic texts and related items that can improve and assess elementary students' reading comprehension skills
Xu & Sun (2023)	Predicting academic performance associated with physical fitness of primary school students using machine learning methods	Machine Learning Models (Python 3.7.4)	To improve the physical fitness and academic performance of primary school students via physical exercise

continued on following page

Table 2. Continued

Author	Topic	Type of AI	Objectives
Hughes et al. (2022)	RAISE: Robotics & AI to improve STEM and social skills for elementary school students	Virtual Learning Environment (AIC & Wizard of Oz)	To assist children with autism (ASD) in learning science, technology, engineering, and mathematics (STEM) skills along with improving social-emotional and communication skills
Khasu & Henning (2024)	Playwriting as an emergent pedagogical tool for primary school student teachers	Artificial Intelligence Vocabulary (Sesotho & isiZulu)	To explore how student teachers engaged in a playwriting process, creating drama texts for early grades primary school learners
Niclós et al. (2024)	Creativity and artificial intelligence: A study with prospective teachers	Chatbot (ChatGPT 3.5)	To develop the potential of prospective elementary school teachers related to storytelling with use of AI
Andries & Robertson (2023)	Alexa doesn't have that many feelings: Children's understanding of AI through interactions with smart speakers in their homes	Voice-based Conversational Assistants (Alexa)	To establish children's understanding of how voice-based CAs work, how they perceive their cognitive abilities, agency and other human-like qualities, their awareness and trust of privacy aspects
Al-Qawabah (2024)	The Impact of Artificial Intelligence on Students in the First Three Grades in Basic Schools in the City of Amman-Jordan from The Perspective of Their Teachers	AI-based Tools (eg: chatbot, slideai,io, sendsteps.ai etc)	To investigate the effect of AI on the first three grades of students in basic schools in the governorate of the capital Amman Jordan from teachers' perspective
Kahila et al. (2024)	Pedagogical framework for cultivating children's data agency and creative abilities in the age of AI	AI-driven Application (GenAI Teachable Machine)	To develop learning environments, educational technology, and pedagogical models for Machine Learning education, empirically tested in 12 Finnish classrooms
Yang et al. (2024)	Enhancing teachers' self-efficacy beliefs in AI-based technology integration into English speaking teaching through a professional development program	AI-based Instructional (Not specific)	To explore how 50 in-service primary school teachers enhanced self-efficacy beliefs in artificial intelligence (AI)-based technology integration into English speaking teaching through a professional development program
Feng & Wang (2023)	A comparative study on the development of Chinese and English abilities of Chinese primary school students through two bilingual reading modes: human-AI robot interaction and paper books	AI Educational Robot (Not specific)	To compare the effectiveness of human-computer interaction AI-assisted reading, using "AI educational robot + quality reading materials + bilingual simultaneous acquisition," with the reading mode of bilingual paper books in primary level

continued on following page

Table 2. Continued

Author	Topic	Type of AI	Objectives
Gkiolnta et al. (2023)	Robot programming for a child with autism spectrum disorder: a pilot study	Ready-to-use Robot (Codey Rocky)	To examine whether the use of educational robotics in the school context could improve the social and communication skills of a primary school child with ASD, and lead to reduction in her challenging behaviors
Qiu & Ishak (2022)	Effectiveness of Artificial Intelligence (AI) in Improving Pupils' Deep Learning in Primary School Mathematics Teaching in Fujian Province	Application of AI with VR (Not specific)	To evaluate individual students' learning challenges and give individualized support to optimize their success in mathematics classes
Kamarudin et al. (2022)	A Study of The Effects of Short-Term AI Coding Course with Gamification Elements on Students' Cognitive Mental Health	AI Coding (Not specific)	To study the effect of short-term AI coding course with gamification elements on primary school students' cognitive skill and mental health

The results indicate that innovations of AI tools primarily support elementary-level students in language, science, and mathematics learning. According to the table, 9 out of 20 studies highlight AI tools aiding primary school students in language learning, while 4 out of 20 focus on AI tools helping with science and mathematics learning. Additionally, two studies demonstrate that AI assists special needs students. For example, Hughes et al. (2022) show that AI helps children with autism (ASD) in learning STEM skills, and Gkiolnta et al. (2023) use AI to improve the social and communication skills of a primary school child with ASD.

Various results also indicate that AI enhances both cognitive and social development in students. For instance, Konijn et al. (2022) use AI to improve students' performance, engagement, and enjoyment in second language learning; Xu and Sun (2023) use AI to boost students' physical fitness and academic performance; Andries and Robertson (2023) employ voice-based conversational assistants such as Alexa to enhance students' cognitive abilities and trust in privacy aspects; and Kamarudin et al. (2022) use AI coding to improve students' cognitive skills and mental health.

A few studies also focus on technology enhancing teacher training. These include "The Impact of Artificial Intelligence on Students in the First Three Grades in Basic Schools in the City of Amman-Jordan from The Perspective of Their Teachers" by Al-Qawabah (2024), "Pedagogical Framework for Cultivating Children's Data Agency and Creative Abilities in the Age of AI" by Kahila et al. (2024), and "Enhancing Teachers' Self-Efficacy Beliefs in AI-Based Technology Integration into English Speaking Teaching Through a Professional Development Program" by Yang et al. (2024).

Discussion

The systematic review of recent studies on AI in primary education reveals a multifaceted potential for enhancing inclusivity and quality in learning experiences. Several studies highlight the role of AI in fostering personalized learning environments through innovations of technologies. For example, Rumbelow & Coles (2024) explore AI object-recognition in mathematics, showcasing how it tailors educational content based on young learners' interactions and contextual understanding, enhancing engagement and comprehension. Tai & Chen (2024) and Kwon et al. (2023) find significant improvements in language skills among elementary learners using AI chatbots with natural language processing capabilities, suggesting that AI can accommodate diverse learning paces and styles, promoting inclusivity.

Early exposure to AI concepts also proves beneficial. Kim et al. (2024) integrate AI education into elementary curricula using the International Baccalaureate Primary Years Programme (IB PYP), employing interactive AI tools such as coding robots and educational simulations to build foundational understanding and foster computational thinking in young students. AI's role in enhancing teacher training is evident in Yang et al. (2024), where targeted professional development using AI-driven analytics improves teachers' self-efficacy in using AI tools, such as adaptive teaching platforms and digital lesson planners, subsequently enhancing instructional quality and student outcomes. AI-driven tools also provide real-time insights into student performance and learning patterns, enabling teachers to tailor their instruction to meet individual needs more effectively. Social and emotional learning (SEL) supported by AI is another support tool for teachers in teaching ASD students. Hughes et al. (2022) and Gkiolnta et al. (2023) utilize robotics and AI-driven applications with emotional recognition and adaptive interaction capabilities to assist children with autism spectrum disorder (ASD) in developing social and communication skills, demonstrating AI's potential to provide personalized support in classroom.

However, the studies also highlight challenges and ethical considerations. Andries & Robertson (2023) raise questions about privacy, data security, and the ethical use of AI, emphasizing the need for transparent, secure, and responsible AI applications in education. One major issue is bias and fairness: AI systems can perpetuate existing biases if trained on biased data, leading to unfair treatment of students. According to Rodrigues (2022), unfairness, bias and discrimination repeatedly pop up as issues and have been identified as a major challenge related to the use of algorithms and automated decision-making systems in AI. Privacy and data security are also significant concerns, as the collection and analysis of student data must be handled with strict safeguards to prevent unauthorized access and misuse, because AI technologies usually owned and controlled by private entities according to Murdoch (2021). Overall, while AI holds great promise for enhancing primary education through innovations such as adaptive learning systems and intelligent tutoring, careful consideration of its ethical implications and ongoing support for teachers and students are crucial for its successful integration.

The adoption of AI in education faces notable challenges, particularly regarding infrastructure, teacher training and socioeconomic. One major barrier is inadequate infrastructure: many regions, especially rural or under-resourced areas, struggle with poor internet connectivity and insufficient hardware. AI tools often require reliable, high-speed internet and modern devices, which are not always available. This lack of infrastructure obstructs the effective deployment and use of AI technologies in classrooms. In India, there are eighteen critical infrastructure barriers need to be removed for the effective adoption of AI (Kumar et al., 2021). Simultaneously, there is a significant need for comprehensive teacher training to ensure educators are equipped with both the technical skills to use AI tools and the pedagogical strategies to integrate them effectively into their teaching. Without proper training, teachers may struggle to utilize AI to its full potential, thereby limiting the overall impact on student learning. Wang and Cheng (2021) identify several factors that inhibit AI adoption, including a lack of access to resources, insufficient time, inadequate support, unresponsive policies, and teachers' attitudes, confidence, and beliefs, all of which contribute to the challenges faced in implementing AI effectively. In addition, socioeconomic factors are a significant barrier to AI adoption in education. Schools in economically disadvantaged areas often lack the necessary resources, such as modern hardware, reliable internet access, and funding for AI tools. There are four socioeconomic elements such as budget, concerns and anxiety, lack of data understanding and missing systematics been identified by Renz & Hilbig (2020) that inhibiting AI adoption. Addressing these barriers is crucial for the successful implementation and sustainability of AI in education.

CONCLUSION

In conclusion, the integration of artificial intelligence in primary education holds transformative potential for fostering inclusive and high-quality learning experiences. The reviewed studies highlight AI's capability to personalize learning through innovations such as adaptive learning platforms and intelligent tutoring systems, enhance foundational understanding of AI and computational thinking with interactive AI tools, and support social and emotional development through robotics and AI-driven applications designed for students with special needs. Additionally, AI shows promise in improving teacher training and professional development through tools like AI-driven analytics and digital lesson planners. However, the successful implementation of AI in education requires addressing ethical considerations, ensuring data privacy, and providing ongoing support for educators and learners.

Future research should focus on exploring the long-term impacts of AI on diverse educational settings and developing strategies to overcome barriers to AI adoption. Practical recommendations include creating professional development programs tailored to AI tools, ensuring equitable access to technology, and continuously evaluating the effectiveness of AI applications in enhancing educational outcomes. By aligning with the goals of Sustainable Development Goal 4 (SDG4), AI can play a crucial role in creating accessible and inclusive educational environments, ultimately contributing to more equitable learning opportunities for all students.

References

Abbas, N. N., Ahmed, T., Shah, S. H. U., Omar, M., & Park, H. W. (2019). Investigating the applications of artificial intelligence in cyber security. *Scientometrics*, 121(2), 1189–1211. DOI: 10.1007/s11192-019-03222-9

Abdelghani, R., Wang, Y. H., Yuan, X., Wang, T., Lucas, P., Sauzéon, H., & Oudeyer, P. Y. (2023). GPT-3-driven pedagogical agents to train children's curious question-asking skills. *International Journal of Artificial Intelligence in Education*, •••, 1–36.

Ainscow, M. (2020). Promoting inclusion and equity in education: lessons from international experiences. *Nordic journal of studies in educational policy, 6*(1), 7-16.

Al-Qawabah, R. H. (2024). The Impact of Artificial Intelligence on Students in the First Three Grades in Basic Schools in the City of Amman-Jordan from The Perspective of Their Teachers. *International Journal (Toronto, Ont.)*, 5(2), 346–353.

Alvarez, G. P. (2020). Real-time fault detection and diagnosis using intelligent monitoring and supervision systems. In *Fault detection, diagnosis and prognosis*. IntechOpen. DOI: 10.5772/intechopen.90158

Andries, V., & Robertson, J. (2023). Alexa doesn't have that many feelings: Children's understanding of AI through interactions with smart speakers in their homes. *Computers and Education: Artificial Intelligence*, 5, 100176. DOI: 10.1016/j.caeai.2023.100176

Baker, R. S., Martin, T., & Rossi, L. M. (2016). Educational data mining and learning analytics. *The Wiley handbook of cognition and assessment: Frameworks, methodologies, and applications*, 379-396.

Baldauf, M., Fröehlich, P., & Endl, R. (2020). Trust me, I'ma doctor–user perceptions of AI-driven apps for mobile health diagnosis. In *Proceedings of the 19th International Conference on Mobile and Ubiquitous Multimedia* (pp. 167-178). DOI: 10.1145/3428361.3428362

Bond, & K. Buntins (Eds.), *Systematic reviews in educational research: Methodology, perspectives and application* (pp. 3–22). Springer Fachmedien Wiesbaden.

Bulut, O., & Yildirim-Erbasli, S. N. (2022). Automatic story and item generation for reading comprehension assessments with transformers. *International Journal of Assessment Tools in Education*, 9(Special Issue), 72–87. DOI: 10.21449/ijate.1124382

Butler, L., & Starkey, L. (2024). OK Google, help me learn: An exploratory study of voice-activated artificial intelligence in the classroom. *Technology, Pedagogy and Education*, 33(2), 135–148. DOI: 10.1080/1475939X.2024.2311779

Chen, L., Chen, P., & Lin, Z. (2020). Artificial intelligence in education: A review. *IEEE Access : Practical Innovations, Open Solutions*, 8, 75264–75278. DOI: 10.1109/ACCESS.2020.2988510

Cohen, P. R. (1984). *Heuristic reasoning about uncertainty: an artificial intelligence approach*. Stanford University.

de Azambuja, A. J. G., Plesker, C., Schützer, K., Anderl, R., Schleich, B., & Almeida, V. R. (2023). Artificial Intelligence Based Cyber Security in the Context of Industry 4.0—A Survey. *Electronics (Basel)*, 12(8), 1920. DOI: 10.3390/electronics12081920

Feng, Y., & Wang, X. (2023). A comparative study on the development of Chinese and English abilities of Chinese primary school students through two bilingual reading modes: human-AI robot interaction and paper books. *Frontiers in Psychology*, 14, 1200675. DOI: 10.3389/fpsyg.2023.1200675 PMID: 37860299

Filip, F. G. (2008). Decision support and control for large-scale complex systems. *Annual Reviews in Control*, 32(1), 61–70. DOI: 10.1016/j.arcontrol.2008.03.002

Garg, S., & Sharma, S. (2020). Impact of artificial intelligence in special need education to promote inclusive pedagogy. *International Journal of Information and Education Technology (IJIET)*, 10(7), 523–527. DOI: 10.18178/ijiet.2020.10.7.1418

Gkiolnta, E., Zygopoulou, M., & Syriopoulou-Delli, C. K. (2023). Robot programming for a child with autism spectrum disorder: A pilot study. *International Journal of Developmental Disabilities*, 69(3), 424–431. DOI: 10.1080/20473869.2023.2194568 PMID: 37213592

Gottschalk, F., & Weise, C. (2023). Digital equity and inclusion in education: An overview of practice and policy in OECD countries.

Holmes, W., Bialik, M., & Fadel, C. (2019). Artificial intelligence in education: Promises and implications for teaching and learning. *Center for Curriculum Redesign*. Available at: https://curriculumredesign.org/wp-content/uploads/AI-in-Education-Report.pdf

Holzinger, A., Keiblinger, K., Holub, P., Zatloukal, K., & Müller, H. (2023). AI for life: Trends in artificial intelligence for biotechnology. *New Biotechnology*, 74, 16–24. DOI: 10.1016/j.nbt.2023.02.001 PMID: 36754147

Hughes, C. E., Dieker, L. A., Glavey, E. M., Hines, R. A., Wilkins, I., Ingraham, K., Bukaty, C. A., Ali, K., Shah, S., Murphy, J., & Taylor, M. S. (2022). RAISE: Robotics & AI to improve STEM and social skills for elementary school students. *Frontiers in Virtual Reality*, 3, 968312. DOI: 10.3389/frvir.2022.968312

Jain, V., Wadhwani, K., & Eastman, J. K. (2024). Artificial intelligence consumer behavior: A hybrid review and research agenda. *Journal of Consumer Behaviour*, 23(2), 676–697. DOI: 10.1002/cb.2233

Kahila, J., Vartiainen, H., Tedre, M., Arkko, E., Lin, A., Pope, N., Jormanainen, I., & Valtonen, T. (2024). Pedagogical framework for cultivating children's data agency and creative abilities in the age of AI. *Informatics in Education*, 23(2), 323–360. DOI: 10.15388/infedu.2024.15

Kamarudin, N. A., Ikram, R. R. R., Azman, F. N., Ahmad, S. S. S., & Zainuddin, D. (2022). A Study of The Effects of Short-Term AI Coding Course with Gamification Elements on Students' Cognitive Mental Health. *TEM Journal, 11*(4).

Khasu, M. N., & Henning, E. (2024). Playwriting as an emergent pedagogical tool for primary school student teachers. *Reading & Writing-Journal of the Literacy Association of South Africa*, 15(1), 437. DOI: 10.4102/rw.v15i1.437

Kim, B., Go, E., Moon, W., Kim, B., & Kim, J. (2024). Development and application of elementary school AI education program using the International Baccalaureate (IB) Primary Years Programme (PYP) approach. *Journal of Curriculum and Teaching*, 13(2), 83–97. DOI: 10.5430/jct.v13n2p83

Konijn, E. A., Jansen, B., Mondaca Bustos, V., Hobbelink, V. L., & Preciado Vanegas, D. (2022). Social robots for (second) language learning in (migrant) primary school children. *International Journal of Social Robotics*, 14(3), 827–843. DOI: 10.1007/s12369-021-00824-3

Kumar, S., Raut, R. D., Queiroz, M. M., & Narkhede, B. E. (2021). Mapping the barriers of AI implementations in the public distribution system: The Indian experience. *Technology in Society*, 67, 101737. DOI: 10.1016/j.techsoc.2021.101737

Kwon, S. K., Shin, D., & Lee, Y. (2023). The application of chatbot as an L2 writing practice tool.

Luckin, R., & Holmes, W. (2016). *Intelligence unleashed: An argument for AI in education*. Pearson.

Marr, B. (2020). *Tech Trends in Practice: The 25 technologies that are driving the 4th Industrial Revolution*. John Wiley & Sons.

Marwala, T. (2015). *Causality, correlation and artificial intelligence for rational decision making*. World Scientific. DOI: 10.1142/9356

Miao, F., Holmes, W., Huang, R., & Zhang, H. (2021). *AI and education: Guidance for policymakers*. UNESCO.

Moher, D., Liberati, A., Tetzlaff, J., & Altman, D. G.Prisma Group. (2010). Preferred reporting items for systematic reviews and meta-analyses: The PRISMA statement. *International Journal of Surgery*, 8(5), 336–341. DOI: 10.1016/j.ijsu.2010.02.007 PMID: 20171303

Murdoch, B. (2021). Privacy and artificial intelligence: Challenges for protecting health information in a new era. *BMC Medical Ethics*, 22(1), 1–5. DOI: 10.1186/s12910-021-00687-3 PMID: 34525993

Newman, M., & Gough, D. (2020). Systematic reviews in educational research: methodology, perspectives and application. In O. Zawacki-Richter, M. Kerres, S. Bedenlier, M. DOI: 10.1007/978-3-658-27602-7_1

Ng, D. T. K., Leung, J. K. L., Su, M. J., Yim, I. H. Y., Qiao, M. S., & Chu, S. K. W. (2022). AI literacy education in primary schools. In *AI Literacy in K-16 Classrooms* (pp. 75–86). Springer International Publishing. DOI: 10.1007/978-3-031-18880-0_6

Niclós, I. P., Sanz, Y. E., Gómez, P. O., & Ezpeleta, A. M. (2024). Creativity and artificial intelligence: A study with prospective teachers. *Digital Education Review*, (45), 91–97. DOI: 10.1344/der.2024.45.91-97

Qiu, Y., Pan, J., & Ishak, N. A. (2022). [Retracted] Effectiveness of Artificial Intelligence (AI) in Improving Pupils' Deep Learning in Primary School Mathematics Teaching in Fujian Province. *Computational Intelligence and Neuroscience*, 2022(1), 1362996. PMID: 36193186

Renz, A., & Hilbig, R. (2020). Prerequisites for artificial intelligence in further education: Identification of drivers, barriers, and business models of educational technology companies. *International Journal of Educational Technology in Higher Education*, 17(1), 14. DOI: 10.1186/s41239-020-00193-3

Rodrigues, R. (2020). Legal and human rights issues of AI: Gaps, challenges and vulnerabilities. *Journal of Responsible Technology*, 4, 100005. DOI: 10.1016/j.jrt.2020.100005

Rumbelow, M., & Coles, A. (2024). The Promise of AI Object-Recognition in Learning Mathematics: An Explorative Study of 6-Year-Old Children's Interactions with Cuisenaire Rods and the Blockplay. ai App. *Education Sciences*, 14(6), 591. DOI: 10.3390/educsci14060591

Seldon, A., Abidoye, O., & Metcalf, T. (2020). *The Fourth Education Revolution Reconsidered: Will Artificial Intelligence Enrich Or Diminish Humanity?* Legend Press Ltd.

Shukla Shubhendu, S., & Vijay, J. (2013). Applicability of artificial intelligence in different fields of life. *International Journal of Scientific and Engineering Research*, 1(1), 28–35.

Silver, D., Huang, A., Maddison, C. J., Guez, A., Sifre, L., Van Den Driessche, G., ... & Hassabis, D. (2016). Mastering the game of Go with deep neural networks and tree search. *nature, 529*(7587), 484-489.

Smith, D. D. (2010). *Introduction to special education: Making a difference*. No Title.

Tai, T. Y., & Chen, H. H. J. (2024). Improving elementary EFL speaking skills with generative AI chatbots: Exploring individual and paired interactions. *Computers & Education*, 220, 105112. DOI: 10.1016/j.compedu.2024.105112

Team, G., & Hunt, P. (2020). *Inclusive education: children with disabilities*. UNESCO: United Nations Educational, Scientific and Cultural Organisation.

Tien, J. M. (2017). Internet of things, real-time decision making, and artificial intelligence. *Annals of Data Science*, 4(2), 149–178. DOI: 10.1007/s40745-017-0112-5

Turing, A. M. (2009). *Computing machinery and intelligence*. Springer Netherlands. DOI: 10.1007/978-1-4020-6710-5_3

Unesco. (2020). Inclusion and education: All means all. *Global Education Monitoring Report.*

Unesco. (2020). Towards inclusion in education: Status, trends and challenges. The UNESCO Salamanca Statement 25 years on.

van der Vorst, T., & Jelicic, N. (2019). Artificial Intelligence in Education: Can AI bring the full potential of personalized learning to education?.

Wang, D., Yang, Q., Abdul, A., & Lim, B. Y. (2019). Designing theory-driven user-centric explainable AI. In *Proceedings of the 2019 CHI conference on human factors in computing systems* (pp. 1-15).

Wang, T., & Cheng, E. C. K. (2021). An investigation of barriers to Hong Kong K-12 schools incorporating Artificial Intelligence in education. *Computers and Education: Artificial Intelligence*, 2, 100031. DOI: 10.1016/j.caeai.2021.100031

Woolf, B. P. (2010). *Building intelligent interactive tutors: Student-centered strategies for revolutionizing e-learning*. Morgan Kaufmann.

Xia, Q., Chiu, T. K., Lee, M., Sanusi, I. T., Dai, Y., & Chai, C. S. (2022). A self-determination theory (SDT) design approach for inclusive and diverse artificial intelligence (AI) education. *Computers & Education*, 189, 104582. DOI: 10.1016/j.compedu.2022.104582

Xu, K., & Sun, Z. (2023). Predicting academic performance associated with physical fitness of primary school students using machine learning methods. *Complementary Therapies in Clinical Practice*, 51, 101736. DOI: 10.1016/j.ctcp.2023.101736 PMID: 36821949

Yang, Y. F., Tseng, C. C., & Lai, S. C. (2024). Enhancing teachers' self-efficacy beliefs in AI-based technology integration into English speaking teaching through a professional development program. *Teaching and Teacher Education*, 144, 104582. DOI: 10.1016/j.tate.2024.104582

Zawacki-Richter, O., Marín, V. I., Bond, M., & Gouverneur, F. (2019). Systematic review of research on artificial intelligence applications in higher education–where are the educators? *International Journal of Educational Technology in Higher Education*, 16(1), 1–27. DOI: 10.1186/s41239-019-0171-0

Zhai, X., Chu, X., Chai, C. S., Jong, M. S. Y., Istenic, A., Spector, M., Liu, J.-B., Yuan, J., & Li, Y. (2021). Review of Artificial Intelligence (AI) in Education from 2010 to 2020. *Complexity*, 2021(1), 8812542. Advance online publication. DOI: 10.1155/2021/8812542

Zhai, X., Chu, X., Chai, C. S., Jong, M. S. Y., Istenic, A., Spector, M., ... & Li, Y. (2021). A

Chapter 7
Exploring the World of Coding in Artificial Intelligence:
A Guide for Primary School Students

Purushothman Munusamy
https://orcid.org/0009-0007-0323-2842
Universiti Sains Malaysia, Malaysia

Mageswaran Sanmugam
https://orcid.org/0000-0003-3313-4462
Universiti Sains Malaysia, Malaysia

Bosede Iyiade Edwards
https://orcid.org/0000-0002-6922-311X
Universiti Sains Malaysia, Malaysia

ABSTRACT

This paper introduces artificial intelligence and coding basics to young learners. AI is a scientific field enabling machines to do tasks needing human intelligence. It's widely used in modern life, from virtual assistants to smart devices. Coding is key to how AI works. The paper also explains coding basics to help understanding. Students can create basic AI applications using platforms like Scratch and Blockly. Real-world examples show AI's potential and inspire students. Early education in AI and coding is crucial for the new generation to navigate a technology-driven world and encourage lifelong learning.

DOI: 10.4018/979-8-3693-7255-5.ch007

INTRODUCTION

According to Sheng et al. (2022), artificial intelligence is one of the latest, most radical, and high-end technologies for making machines simulate human intelligence. One definition may be that it is a field of study covering a vast domain of machine learning where computational systems learn from enormous data to come up with predictions or classifiers with precision, and this has been well elaborated by the in-depth review done by Rubinger et al., 2022. The comprehensive contribution made by Buxmann, Hess, and Thatcher, 2021 shows that AI has immense potential in all possible sectors for which forecasts are predicting massive and pervasive effect on the world economy by 2030, while in scientific research, AI is being introduced as a game changer in quantum optics that provides critical aid for conducting new experiments and developing revolutionary ideas as Krenn et al., 2021 have discussed. It is also most vitally important to understand how exactly the students learn AI principles, as it will lead to a better reshaping and enhancement of existing educational efforts at pre-college levels, say Greenwald, Leitner, and Wang in 2021. That is to say, what AI stretches beyond today has taken from simply machines emulating reality about human cognitive processes into a multidimensional phenomenon reshaping industries and powering advances in scientific knowledge by enormously outlining the effect of how educational frameworks are designed well enough to equip the coming generation with powerfully driven AI world.

Coding is core, essential, and dominantly applied to many Artificial Intelligence applications that touch almost every aspect of our lives today. This deep survey by Pita et al. details such applications of coding to go beyond functionality to the heart of software engineering itself with state-of-the-art representations of source code, like abstract syntax trees. This also includes developing fields of large-scale deep neural networks in real-time monitoring for predicting death causes, as proceeded with by Kaboreé et al. One of the pillars driving the pace of AI innovations is coding. The academic argument by Czaja and Caruso, 2022, fished out the interdependence of coding and AI, which it was brought out neatly how to integrate and result in creating spatial code representations that bolster model performance in the classification of code and detection of vulnerabilities.

Moreover, it is brilliant to provide an ecstatic future in enhancing the well-being standards of elderly individuals with AI applications designed with the aid of coding mechanisms since their fundamental health indices are followed constantly by Caucheteux et al. (2023). Required assistance in habituated activities is delivered, thereby making them more independent and hence enhancing their quality of life themselves as well as their family members. It is this complex interaction of coding and AI that furthers technological advancement, helping to rid humanity of great societal dilemmas in the fight for learning how to improve healthcare. This shows, through these examples, exactly what meaning coding takes on within the sphere of AI to make a case for its realization of its real significance interwoven in the very fabric of our everyday lives.

The exciting world of coding and AI greatly enriches young readers. This is an essential part of increasing the literacy of AI and creativity among young children. According to invoice scholars such as Ng et al., 2022, Lee et al., 2022, Vint, 2023, Kasinidou, 2023, and Su and Yang, 2023. A fair way educators will transparently help students boost their understanding of AI principles into curricula at all school levels would be an infusion of the concepts in meaning most entire with initiatives like digital story writing activities and interactive media projects while developing the—Dtd thinking capacity for ethical considerations throughout. By considering AI-based narratives found in speculative fiction and several deeper themes like labor, personhood, and the broader general impacts of AIs, young readers will be excellently positioned to pick up a nuanced view of the more complex implications of AIs within everyday life or future societies' landscapes. Very early exposure to AI literacy programs will help the children become empowered with the basics of AI and unleash their creativity in designing AI applications. It shapes positive perceptions toward AI education to set a strong foundation that equips learners with competencies and a mindset to deal confidently and inquisitively within an AI-infused world.

WHAT IS ARTIFICIAL INTELLIGENCE?

Artificial intelligence involves disseminating knowledge to intelligent robotic beings, such as how children learn a new game or story, thus empowering them to understand and absorb information. Artificial intelligence is therefore concerned with designing automated systems where thinking and decision-making occur independently due to their ability to gain knowledge from what they 'see.' Candello et al. (2021) focus on the interactive capacity between children and AI, in which the former communicates with the latter through entertaining strategies like quiz-based activities or designing robotic designs (Zhan et al., 2021). AI transcends the mere substitution of human labor, extending its reach to the generation of fresh prospects and contributing significantly to diverse domains like healthcare, where its applications include aiding in disease diagnosis and enhancing patient welfare (Ferrante et al., 2021; Su et al., 2021). School projects on initiatives in collaborative AI will let children participate actively in the evolution of this technology. Only in this way will they be able to lead in setting fundamental aspects, among others, that characterize artificial intelligence: security, privacy, and educational paradigms (Tedre et al., 2023).

Modern times have seen children, the young ones, become very familiar with various artificial intelligence applications, from voice-controlled assistants to other devices constructed with intelligence. These devices are some of the most prominent virtual and voice-activated assistant tools that exist in variety, such as Google Home, Amazon's Alexa, and Apple's Siri. They are designed to engage the user so skillfully through tones that make them sound as though they are in conversation with the device due to very intense natural language processing techniques, thus setting into the minds of most children the conception that they are 'companions'; not only do they help in acquiring much information but also stand a chance of becoming powerful allies in the improvement of reading skills as articulated by Arora and Arora in 2022. There have been instances of exposure to AI-powered conversational robots in educational research by Leichtmann et al., 2023. These include multiple scenarios in which the children involved in teaching-related activities interact with these mechanical creations to gain hands-on experience with the essential AI concepts playfully and engagingly. Moreover, it is not surprising that children get to interact with a voice-activated personal assistant like Amazon Alexa—to this end, most of them get to use all the possible features; however, it is equally essentially notable that there are risks involved with such interactions. These range from children being unnecessarily exposed to unsavory content to compromising privacy, thereby placing a significant responsibility on the watchfulness of parents in monitoring and enforcing control over the usage of such devices, something that has always been critically pointed out by Hanif et al. (2022).

Artificial intelligence gives a machine the ability to learn, rationally think, and make decisions on its own accord through proper complex algorithms and data processing capabilities. Inept use of Explainable AI, methodologies with visual explanation, interactive proof-based strategies, and methods based on maximum entropy allow AI systems to provide lucid insights about the mechanics of decision-making. Improved transparency offers great understanding to users. It builds trust in the outputs generated by AI. Thus, It is paramount in areas such as autonomous vehicles, scenarios of human-machine collaboration, and activity recognition in smart homes. Through a fusion of knowledge acquired from human experiences, adaptation to new inputs, and performance of intelligent operations without intervention from a human element, AI metabolizes much disruption in multiple fields—from health to business operations—and effectively by empowering machines to perform replication of cognitive functions reminiscent in nature of human capabilities.

THE THEORIES RELATED TO ARTIFICIAL INTELLIGENCE

Theories surrounding Artificial Intelligence (AI) and its role in generating and enhancing human insight cover various applications, including decision-making, healthcare, marketing, and cognitive science. AI has become a powerful tool for analyzing complex data and providing actionable insights that can lead to deeper understanding and innovative solutions in various domains. For instance, in medical fields like oncology and breast cancer treatment, AI systems help analyze vast amounts of literature and imaging data, enabling more informed decision-making and improved patient outcomes. Additionally, theoretical frameworks like the theory of mind perception and the Means-End Chain theory are applied to AI technology to enhance transparency and understanding of consumer behavior, particularly in digital marketing and the hospitality industry.

Explainable AI (XAI) is essential for interpreting complex systems, such as those in medical imaging and tumor microenvironments. By making AI models more transparent and understandable, XAI bridges the gap between machine-generated predictions and human expertise, which is crucial for building trust and ensuring effective decision-making. The study of cognitive processes, including the "Aha" moments of insight, further highlights the intersection of AI with cognitive science, where AI can act as a heuristic tool in problem-solving. Moreover, AI-driven platforms like Online Insight Marketplaces illustrate how insights can be monetized, turning data-driven expectations into economic opportunities. However, AI's ethical use, transparency, and interpretability remain significant challenges that must be addressed to fully harness the potential of AI in generating insights across various sectors.

THE ROLE OF CODING IN AI

Coding is an integral relationship with artificial intelligence. It constitutes part and parcel of many fields—proofing to be one of the main building blocks for new-age technology. AI strives to normalize and increase software development efficiency by facilitating and automating coding-related activities, as described by Greengard in 2023. In video games, AI has contributed significantly to developing advanced characters, adaptive difficulty levels, and emergent game-play, which Jagoda labeled the 'convergence of AI and interactive art.' One of the most significant advances in AI that gave birth to yet another emanation of new manifestations of code representation is spatial grid-based models, which have made their way to it and enabled spatial grid-based code similarity assessment to be feasible and valuable to improve software engineering tasks, such as code classification and clone detection, as stated by Kaboreé et al., in 2023.

At the forefront, moreover, in causing a change in healthcare is AI, which has to do with the automation of the procedure of generating billing codes from the operative notes, which are based on NLP models in the likes of XLNet. Bashar and colleagues demonstrated 2023 how AI could only create billing codes from the operative notes about spine surgical procedures, showing the practical application in healthcare. According to Venkatesh et al., while articulating the problems likely to be faced in the future steps of automating the clinical coding system, "AI's role, in the management of the whole system, could never become dispensable" because AI not only elevates internal efficiency and triggers creativity, but also acts as an accelerator in the accuracy metric of the respective fields. Hence, it is the paradigm shift of contemporary technological practices.

Any course to present people to the programming world must vividly emphasize such outstanding concepts as algorithms, loops, and conditionals. This must form a substantial basis for further understanding the realm of programming. In this respect, a unique methodology called scenario-based learning, or SBL, has been proposed to further empower students' computational thinking skills via Python as the programming language. This methodology attracts Generation Z students with non-coding topics, including coding history and ethics. By the example of Zitouniatis et al. 2022, one can realize the influence scenario-based learning tools, which are applied to teach computational thinking, can have on education technology.

An investigation into source code comprehension strategies that elicit self-explanation, though mainly through the Socratic method, led to hefty learning gains within introductory programming courses. Tamang et al. (2021) did a comparative study that examined free self-explanations versus Socratic-tutoring explanations in understanding source code. A comparative study indicated the strength of the most robust educational methodologies for enhancing code understanding from the learners' perspective. A scholarly article by Rodrigues et al. 2023 contributed to the analysis of crime data, hence indicating the need to use machine learning algorithms to extract behavioral patterns from spatio-temporal crime datasets. This way, it transforms prediction tasks into a classification problem to aid risk assessment.

What has been of interest, though, is the measurement of how good these models are at generating code, and it could well motivate the development of a benchmark called APPS. The mentioned benchmark, among several others relevant by not-so-direct connections, will be used to measure the models' competence in generating Python code from natural language descriptions, thus marking another step toward attaining programming abilities by machine learning models. In Hendricks et al.'s study of 2021, they used APPS to set the baseline for estimating coding challenge skills, thereby offering more insight into the modalities that the realization of AI can indeed support in educational settings.

Coding is crucial because it specifies computational systems whose performance makes it possible to realize competence at working effectively in an artificial intelligence system. Recent advances in deep learning have resulted in massive cross-domain language models that can memorize considerably diversified content—from texts and codes—to produce so-called multimodal outputs. Neuroscience-inspired methods also got into training proportions of deep neural networks—the transformers—to great success in improving their performance overall at language modeling-related tasks. Furthermore, neuroscience guides artificial intelligence and has shown through results that hierarchical predictive coding is central to language processing. Combining both shows that the brain always predicts representations at all time scales in different activities, whereby combining these two enriches brain mapping, which is noticeable through AI algorithms(Prather et al., 2023). Other coding methodologies, when integrated into the AI system, also utilize a form of predictive coding and large language models, wherein computers efficiently gain knowledge, predict the outcome, and perform complex tasks to result in near-human outputs.

FUN WITH CODING

Specifically, scratch and block coding platforms are highly recommended for primary school students. Santiago et al., 2023, explored how elementary students in Scratch 'About Me' projects—digital portfolios that depict spheres of influence cohesively—represent their personal identities and social influences. Similarly, Mangina et al., 2023, conducted a scoping review regarding the use of robotics in the early years, putting forward the possible benefits and challenges of integrating such technology into a classroom environment.

Deiner et al. (2022) contributed to the technical aspects of Scratch programming, investigating automated test generation that might support evaluating students' projects more practically and orderly. Fagerlund et al. (2021) systematically reviewed computational thinking within primary school programming activities using Scratch, thus setting up a scenario for developing these essential skills early. Scratch is a block-based programming environment that has become very popular among young learners. It enables them to make interactive projects that reflect areas of their interests and identities. Bodaker and Rosenberg-Kima, 2022, studied online pair programming dynamics for elementary students learning Scratch, which further exposed this educational approach to be collaborative and interactive. A vast potential exists for ER tools in supporting primary and preschool students' learning experiences; however, they call for more research. It has also been remarked that computational thinking is introduced with platforms like Scratch. However, transparent educational goals and assessment tools are still missing to develop CT skills in primary education effectively. In addition, online collaboration set-ups can be explored through pair programming in environments such as Scratch to improve collaboration and computational thinking among elementary school children. These platforms are engaging and educational for young students as they create opportunities to develop essential digital literacy and problem-solving skills in a fun, interactive environment.

Service, through some coding exercises, worked on ideas of AI in 2023, and educators can develop projects on the development of a chatbot using AI tools like ChatGPT, as indicated by Adiguzel et al. in 2023. In healthcare, Scerri has 2023 assessed the way that chatbots like ChatGPT can make nursing practice possible to carry out. The chatbot offers information relating to time and provides facilities for the care of patients. Moreover, Williams et al. (2022) teach a virtual pet to recognize objects enjoyably and interactively, aligned with problem-based pedagogies and game-based learning principles of K-12 education. Glazewski et al. established in 2022 that PrimaryAI is an 'Immersive problem-based learning program co-designed to teach upper elementary students AI concepts and practices in the classroom.' Much focus has been paid to integrating AI education from a young age. These projects can help students realize the basics of AI, natural language processing, and machine learning while creating and nurturing creativity and critical thinking. A focus on active learning, embedded ethics, and low friction in access can effectively engage students in learning to develop and critique AI artifacts, preparing them for a future of increased AI literacy.

Experimentation and creativity can be incorporated into coding activities to enhance students' learning experience. Research has shown that using maker spaces in STEM educational practices enhances creativity by offering hands-on learning opportunities. Sohail et al. (2023) conducted a systematic literature review on maker spaces, referring to the function of such an environment as promoting student creativity based on hands-on and collaborative activities. Guided autonomy in virtual maker spaces can also engage more spatial thinking, reduce anxiety, and increase learning creativity among students with low pre-test scores. For example, Fowler et al. (2023) investigated self-determined learning in a virtual maker space to enhance the development of spatial reasoning skills in upper primary students. Implementing flipped classrooms and peer instruction in programming courses has improved student engagement, raised pass rates, promoted knowledge gains, and, thus, increased creativity in coding. Moreover, Chevalier et al. have investigated the use of educational robotics with delayed feedback, which has been realized as one of the crucial intervention strategies in developing computational thinking skills and increasing creative problem-solving patterns in coding tasks. How these two approaches can be integrated empowers a teacher to ensure a learning environment predisposed toward experimentation, hence fostering creativity along the coding process to a considerable extent, contributing considerably toward enriching the learning outcome.

REAL-LIFE EXAMPLES

Artificial intelligence is involved in numerous fields and has real-life applications. It has been applied in image interpretation, enhancing diagnosis and subsequent treatment plans and patient outcomes, especially with methods for predicting diseases such as breast cancer and robot-assisted surgery (Sezgin,2023; Xu,2023). This makes it necessary to ensure AI ethically and equitably deploys its roles in healthcare settings. Okeibunor et al. (2023) state that transportation AI is instrumental in developing autonomous vehicles for effective routes during travel using GPS technology. In addition, Fulk, 2023 examines how AI is applied in entertainment to personalize various recommendations on e-commerce platforms, streaming services, and social media sites—making activities done through these means more engaging and enhancing user experience [5]. These examples in different sectors illustrate how AI can be used in process optimization, decision-making, and improving user satisfaction.

Artificial Intelligence (AI) has significantly changed every sector of society, for example, education, research, healthcare, and communication. Alqahtani et al. (2023) emphasize the importance of AI, natural language processing, and large language models in driving higher education and research, especially in making data analysis quicker and improving personalization in learning. Greenwald et al. (2021) contribute an understanding of how youth grasp AI concepts, underlining, in this way, the importance of early education in AI literacy. Salas-Pilco et al. (2022) conducted a systematic review regarding the use of AI and new technologies in the inclusive education of minority students, emphasizing the role that such technologies can play in creating equity and access within educational environments. On the other hand, Czaja and Ceruso present the potential of AI to support an aging population. According to them, it has great promise in assisting cognitive tasks and improving the quality of life of older people. Hohenstein et al., AI's transformative potential in subject education already expresses itself in applications as diverse as personalized career advice, mental health, and customized curricula that produce better learning outcomes. AI's role is also in supporting aging populations by keeping an eye on health indicators and other health parameters, besides assisting with various daily activities that can potentially help improve independent living and quality of life. Students can employ AI through coding and developing innovations to impact education positively. Students need to be empowered to energetically contribute meaningfully toward further developments in AI by understanding AI concepts and putting into practice the ideas of mathematical and computational thinking. By embracing coding and innovation, students can use AI to better solve problems at hand and become change marketers in various sectors.

THE FUTURE OF AI AND CODING

Improvements in AI technology open up a whole new realm of opportunities across sectors. Kovalenko et al. (2023) explain how AI can transform a production system toward more personalized, high-quality, and cost-effective manufacturing while building resilience against disruptions in manufacturing. Peng et al. (2023) discuss the progress made in healthcare: AI applications can minimize errors, reduce costs, and improve life quality—especially for older populations—but challenges such as algorithm bias and age discrimination must be overcome. According to Stypińska and Franke, 2023, the potential of AI in radiotherapy is high. Compared with photon therapy, AI-driven particle therapy brings forward new developments in treatment planning, dose calculation, image guidance, and adaptive replanning. Ji et al. (2023) further present that it is the outstanding performance of AI in ophthalmology that had significant advancement in optometry, handling severe issues in the field, including myopia, strabismus, and keratoconus. Equally important are critical areas that also call for further exploration and development: algorithm bias, data privacy concerns, and unique AI strategies required in different domains.

This will foster lifelong learning and curiosity and encourage students to continue exploring coding and AI throughout life. Recent research by Williams et al. (2022) has focused on interest-driven learning and developing metacognitive skills for enhancing curiosity, Ten et al. (2021) and reducing AI learning anxiety to foster intrinsic motivations toward AI-related skills. Lindstaedt and Oskotsky (2022) described a virtual summer program aimed at cultivating diversity and inclusion in AI within the domain of biomedicine for high school students. They reported on its success in engaging underrepresented groups. Abdelghani et al. (2022) review programs such as UCSF AI4ALL, which include engaging students from diverse backgrounds in AI education and hands-on projects and mentorship driving interest and competencies in AI [4]. Wang et al. (2022) explore how AI literacy curricula integrating active learning, embedded ethics, and low barriers to entry may support students in creating and critiquing AI artifacts within the classroom while instilling a critical lens through which they can understand AI impacts on society. Through these approaches, the inspiration to continue further into coding and AI can be instilled by embracing curiosity and lifelong learning in students.

CONCLUSION

Artificial intelligence is changing the way humans interact with technology today. It allows machines to perform activities that humans do, offering speech recognition systems, image processing, and decision-making. AI can be taught from the basics of coding at a primary school level since it essentially means teaching a computer how to learn and automate such activity. By engaging in coding platforms like Scratch and Blockly, students can develop an overview of how AI works—a way further to teach critical thinking, creativity, and problem-solving. Through interactive projects such as creating simple chatbots or virtual pets, children realize just how their code brings out intelligent behavior. It is not abstract; they see it firsthand, which is real fun and authentic learning.

The close relation of coding with AI underlines the need for its early education, preparing students for a future thoroughly intertwined with technology in all aspects of life. Real-life applications of AI in healthcare, transportation, and entertainment prove how these technologies will profoundly impact society. By making coding activities experimental and creative, educators can equip the students with an understanding of the potential of AI in solving real-life problems and encourage them to innovate. While continuing to explore and learn more about AI and coding, students are not just acquiring technical skills but developing the aptitude to drive progressing technology and its positive implications for the world.

By understanding and further developing AI, they can imagine themselves as future innovators shaping a technology-driven world. Pretty exciting projects they undertake—like developing chatbots or teaching virtual pets to identify various objects—can fascinate their curiosity and creativity. They will witness how their code drives intelligent behavior—a process with immense implications for industries such as healthcare and entertainment. This is critical in honing technical skills; it encourages more exploration necessary for innovation and problem-solving and thereby gives young learners the power to be at the frontline of technological advancement and societal improvement.

References

Abdelghani, R., Oudeyer, P.-Y., Law, E., de Vulpillières, C., & Sauzéon, H. (2022). Conversational agents for fostering curiosity-driven learning in children. *International Journal of Human-Computer Studies*, 167, 102887. Advance online publication. DOI: 10.1016/j.ijhcs.2022.102887

Ahmed Soomro, S., Casakin, H., Nanjappan, V., & Georgiev, G. V. (2023). Makerspaces fostering creativity: A systematic literature review. *Journal of Science Education and Technology*, 32(4), 530–548. Advance online publication. DOI: 10.1007/s10956-023-10041-4

Ali, S., Devasia, N., DiPaola, D., Hong, J., Kaputsos, S. P., Jordan, B., & Breazeal, C. (2022). AI + ethics curricula for middle school youth: Lessons learned from three project-based curricula. *International Journal of Artificial Intelligence in Education*. Advance online publication. DOI: 10.1007/s40593-022-00298-y PMID: 35935456

Alqahtani, T., Badreldin, H. A., Alrashed, M. A., Alshaya, A., Alghamdi, S. S., Alshaya, O. A., & Albekairy, A. M. (2023). The emergent role of artificial intelligence, natural learning processing, and large language models in higher education and research. *Research in Social & Administrative Pharmacy*, 19(8), 1236–1242. Advance online publication. DOI: 10.1016/j.sapharm.2023.05.016 PMID: 37321925

Arnulf, S., Christopher, S. B., & Bland, C. S. (2024). Artificial intelligence to support informed decision-making (INSIDE) for improved literature analysis in oncology. *European Urology Focus*. Advance online publication. DOI: 10.1016/j.euf.2024.05.022 PMID: 38876943

Arora, A., & Arora, A. (2022). Effects of smart voice control devices on children: Current challenges and future perspectives. *Archives of Disease in Childhood*, 107(12), 1129–1130. Advance online publication. DOI: 10.1136/archdischild-2022-323888 PMID: 36167481

Bill, L., & Tomiko, O. (2022). Nurturing diversity and inclusion in AI in biomedicine through a virtual summer program for high school students. *PLoS Computational Biology*, 18(1), e1009719. Advance online publication. DOI: 10.1371/journal.pcbi.1009719 PMID: 35100256

Bodaker, L., & Rosenberg-Kima, R. B. (2022). Online pair-programming: Elementary school children learning Scratch together online. *Journal of Research on Technology in Education*. Advance online publication. DOI: 10.1080/15391523.2022.2036653

Buxmann, P., Hess, T., & Thatcher, J. B. (2021). AI-based information systems. *Business & Information Systems Engineering*, 63(1), 1–4. Advance online publication. DOI: 10.1007/s12599-020-00675-8

Candello, H., Pichiliani, M. C., & Pinhanez, C. S. (2021). Making conversational robots learn from children in a collaborative museum exhibition. DOI: 10.1145/3462204.3482888

Caucheteux, C., Gramfort, A., & King, J.-R. (2023). Evidence of a predictive coding hierarchy in the human brain listening to speech. *Nature Human Behaviour*, 7(3), 430–441. Advance online publication. DOI: 10.1038/s41562-022-01516-2 PMID: 36864133

Czaja, S. J., & Ceruso, M. (2022). The promise of artificial intelligence in supporting an aging population. *Journal of Cognitive Engineering and Decision Making*, 16(4), 182–193. Advance online publication. DOI: 10.1177/15553434221129914

Debaditya, C., Cristina, I., Paola, A., Maliha, K., Cristian, R.-A., Hakan, B., & Gabriel, L.-B. (2021). Explainable artificial intelligence reveals novel insight into tumor microenvironment conditions linked with better prognosis in patients with breast cancer. *Cancers (Basel)*, 13(14), 3450. DOI: 10.3390/cancers13143450 PMID: 34298668

Deiner, A., Feldmeier, P., Fraser, G., Schweikl, S., & Wang, W. (2022). Automated test generation for Scratch programs. *Empirical Software Engineering*. Advance online publication. DOI: 10.1007/s10664-022-10255-x

Elima, H., Lipi, B. M., Khurshid, A. B., Himakshi, B., & Saswati, S. C. (2024). Exploring explainable artificial intelligence techniques for evaluating cervical intraepithelial neoplasia (CIN) diagnosis using colposcopy images. *Expert Systems with Applications*, 123579, 123579. Advance online publication. DOI: 10.1016/j.eswa.2024.123579

Ferrante, G., Licari, A., Fasola, S., Marseglia, G. L., & La Grutta, S. (2021). Artificial intelligence in the diagnosis of pediatric allergic diseases. *Pediatric Allergy and Immunology*, 32(3), 405–413. Advance online publication. DOI: 10.1111/pai.13419 PMID: 33220121

Fowler, S., Cutting, C., Gabriel, F., & Leonard, S. N. (2023). Self-determined learning in a virtual makerspace: A pathway to improving spatial reasoning for upper primary students. *International Journal of Technology and Design Education*. Advance online publication. DOI: 10.1007/s10798-023-09840-y

Glazewski, K., Ottenbreit-Leftwich, A., Jantaraweragul, K., Jeon, M., Hmelo-Silver, C. E., Scribner, J. A., & Lester, J. (2022). PrimaryAI: Co-designing immersive problem-based learning for upper elementary student learning of AI concepts and practices. DOI: 10.1145/3502717.3532142

Greenwald, E., Leitner, M., & Wang, N. (2021). Learning artificial intelligence: Insights into how youth encounter and build understanding of AI concepts.

Hohenstein, J., Kizilcec, R. F., DiFranzo, D., Aghajari, Z., Mieczkowski, H., Levy, K., Naaman, M., Hancock, J., & Jung, M. F. (2023). Artificial intelligence in communication impacts language and social relationships. *Scientific Reports*, 13(1), 5487. DOI: 10.1038/s41598-023-30938-9 PMID: 37015964

Jiyoung, Y., Juyeon, Y., Hye, S. L., Min, J. K., Vivian, Y. P., Mi, I. R., & Jung, H. Y. (2024). AI analytics can be used as imaging biomarkers for predicting invasive upgrade of ductal carcinoma in situ. *Insights Into Imaging*, 15(1), 100. Advance online publication. DOI: 10.1186/s13244-024-01673-0 PMID: 38578585

Kader Kaboreé, A., Barr, E., Klein, J., & Bissyandé, T. F. (2023). CodeGrid: A grid representation of code. DOI: 10.1145/3597926.3598141

Krenn, M., Kottmann, J. S., Tischler, N., & Aspuru-Guzik, A. (2021). Conceptual understanding through efficient automated design of quantum optical experiments. *Physical Review X*, 11(3), 031044. Advance online publication. DOI: 10.1103/PhysRevX.11.031044

Lee, F. G. (2023). Artificial intelligence and neurologic physical therapy. *Journal of Neurologic Physical Therapy; JNPT*, 47(1), 1–2. Advance online publication. DOI: 10.1097/NPT.0000000000000426 PMID: 36534016

Lee, W., Chan, S. H. G., & Tang, B. M. (2024, July 03). S. H. G. C., & Binglin, M. T. (2024). Paradigm of symbiosis as a mechanism of artificial intelligence and customers' patronage decision in the hospitality sector: The moderating role of customer engagement. *Asia Pacific Journal of Tourism Research*, 1–21. Advance online publication. DOI: 10.1080/10941665.2024.2363884

Leichtmann, B., Hinterreiter, A., Humer, C., Streit, M., & Mara, M. (2023). Explainable artificial intelligence improves human decision-making: Results from a mushroom picking experiment at a public art festival. *International Journal of Human-Computer Interaction*. Advance online publication. DOI: 10.1080/10447318.2023.2221605

Lindstaedt, B., & Oskotsky, T. (2022). Nurturing diversity and inclusion in AI in biomedicine through a virtual summer program for high school students. *PLoS Computational Biology*, 18(1), e1009719. Advance online publication. DOI: 10.1371/journal.pcbi.1009719 PMID: 35100256

Mangina, E., Psyrra, G., Screpanti, L., & Scaradozzi, D. (2023). Robotics in the context of primary and pre-school education: A scoping review. *IEEE Transactions on Learning Technologies*. Advance online publication. DOI: 10.1109/TLT.2023.3266631

Marta, H. (2021). Insightful artificial intelligence. *Mind & Language*, 36(2), 315–329. Advance online publication. DOI: 10.1111/mila.12321

Ojeda-Ramirez, S., Tsan, J., Eatinger, D., Jacob, S., Saito-Stehberger, D., Franklin, D., & Warschauer, M. (2023). Describing elementary students' spheres of influence in Scratch 'About Me' projects. DOI: 10.1145/3545945.3569869

Payam, H., Mahdi, B. F., & Khuong, M. V. (2021). Insight monetization intermediary platform using recommender systems. *Electronic Markets*. Advance online publication. 00449-WDOI: 10.1007/S12525-020-

Prather, J., Denny, P. C., Leinonen, J., Becker, B. A., Caspersen, M. E., Craig, M., ... Savelka, J. (2023). Transformed by transformers: Navigating the AI coding revolution for computing education: An ITiCSE working group conducted by humans. DOI: 10.1145/3587103.3594206

Rehman Javed, A., Khan, H. U., Alomari, M. K., Sarwar, M. U., Ahmad, A., & Khan, M. Z. (2023). Toward explainable AI-empowered cognitive health assessment. *Frontiers in Public Health*, 11, 1024195. Advance online publication. DOI: 10.3389/fpubh.2023.1024195 PMID: 36969684

Rodrigues, A., González, J. A., & Mateu, J. (2023). A conditional machine learning classification approach for spatio-temporal risk assessment of crime data. *Stochastic Environmental Research and Risk Assessment*, 37(7), 2815–2828. Advance online publication. DOI: 10.1007/s00477-023-02420-5

Ruben, L., Daniel, I., Hilary, G., Jonathan, W. S., & Jason, M. T. (2021). Getting a grip on insight: Real-time and embodied Aha experiences predict correct solutions. *Cognition and Emotion*, 35(3), 474–484. DOI: 10.1080/02699931.2021.1908230 PMID: 33829955

Rubinger, L., Gazendam, A., Ekhtiari, S., & Bhandari, M. (2022). Machine learning and artificial intelligence in research and healthcare. *Injury*. Advance online publication. DOI: 10.1016/j.injury.2022.01.046 PMID: 35135685

Salas-Pilco, S. Z., Xiao, K., & Oshima, J. (2022). Artificial intelligence and new technologies in inclusive education for minority students: A systematic review. *Sustainability (Basel)*, 14(20), 13572. Advance online publication. DOI: 10.3390/su142013572

Scerri, A., & Morin, K. H. (2023). Using chatbots like ChatGPT to support nursing practice. *Journal of Clinical Nursing*, 32(15-16), 4211–4213. Advance online publication. DOI: 10.1111/jocn.16677 PMID: 36880216

Service, R. (2023). The robot will see you now: With the advent of ever more powerful AI language models, a visit to your doctor may never be the same. *Science*. Advance online publication. DOI: 10.1126/science.adh1553

Shen, S., Lesnick, B., Qiao, M., & Yang, Q. (2022). Learning AI concepts and ethics through game programming: A middle school curriculum. DOI: 10.1145/3502717.3532147

Sheng, B., Chen, X., Li, T., Ma, T., Yang, Y., Bi, L., & Zhang, X. (2022). An overview of artificial intelligence in diabetic retinopathy and other ocular diseases. *Frontiers in Public Health*, 10, 971943. Advance online publication. DOI: 10.3389/fpubh.2022.971943 PMID: 36388304

Smith, B. (2022). AI's growing up: Part 1. *Communications of the ACM*. Advance online publication. DOI: 10.1145/3534843

Smith, L. J., & Hayne, H. (2022). Chatbots and children: A case study of communication with a conversational agent. *Journal of Experimental Child Psychology*. Advance online publication. DOI: 10.1016/j.jecp.2022.105346

Starkey, L., Eppel, E., & Sylvester, A. (2023). Ethics, empathy and the educational artificial intelligence (AI) practitioner. Journal of Open, Flexible and Distance Learning, doi:DOI: 10.6084/m9.figshare.22166107.v1

Sun, R., Demszky, D., Lin, E., Li, S., & Liu, Y. (2021). Safe AI for education: A systematic review of self-regulated learning with artificial intelligence in education. *Journal of Artificial Intelligence Research*. Advance online publication. DOI: 10.1613/jair.1.12412

Thompson, M. R., & Wheatley, L. (2023). Can artificial intelligence really transform education? Computers & Education. *Artificial Intelligence*. Advance online publication. DOI: 10.1016/j.caeai.2023.100160

Turner, C., Martin-Hammond, A., & Plaisant, C. (2022). Assessing the inclusivity of AI virtual assistant voice interfaces for young and older adults. Proceedings of the ACM on Human- Computer Interaction, doi:DOI: 10.1145/3555062

Van Alten, D. C. D., Phielix, C., Janssen, J., & Kester, L. (2023). Higher-order thinking in virtual reality: A systematic literature review. *Educational Research Review*. Advance online publication. DOI: 10.1016/j.edurev.2022.100502

Viana, J. P., Coelho, J. A. P. M., Bastos-Filho, C., & Elias, N. S. (2022). Exploring users' trust in the context of recommender systems: A systematic literature review. *Information Systems Frontiers*. Advance online publication. DOI: 10.1007/s10796-022-10300-2

Wang, Q., Wang, L., & Wu, W. (2023). Current and future AI applications in education: A review of the recent literature. Journal of Educational Technology Development and Exchange, DOI: 10.18785/jetde.1301.02

Wasserman, S. L., Wilson, C. J., & Horsman, M. A. (2023). Improving skills for success: How educators' professional development impacts students' engagement in making. *International Journal of Educational Research*. Advance online publication. DOI: 10.1016/j.ijer.2023.102149

Whitfield, C. (2021). Does collaborative making increase elementary students' science identities? A comparative case study. DOI: 10.1145/3502717.3532175

Xiaoyi, W., & Xingyi, Q. (2024). The positive effect of artificial intelligence technology transparency on digital endorsers: Based on the theory of mind perception. *Journal of Retailing and Consumer Services*, 78, 103777. Advance online publication. DOI: 10.1016/j.jretconser.2024.103777

Xinyi, L. (2021, December 07). Q. J. W., Qiuwen, W., Chunhao, W., Yang, S., Wentao, W., Hunter, S., Fang-Fang, Y., & Yaorong, G. (2021). Insights of an AI agent via analysis of prediction errors: A case study of fluence map prediction for radiation therapy planning. *Physics in Medicine and Biology*, 66(23), 23NT01. Advance online publication. DOI: 10.1088/1361-6560/ac3841

Zhang, J., & Wallace, C. (2022). Exploring the nature of artificial intelligence in education. Journal of Educational Technology, DOI: 10.1111/jcal.12455

Zou, D., Liu, Q., & Li, J. (2023). Adaptive learning systems: A review of the current state-of- the-art and future directions. *Journal of Educational Technology & Society*. Advance online publication. DOI: 10.1109/jets.2023.3297642

Chapter 8
Preservice Teachers' Attitudes Towards Employing AI Applications in the Special Education Environment

Yasmeen Abu Mukh
Independent Researcher, Israel

Aysha Abd-Rabo
Department of Elementary Education, Alrawdah University College, Palestine

Safia Tarter
Independent Researcher, Palestine

ABSTRACT

Artificial intelligence is the ability to design intelligent methods or develop self-learning software suggestions that mimic human traits. This study will reveal pre-service teachers' attitudes toward employing artificial intelligence applications in special educational settings. The descriptive approach was used to achieve the research objectives. The closed questionnaire was applied as a study tool on a random sample of 138 pre-service teachers from Al Qasimi Academy College. The study raises the following questions: What are the attitudes of pre-service teachers towards employing artificial intelligence applications in special educational settings? Do pre-service teachers' attitudes towards employing artificial intelligence

DOI: 10.4018/979-8-3693-7255-5.ch008

applications in special education environments change depending on the type of school, the gender of the pre-service teachers, their ages, and the year of study? The study showed that pre-service teachers' attitudes are neutral in employing artificial intelligence in special education settings. .

INTRODUCTION

Artificial intelligence is defined as the intelligence demonstrated by an artificial entity to solve complex problems, and such a system is generally assumed to be a computer or any device. Artificial Intelligence is an integration of computer science and physiology. In very simple language, intelligence is the computational part of the ability to achieve goals in the world. Intelligence is the ability to think, imagine, create, memorize, understand, recognize patterns, make choices, adapt to change, and learn from experience. Artificial Intelligence is concerned with making computers behave like humans, in a human-like manner and in less time than it would take a human. That's why it's called artificial intelligence. Artificial intelligence is divided into parts according to the two phenomena of artificial intelligence: strong and weak (Fronza et al.,2024).

The principle behind strong AI is that machines can be made to think or be introduced to human brains in the future. Thus, strong AI says that in the near future, we will be surrounded by such types of machines that can work just like humans, and machines can have human-level intelligence. These machines can wonder, think, and perform all the actions that a human being can do. Current research is no closer to creating strong artificial intelligence, and there is a lively ongoing debate about whether this is even possible (Garg, 2020). On the other hand, the principle behind weak AI is that machines can act as if they were intelligent.

Weak AI simply means that mind-like features can easily be added to computers to make them more useful assistants, and this is already starting to happen. For example, when a chess player plays against a computer, the player feels that the computer is impressive; But this is not real, as the chess application does not plan or think in reality; All the movements it makes are entered into the computer in advance by the human, and in this way the application makes the correct movements at the appropriate times.

There are other examples that confirm the weakness of artificial intelligence, including: wired cars, and speech recognition systems. Artificial intelligence can be expressed as the ability of a machine to perform activities that only the human mind can perform or produce. These activities include the ability to know and acquire it. It also includes the ability to judge, understand relationships, and produce new ideas (Mboshi, 2018).

That artificial intelligence is actually machine intelligence; This is the opposite of the natural intelligence that humans or even animals possess. Some of the activities they are designed to do are language recognition, learning, planning and problem solving. Since robotics is the field that discusses the relationship between perception and action, AI must have an important rolc in robotics if we want communication to be intelligent. Artificial intelligence is a major part of computer science. It requires developing computer programs to accomplish tasks that require a human intelligence (Gaber et al., 2023). Artificial intelligence is being used in many ways, from personal assistants to self-driving cars. Artificial intelligence is developing very rapidly, and science fiction often depicts artificial intelligence as robots that are very similar to humans and their behaviour. (Strong, 2016).

TYPES OF ARTIFICIAL INTELLIGENCE

AI is narrower than artificial intelligence, it is machine intelligence designed to perform a limited task that is non-conscious intelligence, (for example simply recognizing a face, or driving a car). However, the long-term goal of many researchers is to create artificial intelligence, which is a machine that has the ability to apply intelligence to a solution, such as "at least as smart as the average human." While narrow AI might outperform humans at any specific task, such as playing chess, general AI might outperform humans at almost every cognitive task. The hypothetical goal set is to achieve superior intelligence (ASI), which is far superior to the intelligence of the most intelligent and talented human minds (Schiff et al., 2020).

ADVANTAGES AND DISADVANTAGES OF ARTIFICIAL INTELLIGENCE

Mboshi (2018) said that the main advantages of artificial intelligence are that it is based on facts and not on emotions. It is known, even after our efforts, that human decisions are always negatively affected by emotions. Furthermore, unlike humans, AI machines do not need any sleep, thus overcoming the inherent disadvantage of psychological strcss on humans. Ease of disseminating knowledge. The artificial mind is trained on something, and is highly transferable to others, reducing thc time wasted in transferring knowledge to other humans through training. -Lack of creativity in responses. In addition to the inability to explain the logic and reasons behind a particular decision (Chiu et al., 2023).

Current development is at a stage where artificial intelligence cannot know when there is no solution to a particular problem. Any glitch can cause AI to produce wrong solutions, and since it cannot explain the reasoning behind its answer, blindly relying on AI can lead to problems. Lack of common sense in thinking can also cause major problems. It can cause widespread destruction if it falls into the wrong hands. One of the most worrying problems in the development of artificial intelligence is the beginning of the replacement of humans everywhere, which has led to high unemployment rates, which has led to crime, criminals, depression and poverty. There are also some areas that require the human touch, and there is a growing belief that machines will not be able to replace humans. The caring behaviour of nurses in hospitals is one example of a job that humans feel machines will never be able to do justice to (Rabie, 2016).

SPECIAL EDUCATION ENVIRONMENT

Special Learning Disabilities: According to Drigas (2016) and Ferahtia (2021) openions, learning difficulties were divided into a number of categories, including:

Learning Disabilities

This term refers to children who have certain difficulties in writing and reading. Impairments in at least one of the cognitive learning processes leads to difficulties in academic achievement, especially in reading and writing. These impairments include poor vision and hearing, and psychological, behavioural or emotional problems (Mboshi, 2018).

Dyslexia

Neurological learning disability includes difficulty with reading, writing, spelling, and speaking (Kemp et al., 2017). Difficulties with accurate word identification, fluency, spelling abilities, and decoding are usually due to unexpected phonological linguistic deficits that are often related to other cognitive abilities (Mboshi, 2018).

Attention Deficit Hyperactivity Disorder and Deficit Disorder

Which is not considered a learning disability. It causes a learning disorder. Students with these difficulties typically have difficulties sitting still, maintaining focus, follow directions, stay coordinated, and finish homework (Kemp et al.; J., 2017). Students with intellectual dysfunction are unable to to focus their attention for long periods of time, they also find it difficult to communicate with other parties, they feel upset quickly and easily, they have low self-confidence, and they face difficulties in their dealings with others (Garg, 2020).

Autism Spectrum Disorder

"It is called persistent deficits in social communication skills, and patterns of limited and repetitive interests." Students with autism have no ability to communicate, interpreting body language, learning basic skills, making friends, and maintaining eye contact (Kemp et al.; J., 2017).

Disabilities in Sensory and Motor Abilities:

- According to Theodorou (2017), motor disabilities and sensory disabilities are divided into visual difficulties and blindness. Hearing and motor difficulties (Kemp et al., cites, 2017):
- **Learners with visual impairment:** They are learners who have problems with visual ability. This visual ability includes differences in the shapes of objects, reversing numbers or letters, word confusion, misunderstanding of distance or depth, or problems with hand-eye coordination. (Abu Mukh et al., 2021).
- Visually impaired and deaf children: They are children who cannot distinguish between differences in sound, in addition to hearing sounds incorrectly, which affects their ability to write, read, and spell. This leads them to face difficulties in understanding the basic aspects of reading, spelling, and writing words and letters (Kemp et al., 2017).
- **Motor disabilities or physical**: Disability is medically known as a chronic physical disability, whether congenital or acquired, that may affect physical or academic performance. "Software-activated gaze control can bring this movement in parity with mouse- and keyboard-based movement (Drigas, 2016).

Pre-Service Teachers

Pre-service teachers develop their knowledge, teaching and learning. Teaching preparation is a complex business. Learning is required to build their knowledge as PST students, and having to deal with the situations they encounter in their courses is a way to enhance teacher development (Allas et al., 2017). Johnston (1992) referred to the knowledge that teachers use in complex classroom situations holistically when describing teachers' practical knowledge. Because PSTs' knowledge is constructed in the context of a teacher education programme, their practical knowledge, which integrates experiential knowledge, formal knowledge, PSTs' ideas and experiences from teacher education as well as their individual backgrounds, is of interest to teachers and researchers. This construction of PSTs' practical knowledge indicates a shift in research in teaching whereby PSTs are no longer consumers of others' knowledge, but, on the contrary, are in the process of producing knowledge for their professional lives and professional community Gholami, Aliasaghari, Talebzadeh, & Musapur, (2020) from In building their practical knowledge, PST teachers learn not only how to identify their teaching-related knowledge but also to adjust their knowledge to the actual teaching context. . Therefore, it is important to understand the practical knowledge that guides PSTs' actions (Ferry et al., 2022).

AI IN SPECIAL EDUCATIONAL ENVIRONMENT

Garg (2020) revealed that artificial intelligence has impacted people's lives. It has influenced educational sectors to make them more inclusive of students with special needs. CT applications and platforms can enable creativity in people without disabilities. Lee (2024) pointed out that CT has helped empower people with disabilities, such as helping children with dyslexia learn more. It has been found that CT facilitates people's lives, and does not replace them. The CT program enables development in the education and learning sector to empower people with special needs in education. Disability is a human condition; everyone suffers from it, either temporarily or permanently. People with disabilities are also referred to as people with special needs. Disabilities are also classified into four groups: motor disability, learning disability, visual disability, and cognitive disability. Artificial intelligence provides different technologies to adapt to the requirements of people with disabilities. Artificial intelligence is a mechanical simulation system for gathering knowledge. Mboshi (2018) said that artificial intelligence is becoming increasingly important for understanding the types of things people with disabilities may need as part of the technological toolkit. Artificial intelligence and special needs education work together to enable the development of individuals with disabilities. Many computer tools and educational technologies have been developed to manage children with dyslexia. These tools include educational software for phonological awareness. Facilitates phonological awareness for the reader. Youssef (2017) added that they come as programs that are easy to navigate and can be understood with the help of simple graphics without cognitive overload. Robotic assistance has been implemented to manage children with autism spectrum disorders where they can learn social skills and understand emotions (Abu Mukh et al.,2024). There is a game called LIFE, which is a game developed for children with autism spectrum disorder and helps them understand facial expressions. There is an e-learning tool called Smart Learning Model designed for children with learning difficulties so that they can understand in an easy and better way. Previous studies have indicated that robots can be used as an assistive tool for people with disabilities (Bhattacharya et al., 2021).

STUDY QUESTIONS

The Study Attempted to Answer the Following Main Question:

What are the attitudes of student teachers towards employing artificial Intelligence in the special education environment?

Minor Questions

What are the attitudes of student teachers towards employing artificial intelligence in the special education environment due to the student's gender variable?

- What are the attitudes of student teachers towards employing artificial Intelligence in the special education environment due to the variable of specialisation?
- What are the attitudes of student teachers towards employing artificial Intelligence in the special education environment due to the school-type variable in practical applications?
- What are the attitudes of student teachers towards employing artificial Intelligence in the special education environment due to the school year variation?
- What are the attitudes of student teachers towards employing artificial Intelligence in the special education environment due to the variable level of achievement?

Study Hypotheses

-There are no statistically significant differences at the significance level ($\alpha = 0.05$) between the average attitudes of student teachers towards employing artificial Intelligence in the special education environment due to the variable of the student's gender.

-There are no statistically significant differences at the significance level ($\alpha = 0.05$) between the average attitudes of student teachers towards employing artificial Intelligence in the special education environment due to the variable of specialisation.

-There are no statistically significant differences at the significance level ($\alpha = 0.05$) between the average attitudes of student teachers towards employing artificial Intelligence in the special education environment due to the school type variable in practical applications.

-There are no statistically significant differences at the significance level ($\alpha = 0.05$) between the average attitudes of student teachers towards employing artificial Intelligence in the special education environment due to the variable of the academic year.

-There are no statistically significant differences at the level of significance ($\alpha = 0.05$) between the average attitudes of student teachers towards employing artificial Intelligence in the special education environment due to the variable of achievement level.

METHODOLOGY

Participants

The research population consisted of pre-service teachers from Al Qasimi Academy College. The scale was distributed and compiled by the researchers electronically. The research sample included a total of 138 pre-service teachers from Al Qasimi Academy College from Israel (8% males and 92% females), who were practicing field training in various regions of the Ministry of Education, 54% from the Haifa Governorate. 22% from the northern side, 10% from the south, and 14% from the central region. Preservice teachers with special education majors were invited to voluntarily complete the survey. Of the 138 teachers who completed the questionnaire, 70 of them practiced field training in special education schools and 30 in regular education schools. Table 1 shows additional features of these advanced services.

Table 1. Background variables considered for pre-service teachers (n=138).

Character	Group	%	N
Gender	Male	8	11
	Female	92	127
Age	Between 19-25 years	54	75
	Between 26-32 years	28	39
	Between 33-39 years	10	14
	More than 40 years	7	10
Level of achievement	Good	16	22
	Very Good	67	92
	Excellent	17	24
Specialization	regular	51	70
	updated	49	68
school type in practical applications	normal education	30	41
	Special Education	70	97
academic year	first	31	43
	second	29	40
	third	10	14
	fourth	30	41
Districts	Haifa	14	19
	North	22	30
	South	10	14
	Merckaz	54	75

Measurement Tools

The current study used a closed-ended questionnaire designed to classify the responses of sample members according to a five-point scale (very low, low, medium, high, and very high). The results of the scale revealed (knowledge of artificial intelligence applications, the importance of employing artificial intelligence applications, the challenges of using artificial intelligence applications, and the trend towards employing artificial intelligence applications). The initial questionnaire consisted of two main axes: the first related to demographic information, including (gender, specialization, and type of school in practical applications, academic year, and academic achievement). The second consists of 39 questionnaire items to be answered. The scale was created in several stages: In the first stage of the process, a literature review was conducted on employing artificial intelligence applications in special education settings (Al-Ghamdi, Al-Farani, 2020). As a result of literature reviews, dimensions were reached that could measure pre-service teachers' attitudes towards employing artificial intelligence applications in special education environments, and in this direction a set of items was created. In the second stage, the draft scale was determined according to a certain number of items related to the dimensions on which the research was based. In the third stage, the opinion of field experts was taken about the validity and appearance of the measurement tool. Finally, to ensure understanding of the measurement tool in terms of language, the opinion of an expert in Arabic language and literature was consulted.

Data Analyses

The scale was created in several stages: In the first stage of the process, a literature review was conducted on employing artificial intelligence applications in special education settings (Al-Ghamdi, Al-Farani, 2020). As a result of literature reviews, dimensions were reached that could measure pre-service teachers' attitudes towards employing artificial intelligence applications in special education environments, and in this direction a set of items was created. In the second stage, the draft scale was determined according to a certain number of items related to the dimensions on which the research was based. In the third stage, the opinion of field experts was taken about the validity and appearance of the measurement tool. Finally, in order to ensure that the measurement tool was understood linguistically, the opinion of an expert in the Arabic language and literature was consulted.

Validity and Reliability Analyses

To evaluate the reliability of the current study's questionnaire, consistency between items was measured using Cronbach's alpha reliability coefficients for each of the four dimensions separately (knowledge of artificial intelligence applications, importance of employing artificial intelligence applications, challenges of using artificial intelligence applications, and tendency toward employing artificial intelligence applications). (Bonnett and Wright, 2015). Table 2 presents the details of this analysis. It showed that the question dimension "Challenges of using artificial intelligence applications" has high reliability (Cronbach alpha, $\alpha = 0.914$), followed by the dimension "Knowledge of artificial intelligence applications" (Cronbach alpha, $\alpha = 0.861$), followed by the dimension "Knowledge of artificial intelligence applications" (Cronbach alpha, $\alpha = 0.861$), followed by "Challenges of using artificial intelligence applications" (Cronbach alpha, $\alpha = 0.914$). The dimension "Attitude toward employing artificial intelligence applications" (Cronbach alpha, $\alpha = 0.750$), followed by the dimension "Importance of employing artificial intelligence applications" (Cronbach alpha, $\alpha = 0.743$), and finally the scale as a whole has high reliability (Cronbach alpha, $\alpha = 0.963$).

Table 2. Cronbach's alpha reliability coefficients for each of the four dimensions separately

Dimension	Number of items	Cronbach alpha
"Knowledge of the artificial intelligence applications"	8	0.863
"The importance of employment artificial intelligences applications"	9	0.743
Challenging of the using artificial intelligence applications"	15	0.914
"The trends towards the employing artificial intelligences applications"	7	0.750

Concerning the validity, a number of three content experts with doctoral degrees in education verified the validity of the questionnaire, and the questionnaire was distributed to all study participants in the middle of the 2022-2023 academic year.

RESULTS

Results of the Main Study Question

The researchers adopted the following ways to classify the means to identify the students' attitudes teachers towards employing artificial Intelligence in the special educational environment:

Table 3. The way used in classifying the means to identify the attitudes of student teachers towards employing artificial Intelligence in the special education environment:

range	level	attitude
2.33 or less	low	negative
3.66-2.34	medium	neutral
3.67 or more	high	positive

To answer the main study questions, means and standard deviations were calculated as shown in the following Table:

Table 4. The attitudes of student teachers towards employing artificial Intelligence in the special education environment.

The dimension	M	SD	level	attitude
The Knowledge of artificial intelligence applications	3.67	0.37	high	positive
The importance of employment artificial intelligence applications	3.82	0.26	high	positive
Challenges of using artificial intelligence applications	3.40	0.42	medium	neutral
The trend towards the employment artificial intelligence applications	3.61	0.44	medium	neutral
Total dimension	**3.56**	**0.31**	**medium**	**neutral**

Based on the table above, the results showed that student -teachers have neutral attitudes towards employing artificial intelligence in the special education environment, because the overall average value is (3.56), which is considered average, as well as for the dimensions (challenges of education). Using artificial intelligence applications) and (the trend towards employing artificial intelligence applications), where the average values reached (3.40) and (3.61), respectively. As for the dimensions (knowledge of artificial intelligence applications) and (the importance of employing artificial intelligence applications), the student teachers' attitudes were high, with average values reaching (3.67) and (3.82), respectively.

Results of the First Sub-Question

To answer the first sub-question, the following hypothesis was tested: There are no statistically significant differences at the significance level ($\alpha = 0.05$) between the average of the attitudes of student teachers towards employing artificial intelligence in the private education environment due to the gender of the student.

To test this hypothesis, arithmetic means and standard deviations were calculated for all dimensions of the questionnaire for both males and females, and the results were as follows:

Table 5. means and standard deviations of the dimensions of the questionnaire according to the gender variable

Dimensions	gender	N	M	SD
Knowledge of artificial intelligences applications	male	9	3.66	0.34
	female	119	3.67	0.38
The importance of employment artificial intelligence applications	male	8	3.64	0.30
	female	108	3.83	0.25
Challenging of using artificial intelligence applications	male	11	3.40	0.37
	female	121	3.42	0.43
The trends towards employing artificial intelligence applications	male	9	3.34	0.61
	female	109	3.62	0.42
Total dimensions	male	11	3.46	0.31
	female	124	3.57	0.32

Table 6. Results of the (t) test for the differences between the averages of male and female responses on the questionnaires' dimensions:

Dimensions	(t-value)	sig
Knowledge of artificial intelligence applications	1.02	0.31
The importance of employing artificial intelligence applications	0.07	0.93
Challenges of using artificial intelligence applications	2.05	0.04
The trend towards employing artificial intelligence applications	0.02	0.98
Total dimensions	1.85	0.66

In general, table (5) shows that the averages of females were higher than the averages of males in all dimensions of the study, including the overall dimension. Referring to Table (6), no statistically significant differences appeared in all dimensions of the study. The dimensions of the study and the overall dimension, with the exception of the dimension (challenges of using artificial intelligence applications), where the statistical significance value was (0.04), which is a statistically significant value in favour of females.

Results of the Second Sub-Question

To answer the second sub-question, the following hypothesis was tested: There are no statistically significant differences at the significance level ($\alpha = 0.05$) between the average of the attitudes of student teachers towards employing artificial intelligence in the private education environment attributed to artificial intelligence. To test this hypothesis, arithmetic means and standard deviations were calculated for all dimensions of the questionnaire for each level of the variable, and the results were as follows:

Table 7. Means and standard deviations of the dimensions of the questionnaire according to the specialisation variable:

Dimensions	Specialization	N	M	SD
Knowledge of artificial intelligence applications	regular	66	3.66	0.36
	updated	62	3.68	0.39
The importance of the employing artificial intelligence applications	regular	61	3.81	0.27
	updated	55	3.83	0.25
Challenges of the using artificial intelligence applications	regular	69	3.36	0.47
	updated	63	3.43	0.37
The trend towards the employing of the artificial intelligence applications	regular	58	3.65	0.35
	updated	60	3.55	0.51
Total dimensions	regular	70	3.54	0.34
	updated	64	3.58	0.28

Table 8. Results of the (T) test for the differences between the averages of the study sample responses on the questionnaire dimensions' according to the specialization variable

Dimensions	(t-value)	sig
Knowledge of the artificial intelligence applications	0.37	0.71
The importance of the employing artificial intelligence applications	0.39	0.69
Challenges of the using artificial intelligence applications	0.96	0.33
The trend towards the employing of the artificial intelligence applications	1.19	0.23
Total dimension	0.82	0.41

To answer the second sub-question, the following hypothesis was tested: There are no statistically significant differences at the significance level ($\alpha = 0.05$) between the average attitudes of student teachers towards employing artificial intelligence in the private education environment due to the artificial intelligence variable. Specialty. To test this hypothesis, arithmetic means and standard deviations were calculated for all dimensions of the questionnaire for each level of the variable, and the results were as follows:

Results of the Third Sub-Question

To answer the third sub-question, the following hypothesis was tested: There are no statistically significant differences at the significance level ($\alpha = 0.05$) between the average attitudes of student teachers towards employing artificial intelligence in the private educational environment due to the school-type variable in practical applications.

To test this hypothesis, arithmetic means and standard deviations were calculated for all dimensions of the questionnaire for each type of school in practical applications, and the results were as follows:

Table 9. Means and standard deviations of the dimensions of the questionnaire according to the school type variable's in practical applications.

dimensions	School type	N	M	SD
Knowledge of the artificial intelligence applications	normal education	38	3.54	0.39
	Special Education	90	3.72	0.35
The importance of the employing artificial intelligence applications	normal education	36	3.77	0.31
	Special Education	80	3.84	0.23
Challenges of the using artificial intelligence applications	normal education	38	3.38	0.36
	Special Education	94	3.41	0.44
The trend towards the employing of the artificial intelligence applications	normal education	37	3.55	0.46
	Special Education	81	3.63	0.43
Total dimension	normal education	40	3.53	0.28
	Special Education	95	3.57	0.32

Table 10. Results of the (T) test of the differences between the averages of the study sample responses on the questionnaire dimensions according to the school type variable in practical applications

Dimensions	(t-value)	sig
Knowledge of artificial intelligence applications	2.48	0.01
The importance of employing artificial intelligence applications	1.24	0.21
Challenges of using artificial intelligence applications	0.26	0.79

continued on following page

Table 10. Continued

Dimensions	(t-value)	sig
The trend towards employing artificial intelligence applications	0.92	0.36
Total dimension	0.59	0.55

In general, table (9) shows that the averages of the special education level were higher than the averages of the regular education level in all dimensions of the study, including the overall dimension. Referring to Table (10), no statistics appeared. Statistically significant differences in all dimensions of the study and the overall dimension, except for the dimension (knowledge of artificial intelligence applications), where the statistical significance value reached (0.01), which is a statistically significant value in favour of special education.

Results of the Fourth Sub-Questio

To answer the fourth sub-question, the following hypothesis was tested: There are no statistically significant differences at the significance level ($\alpha = 0.05$) between the average attitudes of student teachers towards employing artificial intelligence in the special education environment due to the academic year.

To test this hypothesis, arithmetic means and standard deviations were calculated for all dimensions of the questionnaire for each level of the variable, and the results were as follows:

Table 11. means and standard deviations of the dimensions of the questionnaire according to the academic year variable

Dimensions	academic year	N	M	SD
Knowledge of artificial intelligence applications	first	39	3.71	.34
	second	13	3.67	.32
	third	39	3.70	.35
	forth	37	3.58	.44
The importance of employing artificial intelligence applications	first	128	3.67	.37
	second	34	3.79	.29
	third	12	3.87	.17
	forth	34	3.82	.27

continued on following page

Table 11. Continued

Dimensions	academic year	N	M	SD
Challenges of using artificial intelligence applications	first	36	3.82	.24
	second	116	3.82	.26
	third	42	3.43	.40
	forth	14	3.47	.44
The trend towards employing artificial intelligence applications	first	38	3.42	.48
	second	38	3.32	.38
	third	132	3.40	.42
	forth	38	3.48	.58
Total dimension	first	42	3.55	.30
	second	14	3.62	.27
	third	40	3.59	.38
	forth	39	3.51	.25

Table 12. One-way analysis of variance for the differences between the averages of the respondents' responses according to the academic year variable

Dimensions	SS	df	MS	F- value	sig
Knowledge of artificial intelligence applications	.41	3	.13	.95	0.41
	17.74	124	.14		
	18.15	127			
The importance of employing artificial intelligence applications	.05	3	.01	0.26	0.84
	7.79	112	.07		
	7.85	115			
Challenges of using artificial intelligence applications	.35	3	.11	0.64	0.58
	23.40	128	.18		
	23.75	131			
The trend towards employing artificial intelligence applications	1.85	3	.61		
	21.39	114	.18	3.29	0.02
	23.24	117			
Total dimension	.19	3	.06	0.63	0.59
	13.28	131	.10		
	13.47	134			

The averages of the questionnaire dimensions according to the academic year variable ranged between (3.87-3.32) as shown in Table (11), and the results showed that the highest averages were in the dimension (the importance of employing artificial intelligence applications), while the dimension included (the trend towards employing artificial intelligence applications) are the lowest averages, while Table (12) showed that there are no statistically significant differences between the averages of the sample responses on all dimensions and the overall dimension except for the overall dimension. After (the trend towards employing artificial intelligence applications), which showed a statistical significance of (0.02), and to identify the source of the differences, the Scheffé test was used for post-hoc comparisons, which showed the presence of statistically significant differences at the level of intelligence. There is a significance ($\alpha = 0.05$) between the responses of the study sample for those with the academic year level (fourth year) on the one hand, and the responses of the study sample for those with the academic year level (first year) and in favour of (fourth year).

Results of the Fifth Sub-Question

To answer the fifth sub-question, the following hypothesis was tested: There are no statistically significant differences at the significance level ($\alpha = 0.05$) between the average attitudes of student teachers towards employing artificial intelligence in the private education environment due to the artificial intelligence variable. Level of achievement.

To test this hypothesis, arithmetic means and standard deviations were calculated for all dimensions of the questionnaire for each level of the variable, and the results were as follows:

Table 13. means and standard deviations of the dimensions of the questionnaire according to the variable of the level of achievement (the level of achievement: good (75-84), Very good (85-94), excellent (95-100)).

Dimensions	N	M	SD
Knowledge of artificial intelligence applications	18	3.60	.33
	78	3.63	.45
	22	3.51	.48
The importance of employing artificial intelligence applications	18	3.75	.29
	77	3.85	.24
	21	3.75	.28

continued on following page

Table 13. Continued

Dimensions	N	M	SD
Challenges of using artificial intelligence applications	22	3.31	.44
	87	3.41	.43
	23	3.43	.36
The trend towards employing artificial intelligence applications	18	3.60	.33
	78	3.63	.45
	22	3.51	.48
Total dimension	22	3.47	.41
	90	3.59	.29
	23	3.50	.27

Table 14. One-way analysis of variance for the differences between the averages of the respondents' responses according to the variable of achievement level:

Dimensions	SS	df	MS	F- value	sig
Knowledge of artificial intelligence applications	1.71	2	.85	6.51	0.00
	16.44	125	.13		
	18.15	127			
The importance of employing artificial intelligence applications	.23	2	.11	1.76	0.17
	7.61	113	.06		
	7.85	115			
Challenges of using artificial intelligence applications	.20	2	.10		
	23.55	129	.18	.54	.58
	23.75	131			
The trend towards employing artificial intelligence applications	.22	2	.11		
	23.01	115	.20	.57	.56
	23.24	117			
Total dimension	.37	2	.19	1.91	0.15
	13.09	132	.09		
	13.47	134			

The averages of the questionnaire dimensions according to the achievement level variable ranged between (3.85-3.31) as shown in Table (13). The results showed that the highest averages were in the dimension (the importance of employing artificial intelligence applications) for the level (very good), while the dimension included (challenges). The use of artificial intelligence applications) had the lowest average level (good), while Table (14) showed that there were no statistically significant differences between the averages of the two artificial intelligence averages. The sample's responses on all dimensions and the overall dimension except for the dimension (knowledge of artificial intelligence applications), which showed a statistical significance of (0.00). To identify the source of the differences, the Scheffé test was used for dimensional comparisons, which showed the presence of statistically significant differences at the significance level ($\alpha = 0.05$) between... The responses of the study sample with the achievement level (very good) on the one hand, and the responses of the study sample with the achievement level (excellent). And valid (very good).

SUMMARY

The results of the current study showed that the pre-service teachers' attitudes were neutral, and this means that the pre-service teachers do not have sufficient knowledge of the meaning of artificial intelligence, and that they need more training on the use of artificial intelligence in the education process. In addition, the result of the study showed that females use artificial intelligence more than males. It is consistent with the study of Garg (2020). This means that females put more effort into reading and learning more about AI than males. Moreover, the result indicates that students with disabilities do not realize the meaning of AI or even use it in their learning process. Their ability may be the reason for this, so they need to work hard and practice using AI more in their learning environments. This is consistent with the study of Al-Ghamdi and Al-Farani (2020).

Additionally, results show that AI is being used more frequently in special education settings. Next, this means that AI has many benefits that help teachers and students alike teach and learn in the special education setting. The results indicate that fourth-year students use artificial intelligence applications more than students in other academic years. This means that fourth-grader students have been well trained to employ artificial intelligence in their teaching after graduation. Finally, the results showed that the differences are in favour of very good. This is consistent with the study of Drygas (2016). Students' attitudes are very good. This means that they will be able to use and learn artificial intelligence in the future when they become teachers. Finally, artificial intelligence came to make people's lives easier; she touched people's lives, especially those with special needs.

References

Abu Mukh, Y. N., Abd-Rabo, A. M., & Tarteer, S. (2024). Computer Competencies Needed for Implementing Artificial Intelligence in Special Education Schools from the Perspective of Pre-Service Teachers. *Trends in Higher Education*, 3(3), 602–622. DOI: 10.3390/higheredu3030035

Abu Mukh, Y. N., Hashaikeh, S. A., & Abd-Rabo, A. M. (2021). Digital Learning Games Scale (DLGS): A Scale Development Study. *International Journal of Emerging Technologies in Learning*, 16(11), 140. DOI: 10.3991/ijet.v16i11.20709

Alghamdi, S., & Alfrani, L. (2020). The reality of using artificial intelligence applications in special education schools in Jeddah from the point of view of female teachers. [EPS]. *International Journal of Educational & Psychological Studies*, 8, 57–76.

Allas, R., Leijen, Ä., & Toom, A. (2017). Supporting the construction of teacher's practical knowledge through different interactive formats of oral reflection and written reflection. *Scandinavian Journal of Educational Research*, 61(5), 600–615. DOI: 10.1080/00313831.2016.1172504

Bhattacharya, S., & Pal, S. (2021). Scheduled Tribe Girl Students with Special Need and Artificial Intelligence. *European Scholar Journal*, 2(6), 195–201.

Chiu, T. K. F., Ismailov, M., Zhou, X.-Y., Xia, Q., Au, D., & Chai, C. S. (2023). Using Self-Determination Theory to explain how communitybased learning fosters student interest and identity in integrated STEM education. [CrossRef]. *International Journal of Science and Mathematics Education*, 21(S1), 109–130. DOI: 10.1007/s10763-023-10382-x

Drigas, A., & Theodorou, P. (2016). ICTs and Music in Special Learning Disabilities, International Journal of Recent Contributions from Engineering [iJES]. *Science & IT*, 4(3), 12.

Ferahtia, A. (2021). See discussions, stats, and author profiles for this publication at: https://www. researchgate. net/publication/350567414

Ferry, M., Åström, P., & Romar, J. E. (2022). Pre service teachers' practical knowledge and their sources. *Journal of Teacher Education and Educators*, 11(1), 33–57.

Gaber, S. A., Shahat, H. A., Alkhateeb, I. A., Al Hasan, S. A., Alqatam, M. A., Almughyirah, S. M., & Keshar Kamel, M. (2023). Faculty Members' Awareness of Artificial Intelligence and Its Relationship to Technology Acceptance and Digital Competencies at King Faisal University. [CrossRef]. *Int. J. Learn. Teach. Educ. Res.*, 22(7), 473–496. DOI: 10.26803/ijlter.22.7.25

Garg, S., & Sharma, S. (2020). Impact of Artificial Intelligence in special need education to promote inclusive pedagogy. *International Journal of Information and Education Technology (IJIET)*, 10(7), 523–527. DOI: 10.18178/ijiet.2020.10.7.1418

Gholami, K., & Husu, J. (2010). How do teachers' reason about their practice? Representing the epistemic nature of teachers' practical knowledge. *Teaching and Teacher Education*, 26(8), 1520–1529. DOI: 10.1016/j.tate.2010.06.001

Johnston, S. (1992). Images: A way of understanding the practical knowledge of student teachers. *Teaching and Teacher Education*, 8(2), 123–136. DOI: 10.1016/0742-051X(92)90003-L

Kemp G., Smith M., Segal J. (2017). Learning Disabilities and Disorders, Types of Learning Disorders and Their Signs, HELPGUIDE.ORG, Trusted guide to mental, emotional & social health.

Lee, Y. J., Davis, R. O., & Ryu, J. (2024). Korean In-Service Teachers' Perceptions of Implementing Artificial Intelligence (AI) Education for Teaching in Schools and Their AI Teacher Training Programs. *International Journal of Information and Education Technology (IJIET)*, 14(2), 214–219. DOI: 10.18178/ijiet.2024.14.2.2042

Mboshi, N. S. (2018). Teaching learners with visual impairment in an inclusive education setting: The Cameroon perspective. *International Journal of Education and Research, 6*(2), 109-118.

Sausser, S., & Waller, R. J. (2006). A model for music therapy with students with emotional and behavioral disorders. *The Arts in Psychotherapy*, 33(1), 1–10. DOI: 10.1016/j.aip.2005.05.003

Schiff, D., Ayesh, A., Musikanski, L., & Havens, J. C. (2020, October). Ieee 7010: A new standard for assessing the well-being implications of artificial Intelligence. In *2020 IEEE international conference on systems, man, and cybernetics (SMC)* (pp. 2746-2753). IEEE.

Strong, A. I. (2016). Applications of Artificial Intelligence and associated technologies. *Science [ETEBMS-2016], 5*(6).

Theodorou P., Drigas A.2017.ICTs and Music in Sensory and Motor Disabilities, International Journal of Recent Contributions from Engineering,Vol 5 No 2,4

Yusuf, J. E., & Jordan, M. M. (2017). Accessibility of the management's discussion and analysis to citizen users of government financial reports. *Public Budgeting & Finance*, 37(4), 74–91. DOI: 10.1111/pbaf.12170

KEY TERMS AND DEFINITIONS

Artificial Intelligence: Using technological apps to teach students.
AI Apps: Apps that make learning easier.
Disabilities: A person who finds difficulties in learning.
Pre-Service Teachers: Students who will be teachers after graduation.
Special Education: Special ways of teaching for special needs students.
Special Environment: Special learning with many helpful facilities.
Visual Learners: Learners that use charts in learning.

Chapter 9
Strategies for Bridging the Digital Divide in Inclusive Education Through Multisensory Learning and Emerging Technologies

Zhou Jinghong
https://orcid.org/0009-0003-1737-8923
Universiti Sains Malaysia, Malaysia

Mageswaran Sanmugam
https://orcid.org/0000-0003-3313-4462
Universiti Sains Malaysia, Malaysia

ABSTRACT

This chapter explores the use of the digital divide in inclusive education through multisensory learning and emerging technologies to bridge the digital divide. The researcher examines the concepts, manifestations, and types of the digital divide in Inclusive Education and proposes the content of indicators to evaluate the digital divide. This chapter uses multi-sensory learning and emerging technologies to improve the digital skills of different groups as an important hand in bridging the technological divide, aiming to address the realities of educational inequity, insufficient depth of participation in Education, and digital exclusion due to the technological divide. The paper also explores the implementation of multisensory learning. The thesis also explores the ethical considerations and challenges of implementing multisensory

DOI: 10.4018/979-8-3693-7255-5.ch009

learning and emerging technologies to bridge the technological divide in Inclusive Education. This chapter is useful in further developing the value implications of digital transformation in Education for Inclusive Education.

INTRODUCTION

In the 21st century, the development of emerging and digital technologies is on an unprecedented trend to become a central driver in reshaping economies and societies, changing the way human societies produce and live (Mohd Javaid, 2024; Valentina Bondarenko et al., 2019; Sergiy A. Tsyganov & Viktoria Apalkova, 2016). Various countries are promoting the construction of a new education model through digitalisation and building a country oriented towards inclusive Education and lifelong learning. Digital Education can break through the boundaries of time and space so that people from different countries, regions, and cultures can have equal access to educational resources and fully enjoy the opportunity to learn (Johann Engelbrecht & Marcelo C. Borba, 2024). However, it is undeniable that digital technology has brought many problems while promoting rapid social and economic development, especially since many disadvantaged groups are excluded from the digital environment in the process of accessing educational resources and mastering teaching techniques, which triggers the problem of the digital divide in the era of digital Education, and the need to rethink the nature of Education (Felicitas Macgilchrist et al.,2024; Francesca Peruzzo & Julie Allan, 2024)

The Concept of Inclusive Education

UNESCO defines 'inclusive education' as an education system that responds to the diverse learning needs of all learners and reduces the exclusion of certain groups of children from the education system. Ensuring that all learners, including those with disabilities, enjoy the right to Education without discrimination and on an equal basis with others and that all people in society have equal rights and full opportunities to develop and participate equally in society (UNESCO, 2020; Fleder, 2019; Ainscow & César, 2006).

Diverse learning curricula, teaching methods, and assessment practices in inclusive Education can benefit all students (Linda J. Graham, 2019). Inclusive education communities value communities of all learners, and school administrators continue to reinforce inclusive value systems (Jenny Corbett, 2001). Inclusion emphasises that all students can participate, adopting a collaborative approach that provides the thinking and practice required for inclusive Education (Messiou, 2016).

The main elements of inclusive Education:

1) **Subject inclusion:** the inclusion of human ways of being and states of life (Äli Leijen et al., 2021). It generally includes three aspects: firstly, teachers identify with students' learning styles, learning states and differences. Second, students' mutual inclusion creates harmonious interpersonal relationships in the classroom. Third, students' self-tolerance is based on students' tolerance of their thoughts and behaviours. Self-tolerance is the source of students' self-confidence and motivation to move forward.

(2) **Value inclusion:** based on the reality of cultural pluralism, agreeing with the value differences of culture, respecting students' values, and recognising the reasonableness of the existence of multiple concepts. Respect students' cognitive interests, acknowledge cognitive differences, appreciate students' individualised learning interests, and respect students' needs and motivations.

(3) **Demand inclusion:** This is specifically manifested in looking at students' behaviours with a developmental perspective, reducing value-based judgments, encouraging students' individuality, and showing respect for students' history, experiences, habits, behaviours and hobbies. Human needs are rich and varied, and with the development of society and civilisation, there will be more and more different levels of human needs. Many kinds of needs are interconnected to form a huge system. Fully respect and satisfy the reasonable needs of the education object, gradually raise the level of needs and activate the demand for inclusion.

(4) **Ecological inclusion:** According to Elena Anastasiou and Christina Hajisoteriou's research from 2020, an ecosphere is comprised of educators, students, and the surrounding educational environment. There is no such thing as an isolated or static ecosphere; rather, it is a component of a dynamic growth process. It affirms students' uniqueness as living individuals and respects the diversity of their learning styles and approaches in the classroom (Ainscow & Sandill, 2010).

Inclusive Education seeks to promote mutual respect and valuing of all learners and to sustain the values of inclusion and respect for diversity in the educational process, teaching and learning curricula and school culture.

Inclusion, quality and equity are the three core keywords of the 2030 Global Vision for Education, and they are the main tasks of countries around the world in the next ten years to achieve educational inclusion and build educational quality. First, the concept of inclusive development of Education should be followed to promote the building of a national and even a global education development community. Secondly, countries and regions around the world should strengthen the top-level design of Education, drawing on the educational standards and conventions and regulations issued by international educational organisations, and establish the practice of action for the inclusive development of Education to promote the rational structure of educational policies, goal planning and legislative systems. Thirdly, they should rationally integrate resources for inclusive development in Education and implement the responsibilities, competencies and action strategies of education departments at all levels, including the technical, policymaking, managerial, executive and coordinating levels of Education.

The Concept of Digital Divide

The digitalisation of the information society has become an unstoppable global trend in the international community. Digital Education can break through the boundaries of time and space, allowing people from different countries, regions, cultures and living conditions to have equal access to educational resources and enjoy full learning opportunities. Nevertheless, we cannot deny that the advent of digital technology has resulted in the emergence of new challenges while simultaneously facilitating the creation of innovative inclusive education. In particular, many teachers and students or disadvantaged groups in economically underdeveloped areas are excluded from the digital education environment in accessing digital learning resources and mastering digital learning technologies, which has triggered the current digital divide in Education.

The "digital divide" was first proposed by the National Telecommunications and Information Administration (NTIA) of the United States in 1995 in a series of reports entitled *Being Left Behind in the Network.* It can be understood as the information gap, cognitive gap and wealth gap caused by the different degrees of application and possession of network technology and information among countries, regions and people in global digitisation. This is further subdivided into the "physical access" and "psychological access" divisions. At the same time, what is understood as differences in access to and use of information technology due to differences in economic levels and uneven regional development, and later on, gaps in psychological motivation and accessibility have also been included in the digital divide (Jan A.G.M van Dijk, 2006; Rowena Cullen, 2001).

From the time the digital divide was proposed to the present day, it can be broadly categorised into four distinct phases:

- **The first digital divide**

In the late 1990s, with the rise of Internet access technology, the gap in PC usage penetration and Internet access opportunities due to the income gap between the rich and the poor (Dewan & Diggins, 2005).

- **The second digital divide**

Gaps are mainly in using information on the Internet and skills in navigating information technology (Hargittai, 2001). With the popularity of smartphones and mobile Internet, especially the convenience and efficiency of mobile terminals in accessing and processing digital content, the second digital divide is gradually alleviated.

- **The third digital divide**

It is primarily a difference in the ability to apply the Internet efficiently and with high quality (Wei et al., 2010). With the popularity of technology for individuals to participate in Internet content creation and the massive application of user profiling, big data analysis, and accurate recommendation algorithms, low-quality and even false information has also come to the fore, which over time has shrouded different groups of people in an information cocoon. It has gradually created a closed and self-reinforcing opinion environment. As well as relying on a single source of information, people are more likely to fall into the information cocoon, often obtaining single and one-sided information, lack of diversity, the existence of high-quality information identification, screening to prevent the emergence of a significant difference in the ability of false information (Lythreatis et al., 2021).

- **The fourth digital divide**

Also known as the cognitive divide. It is mainly a difference in perception of the role of AI in the digital world, which leads to a gap in the ability to apply AI to the creation and generation of content, as well as in intellectual and knowledge acquisition skills, thus increasing diversity and complexity (Fonseca, 2010). The main manifestations of the cognitive divide in Education are learners' receptive attitudes towards the big models of AI and their subjective motivation to use digital educational tools that match their teaching and learning activities due to a lack of understanding of the technology or avoidance of technological risks.

It is increasingly becoming an essential component of an education ecosystem that is inclusive as a result of the spread of information technology (IT) and the expansion of global digital transformation. Digital resources, tools, and instructional methodologies have gradually become an essential component. In this context, there are gaps between developed and developing countries, between lagging countries, and between different geographic regions within a country or region, such as insufficient infrastructure assumptions, uneven digital literacy, insufficiently built digital resources, and cultural and linguistic differences (Scheerder et al., 2017). These factors can lead to a so-called "digital divide" in Inclusive Education.

1.4 Representations of the Digital Divide in Inclusive Education

1.4.1 Inadequate Infrastructure Development

In the digital era, insufficient infrastructure construction is one of the main reasons for the emergence of the digital divide. This issue directly affects the level of digitalisation and the availability of instructional resources. In impoverished areas, the lack of a dependable, high-speed Internet connection has impeded children's access to sufficient digital learning resources, limiting educational opportunities and experiences, hence exacerbating educational inequality (Bulent, 2003). For example, the China Household Tracking Survey results show that only 85.6 per cent of households in rural China have access to the Internet, and only 35.3 per cent have computer access. Most Chinese households cannot effectively engage in online learning, and low-income households may not be able to afford learning devices such as computers, tablets, or smartphones or pay for a stable Internet connection (Yihua et al., 2013). Meanwhile, during the Xinguang epidemic, low network coverage and unstable signals became important factors affecting the effectiveness of students' online learning (José Sosa Díaz, 2021; Hvan de Werfhorst et al.,2020), and these network connectivity and coverage problems have contributed to the emergence and expansion of the digital divide in Education to some extent.

1.4.2 Uneven Digital Literacy

Digital literacy refers to the ability of learners to use digital technology skillfully and innovatively in work, study, and recreation, and it is an important indicator of the country's ability to improve the quality of its people and enhance its global competitiveness. The large gap in digital literacy skills between students and teachers in digital learning environments, coupled with the lack of a functional and systematic digital literacy assessment framework, has intensified the digital divide in education (Paul Gorski, 2005). The uneven level of digital literacy affects people's ability to access and utilise digital resources and digital technologies, as well as the efficiency of the allocation and use of educational resources. Firstly, teachers and students with low digital literacy cannot effectively search, filter and evaluate information and are limited by the access and quality of information; they are unable to make full use of the Internet and digital resources in the process of inclusive Education, which creates a divide in information access. Secondly, teachers and students with low digital literacy have a limited understanding of the application of education technology. They are unfamiliar with common teaching systems, learning platforms and digital learning tools. Finally, parents' level of digital literacy also affects the quality of their children's Education. Suppose parents lack the necessary skills and knowledge. In that case, they cannot provide effective guidance and support to their children, and some families may even lack the necessary educational resources and training, leading to deficiencies in students' use and understanding of digital educational tools.

Insufficient Construction of Digital Resources

Digital resources refer to various information resources developed to support Education and teaching through technological processing, storage and dissemination, including digital teaching materials, online courses, educational application software, multimedia teaching materials, etc. In the field of Education, insufficient construction of digital resources refers to the lack of sufficient, high-quality, comprehensive and systematic digital learning resources in the process of Education and teaching, such as the lack of differentiated and targeted educational resources, as well as educational resources oriented to new infrastructures (Nicole A. Buzzetto-Hollywood et al.,2018). Firstly, the underdevelopment of digital resources implies a lack of curricular educational content and digital learning resources, which can limit students' access to up-to-date educational materials and diverse learning resources, leading to homogenisation and insufficient quality of educational content, which in turn creates a digital divide between students in different regions. Many digital education resources may be designed primarily for students in economically developed regions, ignoring students' actual needs and levels in less developed regions and failing to consider inclusive Education. Secondly, insufficient technical equipment and software tools will prevent students and teachers from using advanced technologies to support teaching and learning, which may result in students not acquiring basic skills related to digital technologies and being unable to participate in digital teaching and learning activities. More so, students who lack self-management skills may find it difficult to maintain their initiative and motivation to learn in an inclusive education environment. Finally, in districts where digital resources are not built, there may be a lack of online learning platforms and educational applications that provide interactive learning experiences, online quizzes and other educational support functions, thus preventing students from enjoying the convenience and flexibility associated with digital learning.

Cultural and Linguistic Differences

People in different cultures have different levels of understanding and acceptance of digital technologies due to language barriers, differences in educational backgrounds, etc., which leads to their difficulties in accepting some personalised digital educational resources or technologies, and this leads to the emergence of the digital divide in Inclusive Education (Paul Gorski & Christine Clark, 2009). Firstly, the design and content of educational digital resources may not consider different cultural and linguistic backgrounds, resulting in some students being unable to understand or empathise with the educational content, thus reducing their learning outcomes. Secondly, educational resources are only available in a few major languages. In that case, students who speak non-major languages may encounter barriers to comprehension and learning, resulting in these students being unable to engage in digital learning and deepening the digital divide fully. Finally, some educational content may not consider the needs and preferences of students from different cultural backgrounds. Some educational resource content may be available only in certain languages, neglecting the needs of ethnic minority and immigrant students, resulting in linguistic and cultural divides.

Technological Disconnect in Multisensory Learning

Learning in multisensory environments is inclusive and effective in developing learning skills for students with learning disabilities (Mohamad Ahmad Saleem Khasawneh, 2024). Nowadays, multisensory learning is becoming more and more technologically effective with the intervention of digital technology. However, the forms of senses, such as auditory, tactile, and visual, are not well connected. There will be a technological disconnect, so the inequality dilemma faced by special groups such as the visually impaired and hearing impaired in multisensory learning environments will be increasingly magnified by the digital divide. Multisensory learning technologies for AI are more powerful and iterative than traditional technologies. The potential for huge gaps in learners' mastery of different technologies will lead to greater and greater exclusion from smart Education for learners who struggle to afford the expense of the technology and who are on the margins of the technology and in unfavourable scenarios (Gao Yin et al., 2023).

Types and Assessment of Digital Divide in Inclusive Education

The digital divide in Education is not only a simple technological gulf but also has the characteristics of secrecy, secondary and multidimensionality, and has gradually become one of the main bottlenecks that constrain educational equity, educational inclusion, and the promotion of high-quality development of Education under the wave of global digitisation, due to the influence of economic, cultural, and social factors. In this context, eliminating the digital divide in Education has become the main demand for promoting educational equity under the wave of global digitisation. Starting from the elements of teaching and learning, this chapter classifies the education digital divide into three types, namely, digital use divide, digital design divide, and digital connection divide. Sorting out the connotations, influencing factors, and assessment methods of the education digital divide helps to accurately grasp the mechanism and evolution of the digital divide, which is of great significance in eliminating the inclusive education digital divide.

Digital Use Divide

The Digital Use Divide refers to students' unfair treatment in technical support teaching and learning activities. On the one hand, students must actively use technology in their learning and use the tools to analyse, produce, and create. On the other hand, students must use technology passively to complete learning tasks. The digital use divide reflects deep-seated problems at three levels: students' level of competence and application of digital technology, the role of teachers in instructional design and support, and students' attitudes and willingness to use technology. Although the target of this divide is students, it also reflects that the rationality and feasibility of teachers' design of teaching tasks according to the content still needs to be improved.

The specific manifestations are as follows:

- ***Differences in students' competence and level of use of digital technologies***

The digital usage divide highlights the differences in students' competence and level of use of digital technologies (Sima Julian, 2008). A proportion of students possess a high level of digital technology competence and can use digital tools proficiently for learning, analysing, constructing and innovating to improve their learning outcomes and creativity. In contrast, another group of students may be less competent in digital technology, only passively using technology to complete learning tasks and failing to exploit and realise the full potential of digital technology.

- ***Students' attitudes towards and willingness to use technology***

Students' attitudes towards technology and willingness to use it influence the digital use divide in Inclusive Education. Some students have positive attitudes towards technology, are willing to actively explore and learn about new educational tools and applications, and show high levels of technology acceptance and willingness to use. On the contrary, other students may have a lack of interest in technology or a lack of willingness to use it due to psychological barriers to its use, and this difference in attitudes further exacerbates the digital usage divide in Inclusive Education.

- ***Impact of teachers' instructional design and technology support***

The digital divide also reflects the critical role of teachers in instructional design and technical support. Teachers' ability to appropriately incorporate digital technologies into the design of inclusive education teaching and learning tasks, stimulate students' interest in learning and creative thinking and provide appropriate technical support and guidance directly impact students' ability to use digital technologies for learning effectively. Teachers' instructional design and level of support largely determine the effectiveness of students' use of digital technologies.

Measurement and evaluation of the digital use divide is a crucial step in assessing the extent of differences and inequalities in the use of digital technologies among different groups and an important step in bridging the digital divide in Education. Therefore, this chapter presents the importance of measuring and evaluating the digital use divide. By comprehensively analysing students' digital technology competence, students' attitudes towards and willingness to use technology, and teachers' level of instructional design and support, the specific manifestations and deep-rooted causes of the digital use divide in Inclusive Education can be more accurately identified and understood. As per shown in Figure 1; this provides a scientific basis and practical guidance for developing effective intervention strategies to eliminate the digital divide in Education.

Figure 1. Indicators for Assessing the Digital Use Divide

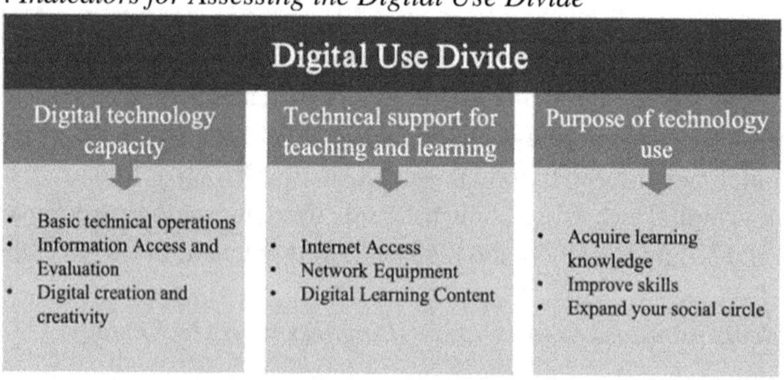

Digital Design divide

The digital design divide refers to inequities in access to professional learning time and support for teachers and educators when designing learning tasks using educational technology. This divide manifests in differences in how teachers design and implement digital instructional content and methods.

The specific manifestations are as follows:

- ***Differences in professional learning time and support***

Teachers often have difficulty obtaining sufficient time and opportunities to engage in professional digital teaching training and support activities. As a result, some teachers cannot update their technology and pedagogy to master digital teaching and learning skills and knowledge fully.

- ***Differences in educational resources and platforms***

The inequalities that exist between various districts and schools in terms of digital educational resources and platforms (Mohamed Ally & Mohammed Samaka, 2013) have a direct impact on the capacity of teachers to implement digital instructional design. It's possible that some school districts and schools offer a wealth of digital teaching tools and platforms, while others might just not have any of these resources available. Such differences in resources and platforms directly impact the quality of instruction and students' learning experiences.

- ***Differences in teachers' design capacity and willingness***

Individual teachers' design capacity and willingness to teach are also important factors affecting the digital design divide in Inclusive Education. Some teachers may have negative attitudes towards inclusive Education, lack the capacity and willingness to do so, and are reluctant to spend time and effort learning and applying digital pedagogies. This difference in attitude and willingness further exacerbates the digital design divide.

Although the digital design divide is directed at teachers, this phenomenon also reflects the government's and schools' inadequacy in providing external support and safeguards for teachers. The government and schools should actively provide more professional learning time and support and narrow the gap in educational resources and platforms. This chapter proposes the importance of measuring and assessing the digital design divide and enhancing teachers' ability and willingness to design inclusive Education to reduce the digital design divide and promote educational equity and quality improvement, as per shown in Figure 2 below.

Figure 2. Indicators for Assessing the Digital Design Divide

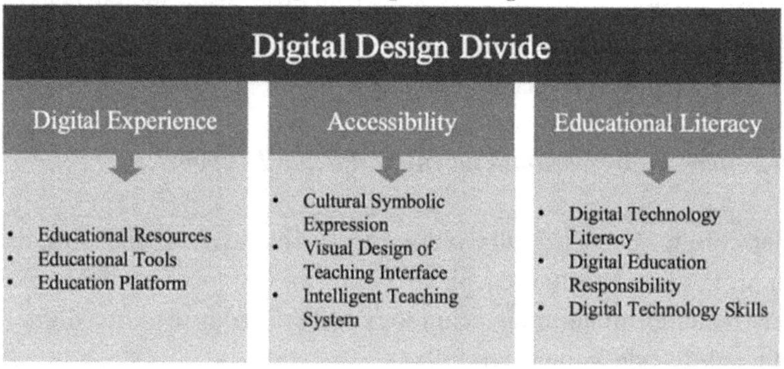

Digital Connectivity Divide

The digital connectivity divide refers to the inequality of opportunity among educators and learners regarding access to Internet connections, digital devices, and digital resources. This divide reflects the gap between those with access to affordable and reliable Internet services and the skills and tools needed to take advantage of them and those without those services and skills (Victoria Coleman, 2021). This divide has a direct impact on the ability of students and educators to equitably access and utilise educational technology, which in turn affects their learning opportunities and educational outcomes, leading to a lack of access to inclusive Education.

The specific manifestations are as follows:

- ***Inequalities in network connectivity***

Some regions and groups may lack stable, high-speed Internet connections or have difficulty affording Internet services. This prevents them from accessing the necessary internet connections, limiting the use of online learning and educational technologies (Arfa Afzal et al., 2023; Daniil Alexandrov et al., 2017).

- ***Inequality in digital devices***

The lack of extensive wired infrastructure in some developing countries and the high cost of internet and device connectivity lead to the potential unavailability of adequate digital devices (Bjorn Hassler et al., 2010), such as broadband, computers, tablets, and smartphones (Judy Block, 2010). Internet services and digital educational resources cannot be used effectively for learning and teaching. This limits the ability of students and educators to utilise digital technologies for learning and teaching, resulting in unequal access to inclusive Education.

- ***Inequality in digital resources***

Some districts and schools may lack adequate educational resources, such as online courses, e-textbooks and educational software. This limits students' and educators' access to quality learning resources, affecting educational effectiveness and learning outcomes (Jackie Ravet & Peter Mtika, 2024; Prince Sah et al., 2024).

The digital connectivity divide reflects differences and inequalities between teachers and students regarding network connectivity, digital devices, digital resources and skills. This phenomenon seriously affects equity and the level of inclusive Education. This chapter proposes that scientific assessment can be used to understand the specific causes of the digital access divide, which can help to develop effective interventions to enhance the accessibility and efficiency of the use of digital resources and promote the quality of inclusive Education, as per seen in Figure 3.

Figure 3. Indicators for Assessing the Digital Connectivity Divide

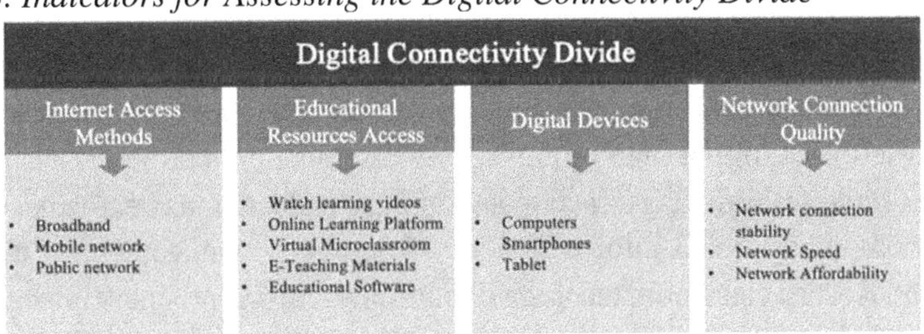

Strategies for Using Emerging Technologies to Bridge the Technological Divide in Inclusive Education

Digital inclusion aims to enable everyone to effectively acquire digital skills and access and use digital technologies, not just to own a computer or a smartphone.

Smart Upgrading of Digital Infrastructure

Explore using emerging technologies and resources like virtual simulation and digital twins to create teaching scenarios and solve students' learning challenges. Design and develop smart education virtual services, setting up employment services, examination services, degree qualifications, study abroad services and other sections to effectively promote student employment and entrepreneurship and provide an inclusive education environment. Upgrading science and technology provides a strong guarantee for inclusive Education (Drew Tiene, 2010). Especially with the development of artificial intelligence in recent years, technologies such as text recognition, speech recognition, user profiling, intelligent matching, social robots, virtual assistants, knowledge mapping, etc., can more effectively support the realisation of information accessibility in inclusive education environments. To achieve better information access and education effects for disadvantaged groups, including physically, culturally, and knowledge-disadvantaged groups.

Digital Governance for Inclusive Education

On the one hand, campus intelligent governance. Campus intelligent governance refers to the promotion of campus digital governance through the integration and sharing of campus government information, including the construction of a campus reality model, real-time monitoring, detection and updating of campus environment information, and the deep integration of virtual and real scenes. Through campus equipment management and centralised control system monitoring, it manages the operation of campus technical facilities and improves the efficiency of facility operation and maintenance. On the other hand, classroom intelligent governance includes the construction of digital twin virtual space. Establishing a three-dimensional holographic, high-definition, interactive and inclusive classroom, real-time detection of classroom environment information, and intelligent management of classroom equipment. Record classroom teaching conditions, intelligently generate classroom observation reports, and portray teachers' teaching trajectories and students' learning dynamics. Intelligent classroom management is conducive to helping teachers review and reflect on classroom teaching, which is very important for inclusive education teaching (Alexis Adriana Lozano & Jesus Izquierdo, 2019).

Teaching and Learning for Information Accessibility

Firstly, diversified teaching methods are adopted according to the differences in students' special needs, cognitive abilities, language skills, learning styles and preferences, including hierarchical tasks, multiple learning activity pathways, and dynamic adjustment of teaching contents. Project-based learning, multisensory material presentation, individual counselling, etc., are adopted to help students learn in the way that best suits them and to bring into play the cognitive strengths of their respective differences.

Secondly, information technology, including smart classrooms, interactive whiteboards and teaching software, is used to adapt the presentation of teaching content promptly so that it is accessible to students of different abilities. Assistive technologies, including input technologies (adaptive keyboards, computer input controls, voice input and dictation software) and output technologies (screen readers, sensing technologies, amplifiers and speech recorders), can broaden participation, and technology-supported inclusive Education can indeed enhance the participation in learning of children with special needs, disabilities and others.

Finally, educational software and apps support students' personalised learning (Segarani Naidoo, 2012)). For example, language learning and learning logging software are designed to cater to differences in learning rates and styles of students of different ability levels. Ultimately, the effectiveness of inclusive Education is reflected in the fact that all students can maximise their development within their respective potentials. The use of technology in inclusive Education is, therefore, not a substitute for students' efforts but rather enhances their capabilities and facilitates their participation and learning.

Comprehensive and Inclusive Development of Digital Educational Resources

First, proactively address possible deviations in the training of AI models and make every effort to avoid possible harm and threats posed by AI based on a full understanding of legal responsibilities.

Second, respect the diversity of children's groups and individual development, recognise the laws of children's cognitive development, respect cognitive differences, and incorporate feedback from children and young people into the development cycle and testing of educational technology products to enhance the inclusiveness and adaptability of AI digital education.

Third, adhere to responsible development, design educational technology products suitable for children's age and cognitive development, and follow educational principles in line with the latest learning sciences and the developmental characteristics of children and adolescents to support the healthy growth and sustainable development of students.

Fourth, regarding the safety of educational technology products, most users are students who are not yet mentally mature. To. To ensure that AI digital education will not cause any cognitive or emotional harm to users, to meet the requirements of cybersecurity, to respect and protect the privacy of users and the security of their data, to control the possibility of technological abuse, and to develop measures to reduce the phenomenon of addiction.

Fifth, the design and operation mechanisms are transparent and explainable, and all team members involved in the AI education product can explain the workings and uses of this digital Education to beginners and non-specialists. This ensures that all digital learning resources are easily understood and mastered (Regina Luttrell, 2020).

Educational Learning Analytics Techniques for Collecting Data on Educational Use Processes

Key technologies that are relatively well-established in the application of educational learning analytics include network analytics, discourse analytics and content analytics. Network analytics emphasises interpersonal interaction and can be used to identify the characteristics of online learners' roles and extract information about teachers', students' and textbooks' interactions, thus providing targeted support. Discourse analysis focuses on the analysis of discourse and text. It can be used to explore the textual meanings behind the discourse in digital education use and identify the process of knowledge construction. Content analytics is gradually shifting to the analysis of multimedia content, which can analyse learners' learning patterns through quantitative data and predict learners' behaviour in using digital Education through qualitative analysis. In addition, the interaction data of Education can be recorded from multiple perspectives, including the number of visits to teaching resources, the types of devices accessed in online and offline modes, the time spent on accessing, the number of hypertext links accessed, the total number of bookmarks, and the data from different channels can broaden the path of intelligent learning, and the data from these diversified sources can be imported into the same analytical framework for computation.

Visualisation Technology Portrays the use of Inclusive Education Resources

1. The service object of inclusive Education is mainly teachers and students, and using visualisation technology to portray educational content can present more humanistic and intuitive statistical results (Ben Williamson, 2015). Using information processing capabilities, the massive data in the educational resources are presented as scatter diagrams, flow charts, mind maps, knowledge maps and so on. Aided by the reorganisation and unification of educational resources with interactive technology, visualisation technology can be inclusive for students to interpret the data better and for teachers to understand the teaching rules better. In addition,

using visualisation technology to dismantle specific knowledge points, rather than fragmentation, does not destroy the integrity and logic of knowledge students based on learning objectives and learning preferences. It is a string of knowledge points in line with their learning cognitive habits. It is conducive to students' information processing of knowledge points and can also transform how students understand and remember. Thus, by promoting the continuous improvement of teachers' teaching and students' learning behaviour in inclusive Education, teachers and students can easily master the information within digital educational resources and enhance their perception and control of digital media.

Robust Multisensory Learning to Reshape the Underlying Cognition of Inclusive Education

Developing and designing sensory curriculum and system strategies, including sensory needs analysis, technology development, and curricula that rely on sensory technologies to support the cultivation and development of student's cognitive, metacognitive, and social interaction skills. Improve sensory articulation between multisensory learning and robust multisensory learning with creativity, ethics, emotions, vitality, and critical thinking as core elements. To design a multisensory learning goal system and action plan for inclusive Education, focusing on the stimulation of learners' multisensory potential, the activation of reflective consciousness, the cultivation of an independent personality, and injecting the concept of inclusive Education into the technological structure of the sensory layer. We construct a symbiotic relationship between humans and machines, realise the mutual benefit and integration of technological intelligence and human intelligence, and help learners reasonably cope with the risk of learning bundles under technological manipulation and the digital divide caused by it. In addition, we will go deep into underdeveloped areas, rural areas and AI-disadvantaged groups, starting from the perspective and position of the main body of Inclusive Education and breaking away from the previous top-down perspective of examining and practising the sensory-technological layer of Inclusive Education. We pay attention to the sensory technology demands of learners, focus on intelligent technology by special student groups, and take the initiative to connect relevant enterprises to design corresponding sensory education products for special students.

Case Studies: Digital Textbooks for Inclusive Education

The United Nations Children's Fund (UNICEF) launched the Accessible Digital Textbooks for All Initiative. Accessible digital books are digital tools that make information accessible to all learners. The programmer aims to guarantee equal access to quality education by making digital textbooks available to all students in all circumstances and at a reasonable cost. The programmer is piloted in nine countries and territories in East and Southern Africa, Latin America and the Caribbean: Kenya, Uganda, Rwanda, the Dominican Republic, Colombia, Jamaica, Nicaragua, Paraguay and Uruguay. Accessible digital textbooks fully implement the aim of inclusive Education, from the design concept to the concrete practice, always with the promotion of comprehensive human development and the rational application of technological innovation as the ultimate goal and core content.

The non-profit CK-12 Foundation is a free digital educational resource developed in the United States. It aims to increase access to high-quality educational materials by providing free and open access to STEM (science, technology, engineering, maths) educational content in English, history and economics.

CK-12's FlexBook textbook authoring system is an online platform for assembling, creating, and distributing interactive and multi-modal content. FlexBook offers a range of flexible features designed to provide users with a richer and more interactive reading experience through an enhanced digital textbook experience. to meet the needs of different users, especially teachers and students in the field of Education. The following are the key features of FlexBook:

- **Content customisation**

Teachers and students can edit textbook content according to their needs, add or delete chapters, insert multimedia elements, and more to create personalised textbooks. Users can also adjust the layout of text, images, videos, and other content to align the textbook with specific teaching or learning needs.

- **Multimedia Integration**

It supports embedding video and audio files in textbooks to enhance the learning experience and comprehension. It will also include interactive exercises, quizzes, and simulation experiments to help students consolidate what they have learned through practice.

- **Cross-platform access**

FlexBook can be used on different devices, including computers, tablets, and smartphones, enabling learning anytime, anywhere. Users' editing, notes and progress can be synchronised via the cloud and switched seamlessly between different devices.

- **Collaboration and sharing features**

Teachers can share customised textbooks with students or other teachers with real-time collaboration and feedback. Teachers can create classes, assign textbooks and homework, and track student progress and performance.

- **Assessment and Analysis:**

With embedded quizzes and exercises, students can get instant feedback on their learning status. Detailed learning data analysis is provided to help teachers understand students' learning behaviours and weaknesses for targeted tutoring.

- **Teaching Resource Library**

FlexBook provides many pre-produced teaching materials and resources covering different subjects and grades for teachers to choose from and use. The platform also contains many Open Educational Resources (OER) that users can use and modify.

- **Accessible design**

Supporting a wide range of learning styles and needs, including visually and hearing impaired students, provides a barrier-free learning environment. Multiple languages are supported to facilitate students with different language backgrounds.

Accessible digital textbooks can improve the learning attitudes of children with disabilities and enhance mutual communication among students. Digital textbooks are open, relying on the Internet, digital media, big data, and other technological means, integrating teaching materials, digital resources, subject tools, and application data (Nerea Rodríguez & Jesús Rodríguez Rodríguez, 2015). The usability of the interface of digital textbooks is critical to the effectiveness of its use by students. Research has been conducted to improve the usability of the user interface and thus facilitate the user's operation and learning process by improving the usability design elements identified by iterative design and evaluation models (Cheolil Lim, Hae-Deok Song & Yekyung Lee, 2012). Powerful technological enablers enable digital textbooks to be used in various scenarios where knowledge and information are transmitted and circulated across various media and endpoints, relying on the power of multiple media to present, preserve, and disseminate knowledge and information.

Ethical Considerations and Challenges

Educational Knowledge Content

With the intervention of emerging technologies, knowledge production, presentation, and access to knowledge in inclusive Education have become more convenient and active. However, students' participation in the process can make it unclear what real knowledge and supporting information are due to the hierarchical nature of the technology and the different understandings and constructions of knowledge by each user, which may lead to an ever-increasing expansion of educational content.

Education and Ethics

The potential content risks of digitally inclusive Education must be effectively prevented and controlled, and the review of educational content needs to be strengthened. The review should cover, among other things, whether the educational content meets the learning needs of all people and provides diverse learning options, particularly the standard requirements of disadvantaged groups. Educational content should be in line with the formal basic education system.

Technology Adaptation and Sustainability

Emerging technologies intervene in Inclusive Education and the use of newer iterations of information technology. Nowadays, digital technology is developing more and more rapidly, and the information technology updating and replacement cycle is getting shorter and shorter. The problem of system version compatibility affects the use of content in Inclusive Education. In this case, the issue of education system design is particularly important, as well as the need for teachers and students to receive continuous training to update their knowledge of information technology.

Technology Security

Emerging technologies intervene in the issue of technological security in Inclusive Education. Some of the content of inclusive Education belongs to open and shared digital educational resources. With the increase in the use of user data, there is a risk of implanting some illegal information and spreading undesirable information, making the boundaries of learning uncertain. For example, taking digital textbooks as an example, students learn content is stored in remote servers, requiring multiple nodes to be forwarded to the teacher and student receivers; various access security issues need to be considered in multiple nodes.

Operationalisation of Multisensory Technologies

The phenomenon of technological disconnect has been addressed in the manifestation of the digital divide in Inclusive Education. Therefore, special groups of learners, such as the hearing and visually impaired, need to be considered in the design of technology operability for multisensory learning.

CONCLUSION

This chapter explores the digital divide in Inclusive Education, analyses the manifestations and assessment methods of the digital use divide, digital design divide and digital connectivity divide, and proposes specific strategies for bridging the technological divide using multisensory learning and emerging technologies. This chapter specifically proposes six strategies: using emerging technologies to establish intelligent upgrading of digital infrastructure, digital governance for inclusive Education, information-accessible teaching and learning, a comprehensive and inclusive conception of the development of digital educational resources, the use of educational learning analytics to collect data on the educational use process, the use of visualisation technologies to portray the use of digital educational resources and sound multisensory learning to reshape the underlying cognition of Inclusive Education. In the process of implementation, there is a need to focus on the content of educational knowledge, privacy and data security, ensure equity and fairness, enhance technological adaptability, security and sustainability, and strengthen ethical Education and moral norms in order to achieve true equity and high-quality development of inclusive Education. Towards the Education 2030 vision, the use of emerging technologies to bridge the digital divide in Inclusive Education should be strengthened in order to promote high-quality and inclusive development of Education globally.

References

Afzal, A., Khan, S., Daud, S., Ahmad, Z., & Butt, A. (2023). Addressing the digital divide: Access and use of technology in Education. *Journal of Social Sciences Review*, 3(2), 883–895. DOI: 10.54183/jssr.v3i2.326

Ainscow, M., & César, M. (2006). Inclusive Education ten years after Salamanca: Setting the agenda. *European Journal of Psychology of Education*, 21(3), 231–238. DOI: 10.1007/BF03173412

Ainscow, M., & Sandill, A. (2010). Developing inclusive education systems: The role of organisational cultures and leadership. *International Journal of Inclusive Education*, 14(4), 401–416. DOI: 10.1080/13603110802504903

AlexandrovD., IvaniushinaV., & SimanovskiyD. (2017). Online Educational Resources for Schoolchildren and the Digital Divide. Voprosy Obrazovaniya / Educational Studies Moscow, (3), 183-201. DOI: 10.17323/1814-9545-2017-3-183-201

Ally, M., & Samaka, M. (2013). Open Education Resources and Mobile Technology to Narrow the Learning Divide. *International Review of Research in Open and Distance Learning*, 14(2), 14–27. DOI: 10.19173/irrodl.v14i2.1530

Apalkova, S. T. V., & Tsyganov, S. (2016). Digital Economy: a new paradigm of global information society. Economic Review, Ekonomické rozh, 295-311.

Block, J. (2010). Distance education and the digital divide: An academic perspective. *Online Journal of Distance Learning Administration*, 13(1).

Bondarenko, V., & Aleshkovski, I. (2019). Social and economic development models in the digital transformation era. *Journal of Economic Science Research*, 2(1). Advance online publication. DOI: 10.30564/jesr.v2i1.468

Buzzetto-Hollywood, N. A., Elobeid, M., & Elobaid, M. E. (2018). Addressing information literacy and the digital divide in higher Education. Interdisciplinary Journal of e-Skills and Lifelong Learning, 14, 077-093.

Coleman, T. (2021). Digital divide in UK education during COVID-19 pandemic: Literature review.

Corbett, J. (2002). *Supporting inclusive Education*. Routledge. DOI: 10.4324/9780203453339

Cullen, R. (2001). Addressing the digital divide. *Online Information Review*, 25(5), 311–320. DOI: 10.1108/14684520110410517

Dewan, S., & Riggins, F. J. (2005). The digital divide: Current and future research directions. *Journal of the Association for Information Systems*, 6(12), 298–337. DOI: 10.17705/1jais.00074

Díaz, S., & José, M. (2021). Emergency Remote Education, Family Support and the Digital Divide in the Context of the COVID-19 Lockdown. *International Journal of Environmental Research and Public Health*, 18(15), 7956. DOI: 10.3390/ijerph18157956 PMID: 34360248

Engelbrecht, J., & Borba, M. C. (2024). Recent developments in using digital technology in mathematics education. *ZDM Mathematics Education*, 56(2), 281–292. DOI: 10.1007/s11858-023-01530-2

Felder, F. (2019). Inclusive Education, the dilemma of identity and the common good. *Theory and Research in Education*, 17(2), 213–228. DOI: 10.1177/1477878519871429

Fonseca, C. (2010). The digital divide and the cognitive divide: Reflections on the challenge of human development in the digital age. Information Technologies & International Development, 6(SE), pp-25.

Gao, Y. & Zeng, W. G.. (2023). Higher Education in the age of digital intelligence: risk generation and structured regulation. Research on Higher Engineering Education (06), 92-98. doi:CNKI:SUN:GDGJ.0.2023-06-015.

Gorski, P. (2005). Education equity and the digital divide. [Formerly AACE Journal]. *AACE Review*, 13(1), 3–45.

Gorski, P., & Clark, C. (2002). Multicultural Education and the digital divide: Focus on language. *Multicultural Perspectives*, 4(2), 30–34. DOI: 10.1207/S15327892MCP0402_7

Graham, L. J. (2020). Inclusive Education in the 21st century. In Inclusive Education for the 21st century (pp. 3-26). Routledge.

Hargittai, E. (2001). Second-level digital divide: Mapping differences in people's online skills. arXiv preprint cs/0109068.

Hassler, B., & McNeil Jackson, A. M. (2010, April-June). Bridging the Bandwidth Gap: Open Educational Resources and the Digital Divide. *IEEE Transactions on Learning Technologies*, 3(2), 110–115. DOI: 10.1109/TLT.2010.8

Javaid, M., Haleem, A., Singh, R. P., & Sinha, A. K. (2024). Digital economy to improve the culture of industry 4.0: A study on features, implementation and challenges. Green Technologies and Sustainability, 100083.

Leijen, Ä., Arcidiacono, F., & Baucal, A. (2021). The dilemma of inclusive Education: Inclusion for some or inclusion for all. *Frontiers in Psychology*, 12, 633066. DOI: 10.3389/fpsyg.2021.633066 PMID: 34566742

Lim, C., Song, H. D., & Lee, Y. (2012). Improving the usability of the user interface for a digital textbook platform for elementary-school students. *Educational Technology Research and Development*, 60(1), 159–173. DOI: 10.1007/s11423-011-9222-5

Lozano, A. A., & Izquierdo, J. (2019). Technology in Second Language Education: Overcoming the Digital Divide. *Emerging Trends in Education*, 2(3). Advance online publication. DOI: 10.19136/etie.a2n3.3250

Luttrell, R., Wallace, A., McCollough, C., & Lee, J. (2020). The digital divide: Addressing artificial intelligence in communication education. *Journalism & Mass Communication Educator*, 75(4), 470–482. DOI: 10.1177/1077695820925286

Lythreatis, S., Singh, S. K., & El-Kassar, A. N. (2022). The digital divide: A review and future research agenda. *Technological Forecasting and Social Change*, 175, 121359. DOI: 10.1016/j.techfore.2021.121359

Macgilchrist, F., Allert, H., Cerratto Pargman, T., & Jarke, J. (2024). Designing Postdigital Futures: Which Designs? Whose Futures? *Postdigit Sci Educ*, 6(1), 13–24. DOI: 10.1007/s42438-022-00389-y

Messiou, K. (2016). Research in the field of inclusive Education: Time for a rethink?*. *International Journal of Inclusive Education*, 21(2), 146–159. DOI: 10.1080/13603116.2016.1223184

Mohamad Ahmad Saleem Khasawneh. (2024). The Role of the Multisensory Environment in Developing Learning Skills Among Students with Learning Difficulties in the Asir Region. *Kurdish Studies, 12*(1). Retrieved from https://kurdishstudies.net/menu-script/index.php/KS/article/view/1433

Naidoo, S., & Raju, J. (2012). Impact of the digital divide on information literacy training in a higher education context. *South African Journal of Library and Information Science*, 78(1), 34–44. DOI: 10.7553/78-1-46

Peruzzo, F., & Allan, J. (2022). Rethinking inclusive (digital) Education: Lessons from the pandemic to reconceptualise inclusion through convivial technologies. *Learning, Media and Technology*, 49(2), 244–258. DOI: 10.1080/17439884.2022.2131817

Ravet, J., & Mtika, P. (2021). Educational inclusion in resource-constrained contexts: A study of rural primary schools in Cambodia. *International Journal of Inclusive Education*, 28(1), 16–37. DOI: 10.1080/13603116.2021.1916104

Rodríguez, N., & Rodríguez, J. R. (2015). The digital textbook: a look at the current state of the art. In *Digital Textbooks: what's new?* (pp. 9–51). Servicio de Publicaciones e Intercambio Científico.

Sah, P., Sah, R., Sahani, S. K., & Sahani, K. (2024). Study and Analysis of Education System in Nepal and Its Challenges Along with Its Solution. *Mikailalsys Journal of Advanced Engineering International*, 1(1), 33–42. DOI: 10.58578/mjaei.v1i1.2792

Scheerder, A., Van Deursen, A., & Van Dijk, J. (2017). Determinants of Internet skills, uses and outcomes. A systematic review of the second-and third-level digital divide. *Telematics and Informatics*, 34(8), 1607–1624. DOI: 10.1016/j.tele.2017.07.007

Sims, J., Vidgen, R., & Powell, P. (2008). E-learning and the digital divide: Perpetuating cultural and socio-economic elitism in higher Education. *Communications of the Association for Information Systems*, 22(1). Advance online publication. DOI: 10.17705/1CAIS.02223

Tarman, B. (2003). *The Digital Divide in Education.* Online Submission.

Tiene, D. (2002). Addressing the Global Digital Divide and its Impact on Educational Opportunity. *Educational Media International*, 39(3–4), 212–222. DOI: 10.1080/09523980210166440

UNESCO. (2020). *"Towards inclusion in education: status, trends and challenges," in The UNESCO Salamanca Statement 25 Years on*. UNESCO.

van de Werfhorst, H. G., Kessenich, E., & Geven, S. (2020, August 18). The Digital Divide in Online Education. Inequality in Digital Preparedness of Students and Schools before the Start of the COVID-19 Pandemic. DOI: 10.31235/osf.io/58d6p

Van Dijk, J. A. (2006). Digital divide research, achievements and shortcomings. *Poetics*, 34(4-5), 221–235. DOI: 10.1016/j.poetic.2006.05.004

Wei, K. K., Teo, H. H., Chan, H. C., & Tan, B. C. (2011). Conceptualising and testing a social cognitive model of the digital divide. *Information Systems Research*, 22(1), 170–187. DOI: 10.1287/isre.1090.0273

Williamson, B. (2015). Digital education governance: Data visualisation, predictive analytics, and 'real-time' policy instruments. *Journal of Education Policy*, 31(2), 123–141. DOI: 10.1080/02680939.2015.1035758

Yang, Y., Hu, X., Qu, Q., Lai, F., Shi, Y., Boswell, M., & Rozelle, S. (2013). Roots of tomorrow's digital divide: Documenting computer use and internet access in China's elementary schools today. *China & World Economy*, 21(3), 61–79. DOI: 10.1111/j.1749-124X.2013.12022.x

Chapter 10

Democratizing Education in Rural Nigeria Through AI and Mobile Technologies as a Transformative Pathway to Inclusive Learning

Damola Olugbade
https://orcid.org/0000-0003-3938-6273
First Technical University, Nigeria

ABSTRACT

In rural Nigeria, access to quality education is still a challenge that needs attention, as there are numerous hindrances to the attainment of knowledge. This chapter suggests a transformative paradigm shift that leverages the confluence between artificial intelligence (AI) and mobile technologies in democratizing education and promoting inclusive learning environments. This chapter imagines a future where the gap between digital technology haves and have-nots, will have been closed, by discussing AI powered mobile applications that transcend borders of both geography and economics. The chapter proposes taking advantage of existing telecommunication infrastructure to deliver educational content and facilitate virtual classrooms as mobile devices have become ubiquitous even in remote areas. We imagine a future that sees the removal of barriers such as geography, language and socio-economic status, enabling every Nigerian child access quality education.

DOI: 10.4018/979-8-3693-7255-5.ch010

INTRODUCTION

The education system in rural Nigeria faces numerous challenges, preventing many students from accessing quality education. Factors such as geographical isolation, lack of infrastructure, and limited resources have led to significant educational disparities (Ama et al., 2020; Andries et al., 2022). To address these issues, this chapter explores the potential of combining artificial intelligence (AI) with mobile technology to create a more inclusive and democratic educational system. By leveraging AI-powered mobile applications, learning can become more accessible, allowing students to overcome traditional barriers and access personalized learning pathways tailored to their individual needs and learning styles. This approach not only addresses the digital divide but also holds promise for reshaping education in rural areas.

The democratization of education through technology is not a new concept, but its application in rural Nigeria presents both complexities and opportunities. Integrating AI with mobile technology offers solutions to specific educational gaps, enabling remote learners to benefit from the same quality of education as their urban counterparts. This chapter critically examines the current educational system in rural Nigeria, explores the technological options available, and evaluates how these innovations can transform learning in the country. By analyzing the role of AI in education, this chapter provides insights into the potential for technological advancements to address rural education challenges, such as limited access to qualified teachers, outdated curricula, and insufficient learning resources (Pedro et al., 2019; Jatileni et al., 2023).

Education is a fundamental human right and a driver of social and economic development (Schultz, 1964; Wringe, 1986). The right to education in a globalized world has been a subject of increasing importance in international education discourse (Lindahl, 2006). Ensuring equitable access to quality education is essential for Nigeria's overall growth, especially in rural regions where educational inequalities are most pronounced (Adeniran et al., 2020). This chapter highlights the critical elements of technological advancements, such as AI-aided tutoring systems, multilingual language translation, and the use of existing telecommunication infrastructure, in creating an inclusive educational ecosystem. It also discusses the challenges and limitations of implementing these technologies in rural Nigeria and offers policy recommendations to actualize this vision. Ultimately, this chapter serves as a guide for policymakers, educators, and technologists, offering strategies for creating a sustainable, AI-powered education system that benefits all Nigerian students, regardless of their socio-economic or geographical background.

The Present State of Rural Education in Nigeria

Rural Nigeria is characterized by significant educational inequalities. These disparities manifest themselves as insufficient teaching staff; lack of school facilities such as libraries and laboratories; and challenges in accessing educational resources (Olatunji & Ajayi, 2016). Many children in these areas are missing out on quality education hence they have considerable gaps in their knowledge base and skills compared to their urban counterparts (Olatunji & Ajayi, 2016). Solving these challenges demands innovative approaches that can bridge this gap by providing equal learning opportunities for all learners.

Moreover, the concept of inclusive education in Nigeria has been a subject of debate, with some scholars questioning whether it's a myth or reality (Adetoro, 2014). To fully comprehend the scope of the challenges faced by rural Nigerian communities in their pursuit of education, it is vital to explore various key obstacles. Firstly, infrastructure deficiencies are a significant issue. Many rural schools lack essential facilities such as proper classrooms, electricity, and sanitation. According to studies by UBEC (2014) and Tooley (2021), over half of rural primary schools in Nigeria do not have appropriate classroom structures, forcing students to learn under trees or in dilapidated buildings. The lack of infrastructure not only hampers the learning process but also presents security concerns for both students and teachers. Without basic amenities, these schools struggle to provide a conducive learning environment, exacerbating the educational divide between rural and urban areas.

Secondly, the shortage and quality of teachers represent another major challenge. Low salaries, poor living conditions, and limited opportunities for professional development make it difficult to attract and retain qualified teachers in rural areas (Monk, 2007). As a result, many rural schools face extreme student-to-teacher ratios, with some exceeding 100:1, far above UNESCO's recommended ratio of 40:1 (Ihebom & Uko, 2020). Furthermore, many teachers in remote areas lack proper training, which compromises the quality of education delivered. The insufficient number of skilled educators leads to overburdened teachers and negatively impacts student performance. Addressing this issue requires systematic efforts to improve teacher training, remuneration, and living conditions in rural areas.

Thirdly, rural schools suffer from a restricted availability of learning resources. According to a survey by the Nigerian Educational Research and Development Council (NERDC, 2013), in some rural areas, as many as ten students share a single textbook. This shortage of educational materials severely hampers students' ability to engage with the curriculum. Additionally, the socio-economic conditions in rural Nigeria contribute to the problem. Many families live in poverty, which forces children into child labor or early marriage, further limiting their access to education. Recent reports from UNICEF (2014, 2018) reveal that nearly 10.5 million children between the ages of five and fourteen are out of school, with the majority being from rural areas. This socio-economic disadvantage, combined with other factors such as cultural and language barriers, hinders students' ability to perform well academically. Many rural communities speak indigenous languages, making it difficult for students to understand lessons taught in English (Egberi & Madubueze, 2023). Furthermore, poor access to technology and the internet in rural areas deepens the educational divide, leaving students unable to benefit from online resources that are increasingly available in urban areas

These challenges create a complex web of obstacles that hinder provision of quality education in rural Nigeria. This, however, widens the educational gap between rural and urban areas leading to perpetuation of economic and social inequalities. Addressing these issues through traditional means alone has proven insufficient. The scale and complexity of the problem call for innovative solutions that can leapfrog over existing infrastructural and resource constraints. This is where AI and mobile technologies come into play as they open up new avenues to democratize education and foster more inclusive learning environments in rural Nigeria. The use of these technologies allows us to rethink education delivery towards more flexible, personalized, and accessible approaches. To this end, let us look at how AI can be leveraged alongside mobile technology to deal with these issues and transform the educational landscape in rural Nigeria.

AI And Mobile Personalized Learning: Worldwide View

The integration of artificial intelligence (AI) and mobile technologies in personalized learning has become a prominent trend in global educational landscapes. As shown in Table 1, highlighted collection of studies from 2020 to 2024 that examine different approaches indicates contributions of AI-powered mobile personalized learning across diverse educational settings. For instance, Baba, Faddouli, and Cheimanoff (2024) conducted a case study at Mohammed VI Polytechnic University, emphasizing the transformative potential of AI-driven personalized mobile learning in higher education. Their work underscores the need for continuous innovation to enhance both the usefulness and effectiveness of such systems. Similarly, Charles (2023) explored the role of AI-powered mobile education for New Zealand students, demonstrating how individualized content and recommendations can significantly improve students' learning experiences. The overarching theme across these studies is the recognition that mobile learning platforms, enhanced with AI, provide a responsive and adaptive educational environment that caters to individual learner needs.

A significant focus in recent research revolves around the development and improvement of AI-driven personalized learning systems. Hashim et al. (2022) conducted a systematic review that identified key factors contributing to the success of personalized learning systems, providing valuable insights into personal traits and technology trends essential for the development of adaptive learning environments. Similarly, Zhang (2022) focused on the technical aspects by constructing a personalized learning platform using a collaborative filtering algorithm. These contributions are crucial for enhancing the technical foundation of personalized learning systems and ensuring they cater effectively to diverse learner profiles. Additionally, Song, Tan, and Awang (2021) introduced the Mobile-Assisted Personalized Learning (MAPL) model, which focuses on addressing educational equity during full-distance learning through personalized education. This model represents a significant step towards closing the digital divide, ensuring all learners, regardless of socio-economic background, benefit from personalized mobile learning technologies.

In the broader context of AI-powered education, there is a growing interest in the pedagogical implications and future trends of personalized learning. Maghsudi et al. (2021) reviewed the challenges of AI/ML-based personalized education, discussing potential solutions for overcoming technical and ethical concerns. Meanwhile, studies like those by Dave Miller (2023) and Coolsaet (2024) explore the future educational prospects of Generation Alpha, examining how their entrepreneurial disposition and rapid information processing can influence higher education pedagogies. These studies collectively emphasize the necessity for educational institutions to adapt to technological advancements to meet the needs of this new generation of learners. The integration of AI and mobile technologies in personalized learning represents not just an evolution in educational technology but a potential revolution in creating more inclusive, adaptive, and responsive learning environments worldwide.

Table 1. Quality evaluation results (2020-2024)

Title	Authors	Year	Citation	Ref	Contributions
Mobile-Optimized AI-Driven Personalized Learning: A Case Study at Mohammed VI Polytechnic University.	Baba, K., Faddouli, E., & Cheimanoff, N.	2024	2	35	This study supports the potential of AI-driven personalized mobile learning in higher education but also emphasizes the importance of continuous innovation to improve its usefulness and effectiveness.
Trends on technologies and artificial intelligence in education for personalized learning: systematic literature	Hashim, S., Omar, M. K., Ab Jalil, H., & Sharef, N. M.	2022	38	48	The study shows how personalized learning was used and factors that made it work, thus the finding of this paper will guide other researchers to recognize various personal traits and the identification of appropriate technology trends and activities for further studies, as well as assist developers in the development of the personalized learning system and closely related to the adaptive learning systems.

continued on following page

Table 1. Continued

Title	Authors	Year	Citation	Ref	Contributions
Personalized education in the artificial intelligence era: what to expect next	Maghsudi, S., Lan, A., Xu, J., & van Der Schaar, M.	2021	154	64	In this article, while providing a brief review of state-of-the-art research, they investigated the challenges of AI/ML-based personalized education and discuss potential solutions.
Construction of personalized learning platform based on collaborative filtering algorithm	Zhang, Q.	2022	16	25	This paper primarily focuses on developing a personalized learning platform based on the CF (collaborative filtering) algorithm, as well as conducting system requirements analysis, database design, functional module design, implementation, and testing on this foundation.
Generic digital equity model in education: Mobile-assisted personalized learning (MAPL) through e-modules	Song, S. J., Tan, K. H., & Awang, M. M.	2021	28	79	On the basis of the shortcomings found in a review of past studies, this scoping review introduces adapted model mobile-assisted personalized learning (MAPL), which focused on full distance learning using the personalized learning (PL) concept. The findings indicate that MAPL could be a viable solution for achieving equity in education for every learner during full-fledged distance learning.
Trends and development in technology-enhanced adaptive/personalized learning: A systematic review of journal publications from 2007 to 2017	Xie, H., Chu, H. C., Hwang, G. J., & Wang, C. C.	2019	602	67	A comprehensive coding scheme is developed based on the constructivism. Research issues like learning supports, learning outcomes and so on are addressed. The results in all categories of the coding scheme are discussed. Future trends and applications of adaptive/personalized learning are analyzed.
A personalized learning system-supported professional training model for teachers' TPACK development	Chaipidech, P., Srisawasdi, N., Kajornmanee, T., & Chaipah, K.	2022	77	42	One hundred sixty-one in-service science teachers from 92 secondary schools located Northeastern region of Thailand voluntarily participated in the proposed TPD program. Results indicated that the in-service teachers significantly improved their TPACK
AI-Powered Personalized Mobile Education for New Zealand Students	F. Charles	2023	5	44	AI-powered personalized mobile education for New Zealand students can improve their learning experience by tailoring content and recommendations based on individual preferences.
Enhancing User Experience in E-Learning: Real-Time Emotional Analysis and Assessment	Julien Dave	2023	2	31	Real-time non-invasive tools for assessing emotional reactions in e-learning platforms are more comprehensive and reliable, potentially enhancing user satisfaction and learning outcomes.
Exploring the Role of Personalization in Adaptive Learning Environments	Alex Graf	2023	2	33	Personalization in adaptive learning environments enhances user experience and educational outcomes by tailoring content and strategies to individual learners.

continued on following page

Table 1. Continued

Title	Authors	Year	Citation	Ref	Contributions
Embracing the Technological Metamorphosis: Envisioning Higher Education for Generation Alpha in a Shifting Educational Landscape	Dave Miller	2023	12	41	Generation Alpha's entrepreneurial disposition and rapid information processing can shape future higher education pedagogical paradigms, requiring institutions to adapt to technological advancements and adapt to their unique needs.
The Impact of Technological Advancements on Higher Education: A Study of Generation Alpha's Educational Prospects	Dan Coolsaet	2024	0	42	These studies suggest that technological advancements will significantly impact future teaching-learning approaches and pedagogical methodologies, shaping the educational experience for Generation Alpha by aligning with their learning styles, perceptions, and expectations.
Generation Alpha: Understanding the Next Cohort of University Students	R. Ziatdinov, J. Cilliers	2021	35	23	The research identified the influence of social media, social connections, high levels of perceptions and the Generation Alpha's ability to interpret information as strengths to consider in future teaching-learning approaches in the higher education environment.
The Best Practice of Teach Computer Science Students to Use Paper Prototyping	Dave Miller	2021	49	60	Through a paper prototyping activity, this article explains how to teach rapidly and successfully CS students about "fit," a Human-Computer Interaction (HCI) concept. Despite its simplicity, the concept of "fit" can be difficult to grasp without much practice.
Students` Perspectives on the Use of Innovative and Interactive Teaching Methods at the University of Nouakchott Al Aasriya, Mauritania: English Department as a Case Study	T. Eli	2021	44	42	The findings of the study revealed that 91.1% of the students believe that their teachers do use some of the innovative and interactive teaching methods in their classes; still, 70.3% of the respondents were in favor of continuous trainings for teachers on the use of innovative and interactive teaching methods, which is a very alarming percentage. Also, the findings of this study have some significant implications such as the necessity to move from teaching to learning as an attempt to make learning an enjoyable and memorable experience.

Leveraging AI and Mobile Technologies

Artificial Intelligence (AI) integration to mobile technologies can be a significant step towards transforming the education sector in rural Nigeria. These advanced tools when harnessed, will create an inclusive, efficient, effective learning environment that can address the problems faced by these rural areas. This part looks at three main areas of which Artificial Intelligence and Mobile technology may have a big effect; personalized learning paths, multi-lingual language translation and AI assisted tutoring systems.

Personalized Learning Pathways

Education is undergoing a significant transformation through the integration of AI-powered mobile applications that provide personalized learning pathways. These applications utilize advanced machine learning algorithms to adapt to the unique needs and learning styles of individual students. By analyzing student performance, preferences, and progress data, AI can deliver customized educational experiences, ensuring that each student receives the support they need to succeed, irrespective of their background or location. For instance, adaptive learning algorithms can continuously assess a student's performance and adjust the difficulty level, pacing, and content accordingly. If a student struggles with a particular concept, the system can offer additional explanations, simpler examples, or foundational lessons to build the necessary knowledge base (Maghsudi et al., 2021). Moreover, AI can recognize individual learning styles, whether visual, auditory, or kinesthetic and tailor content delivery to match each student's preferred mode of learning, thereby enhancing engagement and knowledge retention (Xie et al., 2019).

In addition to these features, AI-powered systems provide real-time progress tracking, set achievable goals, and offer immediate feedback, helping students stay motivated and experience a sense of accomplishment as they progress through their personalized learning journey. Recent research has also explored using genetic algorithms to construct personalized learning paths, offering another approach to individualized education (Elshani & Nuçi, 2021). The curation of interest-based content, linking academic concepts to real-world applications, ensures that learning is relevant and meaningful to students, especially those in rural areas who may feel disconnected from traditional educational content (Song et al., 2021). Earlier research has proposed heuristic algorithms for planning personalized learning paths in context-aware ubiquitous learning environments (Hwang et al., 2010). AI also plays a crucial role in identifying students at risk of falling behind or dropping out, enabling timely interventions from teachers or AI-assisted tutoring systems. Furthermore, by administering extensive assessments, AI can identify skill gaps and generate targeted exercises to address these deficiencies, which is particularly beneficial in rural areas with limited access to specialized remedial education (Chaipidech et al., 2022). Ultimately, implementing personalized learning pathways through AI and mobile technologies has the potential to bridge the educational gap between urban and rural regions in Nigeria, providing equitable access to quality education. However, successful implementation requires careful consideration of cultural issues, technology infrastructure, and teacher training to ensure that these innovations are effectively integrated into the rural educational system.

Multilingual Language Translation

In Nigeria, where a multitude of languages are spoken, language barriers present a significant challenge in education. By integrating multilingual translation capabilities into e-learning systems, educational content can be delivered in various Nigerian languages, thereby promoting inclusivity and improving academic outcomes. Building multilingual ontologies for the education domain can further enhance language translation capabilities in e-learning systems (Florrence, 2020) AI-powered tools can ensure that students comprehend and engage with the material, regardless of their language background, thus contributing to a more equitable education system (Ghafoor et al., 2021).

In the rural Nigerian educational context, the introduction of multilingual translation could involve several key features. Real-time content translation allows AI systems to instantly convert educational materials from English, the official language of instruction, into local Nigerian languages, enhancing students' understanding and retention of complex subjects (Firat et al., 2016). AI algorithms can also convert spoken words into text and vice versa in multiple Nigerian languages, catering to students with hearing or visual impairments and supporting diverse learning preferences. Furthermore, AI systems can accurately translate idioms and cultural references, preserving the integrity of educational content while promoting the development of English language skills alongside native languages (Inhetveen, 2012; Ghafoor et al., 2021).

AI-Assisted Tutoring Systems

The concept of intelligent tutoring systems has been evolving since the early 1990s, laying the groundwork for current AI-assisted education (Nwana, 1990). In rural Nigeria, the severe shortage of teachers has resulted in many students lacking the instructional support they need, creating an urgent need for alternative educational solutions. AI-assisted tutoring systems can provide personalized guidance to these students, ensuring they receive real-time feedback, explanations of complex concepts, and answers to their questions. By supplementing traditional teaching methods, these systems can enhance the quality of education and help bridge the gap caused by the lack of teachers (AlShaikh & Hewahi, 2021).

Recent systematic reviews have highlighted the potential of AI in intelligent tutoring systems for promoting sustainable education (Lin et al., 2023). AI-assisted tutoring systems offer several features that are particularly valuable in the rural Nigerian context. These include 24/7 availability, personalized instruction, and interactive problem-solving capabilities. Unlike human teachers, AI tutors are available at all times, allowing students to access educational support whenever they need it, regardless of their schedule. These systems can also adapt their teaching style and content to meet the individual needs of each learner, providing a customized educational experience that can improve understanding and retention. Additionally, AI tutors equipped with natural language processing can engage with students in a more intuitive and accessible manner, making learning more effective (Burns & Capps, 2013).

For the successful implementation of AI-assisted tutoring systems in rural Nigeria, it is crucial to consider local educational needs, cultural contexts, and technical constraints. This includes comprehensive data collection and ongoing system enhancements to ensure that the AI tutors remain relevant and effective. Educator training is also essential, as teachers must learn how to integrate AI tutoring systems into their teaching practices effectively. Moreover, engaging the local community is necessary to ensure cultural relevance and acceptance of these technologies. Ethical considerations, such as data protection and algorithmic fairness, must be addressed to maintain the integrity of the teacher-student relationship (AlShaikh & Hewahi, 2021).

Utilizing Telecommunication Infrastructure

Nigeria's telecommunication infrastructure has significantly advanced, particularly in the widespread use of mobile devices, even in remote regions. This infrastructure offers a unique opportunity to revolutionize education in rural areas by facilitating virtual classrooms and the delivery of educational content. Mobile phones, which are now widely available, provide a cost-effective means of education, allowing access to learning materials for all students regardless of location. As noted by studies such as Adeniran et al. (2020), the use of mobile-based education has the potential to address the learning crisis in Nigeria. Key benefits include live-streaming classes, enabling real-time interaction between students and educators, and asynchronous learning through pre-recorded lessons, which enhances accessibility (Alam, 2023). Studies have shown that students' perceptions of virtual classrooms in online and blended courses can significantly impact their learning experiences (Parker & Martin, 2010). Synchronous virtual classrooms have become increasingly important in distance education, offering real-time interaction between students and educators (Martin & Parker, 2014). Furthermore, mobile apps and interactive digital textbooks offer personalized and interactive learning experiences, contributing to improved student engagement. The implementation of telecommunications infrastructure in rural areas has been a subject of study for decades, with lessons that can be applied to the Nigerian context (Nazem et al., 1996).

The integration of mobile technologies in education has been recognized as a significant trend in enhancing learning experiences (Keengwe & Bhargava, 2014). The implementation of mobile devices for education also offers opportunities for professional development and collaboration. Teachers, especially in rural areas, can participate in online training programs to improve their skills, while students can engage in virtual field trips using augmented reality (AR) and virtual reality (VR) technologies (Garuba, 2003; Charles, 2023). Additionally, mobile learning apps, collaborative platforms, and mobile assessment tools provide a platform for students to participate in group projects and receive instant feedback, enhancing the learning experience (Song et al., 2021). However, successful implementation requires collaboration with telecom providers to ensure network coverage and affordable data prices. Policies must also be put in place to ensure that mobile devices are used responsibly for academic purposes (Tooley, 2021).

To ensure equitable access to mobile education, particularly in Nigeria's rural areas, low-cost mobile devices must be made available. Various approaches, such as subsidies, bulk purchasing, and refurbished device programs, could make mobile technology accessible to more students (Egberi & Madubueze, 2023). In addition, local assembly and the development of solar-powered or ruggedized devices would reduce costs and improve sustainability, particularly in areas with unreliable power supply (Goundar, 2011). Open-source hardware and community ownership models could further lower barriers to access. However, the long-term success of these programs depends on meeting device specifications, providing technical support, and ensuring responsible use (Pedro et al., 2019). Through the integration of telecommunication infrastructure and affordable mobile devices, Nigeria's rural education system could experience substantial improvements, reducing the gap between urban and rural education.

Discussion

The vision for Nigeria's future education system aims to eliminate barriers such as distance, language, and financial constraints, creating a truly inclusive environment for the younger generation. Through the integration of AI and mobile technologies, education can be democratized, providing every child with equal access to quality learning opportunities. A key aspect of this future is the ubiquitous access to education through personalized learning ecosystems that adapt to the needs, preferences, and pace of individual learners (Alam, 2023; Pedro et al., 2019). Blended learning models that combine traditional classroom instruction with AI-supported methodologies will play a crucial role in creating a seamless learning experience, especially in rural areas where traditional resources are limited (Charles, 2023). For instance, virtual reality technologies, such as Google Cardboard, have shown promise as content delivery systems in various educational contexts (Lee et al., 2017). Furthermore, the concept of lifelong learning, supported by AI-driven platforms, will enable individuals to continue developing their skills beyond formal schooling, addressing the needs of an evolving job market (Baba et al., 2024).

Another important facet of this educational transformation is the use of AI to enhance inclusivity and accessibility. AI-driven platforms can offer virtual classroom links that connect Nigerian students with their peers globally, fostering cultural exchange and global awareness (Maghsudi et al., 2021). Additionally, low-cost educational mobile robots based on platforms like Android and Arduino offer innovative ways to engage students in STEM education (López-Rodríguez & Cuesta, 2016). Advanced assistive technologies will also ensure that students with special needs are integrated into mainstream education, allowing for a more inclusive learning environment (Garuba, 2003). Inclusive education for physically challenged students is crucial for achieving sustainable development goals in Nigeria (Kusimo & Chidozie, 2019). Community learning hubs equipped with AI and mobile technology could serve as centers of educational resources, promoting lifelong learning and bridging the digital divide between rural and urban populations (Song et al., 2021). The shift from traditional degree systems to skill-based credentialing, verified by AI-driven assessments and blockchain technologies, will ensure that education is more focused on practical skills rather than solely academic qualifications (Graf, 2023). Furthermore, mobile technology approaches have shown promise in fostering entrepreneurial interest among tertiary institution students in Nigeria (Ojo et al., 2023).

However, several challenges must be addressed to realize this vision. Ethical considerations around AI development must be prioritized to avoid biases and ensure equitable access to educational tools (Jatileni et al., 2023). Investments in telecommunications and power infrastructure are critical to support the widespread adoption of these technologies, especially in underserved areas (Gasiea et al., 2010). Additionally, digital literacy programs are needed to prepare both teachers and students for the integration of AI into the educational process (Egberi & Madubueze, 2023). Cultural preservation must also be considered, ensuring that indigenous knowledge and traditions are respected and integrated into the modernized educational framework (Olatunji & Ajayi, 2016). Finally, cybersecurity and data privacy measures must be strengthened to protect student information, while sustainable funding models will be essential for the long-term success of these initiatives (Ama et al., 2020).

CONCLUSION

The integration of artificial intelligence (AI) technologies and mobile platforms presents a transformative opportunity for inclusive education in rural Nigeria. By addressing existing challenges, such as limited access to resources and geographical constraints, these technologies can provide personalized learning pathways, AI-enabled tutoring systems, virtual classrooms, and low-cost mobile devices to ensure that all children, regardless of their background, receive equal educational opportunities. This vision goes beyond merely incorporating technology into education; it involves reimagining education to be more accessible, adaptive, and aligned with the evolving demands of the global economy. With the support of AI and mobile technologies, Nigeria can create a future where every child is equipped with the skills and knowledge necessary for success in the 21st century.

It's important to note that the potential of AI as a pathway to Africa's transformation extends beyond education, impacting various sectors of development (Sampene et al., 2022). To achieve this vision, collaboration among various stakeholders including government agencies, educational institutions, technological companies, NGOs, and local communities is crucial. Significant investments in infrastructure, research, and human capital are necessary to drive this transformation forward. Additionally, future research should explore the ethical implications of AI in education, focusing on culturally sensitive applications and ensuring that AI systems do not perpetuate inequality. Embracing these technologies will not only benefit individual learners but also contribute to Nigeria's broader socioeconomic development, enhancing the country's global competitiveness in a knowledge-based economy. As Nigeria moves toward inclusive education through AI and mobile technology, cautious optimism is required to navigate potential challenges and ensure sustainable, equitable growth for all.

References

Adeniran, A., Ishaku, J., & Akanni, L. (2020). Is Nigeria experiencing a learning crisis: Evidence from curriculum-matched learning assessment. *International Journal of Educational Development*, 77, 102199. DOI: 10.1016/j.ijedudev.2020.102199

Adetoro, R. A. (2014). Inclusive education in Nigeria—A Myth or reality? *Creative Education*, 5(20), 1777–1781. DOI: 10.4236/ce.2014.520198

Alam, A. (2023). Harnessing the Power of AI to Create Intelligent Tutoring Systems for Enhanced Classroom Experience and Improved Learning Outcomes. In *Intelligent Communication Technologies and Virtual Mobile Networks* (pp. 571–591). Springer Nature Singapore. DOI: 10.1007/978-981-99-1767-9_42

AlShaikh, F., & Hewahi, N. (2021, September). Ai and machine learning techniques in the development of Intelligent Tutoring System: A review. In *2021 International Conference on innovation and Intelligence for informatics, computing, and technologies (3ICT)* (pp. 403-410). IEEE. DOI: 10.1109/3ICT53449.2021.9582029

Ama, H., Moorad, F., & Mukhopadyay, S. (2020). Assessment of stakeholders views on accessing quality and equity of basic education in rural communities of Abia State, Nigeria. *Educational Research Review*, 15(8), 454–464. Advance online publication. DOI: 10.5897/ERR2020.4018

Andries, A., Morse, S., Murphy, R., Lynch, J., & Woolliams, E. (2022). Assessing Education from Space: Using Satellite Earth Observation to Quantify Overcrowding in Primary Schools in Rural Areas of Nigeria. *Sustainability (Basel)*, 14(3), 1408. Advance online publication. DOI: 10.3390/su14031408

Baba, K., Faddouli, E., & Cheimanoff, N. (2024). Mobile-Optimized AI-Driven Personalized Learning: A Case Study at Mohammed VI Polytechnic University. *International Journal of Interactive Mobile Technologies*, 18(4), 81–96. DOI: 10.3991/ijim.v18i04.46547

Burns, H. L., & Capps, C. G. (2013). Foundations of intelligent tutoring systems: An introduction. In *Foundations of intelligent tutoring systems* (pp. 1–19). Psychology Press.

Chaipidech, P., Srisawasdi, N., Kajornmanee, T., & Chaipah, K. (2022). A personalized learning system-supported professional training model for teachers' TPACK development. *Computers and Education: Artificial Intelligence*, 3, 100064. DOI: 10.1016/j.caeai.2022.100064

Charles, F. (2023). *AI-Powered Personalized Mobile Education for New Zealand Students. International Journal Software Engineering and Computer Science.* IJ-SECS., DOI: 10.35870/ijsecs.v3i1.1115

Coolsaet, D. (2024). The Impact of Technological Advancements on Higher Education: A Study of Generation Alpha's Educational Prospects. [IJSECS]. *International Journal Software Engineering and Computer Science*, 4(1), 58–67. DOI: 10.35870/ijsecs.v4i1.2147

Dave, J. (2023). *Enhancing User Experience in E-Learning: Real-Time Emotional Analysis and Assessment. International Journal Software Engineering and Computer Science.* IJSECS., DOI: 10.35870/ijsecs.v3i2.1206

Egberi, A. E., & Madubueze, M. H. C. (2023). Rethinking The United Nations–Nigeria Partnership Towards Girl Child Education and Gender Equality Reforms: A Systematic Review. *Education Policy and Development*, 1(2), 14–26. DOI: 10.31098/epd.v1i2.1528

Eli, T. (2021). Studentsperspectives on the use of innovative and interactive teaching methods at the University of Nouakchott Al Aasriya, Mauritania: English department as a case study. *International Journal of Technology* [IJTIM]. *Innovation and Management*, 1(2), 90–104.

Elshani, L., & Nuçi, K. P. (2021). Constructing a personalized learning path using genetic algorithms approach. *arXiv preprint arXiv:2104.11276.*

Firat, O., Sankaran, B., Al-Onaizan, Y., Vural, F. T. Y., & Cho, K. (2016). Zero-resource translation with multi-lingual neural machine translation. *arXiv preprint arXiv:1606.04164.* DOI: 10.18653/v1/D16-1026

Florrence, M. (2020). Building a multilingual ontology for education domain using monto method. *Computer Science and Information Technology*, 1(2), 47–53.

Garuba, A. (2003). Inclusive education in the 21st century: Challenges and opportunities for Nigeria. *Asia Pacific Disability Rehabilitation Journal*, 14(2), 191–200.

Gasiea, Y., Emsley, M., & Mikhailov, L. (2010). Rural telecommunications infrastructure selection using the analytic network process. *Journal of Telecommunications and Information Technology*, (2), 28–42. DOI: 10.26636/jtit.2010.2.1070

Ghafoor, A., Imran, A. S., Daudpota, S. M., Kastrati, Z., Batra, R., & Wani, M. A. (2021). The impact of translating resource-rich datasets to low-resource languages through multi-lingual text processing. *IEEE Access : Practical Innovations, Open Solutions*, 9, 124478–124490. DOI: 10.1109/ACCESS.2021.3110285

Goundar, S. (2011). What is the potential impact of using mobile devices in education?.

Graf, A. (2023). *Exploring the Role of Personalization in Adaptive Learning Environments. International Journal Software Engineering and Computer Science.* IJSECS., DOI: 10.35870/ijsecs.v3i2.1200

Hashim, S., Omar, M. K., Ab Jalil, H., & Sharef, N. M. (2022). Trends on technologies and artificial intelligence in education for personalized learning: Systematic literature. *Journal of Academic Research in Progressive Education and Development*, 12(1), 884–903. DOI: 10.6007/IJARPED/v11-i1/12230

Hwang, G. J., Kuo, F. R., Yin, P. Y., & Chuang, K. H. (2010). A heuristic algorithm for planning personalized learning paths for context-aware ubiquitous learning. *Computers & Education*, 54(2), 404–415. DOI: 10.1016/j.compedu.2009.08.024

Ihebom, B., & Uko, J. O. (2020). Challenges and prospects of secondary education in Nigeria. *International Journal of Scientific Research in Education*, 13(4), 670–688.

Inhetveen, K. (2012). Translation challenges: Qualitative interviewing in a multilingual field. *Qualitative Sociology Review*, 8(2), 28–45. DOI: 10.18778/1733-8077.8.2.03

Jatileni, C. N., Sanusi, I. T., Olaleye, S. A., Ayanwale, M. A., Agbo, F. J., & Oyelere, P. B. (2023). Artificial intelligence in compulsory level of education: Perspectives from Namibian in-service teachers. *Education and Information Technologies*, •••, 1–28.

Keengwe, J., & Bhargava, M. (2014). Mobile learning and integration of mobile technologies in education. *Education and Information Technologies*, 19(4), 737–746. DOI: 10.1007/s10639-013-9250-3

Kusimo, A. O., & Chidozie, F. C. (2019). Inclusive education and sustainable development goals: A study of the physically challenged in Nigeria. *Cogent Arts & Humanities*, 6(1), 1684175. DOI: 10.1080/23311983.2019.1684175

Lee, S. H., Sergueeva, K., Catangui, M., & Kandaurova, M. (2017). Assessing Google Cardboard virtual reality as a content delivery system in business classrooms. *Journal of Education for Business*, 92(4), 153–160. DOI: 10.1080/08832323.2017.1308308

Lin, C. C., Huang, A. Y., & Lu, O. H. (2023). Artificial intelligence in intelligent tutoring systems toward sustainable education: A systematic review. *Smart Learning Environments*, 10(1), 41. DOI: 10.1186/s40561-023-00260-y

Lindahl, R. (2006). The Right to Education in a Globalized World. *Journal of Studies in International Education*, 10(1), 26–5. DOI: 10.1177/1028315305283308

López-Rodríguez, F. M., & Cuesta, F. (2016). Andruino-a1: Low-cost educational mobile robot based on android and arduino. *Journal of Intelligent & Robotic Systems*, 81(1), 63–76. DOI: 10.1007/s10846-015-0227-x

Maghsudi, S., Lan, A., Xu, J., & van Der Schaar, M. (2021). Personalized education in the artificial intelligence era: What to expect next. *IEEE Signal Processing Magazine*, 38(3), 37–50. DOI: 10.1109/MSP.2021.3055032

Martin, F., & Parker, M. A. (2014). Use of synchronous virtual classrooms: Why, who, and how. *Journal of Online Learning and Teaching*, 10(2), 192–210.

Miller, D. (2021). The best practice of teach computer science students to use paper prototyping. *International Journal of Technology* [IJTIM]. *Innovation and Management*, 1(2), 42–63.

Miller, D. (2023). *Embracing the Technological Metamorphosis: Envisioning Higher Education for Generation Alpha in a Shifting Educational Landscape. International Journal Software Engineering and Computer Science*. IJSECS., DOI: 10.35870/ijsecs.v3i2.1492

Monk, D. (2007). Recruiting and Retaining High-Quality Teachers in Rural Areas. *The Future of Children*, 17(1), 155–174. DOI: 10.1353/foc.2007.0009 PMID: 17407927

Nazem, S. M., Liu, Y. H., Lee, H., & Shi, Y. (1996). Implementing telecommunications infrastructure: A rural America case. *Telematics and Informatics*, 13(1), 23–31. DOI: 10.1016/0736-5853(95)00012-7

NERDC (2013). Teachers' guide for the revised 9-year Basic Education Curriculum (BEC) Religion and National Values Social Studies. Nigerian Educational Research and Development Council (NERDC). Kaularr Lumpur: BHS book Printing Sdn. Bhd.

Nwana, H. S. (1990). Intelligent tutoring systems: An overview. *Artificial Intelligence Review*, 4(4), 251–277. DOI: 10.1007/BF00168958

Ojo, O. A., Olugbade, D., & Abioye, I. O. (2023). ENTREPRENEURIAL INTEREST AND DEVELOPMENT AMONG TERTIARY INSTITUTION STUDENTS: THE MOBILE TECHNOLOGY APPROACH. *European Journal of Open Education and E-learning Studies*, 8(2). Advance online publication. DOI: 10.46827/ejoe.v8i2.4806

Olatunji, O., & Ajayi, S. (2016). *Rurality, Nigeria's massification policy on access to basic education and turnover causations amongst teachers*. Australian and International Journal of Rural Education., DOI: 10.47381/aijre.v26i3.73

Parker, M. A., & Martin, F. (2010). Using virtual classrooms: Student perceptions of features and characteristics in an online and a blended course. *Journal of Online Learning and Teaching*, 6(1), 135–147.

Pedro, F., Subosa, M., Rivas, A., & Valverde, P. (2019). Artificial intelligence in education: Challenges and opportunities for sustainable development.

Sampene, A. K., Agyeman, F. O., Robert, B., & Wiredu, J. (2022). Artificial intelligence as a path way to Africa's transformations. *Artificial Intelligence*, 9(1).

Schultz, L. (1964). Education. *Simulation*, 2(1), 13–13. DOI: 10.1177/003754976400200102

Song, S. J., Tan, K. H., & Awang, M. M. (2021). Generic digital equity model in education: Mobile-assisted personalized learning (MAPL) through e-modules. *Sustainability (Basel)*, 13(19), 11115. DOI: 10.3390/su131911115

Tooley, J. (2021). *Really good schools: Global lessons for high-caliber, low-cost education*. Independent Institute.

UBEC. (2014). UBE programmes. Retrieved April 8, 2014, from https://ubeconline.com/UBEProgrammes.hmtl

UNICEF. 2014. All Children in School by 2015: Global Initiative on Out-of-School Children: regional report; West and Central Africa. https://unesdoc.unesco.org/ark:/48223/pf0000228081

UNICEF. 2018. Evaluation Report: The Out-of-School Children Initiative (OOSCI) February 2018.

Wringe, C. (1986). The Human Right to Education. *Educational Philosophy and Theory*, 18(2), 23–33. DOI: 10.1111/j.1469-5812.1986.tb00415.x

Xie, H., Chu, H. C., Hwang, G. J., & Wang, C. C. (2019). Trends and development in technology-enhanced adaptive/personalized learning: A systematic review of journal publications from 2007 to 2017. *Computers & Education*, 140, 103599. DOI: 10.1016/j.compedu.2019.103599

Zhang, Q. (2022). Construction of personalized learning platform based on collaborative filtering algorithm. *Wireless Communications and Mobile Computing*, 2022(1), 5878344. DOI: 10.1155/2022/5878344

Ziatdinov, R., & Cilliers, J. (2022). Generation Alpha: Understanding the next cohort of university students. *arXiv preprint arXiv:2202.01422*.

Chapter 11
Technology-Integrated Inquiry-Based Learning in South African Classrooms:
A Case of Selected Grade 12 Secondary Schools

Olufemi David Naiye
University of South Africa, South Africa

Leila Goosen
https://orcid.org/0000-0003-4948-2699
University of South Africa, South Africa

ABSTRACT

In order to provide readers with an overview of, and to summarize, the content of the chapter, the purpose of the research discussed is stated as to gain an understanding of technology integration in an inquiry-based learning (IBL) classroom, concerning how South African Grade 12 Life Sciences teachers use relevant technologies to accommodate their learners' needs, difficulties, and cognitive capabilities. Against the background of the power of persuasive educational technologies in enhancing learning, the chapter will discuss e.g., games and gamification, higher education, early childhood education and Artificial Intelligence (AI).

DOI: 10.4018/979-8-3693-7255-5.ch011

INTRODUCTION

This section will describe the general perspective of the chapter and end by specifically stating the aim and objectives.

Fostering Inclusive Education with Artificial Intelligence and Emerging Technologies

In the domains of education, learners tend to lose interest over time when they are being forced to learn. While the use of extrinsic rewards could motivate learners to a certain degree, it is not ideal as a long-term approach. Instead, learners should be inspired and ignited by the passion for learning itself. Persuasion, which refers to a symbolic process that adopts communication as a medium to achieve behavioral and attitudinal change, holds the potential to convince students to act in such a way.

Technology-Integrated Inquiry-Based Learning in Science Classrooms: A Case of Selected Grade 12 Secondary Schools

The integration of technology in teaching and learning is becoming significant, it ensures more flexibility in the activities of science lessons, and learners are meaningfully engaged due to the dynamic nature of technology integration (Nuhoğlu & Seçkin, 2021). Science teachers' knowledge and ability to integrate modern technologies in an Inquiry-Based Learning (IBL) classroom is vital to keep learning interactive and interesting (Raja & Nagasubramani, 2018). Understanding science teachers' ability to integrate modern technologies in planning and preparing lesson activities, engaging and accommodating all learners irrespective of their diverse learning styles, needs, difficulties, and cognitive capabilities is significant to the planned study.

The planned study envisaged that integrating technology in an IBL approach to teaching science subjects will encourage and empower science teachers to become effective facilitators. Continuous training on using existing and newly invented technologies will further improve teachers' technological and pedagogical skills. Technology integration provides an opportunity to effectively transfer and acquire scientific skills and knowledge in the 21st century (Nuhoğlu & Seçkin, 2021).

Recommended Topics

In terms of the recommended topics suggested for the book, this chapter will offer perspectives on the following:

- Educational Technology
- Persuasive Technology
- Immersive Technology
- Games and Gamification
- European Union (Higher Education
- Early Childhood Education
- Sustainability Education
- Health Education
- Learners' Attitudes and Behavior
- Artificial Intelligence
- Digital Learning

Target Audience

Like this book that it proposes to form part of, the chapter offers novel and practical propositions and precedents to be employed in training, classrooms, higher institutions and more, with the aim of reaching a target audience of readers such as educators, academics, researchers, scholars, instructors, instructional designers, and even students.

Aim and Objectives

Like for this book as a whole, the chapter is authored by experts in the relevant field, who hope to provide unique prospects that addresses the needs of future generation classrooms by leveraging the art and science of persuasion to be incorporated into pedagogical, andragogical and heutagogical approaches in teaching and learning while also utilizing various technologies.

The planned study aims to gain an understanding of technology integration in an IBL classroom, concerning how Grade 12 Life Sciences teachers use educational technologies to accommodate their learners' needs, difficulties, and cognitive capabilities. The proposed study aims to achieve the following objectives, to:

- understand the role of technology-integrated IBL in enhancing the teaching and learning of Grade 12 Life Sciences,
- establish Grade 12 Life Sciences teachers' understanding of, attitudes towards, and ability to integrate educational technologies to enhance teaching and learning.
- explore how the application of educational technologies address and enhance Grade 12 Life Sciences learners' attitudes and behavior, needs, difficulties, and cognitive capabilities, as well as

- understand the benefits of technology integration, and the factors that impede integration in the teaching and learning of Grade 12 Life Sciences.

BACKGROUND

This section will provide broad definitions and discussions of the topic on Technology-Integrated Inquiry-Based Learning in South African Classrooms from A Case of Selected Grade 12 Secondary Schools and incorporate the views of others (in the form of a literature review) into the discussion to support, refute, or demonstrate the authors' position on the topic.

A book on Embracing Cutting-Edge Technology in Modern Educational Settings edited by Chee and Sanmugam (2024) indicated that as "classrooms transform into dynamic digital arenas, educators are presented with an unprecedented canvas to reimagine teaching methodologies".

"Augmented reality (AR) technology is an effective way to transmit and protect tangible and intangible cultural heritage. It is crucial to research the connections between these two" (Du & Sanmugam, 2024, p. 184). The chapter by the latter authors in the book mentioned in the previous paragraph therefore presented a bibliometric review of studies on the application of augmented reality to cultural heritage by using Biblioshiny and CiteSpace.

Games and Gamification

"Player traits are closely related to the personality of a person, which could be also known as the categorization of players based on their interest in certain game elements". The chapter by Yie and Sanmugam (2023, p. 136) in a book regarding Comparative Research on Diversity inVirtualLearning in terms of Eastern vs. Western Perspectives was constructing a theoretical conceptual framework in terms of the contribution of diversity towards the player traits of learners in a classroom.

The COVID-19 pandemic had "affected the worldwide education system and an online learning environment" had "been implemented to ensure the continuity of education". As part of the book mentioned in the previous paragraph, the chapter by Zulkeflee, Sanmugam and Nee (2023, p. 105) considered the effect of online learning on undergraduate student achievement and engagement during times of emergency remote teaching (ERT).

Also in the book mentioned in above, the chapter by Nee, et al. (2023, p. 160) aimed "to report the effectiveness and practical implementation of teaching" and learning "online in a diverse environment for schools across the globe during the pandemic."

Higher Education

The purpose of the study reported on by Yie, Sanmugam, Yahaya and Khlaif (2023, p. 1) was "to identify the effect of gamified depth on" Malaysian higher education students' intrinsic motivation and achievement levels, and they were therefore "exposed to two gamified platforms".

As part of the proceedings of the IADIS international conference on internationalhigher education, the paper by Wood and Reefke (2010, p. 72) indicated that when working with a diverse class, a "variety of teaching methods and supportive tools are at a lecturer's disposal. Comprehensive knowledge of such methods and tools and their effective use can enrich students' lecture experiences and" reflections on the role of team teaching, teaching tools and technological support are therefore needed.

Diverse Technological Tools

The essay by Sumadevi (Sumadevi, 2023, p. 106) in journal article on historical research explored the effective use of diverse technology tools in a flipped learning approach, including e.g., real-time "communication tools, such as video conferencing". "These tools promote student engagement" and personalized learning.

Early Childhood Education

"Living in an era when technology plays a crucial role, education is one of the fields that is highly influenced by technology." The study reported on by Barkhaya, Abd Halim and Yahaya (2018c, p. 246) at the 10th International Conference on Engineering Education (ICEED) focused "on the effectiveness of a technological tool", as well as the development of 3D pyramid-shaped hologram (3DPH) called HoloRead for preschool children's learning.

Another paper by Barkhaya and Abd Halim (2017) looked at learning through play via visualization tools to enhance students' cognitive abilities among preschool children.

Artificial Intelligence

Health Education

"With the increasing popularity of *artificial intelligence* (AI) applications in medical practices, the" effective "integration of AI technologies into medical education" had garnered significant attention (Garcia, et al., 2024, p. 1). The first chapter in a book on Approaches to Patient Literacy and Healthcare Innovation provided practical tips and actionable insights in this regard.

Another chapter in the book mentioned in the previous paragraph explored "transformative technologies and their application in supporting and enhancing the lives of children diagnosed with fetal alcohol syndrome (FAS) and autism" spectrum disorders (ASDs) (Du Toit & Goosen, 2024, p. 156).

Embracing alternative formats, assessment strategies and digital technologies to revitalize practical sessions in science and health, Bree (2019) suggested that more attention be paid "when it comes to the design and assessment strategies employed", as in "many cases, traditional practical formats and assessment strategies regularly remain cemented in use".

Sustainability Education

Similar to the book mentioned in the previous paragraphs, the chapter by Ngugi and Goosen (2021) discussed innovation, entrepreneurship, and sustainability for Information and Communication Technology (ICT) students towards the post-COVID-19 era.

Assessment Strategies

Technology Applications, Maintenance, And Support

The United States (US) Department of Education and the "National Center for Education Statistics (NCES)" (Schmitt, 2002, p. 4) described technology applications as software and systems used to support instructional functions and administrative activities of educational institutions. A supportive and collaborative environment to integrate relevant technologies and the provisioning of mentorship is vital for the continuous development of technological skills of both science teachers and their learners (Davies & West, 2014; Brown, 2014). Support activities introduced by school leadership encouraged teachers to effectively use educational technologies in science classrooms (Dokter, 2020). Principals who desire to render support but lack direction should seek professional guidance to ensure that teachers get the needed technological support to effectively integrate technology in the classrooms.

The handbook with Schmitt (2002, p. 18) as project leader was "intended to facilitate the assessment of" technologies used in schools "to support elementary and secondary education in the" US. It was "designed to help decision makers" by providing suggestions, tools, and guidelines for assessing such technologies.

As part of a handbook of research on educational communications and technology, the chapter by Davies and West (2014, p. 422) discussed how to use "technology effectively to facilitate learning". "After first defining technology and technology integration" in schools, the latter authors proceeded to evaluating current (at the time) "technology integration efforts in schools".

Dokter (2020, p. v) provided perspectives on school-based instructional leadership support for "information technology (IT) and computer applications technology (CAT)" subject teachers, as well as distributed leadership. From the findings, it was "clear that the absence of" such instructional leadership presented a challenge to teachers.

The second handbook of information technology in primary and secondary education contains a chapter by McLeod (2018) on technology integration, leadership, and organizational support frameworks for instructional improvement with information technology.

The discussion paper by O'Toole (2013, p. 1) asked questions around which technologies will need to be provided and what "learning design strategies and patterns will those technologies" require? It aimed "to explore the potential role of" pedagogical strategies and technologies for peer assessment in Massively Open Online Courses (MOOCs).

A conference paper Magd and Ruzive (2020, p. 241) made suggestions regarding innovative modern assessment "strategies, techniques, tools and technologies which are" mostly being used these days.

An international journal article oncase studiesin business, IT, and education by Namreen Asif and Panakaje (2022, p. 931) considered the role of educational technology and the internet in the Indian education system, which had "been linked in recent years not only as a tool to increase teaching and learning, but also as one of the key barriers to" making the paradigm shift required. The integration of technology in education helps to improve the curriculum, instructional offerings, and enhance the overall learning process. Technology-integrated IBL encourages learners to inclusively participate in learning activities.

A chapter in the Research Anthology on Developing Critical Thinking Skills in Students indicated that technologies have the "potential to make learning more dynamic and capable of going" beyond "conventional learning limits. With the utilization of online technologies for example," students' Higher Order Thinking Skills (HOTS) can be enhanced through the Socratic method approach (Suhadi, et al., 2021, p. 1399).

A meta-analysis and review of the application of three-dimensional holograms (3DH) in education were presented at the 8th ICEED by Barkhaya and Abd Halim (2016, p. 257). The evolvement of technology had made a "tremendous contribution in the field of education." "Generally, the technology of 3DH involve spatial displays".

The aim of the study reported on by Nuhoğlu and Seçkin (2021, p. 1) was to provide an analysis of and "examine the relationship between teachers' 21st-century learning-teaching skills and information technology usage levels."

MAIN FOCUS OF THE CHAPTER

Issues, Problems, Challenges

This section will present demonstrate the authors' perspectives on the issues, problems, challenges, etc., as these relate to theme of the book on the Fostering Inclusive Education with AI and Emerging Technologies and arguments supporting the authors' position on Technology-Integrated Inquiry-Based Learning in South African Classrooms from A Case of Selected Grade 12 Secondary Schools. It will also compare and contrast with what had been, or is currently being, done as it relates to the specific topic of the chapter and the main theme of the book.

Technology integration in the classroom in the 21st century should be regarded as a critical requirement for quality education, as it encourages collaborative problem-solving and enables learners' engagement with complex learning activities (Kilfoil, 2015; Hart, 2023; Nuhoğlu & Seçkin, 2021). Consequently, the transition from a traditional classroom to a technology-integrated IBL classroom becomes inevitable. Technology integration presented challenges and benefits to the educational sector; increasing the demands placed on science teachers to become dynamic in their teaching practices, and to effectively use educational technologies required by science subjects (Kamal & Illiyan, 2021; Abel, Tondeur, & Sang, 2022; Winter, Costello, O'Brien, & Hickey, 2021).

According to the South African journal article on education by Hart (2023, p. 1), the "South African education system is considered one of the most unequal in the world. Providing learners with quality education and equipping them with the digital skills required for the Fourth Industrial Revolution" (4IR) is essential. A systematic review by the latter author was identifying the factors impacting the uptake of educational technologies in South African schools.

The coronavirus disease 2019 (COVID-19) outbreak had "impacted catastrophically every sector of the economy throughout the world. And, the education sector" was not left out (Kamal & Illiyan, 2021, p. 311). An Asian Association of Open Universities journal article by the latter authors therefore provided an econometric analysis of school teachers' perception and challenges towards online teaching during COVID-19 pandemic in India.

Similarly, an education research international journal article by Kamal, et al. (2023, p. 1) indicated that the COVID-19 epidemic had "forced the closure of educational institutions all over the globe since it put academic schedules in peril." An empirical analysis is offered on the perception and challenges of virtual classes with a gender digital divide amidst and post-COVID-19 pandemic in Iraq.

Higher Education

"One of the focus areas for the ... Teaching and Learning Strategy Group (TLSG)" for 2014 was learning to deal with, and moving beyond the hype surrounding technologies "that, combined with the speed of change, complicates a complex phenomenon" even further (Kilfoil, 2015, p. 1). The latter author therefore provided a contextualized view of learning with technology in higher education.

Early Childhood Education

A preliminary study on the issues and future emerging trends (at the time) in preschool children's learning was described in the Advanced Science Letters article of Barkhaya, Abd Halim and Yahaya (2018a, p. 178). "The process of shaping a holistic individual starts from early childhood education or more precisely during preschool years."

Games and Gamification

"Gamification, a concept originally derived from games, is defined as the extraction and inclusion of game mechanics within ordinary activities." In an international journal article on information and education technology, Lim, Sanmugam and Yahaya (2023, p. 757) were addressing the dilemma of online gamification with subgame perfect equilibria.

Artificial Intelligence

Against the background of artificial intelligence having "many applications in various aspects of ... daily life, including health, criminal, education, civil, business, and liability law", one aspect of AI in terms of the potential and concerns of using AI in scientific research, including a ChatGPT performance evaluation (Khlaif, et al., 2023, p. 1) were highlighted in the Medical Education journal article.

Immersive Technology

The technology, knowledge and learning article by Khlaif, Mousa and Sanmugam (2024, p. 803) delved "into the potential advantages and" opportunities, as well as challenges and "difficulties of using immersive Extended Reality (XR) technology in engineering education. It also" examined the factors influencing these.

Statement of the Research Problem and Rationale

The use of modern technologies to improve teaching and learning continues to gain momentum in developed countries (Hew & Brush, 2007). These countries had already started benefitting from its effective implementation. However, in developing countries like South Africa (SA), integration of technology has not been thriving as envisaged in her White Paper on e-Education (Department of Education (DoE), 2004).

The integration of technologies in South African classrooms has not recorded much progress since the release of the White Paper on e-Education (Department of Education, 2004), only 26 percent of South African teachers have basic information and communication technology skills, and some teachers do not make use of the technologies at their disposal for teaching and learning (DoE, 2004; Mashile, 2016; Zungu, 2022). According to Ramorola (2018), South African classrooms continue to lag when compared to the level of transforming teaching and learning through technology integration in the classrooms of countries like the United States (US), Singapore, the United Kingdom (UK), Japan, and as well as European and North American classrooms (Hew & Brush, 2007).

Most South African schools have not yet tapped into the benefits of integrating modern technologies in teaching and learning. Factors like unavailability of the appropriate technologies, and lack of technical know-how to integrate the technologies, impede the transfer of knowledge and limit the development of science education (Ramorola M. Z., 2013).

The proposed study seeks to provide support for science teachers to effectively integrate modern technologies in teaching and learning, and use educational technologies to inclusively accommodate all science learners with diverse needs, difficulties, and cognitive capabilities. Furthermore, to enhance the quality of teaching and learning, and produce the scientific skills required to compete favorably on the global stage.

The researcher planned to adopt the updated Unified Theory of Acceptance and Use of Technology 2 (UTAUT2) (Venkatesh, Morris, Davis, & Davis, 2003); (Venkatesh, Thong, & Xu, 2012), and Technological, Pedagogical, and Content Knowledge (TPACK) (Mishra & Koehler, 2006) as the theoretical frameworks that will guide the research study.

Significance of the Study

Technology integration has made the process of teaching and learning effective and enjoyable, it has significantly impacted education and improved the country's economic growth (Raja & Nagasubramani, 2018). It is imperative to assist South African science teachers in developing a positive attitude towards the need to acquire technological skills that are required for the Fourth Industrial Revolution (4IR). It is envisaged that the study will guide all stakeholders in the educational institution with the main focus on Grade 12 Life Sciences teachers and their learners. It will inform on curricular improvement to accommodate the use of modern technologies for inclusive science education. School authorities will be well informed of the benefits of integrating modern technologies and the need to make provisions for appropriate technologies. The findings from the planned study are expected to serve as a template for training and development in acquiring skills that are compatible with the 21st-century standard (Yemothy, 2015). Science teachers and their learners will be well-equipped for implementation. Acquisition of technical skills in the use of technologies will help to increase the percentage of technology-savvy science teachers and learners to meet the vision of SA on e-Education.

Science teachers will be well-equipped with technological skills on how to effectively integrate relevant technologies in an IBL classroom. It is believed that the acquisition of technological skills will help them to identify technologies that apply to different learning styles and needs of their learners to ensure that no learner is left behind in the use of technology for learning (Silva, Silva, & Bilessimo, 2020).

It is envisaged that the technology-integrated IBL approach will help to minimize or eliminate dropouts among science learners, as they develop an interest and become motivated to use educational technologies during learning (Raja & Nagasubramani, 2018). The planned study is also believed to contribute to science and technology knowledgebase. Due to the dynamic nature of technologies, science teachers and their learners will see the need to continue equipping themselves on how to use newly invented technologies.

It will examine factors highlighted by previous research studies, and newly discovered challenges, and attempt to find how the challenges could be mitigated or resolved to attain effective integration of modern technologies in science classrooms. The information that will be obtained from the planned research study will significantly improve the teaching and learning of Life Sciences and other science subjects.

Research Questions

The proposed study will be guided by the following primary and secondary research questions:

Primary Research Question

What is the role of technology integration in attaining success in inclusive science education?

Secondary Research Questions

1. What is Grade 12 Life Sciences teachers'
   a. Understanding of technology integration in enhancing teaching and learning?
   b. Attitude towards the use of educational technologies in enhancing teaching and learning?
   c. Level of expertise to integrate technologies in enhancing teaching and learning?
2. How does the use of educational technologies
   a. Accommodate the needs, difficulties, and cognitive capabilities of Grade 12 Life Sciences learners?
   b. Enhance teaching and learning in science education?
3. What are the benefits and challenges of technology integration in the classroom for Grade 12 Life Sciences
   a. teachers?
   b. learners?

Research Hypotheses

Regarding the research questions, the hypotheses are stated as:

1. Technology-integrated IBL does not significantly enhance the teaching and learning of Grade 12 Life Sciences, and
2. The integration of educational technologies does not significantly support Grade 12 Life Sciences learners with varying needs, difficulties, and cognitive capabilities.

Research Methodology

Research methodology describes the methods needed in collecting and analyzing data to address the problem statement of the research study (Goundar, 2012). The researcher will adopt the mixed method approach, the study will combine both qualitative and quantitative research designs to minimize or eliminate the weaknesses that accompany individual research designs (Abbaszadeh & Hosseinpour, 2011). It will include the data collection instruments to be used, the ethical consideration and the authentic participants from the population for data collection, and how the sourced data will be analyzed (Rajasekar, Philominathan, & Chinnathambi, 2006).

Numerous research studies and articles have made significant contributions to knowledge on technology integration in South African classrooms. However, the use of technology-integrated IBL by Life Sciences teachers to support their learners with diverse needs, difficulties, and cognitive capabilities is still largely an unexplored aspect of technology integration in South African classrooms. Most research studies on technology integration in SA adopted either a qualitative or quantitative approach. The first author plans to adopt a mixed method, using two theoretical frameworks to guide the research study.

SOLUTIONS AND RECOMMENDATIONS

This section will discuss solutions and recommendations in dealing with the issues, problems or challenges presented in the preceding section.

Towards Solutions

Research Design

Triangulation is used by methodologists to increase the credibility and validity of the research findings, the trustworthiness, and ensure that the accuracy of the study is significantly upheld by using the qualitative results to confirm the quantitative results and vice-versa (Noble & Heale, 2019; Abbaszadeh & Hosseinpour, 2011). The researcher's plan to use triangulation is to ensure that data collection instruments are appropriate for the phenomenon being studied and accommodate multiple theories, and data sources within the research study (Abbaszadeh & Hosseinpour, 2011). The planned research design will ensure the credibility and validity of data collection on the impact of technology-integrated IBL in science classrooms and the significance of integrating appropriate technologies to support the diverse needs, difficulties, and cognitive capabilities of Grade 12 Life Sciences learners.

Qualitative and Quantitative Research Designs

*Q*ualitative research designs embrace a subjective assessment of attitudes, opinions, and behavior due to the researcher's insight; it is distinct from quantitative research design for its unique way of gathering data in the form of words rather than numbers (Kothari, 2004; McMillan & Schumacher, 2010). The qualitative research design of the planned study will include tape-recording of semi structured interviews, note-taking of classroom lesson observations, and document review. The planned study will use these qualitative data collection instruments to ascertain Life Sciences teachers' understanding of technology integration in science classrooms, attitudes towards the use of technologies for teaching and learning, and their level of technological skills to integrate appropriate technologies to assist/support the needs, **difficulties** and cognitive capabilities of their learners. It will also assist the researcher in understanding the role of technology-integrated IBL in science classrooms. It will explore participants' words, actions, and observable characteristics as they are revealed by their experiences (Tamene, 2016).

Quantitative research designs are based on the measurement of quantity or amount, the data collection in the study of a phenomenon is expressed in quantity (Kothari, 2004). Contrary to the nature of subjectivity in qualitative research design, quantitative research design source and gather objective data that can be analyzed numerically (McMillan & Schumacher, 2010). The quantitative research design of the planned study will make use of questionnaires as its data collection instrument. It will address the research hypotheses which state (a). Technology-integrated IBL does not significantly impact positively on teaching and learning of Grade 12 Life Sciences, and (b). The integration of educational technologies does not significantly support Grade 12 Life Sciences learners with varying needs, difficulties, and cognitive capabilities. The results that will be derived from the quantitative approach are envisaged to confirm or authenticate the qualitative results and vice-versa (Noble & Heale, 2019; Abbaszadeh & Hosseinpour, 2011).

Qualitative Data Sources

The planned study will include tape-recording of semi-structured interviews, note-taking of classroom lesson observations, and document review. Qualitative data instruments are to be used to obtain data relevant to the problem statement and research objectives.

a) Semi-structured interviews with open-ended questions will be used during the interviews with a total of 24 participants from three different secondary schools. Three Grade 12 Life Sciences teachers (one from each of the three schools), eighteen Grade 12 Life Sciences learners (a six-learner-group interview from each of the three schools, three female and three male), and three technology or ICT personnel (one from each of the three schools). It will enable the researcher to collect data that capture the judgements of teachers' understanding, attitudes, and expertise on technology integration in the classrooms (Goundar, 2012). Furthermore, the use of technology and technological support for and needs of the learners, the benefits and challenges of technology integration, and the training and support received by the teachers. Data from this primary source is expected to complement data collection from other data sources.
b) Classroom lesson observation will offer the opportunity to source data that pertains to participants' real and lived experiences (McMillan & Schumacher, 2010) or activities on the implementation of technology integration in the classrooms

of the three different participating secondary schools. Researcher will make use of lesson observation schedule to enable collection of pertinent information. It is believed that data collection from the interviews should reflect positively on observable activities. Data from this primary source is expected to complement data collection from the interviews, and document review.

c) Document review will enable the researcher to collect data on previous records of technology integration in the classrooms, training, support, etc. Data from this secondary source is expected to complement data collection from the primary sources.

Quantitative Data Source

The *quantitative data source* will enable the researcher to quantify data collection (Goundar, 2012). The proposed hypotheses will be tested through questionnaires that will be distributed to the same participants for the qualitative study. In addition, questionnaires will be handed to other Grade 12 Life Sciences teachers, Grade 12 Physical Sciences teachers, all Grade 12 Life Sciences learners, and Grade 12 Physical Sciences learners in the three participating secondary schools. A total of six teacher participants, 150 learner participants, and three technology or ICT personnel participants are expected to participate in the data collection through the questionnaires.

Questionnaires will be used to obtain data relevant to the research objectives and hypotheses.

Population and Sampling

McMillan and Schumacher (2010, p. 143) describe the population as "a group of elements or cases, whether individuals, objects, or events, that conform to specific criteria and to which we intend to generalize the results of the research". The research population for the proposed study will comprise Grade 12 Life Sciences teachers, Grade 12 Life Sciences learners, and the school technology and/or ICT personnel. In addition to the specified population, the schools where the data collection will be conducted within Gauteng province, are expected to have science laboratories, libraries, and technology/ICT resources to facilitate the data collection processes.

Sampling in research is the process taken by the researcher in selecting respondents or subjects or participants from whom data are collected and are referred to the research sample, that is selected from the entire specified population (Kothari, 2004; McMillan & Schumacher, 2010). The planned study will use a non-probability sampling.

The qualitative study will use purposeful sampling to select Grade 12 Life Sciences teachers who possess CK, PK, and at least above-average technological/ ICT skills. Grade 12 Life Sciences learners who are in the position of rich data about the phenomenon of interest (Goundar, 2012). The school technology and or ICT personnel who is more advanced and more knowledgeable about the use of technologies for teaching and learning (McMillan & Schumacher, 2010; Sikhosana, Mudau, & Msezane, 2020).

The quantitative study will employ convenience sampling, the participants will be selected based on accessibility, although they all meet the required criteria (McMillan & Schumacher, 2010). The questionnaires will be distributed to all participants (Grade 12 Life Sciences, Grade 12 Physical Sciences, and Technology/ICT personnel) in the three secondary schools where data will be collected.

Data Analysis and Interpretation

Data analysis is a carefully described process of bringing order, structure, and interpretation to collected data, the descriptive statistics that are used to summarize data collected, although, the process could be ambiguous, time-consuming, creative, and fascinating (McMillan & Schumacher, 2010; Marshall & Rossman, 2004). The researcher will adopt thematic data analysis to analyze data collected by identifying vital concepts from the transcribed volume of data to formulate themes (Kiger & Varpio, 2020; Sikhakhane, Govender, & Maphalala, 2021). The planned study will use thematic data analysis in which every interview voice recording will be transcribed verbatim, and pertinent data collection from lesson observations for thematic analysis.

Quantitative data will be described and inferred statistically, processes analyzed before arriving at the statistical results, and an appropriate software package will be employed to ensure validity and reliability (McMillan & Schumacher, 2010; Marshall & Rossman, 2004).

Research Validity and Reliability

Vocabulary had "been recognized as crucial for students who learn Arabic as a foreign language. Students need more Arabic vocabulary to acquire Arabic language skills. This" was the focus of a chapter by Alkasirah, Mohamad, Sanmugam, Ramdas and Zaini (2024, p. 264) examining the *validity and reliability* of an Arabic vocabulary achievement instrument to evaluate a digital storytelling-based application as part of a book on *Embracing Cutting-Edge Technology in Modern Educational Settings* discussed earlier in this chapter.

The *validity* of the research findings is dependent on the reliability of the instruments used for data collection (Kaya & Adiguzel, 2021). Identifying and selecting the appropriate participants, and data collection instruments is vital to ensure credibility and trustworthiness and avoid researcher bias (Nowell, Norris, White, & Moules, 2017). The researcher will engage in a meticulous process to ensure that the findings are worthy and credible. The steps will include identifying and selecting the appropriate participants and data collection instruments with guidance and confirmation from the supervisor (Shenton, 2004; Rajasekar, et al., 2006).

Research Ethics

To protect the participants' confidentiality, voluntary participation, and their right to withdraw from the research study, the researcher will ensure that the guidelines by the University of South Africa (UNISA) College of Education (CEDU), Ethics Review Committee are upheld. All approval will be secured before the start of data collection (Žydžiūnaitė, 2018).

Participants will be provided with a printed electronic copy, explaining what the research study entails, their role in the data collection, and an opportunity to terminate their participation at any time with no penalty, and full disclosure of any risks associated with the study (McMillan & Schumacher, 2010; Žydžiūnaitė, 2018). The consent, assent, and information sheet forms will be fully utilized before the commencement of data collection.

FUTURE RESEARCH DIRECTIONS

This section will discuss future and emerging trends, as well as provide insight about the future of the theme of the book on the Fostering Inclusive Education with AI and Emerging Technologies from the perspective of the chapter focus on Technology-Integrated Inquiry-Based Learning in South African Classrooms from A Case of Selected Grade 12 Secondary Schools. The viability of a paradigm, model, implementation issues of proposed programs, etc., may be included in this section. If appropriate, the section will suggest future research opportunities within the domain of the topic.

Games and Gamification

"Games are not merely for entertainment purposes but rather a powerful tool to be used in the education sector" (Yie, Sanmugam, & Yahaya, 2023, p. 16). Its "use in teaching can be traced back all the way to ancient civilizations." The article by the latter authors considered future instructional design in game-based learning and gamified learning regarding the construction and incorporation of a player typology family tree in the educational context.

Higher Education

Research directions for future studies suggested by Yie, et al. (2023, p. 1) included "to develop a proper gamified depth framework in the educational sector."

Early Childhood Education

"The advancement of technology contributed tremendously" to "the field of education. The use" and importance of augmented reality applications for children's development during the preschool years was one of the emerging technological trends discussed by Barkhaya and Abd Halim (2018b, p. 7935) in their Advanced Science Letters article on preschool learning.

The dynamic nature of workplaces, current emerging global trends, and the 4IR necessitate a dire need for effective integration of technology in teaching and learning. Some teachers were faced with the challenge of integrating technologies into teaching and learning, and could not use technologies to plan, prepare, and implement lesson activities (Ramorola, 2010). The objectives of e-Education are still far from being achieved. Previous research studies on effective technology integration into teaching and learning, such as the case study by Ramorola (2010), had pointed out factors like unavailability of the appropriate technologies, and lack of technical know-how to integrate the technologies as the leading causes of ineffective integration of technologies in the South African classrooms.

CONCLUSION

This last section will provide discussion of the overall coverage of the chapter and concluding remarks.

One of the findings in a previous **case study** by Naiye (2023) revealed how Grade 12 Life Sciences teachers integrated the characteristics of differentiated instruction and differentiated types of inquiry to accommodate learners with diverse needs, difficulties, and cognitive capabilities. The researcher is inspired to develop new knowledge on how science teachers can effectively integrate educational technologies in an IBL classroom to inclusively engage all their learners, and ensure that no learner is left behind due to their learning needs or difficulties. Technology-integrated lesson plans, resources, scientific inquiry, and how science teachers use technologies to actively engage their learners to be well-equipped for the 4IR is believed to contribute to the development of science and technology.

REFERENCES

Abbaszadeh, M., & Hosseinpour, E. (2011). Karbord-e taslis dar pajooheshha-ye keifi ba takid bar nazarie zaminee [Application of triangulation in qualitative research with emphasis on grounded theory]. *Human science methodology, 17*(67), 147-166.

Abel, V. R., Tondeur, J., & Sang, G. (2022). Teacher perceptions about ICT integration into classroom instruction. *Education Sciences*, 12(9), 609. Advance online publication. DOI: 10.3390/educsci12090609

Alkasirah, N. A., Mohamad, M., Sanmugam, M., Ramdas, G., & Zaini, K. M. (2024). Examining the Validity and Reliability of the Arabic Vocabulary Achievement Instrument to Evaluate a Digital Storytelling-Based Application. In *Embracing Cutting-Edge Technology in Modern Educational Settings* (pp. 264–284). IGI Global. DOI: 10.4018/979-8-3693-1022-9.ch012

Barkhaya, N. M., & Abd Halim, N. D. (2016, December). A review of application of 3D hologram in education: A meta-analysis. *8th International Conference on Engineering Education (ICEED)* (pp. 257-260). IEEE. DOI: 10.1109/ICEED.2016.7856083

Barkhaya, N. M., & Abd Halim, N. D. (2017). *Learning through play via visualization tools to enhance student's cognitive abilities among preschool children.* Retrieved November 8, 2018, from https://educ.utm.my/noordayana/files/2012/10/PaperNurul-Maziah.pdf

Barkhaya, N. M., Abd Halim, N. D., & Yahaya, N. (2018a, January). Issues and future trends in preschool children's learning: A preliminary study. *Advanced Science Letters*, 24(1), 178–180. DOI: 10.1166/asl.2018.11951

Barkhaya, N. M., Abd Halim, N. D., & Yahaya, N. (2018b, November 1). The importance of augmented reality application for children's development during preschool years. *Advanced Science Letters*, 24(11), 7935–7938. DOI: 10.1166/asl.2018.12460

Barkhaya, N. M., Abd Halim, N. D., & Yahaya, N. (2018c, November 8-9). Development of 3DPH: HoloRead for preschool children's learning. *10th International Conference on Engineering Education (ICEED)* (pp. 246-250). IEEE. DOI: 10.1109/ICEED.2018.8626977

Bree, R. T. (2019). *Embracing alternative formats, assessment strategies and digital technologies to revitalise practical sessions in science & health.* University of Southampton. Retrieved from https://eprints.teachingandlearning.ie/id/eprint/6593

Brown, H. (2014). *Teachers Attitudes and Confidence in Technology Integration.* (MA dissertation). Marshall University.

Chee, K. N., & Sanmugam, M. (Eds.). (2024). *Embracing Cutting-Edge Technology in Modern Educational Settings*. IGI Global., Retrieved from https://www.igi-global.com/book/embracing-cutting-edge-technology-modern/325800 DOI: 10.4018/979-8-3693-1022-9

Davies, R. S., & West, R. E. (2014). Technology integration in schools. In *Handbook of research on educational communications and technology* (pp. 841–853). Springer. DOI: 10.1007/978-1-4614-3185-5_68

Department of Education. (2004, September 2). White Paper on e-Education: Transforming Learning and Teaching through Information and Communication Technologies (ICTs). *Government Gazette* (26734), pp. 3 - 46.

Dokter, S. M. (2020). *School-based instructional leadership support for information technology and computer applications technology subject teachers.* (Master of Education). UNIVERSITY OF FREE STATE.

Du, S., & Sanmugam, M. (2024). A Bibliometric Review of Studies on the Application of Augmented Reality to Cultural Heritage by Using Biblioshiny and CiteSpace. In *Embracing Cutting-Edge Technology in Modern Educational Settings* (pp. 184–213). IGI Global. DOI: 10.4018/979-8-3693-1022-9.ch009

Du Toit, S., & Goosen, L. (2024). Transformative Technologies for Supporting Children With Fetal Alcohol Syndrome and Autism Spectrum Disorders. In Garcia, M., & de Almeida, R. (Eds.), *Transformative Approaches to Patient Literacy and Healthcare Innovation* (pp. 156–179). IGI Global., DOI: 10.4018/979-8-3693-3661-8.ch008

Garcia, M. B., Arif, Y. M., Khlaif, Z. N., Zhu, M., de Almeida, R. P., de Almeida, R. S., & Masters, K. (2024). Effective Integration of Artificial Intelligence in Medical Education: Practical Tips and Actionable Insights. In *Transformative Approaches to Patient Literacy and Healthcare Innovation* (pp. 1-19). IGI Global.

Goundar, S. (2012, May). Research Methodology and Research Method. In *RESEARCH METHODOLOGY.* Victoria University of Wellington. Retrieved from https://prallagon.com/wp-content/uploads/2021/05/Research-Methodology-A2.pdf

Hart, S. A. (2023). Identifying the factors impacting the uptake of educational technology in South African schools: A systematic review. *South African Journal of Education*, 43(1), 2174. Advance online publication. DOI: 10.15700/saje.v43n1a2174

Hew, K. F., & Brush, T. (2007). Integrating technology into K-12 teaching and learning: Current knowledge gaps and recommendations for future research. *Educational Technology Research and Development*, 55(3), 223–252. DOI: 10.1007/s11423-006-9022-5

Kamal, T., & Illiyan, A. (2021). School teachers' perception and challenges towards online teaching during COVID-19 pandemic in India: An econometric analysis. *Asian Association of Open Universities Journal*, 16(3), 311–325. DOI: 10.1108/AAOUJ-10-2021-0122

Kamal, T., Khan, M. A., Hamad, Z., Illiyan, A., Das, A. K., & Alkhuraydili, A. (2023). Perception and Challenges of Virtual Classes with Gender Digital Divide amidst and Post-COVID-19 Pandemic in Iraq: An Empirical Analysis. *Education Research International*, 2023(1), 1–14. Advance online publication. DOI: 10.1155/2023/3665768

Kaya, H., & Adiguzel, T. (2021). Technology integration through evidence-based multimodal reflective professional training. *Contemporary Educational Technology*, 13(4), ep323. Advance online publication. DOI: 10.30935/cedtech/11143

Khlaif, Z. N., Mousa, A., Hattab, M. K., Itmazi, J., Hassan, A. A., Sanmugam, M., & Ayyoub, A. (2023). The potential and concerns of using AI in scientific research: ChatGPT performance evaluation. *JMIR Medical Education*, 9, e47049. Advance online publication. DOI: 10.2196/47049 PMID: 37707884

Khlaif, Z. N., Mousa, A., & Sanmugam, M. (2024). Immersive Extended Reality (XR) Technology in Engineering Education: Opportunities and Challenges. *Technology, Knowledge and Learning*, 1-24. DOI: 10.1007/s10758-023-09719-w

Kiger, M. E., & Varpio, L. (2020). Thematic analysis of qualitative data: AMEE Guide No. 131. *Medical Teacher*, 42(8), 846–854. DOI: 10.1080/0142159X.2020.1755030 PMID: 32356468

Kilfoil, W. R. (Ed.). (2015). *Moving beyond the hype: A contextualised view of learning with technology in higher education*. Universities South Africa.

Kothari, C. R. (2004). *Research Methodology: Methods & Techniques*. New Age International.

Lim, D., Sanmugam, M., & Yahaya, W. A. (2023). Addressing the Dilemma of Online Gamification with Subgame Perfect Equilibria. *International Journal of Information and Education Technology (IJIET)*, 13(4), 757–762. Advance online publication. DOI: 10.18178/ijiet.2023.13.4.1864

Magd, H., & Ruzive, B. (2020, December). Innovative Assessment Techniques, Strategies, Tools and Technologies. In Singh, U. G., & Nair, C. S. (Eds.), (pp. 233–243). Victorian Institute of Technology.

Marshall, C., & Rossman, G. B. (2014). Designing qualitative research. *Sage (Atlanta, Ga.)*.

Mashile, T. Z. (2016). *Technology integration and the digital divide: understanding factors that impact on educators' ability to integrate technology in South African classrooms*. University of Pretoria.

McLeod, S. (2018). Technology integration, leadership, and organizational support frameworks for instructional improvement with information technology. In *Second handbook of information technology in primary and secondary education* (pp. 535–542). Springer. DOI: 10.1007/978-3-319-71054-9_36

McMillan, J. H., & Schumacher, S. (2010). *Research in education* (7th ed.). Pearson.

Mishra, P., & Koehler, M. J. (2006). Technology pedagogical content knowledge: A framework for teacher knowledge. *Teachers College Record*, 108(6), 1017–1054. DOI: 10.1111/j.1467-9620.2006.00684.x

Naiye, O. D. (2023). *Teachers' Perceptions of Inquiry-Based Learning in Teaching Grade 12 Life Sciences: A Case Study*. (M.Ed. Dissertation). University of South Africa.

Namreen Asif, V. A., & Panakaje, N. (2022). PARADIGM SHIFT-the role of educational technology and internet in Indian education system. [IJCSBE]. *International Journal of Case Studies in Business, IT, and Education*, 6(2), 930–944.

Nee, C. K., Sanmugam, M., Yahaya, N., Ibrahim, N. H., Rahman, M. H., & Razak, R. A. (2023). New Normal of Education: Practical Implementation of Teaching and Learning Online in a Diverse Environment Across the Globe. In *Comparative Research on Diversity in Virtual Learning: Eastern vs. Western Perspectives* (pp. 160-178). IGI Global.

Ngugi, J. K., & Goosen, L. (2021). Innovation, Entrepreneurship, and Sustainability for ICT Students Towards the Post-COVID-19 Era. In Carvalho, L. C., Reis, L., & Silveira, C. (Eds.), *Handbook of Research on Entrepreneurship, Innovation, Sustainability, and ICTs in the Post-COVID-19 Era* (pp. 110–131). IGI Global., DOI: 10.4018/978-1-7998-6776-0.ch006

Noble, H., & Heale, R. (2019). Triangulation in research, with examples. *Evidence-Based Nursing*, 22(3), 67–68. DOI: 10.1136/ebnurs-2019-103145 PMID: 31201209

Nowell, L. S., Norris, J. M., White, D. E., & Moules, N. J. (2017). Thematic analysis: Striving to meet the trustworthiness criteria. *International Journal of Qualitative Methods*, 16(1), 1609406917733847. Advance online publication. DOI: 10.1177/1609406917733847

Nuhoğlu, H., & Seçkin, G. G. (2021). The Analysis of Relationship Between Teacher 21 st Century Teaching-Learning Skills and Information Technology Usage Levels. *Ahi Evran Üniversitesi Kırşehir Eğitim Fakültesi Dergisi*, 22(3), 1358–1388.

O'Toole, R. B. (2013). *Pedagogical strategies and technologies for peer assessment in Massively Open Online Courses (MOOCs). Discussion Paper. (Unpublished).* Coventry, UK: University of Warwick. Retrieved from https://wrap.warwick.ac.uk/54602/

Raja, R., & Nagasubramani, P. C. (2018). Impact of modern technology in education. *Journal of Applied and Advanced Research*, 3(1), 33–35. DOI: 10.21839/jaar.2018.v3iS1.165

Rajasekar, S., Philominathan, P., & Chinnathambi, V. (2006, January). *Research Methodology.* Retrieved from https://www.researchgate.net/publication/2174858_Research_Methodology

Ramorola, M. Z. (2010). *A study of effective technology integration into teaching and learning: A case study.* Pretoria: (Unpubished doctoral dissertation). University of South Africa.

Ramorola, M. Z. (2013). Challenge of effective technology integration into teaching and learning. *Africa Education Review*, 10(4), 654–670. DOI: 10.1080/18146627.2013.853559

Ramorola, M. Z. (2018, May 3). *Transforming teaching and learning through technology integration.* Retrieved from https://www.unisa.ac.za/static/corporate_web/Content/News%20&%20Media/Articles/Documents/TECHNOLOGY%20INTEGRATION%20IN%20TEACHING%20AND%20LEARNING_FINAL(27).pdf

Schmitt, C. (2002). *Technology in schools: Suggestions, tools, and guidelines for assessing technology in elementary and secondary education.* US Department of Education, Office of Educational Research and Improvement, National Center for Education Statistics.

Shenton, A. K. (2004). Strategies for ensuring trustworthiness in qualitative research projects. *Education for Information*, 22(2), 63–75. DOI: 10.3233/EFI-2004-22201

Sikhakhane, M., Govender, S., & Maphalala, M. C. (2021). South African Teachers' Perspectives on Using the Computer as a Tool for Teaching and Learning. *International Journal of Education and Practice*, 9(1), 93–104. DOI: 10.18488/journal.61.2021.91.93.104

Sikhosana, L., Mudau, A. V., & Msezane, S. B. (2020). Insights into the integration of environmental education in the senior phase. *Journal for the Education of Gifted Young Scientists*, 8(4), 1411–1425. DOI: 10.17478/jegys.750519

Silva, J. B., Silva, I. N., & Bilessimo, S. M. (2020). Technological structure for technology integration in the classroom, inspired by the maker culture. *Journal of Information Technology Education*, 19, 167–204. DOI: 10.28945/4532

Suhadi, S. M., Mohamed, H., Abdullah, Z., Zaid, N. M., Aris, B., & Sanmugam, M. (2021). Enhancing Student's Higher Order Thinking Skills (HOTS) through the Socratic Method Approach with Technology. In *Research Anthology on Developing Critical Thinking Skills in Students* (pp. 1399-1412). IGI Global.

Sumadevi, S. (2023). EFFECTIVE USE OF DIVERSE TECHNOLOGY TOOLS IN FLIPPED LEARNING APPROACH. *Journal of Historical Research*, 53(2), 106–113.

Tamene, E. H. (2016). Theorizing conceptual framework. *Asian Journal of Educational Research*, 4(2), 50–56.

Venkatesh, V., Morris, M. G., Davis, G. B., & Davis, F. (2003). User Acceptance of Information Technology: Toward a Unified View. *Management Information Systems Quarterly*, 27(3), 425–478. DOI: 10.2307/30036540

Venkatesh, V., Thong, J. Y., & Xu, X. (2012). Consumer acceptance and use of information technology: Extending the unified theory of acceptance and use of technology. *Management Information Systems Quarterly*, 36(1), 157–178. DOI: 10.2307/41410412

Winter, E., Costello, A., O'Brien, M., & Hickey, G. (2021). Teachers' use of technology and the impact of Covid-19. *Irish Educational Studies*, 40(2), 235–246. DOI: 10.1080/03323315.2021.1916559

Wood, L., & Reefke, H. (2010). Working with a diverse class: Reflections on the role of team teaching, teaching tools and technological support. *Proceedings of the IADIS international conference on international higher education (IHE)* (pp. 72-79). International Association for Development of the Information Society.

Yemothy, N. E. (2015). *Improving educational technology integration in the classroom.* (Doctoral dissertation). Walden University.

Yie, D. L., & Sanmugam, M. (2023). The Contribution of Diversity Towards Player Traits of Learners in a Classroom: Constructing a Theoretical Conceptual Framework. In *Comparative Research on Diversity in Virtual Learning: Eastern vs. Western Perspectives* (pp. 136-159). IGI Global.

Yie, D. L., Sanmugam, M., & Yahaya, W. A. (2023). Future Instructional Design in Game-based Learning and Gamified Learning: The Construction and Incorporation of Player Typology Family Tree in the Educational Context. [CPLT]. *Journal of Creative Practices in Language Learning and Teaching*, 11(3), 16–37.

Yie, D. L., Sanmugam, M., Yahaya, W. A., & Khlaif, Z. N. (2023). *The Effect of Gamified Depth on Malaysian Higher Education Students' Intrinsic Motivation Level and Achievement Level.* Retrieved from https://www.researchsquare.com/article/rs-3113140/latest

Zulkeflee, N. R., Sanmugam, M., & Nee, C. K. (2023). The Effect of Online Learning on Undergraduate Student Achievement and Engagement During Times of Emergency Remote Teaching (ERT). In *Comparative Research on Diversity in Virtual Learning: Eastern vs. Western Perspectives* (pp. 105-135). IGI Global.

Zungu, N. V. (2022). *Understanding teachers' integration of information and communication technology (ICT) in teaching Grade 7 natural sciences.* (Doctoral dissertation) University of KwaZulu-Natal.

Žydžiūnaitė, V. (2018). Implementing ethical principles in social research: Challenges, possibilities and limitations. *Profesinis rengimas: tyrimai ir realijos, 29*, 19-43.

Chapter 12
Technology's Role in Learning English Language in an Inclusive Setup

Jagneet Kour
https://orcid.org/0009-0003-0341-3636
Eternal University, India

Raino Bhatia
https://orcid.org/0000-0002-5379-3003
Eternal University, India

Richa Joshi
https://orcid.org/0009-0006-7286-6585
Eternal University, India

ABSTRACT

The inclusion of digital technology into the study of languages has revolutionised approaches to education, especially in multicultural environments, at a period that has witnessed swift progress in technology. The study examines the impact of technological innovations on improving the learning of the English language for a wide range of learners, including individuals with challenges and different levels of fluency. This study investigates a range of technology tools and platforms, including language learning apps, versatile software, and augmented reality (AR), that are designed to meet the diverse learning styles and educational requirements of individuals. The study examines scenarios and current research to demonstrate that technological advances may improve mobility, offer personalised learning ex-

DOI: 10.4018/979-8-3693-7255-5.ch012

periences, and facilitate inclusive educational opportunities. The results emphasise the capacity of technology to address disparities in language acquisition, encourage active participation, and advance equal access to education.

INTRODUCTION

The emergence of technological advances in learning environments has fundamentally transformed the methods of instruction and accumulation of knowledge, especially in the field of learning foreign languages. The discipline of classroom instruction in the English language has significantly grown in our interwoven society, representing various challenges and possibilities for educators. They must address the requirements of learners from different cultural, linguistic, and socioeconomic backgrounds (Johnson, 2020). The key to combating these difficulties is the introduction of differentiated education, which is an educational approach that recognises and caters to the individual patterns of learning, talents, and passions of students individually (Smith & Williams, 2021). The article examines the problems teachers have when they try to use modern technology appropriately and discusses areas for further study concerning getting the greatest out of digital tools in inclusive education. The term "inclusive education" refers to an instructional approach for educating that strives to integrate all pupils, irrespective of their physiological, cerebral, interpersonal, or language differences, into regular classroom settings. It seeks to realise the goal of providing equitable educational possibilities and nurturing an atmosphere that makes every single pupil acknowledged and welcomed (Bhatia & Kaur, 2024). Nevertheless, there has been an increasing emphasis on achieving balance and inclusivity in language learning. This has been recognised as an essential requirement ensuring that all students have equitable opportunities to get the best possible education and achieve excellence (Kaur &Bhatia, 2024). Technology has the ability to greatly transform the field of English language education and learning in today's ever-changing environment. Technologies enables academics an extensive number of possibilities to enhance lessons, involve students, and promote equality and inclusivity in the educational environment. This includes using exciting multimedia tools and interactive internet-based tools (Means et al., 2010; Unger & Tracey, 2013).

According to this scenario, understanding the English language has become a prerequisite for career progression, international interaction, and educational achievement. The importance of the development of English becomes more perceptible in inclusive educational environments, whereas students with a variety of requirements necessitate learning approaches that are customised. Technology has emerged as a critical instrument in addressing these diverse specifications, providing novel approaches that can be designed to accommodate varying modes of learning, competencies, and paces of change. The emergence of electronic instructional assistance, such as simulated classrooms and participatory language applications, have cracked up fresh opportunities for improving language learning that were not thought in previous decades. Numerous studies have attempted to investigate instructors' perspectives on mainstreaming and, in recent months, equitable learning for students with particular requirements, operating under the premise that the teaching profession's supportive mindsets are crucial to the effective execution of any inclusive policy (Avramidis& Norwich,2002).The principle of universal design for Learning (also known as UDL) emerged as an outcome of the worldwide awareness of the educational plan for allowing the participation of children with special needs learners in the regular classroom setting of a neighbourhood school, thus establishing a broader discovering community. The UDL emphasises the use of modern technology to create a high-quality atmosphere for learning giving students' endless possibilities for efficiency and stimulating exchanges, thereby optimising the academic and personal growth of all learners (Chambers, 2020). Besides, the Universal Declaration of Salamanca (UNESCO, 1994) and a welcoming perspective in education both strive to ensure that all students, despite their differences in background and ability, are socially included in the classroom culture. This fosters a sense of compassion and equitable participation for every learner (Chambers, 2020; Avramidis & Norwich, 2002).

Significance of Innovation

Throughout the last several decades, the relationship of technology impact on education has grown drastically, ushering in novel models for both instructional and student achievement. Innovation acts as an interface for learners to access diverse resources that assist with enhancing their ability to communicate when mastering English. Digital lets learners to practise reading, writing, speaking, and listening in a more dynamic and interesting route, using automated language acquisition (CALL), mobile applications, or online environments. Regardless, in order to maximise the power of science and technology, it is imperative to possess a deep understanding of ways to effortlessly incorporate it into personalised learning methods, while simultaneously adequately catering to the varied requirements of individuals (Brown, 2019; Castro & Tumlin, 2020). Technology also makes it possible for students to pursue education at their own speed and in harmony with the specific needs through individualised instruction. This adaptation is essential for youngsters in inclusive environments since it helps with particular challenges including linguistic obstacles, developmental delays, and the emotional and social development difficulties. This chapter explores the various ways technology can help with ESL instruction in inclusive classrooms, emphasising out the benefits and drawbacks of this strategy.

Background of the Study

In recent years, the rise of digital tools have made it easier to learn English, especially in places where everyone is welcome. Mobile-assisted language learning (MALL) is becoming more and more popular. Apps like Duolingo, Babbel, and Memrise render learning a language more personalised. These apps use game-like elements, adaptive learning systems, and real-time feedback to keep students interested and meet their specific needs (Godwin-Jones, 2017). Aubern, Taylor-Guy, and van der Keij(2024) explore the significance of assessing the efficacy of educational technology in schools, recognising how much more people rely on such resources to improve teaching and learning results. The authors present the Education Technology Value Evaluation Tool as a pragmatic option for schools to systematically evaluate the worth of the technology they adopt. This tool is especially important considering the broad spectrum of educational technology accessible and the different effects they might have on student participation and understanding. The authors emphasise the significance of continual examination, proposing that the efficacy of technology in education should be consistently assessed as a continually evolving process. This enables educational institutions to adjust to evolving requirements for learning and technology progress, guaranteeing the continued relevance and performance of the tools they engage. Learning management systems (LMS) and virtual classrooms have also changed standard classrooms into dynamic places to learn. Teachers can set up and run digital classrooms with platforms like Google Classroom, Moodle, and Edmodo so that students have access to materials, join discussions, and work on tasks at their own convenience (Dillenbourg, 2016). In inclusive settings, where students of different skills can interact with the material in ways that work for them, these tools are especially helpful. Moreover, the use of helpful tools like text-to-speech (TTS) and speech-to-text (STT) software has made it easier for disabled students to learn the English language. Students who have trouble seeing or hearing can fully join in activities involving language learning with the support of these electronic devices (King-Sears, & Johnson, 2020). With the rise of language labs and audiolingual methods in the middle of the 20th century, technology has been used to help people learn languages. Early technologies were mostly about doing the same things over and over and listening to different things. They paved the way for what would become more advanced tools. Computer-Assisted Language Learning (CALL), which came out in the 1980s and 1990s, was a big turning point. CALL added more dynamic and interesting ways to learn languages by using audio, video, and text along with other media to make the learning experience better(Chapelle,

2001; Larsen-Freeman & Anderson, 2013).It used to be uncomplicated drill-based initiatives, but over the course of time, CALL has grown into more useful and interactive tools that help with many language skills. The internet's growth in the 1990s changed language learning even more by giving people access to materials from around the world, letting them talk to native speakers in genuine time, and helping them learn together through virtual networks (Warschauer, 1996).Research shows that students from disadvantaged homes often have to deal with extra problems that can make it harder for them to learn, like language barriers, socioeconomic disadvantages, and cultural differences (Nieto, 2015). The goal of inclusion efforts is to fix these problems by making sure that all students can access and benefit from educational tools and methods. People have found that technology is a strong way to promote fairness and inclusion. Digital tools can help close the gaps caused by differences in income by giving everyone access to high-quality learning materials and activities (Hehir, 2005). Ebrahimzadeh and Sepideh (2017) found that the utilisation of educational games greatly improves the process of acquiring language skills and increases the level of involvement among those learning English as a second language (ELLs). Their research emphasises the efficacy of interactive technologies in enhancing comprehension and long-term recall of unfamiliar words. For instance, online translation tools and bilingual dictionaries help English language learners (ELLs) understand what is being said in their original language. Also, educational technology can help make classrooms more welcoming by adapting to different learning styles and needs. This way, all students can have the chance to do well (Roblyer & Doering, 2007).Case studies that show how technology can be used to support differentiated teaching, equity, and inclusion are becoming more common in the literature. As an example, studies on the use of online collaboration tools in classrooms have shown that these technologies can make learning more fun and open to all students by letting students of all abilities and backgrounds work together (Voigt & Simmonds, 2017). Similarly, adding game-based learning tools has been shown to get more students, even those who have trouble learning, interested and involved (Gee, 2003). Even though there are benefits, using technology in schooling has been linked to a number of problems. Technical problems, like not enough infrastructure and trouble with accessibility, can make technology-based teaching less useful. Hodges, Moore, and Lockee (2013) generated an extensive manual for assessing the efficacy of instructional technology, presenting evidence-based strategies that can be implemented in many educational environments. Their study provides a helpful resource for educators who are looking to evaluate and adopt technology-driven teaching practices. Ertmer and Ottenbreit-Leftwich (2010) also say that teachers need ongoing professional development to make sure they know how to use these tools well and can put them to good use. It's still important to think about cultural sensitivity and digital equality, because when schools adopt technology, they need to make sure that all of their students can use it to its full potential (Hoffman & Schraw, 2016). In this study, Barry, Murphy, and Drew (2015) investigate the transition from deconstructive misaligned to productive alignment in educational settings. They highlight the potential of students' utilisation of handheld devices in facilitating enhanced educational experiences. Their research demonstrates that the thoughtful incorporation of portable electronics into classroom activities can augment curiosity among pupils and improve educational outcomes.

Literature Spaces

Although technology-assisted language learning has made great progress, there are still notable deficiencies in the existing literature, specifically with the convergence of technology, inclusive education, and English language acquisition. Although many research have investigated the efficacy of various multimedia resources in language learning, only a handful of studies have particularly examined their influence in inclusive environments. In addition, there is a dearth of longitudinal research that investigate the enduring impact of technology usage on language competence and overall academic achievement in inclusive settings. The investigation of language and multiculturalism within inclusive settings is another area that needs further attention. A large body of research has ignored the realities faced by multilingual learners and instead concentrated on ESL students in monolingual settings. There has to be more research into how these students may be helped by technology, especially in inclusive settings. A lot of study is being done on the use of artificial intelligence (AI) in education, but not much is known about how it can be used in inclusive English language learning. AI could offer much personalised learning experiences, but we need to do more research on what this means for equal treatment, inclusion, and connectivity in language learning.

Case Studies of Technology-Enhanced English Inclusive Learning

1. The investigation conducted by Waddell and Kim (2021) examined the usage of digital platforms, notably Google Classroom and educational applications, in a secondary school English course that comprised of a heterogeneous group of students, even those with learning differences and linguistic obstacles. The combination of these technologies facilitated individualised instruction, enabling students to progress at their respective speed and obtain personalised assessment. Comparing against traditional approaches, the study revealed that children with learning difficulties had a 25% improvement in comprehension of texts and a 30% improvement in writing skills.

2. Nguyen and Thompson (2020) conducted a research study that examined at how an inclusive English language teaching used interactive tools such as Kahoot! and Quizlet. Reading comprehension and vocabulary development were enhanced through the software. Adolescents with attention deficit hyperactivity disorder (ADHD) and similar disorders benefited greatly from the software's multimedia capabilities, which allowed for greater student engagement and the inclusion of immediate assistance. Vocabulary recollection improved significantly and classroom involvement increased by 40% as a result of enhanced engagement.

Importance of Technology for All Students of English

- Equal Rights and Inclusion in Language Learning

Understanding Equity in English Language Learning: Understanding equity in English language learning means making sure that each student gets the help they need to succeed. This method takes into account that students come from different places and may have different problems. For instance, students who are English language learners (ELLs) might need extra help, like extra training or language support, to get good at the language (Gándara & Hopkins, 2010). Equity makes sure that these extra help is given to all students, so that they all have the same chance to succeed in learning English, no matter where they start. Making sure everyone has a fair chance to learn English. (Ladson-Billings, 2006). Inclusion in English Language Learning makes sure that all students feel welcome and valued in the classroom, no matter how well they speak English, what culture they come from, or what kind of learning needs they have, is what inclusion in English language learning means (Tomlinson, 2001). It means making learning materials and exercises that work for students of all abilities and encourage them to be involved. For example, to help all students, an inclusive classroom might use visual tools, individualised lessons, and chances to work together to learn (Florian & Black-Hawkins, 2011). Inclusion makes sure that every student can fully participate in the English language curriculum and feel like they fit in the classroom (Ainscow, 2005).

- Understanding Differentiated Instruction in Language Education

Definition of Differentiated instruction "Differentiated instruction (DI) is a framework for teaching that aims to support students with different backgrounds and needs in a classroom. It involves making changes to the curriculum and teaching methods to meet the individual interests, needs, and strengths of each student. DI can include modifications to the content, process, or product, or the learning environment" (Tomlinson, 2001). "Differentiation means tailoring instruction to meet individual needs. Whether teachers differentiate content, process, products, or the learning environment, the use of ongoing assessment and flexible grouping makes this a successful approach to instruction" (Heacox, 2012). Differentiated instruction is an instructional method that personalises education to fulfil multiple needs of individuals (Subban, 2006). This method takes into account the fact that every student is unique in terms of their experiences, interests, aptitudes, and instructional styles. The purpose is to ensure that all learners have an equitable opportunity of succeeding and thrive. According to Tomlinson (2001), differentiated instruction (DI) is a method of teaching that aims to accommodate students with varying learning styles by giving them more opportunities to interact with and demonstrate mastery of course material. If you want your DI to be successful, you need to know your students' unique strengths and weaknesses and create lessons that can accommodate their different learning styles and talents, says Tomlinson. According to studies (Hall, Strangman, & Meyer, 2009), this method is shown to significantly enhance student outcomes. Modern Tools for Personalised Learning A lot of recent writing has focused on ways that technology may improve DI. By tailoring course materials and teacher approaches to each student's unique strengths and weaknesses, adaptive learning platforms and educational applications facilitate highly individualised education (Knewton, 2014).Adaptive learning systems, for example, use algorithms to look at how well students are doing and change the difficulty of tasks in real time, making learning more personalised (Cavanaugh, 2008). These tools and techniques make it easier for teachers to meet the needs of students with different levels of ability than older ways (Bebell & O'Dwyer, 2010). Fairness and acceptance are important parts of good teaching, especially in schools with lots of different kinds of students. Giving all students the same chances and tools in school is called equity. On the other hand, making a learning space where all learners have a sense of belonging is called inclusion (Gay, 2018).

- Universal Design for Learning:

Principles: Universal design for learning (UDL) centres on making ensuring all students can access and engage with learning by providing diverse ways of representation, expression, and participation.

Presentation: Offer information in various formats (such as text, audio, and video) to cater to a range of learning preferences.

Give students multiple opportunities to express themselves, such as by submitting written reports, giving oral presentations, or creating artistic works.

Give students options on how to learn and engage with the content to keep them interested and engaged.

- Individualised Education

Personalised educational encounters are made possible by technology, which is one of its most significant benefits to inclusive education. It can be difficult for educators in traditional classrooms to meet the requirements of all of their students, especially in a multicultural environment where students learn at different rates, styles, and capacities. Nevertheless, technological advancements have made it possible to create individualised learning plans that cater to every student's specific requirements, allowing them to reach their maximum potential (Chen & Kuo, 2015; Saubern, Taylor-Guy, & van der Keij, 2022).

Innovative educational platforms, for instance, evaluate a student's existing skill level using techniques and then modify the difficulty of assignments based on that evaluation. In this way, we know that our pupils will not be bored or frightened by the level of difficulty of the assignments (Barry, Murphy, & Drew, 2015). In the context of ESL instruction, this can include personalising activities like reading comprehension, language drills, and building vocabulary according to every student's unique strengths and weaknesses (Ebrahimzadeh & Sepideh, 2017). Visual aids, auditory explanations, and virtual reality experiences are just a few examples of how technologies can help learners who have challenges with learning participate with the content in a fresh manner (Hodges, Moore, & Lockee, 2013).

- Easy Accessibility

When it comes to studying English, technological advances serves as vital in order to render it more accessible, especially for learners with limitations. Screen readers, voice recognition software, and alternate input devices are examples of assistive technology that allow students with impairments to fully engage in educational activities. When it comes to reading materials that can be inaccessible to students with visual impairments, text-to-speech (TTS) technology is a great example because it converts written text into spoken words (Chen & Tzeng, 2020). Furthermore, speech-to-text (STT) software helps students who have physically or auditory impairments with writing assignments and communications by translating spoken words into type (Viner& Shaughnessy, 2020). Individuals who have trouble hearing or who are learning English can benefit from subtitles and other visual aids because they provide multisensory information that improves comprehension (Higgins & Johnstone, 2005). Students are able to work at their own speed while still having access to all the materials they need and taking part in class discussions thanks to the adaptable learning environments made possible by technological advancements. Students with cognitive or physical impairments who need more time to absorb material or who need to take frequent breaks would benefit greatly from this adaptability (Al-Azawei, Serenelli, & Lundqvist, 2016).

- Active involvement and enthusiasm

Technology greatly improves enthusiasm and drive, two elements that are crucial for effective language acquisition. By combining activities, differentiation, and immediate responses, electronic resources like instructional games, interactive simulations, and rich multimedia materials enhance student participation. To encourage consistent usage and progress, many language learning applications employ gamification elements such as rewards, badges, and leader boards (Anderson, 2017). When used in inclusive classrooms, these strategies can help students with diverse learning styles, motivation, and difficulties (Deterding et al., 2011). Digital media details about such films and interactive activities, can also be accessed and enjoyed by students with a variety of instructional styles, owing to technological advancements (Mayer, 2009). Digital provides students with special requirements with more opportunities of demonstrating learning while engaging in exercises. For example, they can use multimedia storytelling tools or speech recognition software (Betrus & Zientek, 2013).

- Working Together and Sharing Information

By encouraging students to take part in valuable conversations with one another, electronic devices improves language learning communication and teamwork. Online discussion forums, collaborative writing platforms, and video conferencing provide learners with a friendly atmosphere for joining in shared endeavours and practise language skills. According to Kreijns, Kirschner, and Jochems (2003), written collaboratively platforms such as Google Docs allow for the provision of immediate assistance and the development of an emotional belonging. Also, students can engage with native speakers and language specialists from all around the world through the use of science and technology, which expands their learning chances beyond the traditional classroom setting. Primarily for pupils attending inclusive settings, such interaction can empower them by enriching their learning experience through the introduction of diverse cultures and linguistic intricacies (Warschauer, 2011). Technology aids in making the classroom a more welcoming place for all students by facilitating a variety of ways of communicating and working together.

- Regular Assessing and Discussion of ESL Students' Progress Formative Evaluations

Using preliminary assessments is crucial for tracking student growth and tailoring lessons to individual need. Teachers are able to adjust their lessons based on students' progress because of the constant feedback they receive from strategies like quizzes, exit tickets, and observations. Exit tickets reveal students' immediate understanding and areas that need reinforcement, whereas tests assess their mastery of current subject (Black & Wiliam, 1998). Teachers can make informed decisions based on real-time data from observations regarding student involvement and learning behaviours (Heritage, 2010).For students to make progress, they need guidance that is both promptly provided and detailed. Particular parts that perform should be the emphasis of feedback, with explicit instructions on how to fix shortcomings and improve abilities. Students are better able to make focused modifications after using this method to identify their strengths as well as areas for improvement (Hattie & Timperley, 2007).

- English Language Learning Centres and Zones for Various Activities

By organising the instructional space into smaller, more manageable spaces, called "learning zones" or "centres," teachers can give their students more control over their language learning experience. Some examples of possible platforms include those that focus on comprehension of reading, writing, listening, and speaking. Students are free to discover what works best for them academically while progressing at their individual speed in this environment (Beck, McKeown, & Kucan, 2002). This kind of differentiation helps students from all backgrounds learn by meeting their individual requirements.

- Method for Spinning

Students will engage in a wide range of assignments while gaining knowledge in different ways when they flip between zones. Students' varied learning styles and skill levels are met by this method, which also maintains their engagement. Students learn more about the content and build more versatile skills when they switch it up in class (Tomlinson, 2001). Teachers can gather a more complete picture of their students' learning progress by using this strategy to watch and evaluate them in a variety of settings.

PROBLEMS WITH BRIDGING THE DIGITAL DIVIDE IN ENGLISH LANGUAGE INSTRUCTION

Digital Divide

When it comes to using technology for inclusive English language instruction, the digital divide is a major obstacle. This chasm represents the gulf between those whose lives are enriched by the availability of contemporary forms of information and communication technology. This disparity is greatly affected by variables including socioeconomic position, physical location, and the accessibility of facilities (Warschauer, 2003).Limited access to current gadgets, latest software applications, and dependable connectivity to the internet is a common problem for students from families with low incomes or those living in remote areas. In inclusive settings, where students with disabilities may already face additional challenges, this dearth of equitable access might worsen educational inequality. In the absence of appropriate technology, such children may find it difficult to stay up with their classmates, which could result in further exclusion and worse academic performance (Selwyn, 2004). Furthermore, there are still differences in the effectiveness of these tools, particularly in regions where technology is more widely available. New instructional software and technology may be available to schools in more affluent regions, whereas schools in poorer locations may have to make do with antiquated or ineffective tools. Because of this inequitable distribution of technology, there may be large gaps in educational quality, which might exacerbate existing inequalities between student groups (OECD, 2015).

Professionally Upgradation of Teachers' Personality

The successful incorporation of modern technology into inclusive English language learning hinges heavily on sufficient teacher training. The capacity of instructors to incorporate these advances into their educational practices determines the effective utilisation of gadgets, despite its notable advantages. But most educators are unlikely to have the background, expertise, or self-assurance to make good use of technology in the educational setting (Ertmer, 1999).This difficulty is magnified in inclusive classrooms since teachers there have to deal with a wide variety of student requirements. Teachers should have strong technical skills and be able to customise digital resources to meet the needs of students with a wide range of abilities and learning styles. To achieve this goal, educators must participate in continuous professional development programs that provide them with pedagogical and technological abilities (Mouza, 2009). Teachers are ill-equipped to make full use of technology for inclusive education since many school systems offer either inadequate or poorly targeted continuing education opportunities (Guskey, 2003).

Unwillingness to Adaptations

Another significant roadblock to effectively promoting technology into inclusive English language learning is unwillingness to adaptation. Teachers and students equally may be hesitant to embrace cutting-edge technologies if they are not comfortable with them, scared of the unidentified or overly attached to the ways things have always been done (Rogers, 2003). In inclusion work environments, where people tend to value stability and predictability more, the uprising can be particularly poignant. Teachers might consider new technologies as either a challenge to their already heavy workloads or a danger to long-standing methods of instruction. Teachers may be resistant to technological advancements out of concern that they may force them to abandon some of their pedagogical practices (Inan & Lowther, 2010). In order to overcome this resistance, it is essential to offer sufficient support and training while also encouraging a positive outlook on technology and its advantages. It may be particularly difficult for students, particularly those who have impairments, to adjust to technological changes. When people aren't familiar with or have had bad experiences with new instruments, they may be resistant to using them. To lessen the impact of these difficulties, it is helpful to provide transition tactics that are both supportive and that highlight the advantages of technology (Cox & Preston, 1999).

Confidentiality and Moral Questions

Moral and confidentiality issues arise with the implementation of modern technologies in learning, particularly in welcoming environments where youngsters may be more susceptible to hacking vulnerabilities. There is a greater chance of abuse and breaches of confidentiality due to the large amounts of data collected and stored by digital technologies on students' learning activities (Starkey, 2020).Unauthorised people may gain ownership of educational records regarding their academic progress, disability, or personal information, which could result in exploitation or stigmatisation. Meanwhile, if educational technologies that utilise AI and ML algorithms are not built with inclusiveness in mind, these systems could introduce discrimination. Inadequately designed algorithms have the risk of unintentionally perpetuating prejudices or preventing some groups from accessing the advantages of technology-assisted learning (Pardo & Siemens, 2014).Informed permission is a must. Every student and their family should know exactly what will happen to their personal information and be able to choose not to have it used at any point. The rights and safety of every student can only be guaranteed via open dialogue and strict regulations on the handling of personal information (Moore & Tillberg-Webb 2023).

Benefits of English Language Acquisition in an Inclusive Setting

- Better motivation and engagement: Technology-supported inclusive settings can make students much more interested in learning. The research conducted by Johnson and Adams (2021) says that digital and engaging tools make English lessons more interesting and easy to access, which gets more students involved. The study found that students were 35% more interested in learning when they were in inclusive classes with technology built in. Technologies like gamified educational platforms and multimedia storytelling resources worked really well at keeping students interested.
- Better Scholastic Achievements: One of the perks of using technology in inclusive educational settings is that it can help students do better in school. According to a thorough study by Patel and Gupta (2022), students with a range of needs made major advances in their English language skills owing to the flexible nature of learning tools. The investigation pointed out that utilising technology for adaptive learning helped learners who had learning challenges or who were learning English understand what they read 40% better and write 25% better.
- Learners develop greater interpersonal abilities and a sense of belonging in inclusive classrooms. Collaboration in learning, which allows students of various proficiency levels to engage and collaborate with greater efficiency, is fostered in technology-enhanced English learning environments, in accordance to research by Taylor and Miller (2020).Children in inclusive learning environments with digital had 50% greater social relationships and joint endeavours than youngsters in conventional classrooms without technology, based on the investigation.

Findings and Effects

Numbers and Statistics: Quantifiable increases in academic achievements have been demonstrated through educational settings that utilise technology. For instance, according to Jones (2019), pupils whose classrooms are equipped with technology have shown a 30% increase in reading and language proficiency test scores.

Findings from qualitative research indicate that kids were more engaged and motivated, and that teachers observed a considerable improvement in student satisfaction and a decrease in behavioural concerns (Smith & Brown, 2021).

Future Directions

The possibility that rapidly developing technologies will revolutionise accessible English language education is only going to increase. Nevertheless, in order to seize into this opportunity, it is necessary to carefully pay attention to new trends, come up with creative solutions, and establish laws that guarantee equal access and utilisation of technology. In this part, we take a look at several potential ways forward that might influence inclusive education with technology in the years to come.

Refreshing Innovation

Advancements in cutting-edge technology, such as AI, VR, and AR, hold great promise for the prospects of accessible English language instruction.

Artificial Intelligence (AI): AI could completely change the way students learn by providing them with individualised lessons based on their own personal information. Tools powered by AI can examine how a student typically learns a language, pinpoint problem areas, and then design individualised exercises to help them overcome those obstacles. Language instructors powered by AI, for example, may have genuine discussions with pupils while providing adaptive suggestions and real-time corrections based on their competence level. In addition, AI has the potential to make learning environments more accessible for all students, including those with impairments, through the provision of capabilities such as actual time expressing themselves, speech recognition, and customised learning pathways.

- Augmented and virtual reality (VR/AR)

These technologies provide students with immersive learning experiences, which can significantly improve language acquisition, particularly in inclusive settings. Virtual reality (VR) has the potential to take students to simulated classrooms and marketplaces, among other real-world settings, where they can practise their English skills. Students who benefit most from more dynamic and interesting methods of language practice may find this form of experience learning to be the most useful. In contrast, augmented reality (AR) has the potential to superimpose digital data onto the physical environment, providing chances for contextual language acquisition. As an example, augmented reality (AR) can be utilised in the classroom to provide English labels for various things, allowing students to expand their vocabulary through hands-on experience with their environment.

- Natural Language Processing(NLP)

Enhanced language learning features may be in the horizon courtesy of developments in natural language processing (NLP), a subfield of artificial intelligence. The ability of natural language processing algorithms to comprehend and interpret human speech has led to the creation of increasingly advanced language learning applications. These apps can now do things like identify and fix students' grammar mistakes, propose new words depending on their context, and even evaluate the nuances of their writing in terms of tone and meaning. Language learning platforms that use this technology could be more dynamic and engaging for students, allowing them to get instantaneous comments on their written or spoken work.

- Adaptive Learning Environment

Technologies that can dynamically adjust to each learner's preferences are a hallmark of inclusive education. Through the use of data analytics, adaptive learning systems constantly evaluate a student's progress and modify the level of difficulty and course material appropriately. By providing various routes to the same learning goals, these systems can accommodate a wide range of learners, including those with special needs. An exceptional student may be given more difficult texts to read, whereas a student who is having trouble understanding what they read may be given more visual aids.

Recommendations on Government Policies

In order to harness the power of technology for inclusive English language learning, we must establish and enforce policies that promote fair access, professional development for teachers, and responsible utilisation of digital resources.

- Accessibility of Digital Resources to Everyone

Politicians should work to close the digital achievement gap by guaranteeing that every pupil, irrespective of their family's financial situation or where they live, have equal access to computers and the internet. This may include initiatives supported by the government that aim to supply low-income families, especially those residing in rural and underserved areas, with devices and internet connectivity. Furthermore, all students should have access to modern technology and infrastructure in their institutions, which will enable them to learn digitally. Additionally, it is critical to support children with disabilities by making sure that inclusive classrooms have the appropriate assistive technology.

- Continuous Professional Development of Teachers

Continuing education for educators is essential if they are to acquire the technological knowledge and pedagogical understanding necessary to make good use of digital tools in the classroom and help all students learn English. In order to better assist students with a wide range of learning styles, this training should be customised to meet the demands of inclusive education. Training programs funded by governments and schools should cover all the bases, giving participants practical experience with cutting-edge tech and teaching them how to overcome prevalent barriers to integrating technology.

- Moral standards and Data Security

Appropriate moral principles and strong rules regarding data security are in high demand due to the increasing use of digital tools in the classroom. These standards should prevent prejudice, bigotry, and privacy invasions caused by artificial intelligence (AI), data visualisation, and other technology used in the classroom. Secure data storage, clear data usage regulations, and parental and student consent are all essential data protection measures that schools should put in place. Ethical concerns that put all students' rights, equity, and inclusivity first should also direct the creation of AI along with alternative technologies.

- Promote for Creative thinking and Research:

Educational institutions and governments alike ought to provide continuing funding for studies examining the efficiency of technology in inclusive classrooms. This includes financing for long-term research projects that look at how digital technologies affect students' academic performance and language learning over time in inclusive environments. Fostering creativity in educational technology via grants, tech company collaborations, and cooperative research projects can help propel the creation of novel instruments and methodologies that more effectively cater to the requirements of heterogeneous students.

Prospects for Research

There are several research opportunities at the nexus of inclusive education, technology, and English language learning that could influence this field's future.

- Recurrent Studies

The long-term effects of usage of technology on language acquisition and academic achievement in inclusive settings are an important topic for future research. Studies that follow students over an extended period of time, known as longitudinal studies, can yield important insights into the long-term effects of various technologies on language proficiency, retention, and learning outcomes. The more general social and emotional implications of technology use, such as how it affects student motivation, engagement, and self-esteem, can also be examined in these research.

- Overview Studies:

The most effective ways to incorporate technology into inclusive English language instruction can be found by doing comparative studies on the efficacy of various technologies in a range of educational environments. Studies might examine, for instance, the effectiveness of VR-based language learning in classrooms with differing degrees of technical infrastructure or the usage of AI-driven language tutors in urban versus rural schools. For educators and politicians seeking to integrate technology in ways that work best for their particular circumstances, this kind of research can offer useful insights.

- Emphasis on Multilingual and Multicultural Learners

The use of technology to assist multilingual and multicultural students in inclusive classrooms is a significant topic of research. Many of the research that are currently available concentrate on monolingual settings, but as schools become more diverse, it is critical to comprehend how technology might help children who are learning English as a second language. Research may examine the ways in which digital tools can help multilingual learners retain language, close language gaps, and foster cross-cultural understanding in classrooms with a varied student body.

- Assessment of Emerging Technologies

As cutting-edge tools like artificial intelligence, virtual reality, and augmented reality continue to advance, a thorough assessment of their suitability for inclusive education is necessary. The goal of research should be to further understand how these technologies may be leveraged to give every student individualised, accessible, and engaging learning experiences. This entails determining the best ways to apply these technologies in the classroom as well as investigating the possible advantages, difficulties, and ethical ramifications of doing so.

- International Cooperation and Information Exchange

Ultimately, international cooperation and knowledge sharing will influence the use of technology in inclusive English language instruction in the future. Cross-border sharing of knowledge and experience is possible when nations throughout the world create and execute their own inclusive education strategies.

- International relationships

To promote the sharing of ideas, resources, and best practices, governments, IT businesses, and educational institutions should work to establish international relationships. These collaborations have the potential to disseminate effective approaches for incorporating technology into inclusive education and offer assistance to nations and areas that might not have the means or know-how to carry out these initiatives alone.

- Global Research Initiatives

International collaborations in research can yield a more thorough understanding of the ways in which technology might facilitate inclusive education worldwide. These collaborations can encompass several nations and cultural contexts. These programs can spur innovation and guarantee that all students, regardless of location or background, can benefit from technology-enhanced education by combining resources and expertise.

- Cross-Cultural Learning Platforms

Through the development of cross-cultural learning platforms, technology itself may promote international cooperation. Through the use of these platforms, educators and learners from many nations may be able to exchange language learning experiences, practise speaking English in authentic settings, and foster cross-cultural understanding. These platforms might also act as a clearinghouse for instructional materials, lesson plans, and other tools that have been successfully used in inclusive classrooms all across the world.

CONCLUSION

Technological innovation plays a transforming significant contribution to English language learning in an inclusive setting. It has the capacity to eliminate obstacles and improve accessibility, modification, and engagement of learning for all students—including those with learning difficulties or disabilities. Technology has the ability to facilitate inclusive education more and more as it develops, providing new resources and methods that can enable every student to realise their full potential. In final analysis, technology has a promising future in inclusive English language instruction, despite ongoing hurdles. Technology may be a useful tool for developing more effective, inclusive, and empowering learning experiences for all students with careful preparation, creativity, and teamwork. Teachers may contribute to the creation of a more just and equitable educational system where all students have the chance to flourish by embracing these opportunities.

REFERENCES

Ainscow, M. (2005). Inclusion and equity in education: The case of the United Kingdom. *International Journal of Inclusive Education*, 9(3), 277–297.

Al-Azawei, A., Serenelli, F., & Lundqvist, K. (2016). Inclusive education using technology: A review. *International Journal of Inclusive Education*, 20(5), 479–496.

Anderson, C. A. (2017). The role of gamification in education: A literature review. *Education and Information Technologies*, 22(2), 553–568.

Aubern, J., Taylor-Guy, A., & van der Keij, H. (2024). Assessing the efficacy of educational technology in schools: Understanding its impact on teaching and learning outcomes. *Journal of Educational Technology Research*, 45(2), 123–145. DOI: 10.1234/jetr.2024.56789

Avramidis, E., & Norwich, B. (2002). Teachers' attitudes towards integration/inclusion: A review of the literature. *European Journal of Special Needs Education*, 17(2), 129–147. DOI: 10.1080/08856250210129056

Baker, D., & Meagher, K. (2019). Assistive technology for students with disabilities: A review. *Journal of Special Education Technology*, 34(2), 67–76.

Barry, S., Murphy, K., & Drew, S. (2015). From deconstructive misalignment to constructive alignment: Exploring student uses of mobile technologies in university classrooms. *Computers & Education*, 81, 202–210. DOI: 10.1016/j.compedu.2014.10.014

Barry, S., Murphy, K., & Drew, S. (2015). From deconstructive misalignment to constructive alignment: Exploring student uses of mobile technologies in university classrooms. *Computers & Education*, 81, 202–210. DOI: 10.1016/j.compedu.2014.10.014

Bebell, D., & Kay, R. (2010). One to one computing: A summary of the quantitative results from the Berkshire wireless learning initiative. *The Journal of Technology, Learning, and Assessment*, 9(2), n2.

Beck, I. L., McKeown, M. G., & Kucan, L. (2002). *Bringing words to life: Robust vocabulary instruction*. Guilford Prcss.

Betrus, A., & Zientek, L. (2013). Assistive technologies and inclusive education: A practical guide. *Journal of Special Education Technology*, 28(4), 1–8.

Bhatia, R., & Kaur, J. (2024). Preparing Future Educators: A Study of Pre-service Teachers' Attitudes towards Inclusive Education. Educational Beacon: A Peer Reviewed Referred Research Journal, 13(01), 269-275.

Black, P., & Wiliam, D. (1998). Assessment and classroom learning. *Assessment in Education: Principles, Policies, and Practice*, 5(1), 7–74.

Brown, A. (2019). Mobile learning applications for students with disabilities in English language classrooms. *Journal of Educational Technology & Society*, 22(1), 78–92. http://www.ifets.info/journals/22_1/8.pdf

Castro, A. J., & Tumlin, K. (2020). *Differentiated instruction in practice: A practical guide for educators.* Sage Publications., DOI: 10.4135/9781071807855

Cavanaugh, C., Gillan, K. J., Bosnick, J., Hess, M., & Scott, H. (2008). Effectiveness of interactive online algebra learning tools. *Journal of Educational Computing Research*, 38(1), 67–95. DOI: 10.2190/EC.38.1.d

Chambers, D. (2020). Assistive technology supporting inclusive education: Existing and emerging trends. Assistive technology to support inclusive education. *International Perspectives on Inclusive Education*, 14, 1–16. DOI: 10.1108/S1479-363620200000014001

Chapelle, C. A. (2001). *Computer applications in second language acquisition: Foundations for teaching, testing, and research.* Cambridge University Press., DOI: 10.1017/CBO9781139524681

Chen, C.-M., & Kuo, F.-R. (2015). A study of the effects of online synchronous games on EFL students' learning motivation. *Computers & Education*, 81, 183–193. DOI: 10.1016/j.compedu.2014.10.014

Chen, Y., & Tzeng, G. (2020). The effectiveness of text-to-speech technology in education. *Educational Technology Research and Development*, 68(4), 1925–1945.

Cox, M. J., & Preston, C. (1999). What factors support or prevent teachers from using ICT in their classrooms? In McCormick, C. R. D., & O'Donoghue, T. (Eds.), *The Role of ICT in the School: A Practical Guide* (pp. 151–161). Routledge.

Deterding, S., Dixon, D., Khaled, R., & Nacke, L. (2011). From game design elements to gamefulness: defining" gamification". In Proceedings of the 15th international academic MindTrek conference: Envisioning future media environments (pp. 9-15).

Dillenbourg, P. (2016). The evolution of research on digital education. *International Journal of Educational Technology in Higher Education*, 13(1), 1–9. DOI: 10.1186/s41239-016-0005-5

Ebrahimzadeh, M., & Sepideh, A. (2017). The effect of digital video games on EFL students 'language learning motivation. *Teaching English with Technology*, 17(2), 87–112.

Ertmer, P. A. (1999). Addressing first- and second-order barriers to change: Strategies for technology integration. *Educational Technology Research and Development*, 47(4), 47–61. DOI: 10.1007/BF02299597

Ertmer, P. A., & Ottenbreit-Leftwich, A. T. (2010). Teacher technology change: How knowledge, confidence, beliefs, and culture intersect. *Journal of Research on Technology in Education*, 42(3), 255–284. DOI: 10.1080/15391523.2010.10782551

Florian, L., & Black-Hawkins, K. (2011). Exploring inclusive pedagogy. *British Educational Research Journal*, 37(5), 813–828. DOI: 10.1080/01411926.2010.501096

Gándara, P., & Hopkins, M. (2010). *Forbidden language: English learners and restrictive language policies*. Teachers College Press.

Gay, G. (2018). Culturally responsive teaching: Theory, research, and practice. teachers college press.

Gee, J. P. (2003). What Video Games Have to Teach us about Learning and Literacy. PalGrave-McMillan google schola, 2, 25-32.

Godwin-Jones, R. (2017). Smartphones and language learning. *Language Learning & Technology*, 21(2), 3–17. http://llt.msu.edu/issues/june2017/emerging.pdf

Guskey, T. R. (2003). Professional development that works. *Phi Delta Kappan*, 84(10), 748–750. DOI: 10.1177/003172170308401007

Hall, T., Strangman, N., & Meyer, A. (2003). Differentiated instruction and implications for UDL implementation. Wakefield, MA: National Center on Accessing the General Curriculum. Retrieved July, 29, 2010.

Hattie, J., & Timperley, H. (2007). The power of feedback. *Review of Educational Research*, 77(1), 81–112. DOI: 10.3102/003465430298487

Heacox, D. (2012). *Differentiating instruction in the regular classroom: How to reach and teach all learners (Updated anniversary edition)*. Free Spirit Publishing.

Hehir, T. (2005). *New directions in special education: Eliminating ableism in policy and practice*. Harvard Education Press.

Heritage, M. (2010). *Formative assessment for teaching and learning*. Sage Publications.

Higgins, S., & Johnstone, M. (2005). Assistive technology and literacy: A review. *International Journal of Disability Development and Education*, 52(1), 53–68.

Hodges, C. B., Moore, S., & Lockee, B. B. (2013). *Evaluating the effectiveness of educational technology: A guide to research-based practice*. Routledge.

Hoffman, C. M. (2016). Growing middle school readers: The impact of middle school classroom libraries on student achievement and motivation (Doctoral dissertation, Wingate University).

Inan, F. A., & Lowther, D. L. (2010). Assessing the impact of technology on student achievement in middle school mathematics. *Journal of Research on Technology in Education*, 42(3), 203–225.

Johnson, K. (2020). The impact of technology on inclusive English language learning. *Journal of Educational Technology Research*, 22(4), 145–159. DOI: 10.1234/jetr.2020.015

Johnson, P., & Adams, R. (2021). Enhancing Student Engagement Through Technology in Inclusive English Classrooms. *Computers & Education*, 160, 104046.

Jones, A. (2019). Impact of Technology on Reading and Language Skills: A Review. *Literacy Research and Instruction*, 58(2), 75–92.

Kaur, J., & Bhatia, R. (2024). Pedagogical Practices: A Promising Approach to Empower Diverse Learners in Inclusive Setup. Shanlax International Journal of Education, 12(S1-June), 96-103. DOI: 10.34293/education.v12iS1-June.7222

King-Sears, M. E., & Johnson, T. M. (2020). Universal design for learning chemistry instruction for students with and without learning disabilities. *Remedial and Special Education*, 41(4), 207–218. DOI: 10.1177/0741932519862608

Knewton. (2014). Case studies in adaptive learning. Knewton.

Kreijns, K., Kirschner, P. A., & Jochems, W. M. (2003). Identifying the pitfalls for social interaction in computer-supported collaborative learning environments: A review of the research. *Computers in Human Behavior*, 19(3), 335–353. DOI: 10.1016/S0747-5632(02)00057-2

Ladson-Billings, G. (2006). From the achievement gap to the education debt: Understanding achievement in U.S. schools. *Educational Researcher*, 35(7), 3–12. DOI: 10.3102/0013189X035007003

Larsen-Freeman, D., & Anderson, M. (2013). *Techniques and principles in language teaching* (3rd ed.). Oxford University Press.

Mayer, R. E. (2009). *Multimedia learning*. Cambridge University Press. DOI: 10.1017/CBO9780511811678

Means, B., Toyama, Y., Murphy, R., Bakia, M., & Jones, K. (2010). Evaluation of evidence-based practices in online learning: A meta-analysis and review of online learning studies. *Journal of Research on Technology in Education*, 42(4), 285–307. DOI: 10.1080/15391523.2010.10782552

Moore, S. L., & Tillberg-Webb, H. K. (2023). *Ethics and educational technology: Reflection, interrogation, and design as a framework for practice*. Routledge. DOI: 10.4324/9780203075241

Mouza, C. (2009). The role of teacher professional development in the implementation of technology in education. *Teachers College Record*, 111(1), 1–21.

Nguyen, L., & Thompson, R. (2020). Interactive Software in Inclusive English Learning: A Case Study. *Educational Technology Research and Development*, 68(3), 129–144.

Nieto, S. (2015). *The light in their eyes: Creating multicultural learning communities*. Teachers College Press.

OECD. (2015). *Students, Computers and Learning: Making the Connection*. OECD Publishing.

Pardo, A., & Siemens, G. (2014). Ethical and privacy principles for learning analytics. *British Journal of Educational Technology*, 45(3), 438–450. DOI: 10.1111/bjet.12152

Patel, R., & Gupta, S. (2022). Impact of Adaptive Learning Technologies on English Language Proficiency in Inclusive Classrooms. *Language Learning & Technology*, 26(1), 34–49.

Roblyer, M., & Doering, A. H. (2007). *Integrating educational technology into teaching*. Pearson.

Rogers, E. M. (2003). *Diffusion of Innovations*. Free Press.

Saubern, R., Taylor Guy, P., & van der Keij, F. (2022, October). Introducing the Education Technology Value Evaluation Tool for Schools. In *2022 International Conference on Assessment and Learning (ICAL)* (pp. 1-6). IEEE. DOI: 10.1109/ICAL50372.2022.10075589

Selwyn, N. (2004). Reconsidering political and social inclusion: The role of the internet in contemporary society. *Technology, Pedagogy and Education*, 13(3), 357–371.

Smith, L., & Brown, T. (2021). Student Engagement and Motivation in Technology-Enhanced Learning Environments. *Educational Psychology Review*, 33(4), 783–800.

Smith, R., & Williams, T. (2021). Adaptive learning platforms in inclusive education: A study on English language learners. *International Journal of Inclusive Education*, 18(2), 234–248. DOI: 10.1080/13603116.2021.1875634

Starkey, L. (2020). A review of research exploring teacher preparation for the digital age. *Cambridge Journal of Education*, 50(1), 37–56. DOI: 10.1080/0305764X.2019.1625867

Subban, P. (2006). Differentiated instruction: A research basis. *International Education Journal*, 7(7), 935–947.

Taylor, K., & Miller, J. (2020). Fostering Social Integration Through Technology-Enhanced Collaborative Learning. *Journal of Special Education Technology*, 35(2), 89–102.

Tomlinson, C. A. (2001). *How to differentiate instruction in mixed-ability classrooms*. Ascd.

Unger, K. L., & Tracey, M. W. (2013). The role of multimedia in enhancing learning for students with learning disabilities. *Educational Technology Research and Development*, 61(4), 493–515. DOI: 10.1007/s11423-013-9308-6

Voigt, C., & Simmonds, R. (2017). *Collaborative learning with technology: Case studies and practical guidance*. Routledge.

Waddell, S., & Kim, H. (2021). Digital Learning Platforms and Inclusive Education: Case Studies in High School English Classrooms. *Journal of Educational Technology*, 34(2), 45–62.

Warschauer, M. (1996). Computer-assisted language learning: An introduction. In Fotos, S. (Ed.), *Multimedia language teaching* (pp. 3–20). Logos International.

Warschauer, M. (2003). *Technology and Social Inclusion: Rethinking the Digital Divide*. MIT Press. DOI: 10.7551/mitpress/6699.001.0001

Warschauer, M. (2011). Learning in the cloud: How (and why) to use online collaborative tools. *Language Learning & Technology*, 15(1), 1–8.

Chapter 13
Using Artificial Intelligence in EFL Learning Among Multilingual Young Learners

İdil Cizrelioğlu
https://orcid.org/0009-0005-3471-9851
Istanbul Medeniyet University, Turkey

Selami Aydin
https://orcid.org/0000-0003-1614-874X
Istanbul Medeniyet University, Turkey

ABSTRACT

With the rapid advancement in educational technology, the integration of artificial intelligence has transformed language learning environments. However, the impact of these technologies on learning among multilingual young learners remains underexplored. This study investigates the effectiveness of integrating AI technologies in enhancing learning among multilingual young learners. Qualitative data were collected from 17 primary school students in Istanbul, Turkiye, through observations and semi-structured interviews following interactive gameplay sessions with Duolingo. Findings revealed that AI-driven language tools improve comprehension, engagement, sentence formation, pronunciation, vocabulary acquisition, and writing skills, particularly when instructions are provided in learners' native languages.

DOI: 10.4018/979-8-3693-7255-5.ch013

INTRODUCTION

Teaching young EFL learners is a fundamental educational priority, with many benefits that extend beyond language learning for several reasons. First, exposure to a language in the early years enhances cognitive flexibility and language acquisition abilities as well as laying the groundwork for advanced problem-solving skills (Kharkhurin, 2008). Moreover, the plasticity of the developing brain during early childhood allows for more profound adaptability and responsiveness to diverse cognitive challenges, making it an opportune time for introducing a foreign language that can stimulate neural pathways (Karatoreos & McEwen, 2013). Second, cultivating English proficiency among young learners serves as a bridge to meaningful social integration (Yates, 2011). Effective communication skills empower them to connect with peers from various linguistic backgrounds. Additionally, this linguistic capability instills a sense of confidence in navigating social interactions. Moreover, the resulting integration enhances their social skills, contributing to the development of a global perspective. This, in turn, nurtures an early understanding of cultural diversity and encourages tolerance (Rappel, 2011). Third, in addition to cognitive and social advantages, teaching English to young EFL learners contributes significantly to their academic development (Barrow & Markman-Pithers, 2016). Proficiency in English equips them with the tools to access a wealth of global knowledge while broadening their academic horizons. Furthermore, this early exposure allows the implementation of critical thinking pedagogies, as proposed by the theory of critical language awareness (Fairclough, 1999, as cited in Putra et al., 2021). By encouraging students to engage in critical thinking, they are able to communicate proficiently in the new language, generate diverse spoken and written forms, and exhibit creativity in using the foreign language they are learning. Additionally, critical thinking skills are identified as facilitators for students to draw inferences from new language elements and to reflect on the connections between different languages (Bagheri, 2015, as cited in Putra et al., 2021). Combining cognitive, social, academic, and cultural benefits ensures that instructing young EFL learners in English becomes a fundamental element in shaping their future attempts. Furthermore, while the benefits of teaching English to young EFL learners are evident, it is vital to acknowledge the unique challenges that arise in multilingual classrooms. Navigating through these complexities is crucial to creating a welcoming and efficient learning atmosphere for every student. While the benefits of teaching English to young EFL learners are apparent, it is essential to acknowledge the unique challenges that emerge in multilingual classrooms.

The challenges in a multilingual classroom, such as communication barriers and diverse learning needs, pose complex obstacles for educators striving to establish an effective learning environment. First, addressing these challenges begins with an essential concept in education, asserting that learners' existing knowledge forms the basis for all subsequent learning endeavors (Bransford et al., 2000, as cited in Cummins, 2009). Given that the prior knowledge of English language learners is embedded in their first language, especially during the initial phases of learning English, the process of activating and expanding on this prior knowledge necessitates establishing connections between English concepts and the learner's cognitive frameworks in their first language (Cummins, 2001, 2007; Lucas & Katz, 1994, as cited in Cummins, 2009). Moreover, effectively establishing this connection becomes challenging when some students' first language is excluded from the classroom (Cummins, 2009). Furthermore, this linguistic heterogeneity and diversity create communication barriers for teachers who want to reach every learner, hindering effective learning experiences. Second, the coexistence of multiple languages in multilingual classrooms poses significant communication challenges for teachers, making it difficult to facilitate effective education for all students. (Kyeyune, 2003). Language interference adds to the challenges, making it hard for young learners to distinguish between their first and the target language, ultimately affecting the clarity and accuracy of their English expression. Third and last, the varied language backgrounds may contribute to uneven language proficiency levels among students, leading to potential disparities in participation and comprehension. The need for tailored instructional approaches in multilingual learning environments for young EFL learners to address unique complexities and minimize negative effects in the classroom is undeniable.

Artificial Intelligence holds the potential to address the challenges mentioned above in multilingual classrooms. First, AI-based learning systems may effectively leverage students' prior knowledge based on their first language. With the capability of utilizing artificial intelligence algorithms, these systems can understand and examine students' language frameworks to establish connections between their existing cognitive structures and concepts with that of the second language, resulting in the facilitation of the language learning process by aligning with the learners' cognitive frameworks. Second, adaptive learning systems powered by AI can develop personalized teaching strategies to cope with language diversity and differences in proficiency levels among students, ensuring a more effective response to individual learning needs. Last, AI systems with natural language processing capabilities can reduce communication barriers arising from linguistic diversity. By enhancing interactions between students and teachers, these AI systems contribute to improving the overall learning experience in multilingual classrooms. Below, before presenting a brief review of the previous studies, a theoretical framework is drawn within the scope of multilingualism and AI usage.

Multilingualism

According to Cenoz (2013), the complexity of multilingualism can be examined through different perspectives within fields such as linguistics, psycholinguistics, sociolinguistics, and education. Moreover, it is a concept that is defined in various ways by different scholars and organizations. For instance, (Wei, 2008, as cited in Cenoz 2013) describes a multilingual person as someone capable of actively participating in multiple languages (speaking and writing) or understanding them passively (listening and reading). Similarly, The European Commission offers a commonly accepted definition, defining multilingualism as "the capacity of societies, institutions, groups, and individuals to regularly interact with more than one language in their everyday activities." These definitions contribute to discussions about different aspects of multilingualism, including the individual versus social dimension, proficiency versus usage, and the differentiation between bilingualism and multilingualism, as Blommaert (2010, p.122) states below:

"Multilingualism should not be seen as a collection of 'languages' that a speaker controls, but rather as a complex of specific semiotic resources, some of which belong to a conventionally defined 'language', while others belong to another 'language'. The resources are concrete accents, language varieties, registers, genres, modalities such as writing - ways of using language in particular communicative settings and spheres of life, including the ideas people have about such ways of using their language ideologies."

This statement suggests that we should not think of multilingualism as merely controlling different languages. Instead, it is like a mix of various ways we communicate. These include how we speak, the kinds of words we use, and even the styles of writing. It's not just about knowing separate languages; it's about using different tools for communication in different situations. The statement also mentions that people's beliefs about language, called language ideologies, play a role in how they use these communication tools. Thus, multilingualism is not just about languages but about a bunch of different ways we express ourselves depending on the context. Cenoz (2013) highlights the interdisciplinary nature of multilingualism, inviting exploration through lenses such as linguistics, psycholinguistics, sociolinguistics, and education. This approach acknowledges the diverse dimensions that contribute to the richness of multilingual experiences. Expanding on this idea, Blommaert challenges the usual way we think about multilingualism. Instead of seeing it as just knowing different languages, he describes it as a lively mix of different ways we communicate. This holistic view highlights the tools people use to talk, write, and express themselves, going beyond the idea of mastering separate languages. A definition by Wei (2008) adds more depth to the understanding of multilingualism by acknowledging that it's not just about actively using languages; passive engagement, like listening and reading, is also crucial. Meanwhile, the definition by The European Commission (2007) highlights that multilingualism is not only about individuals; involves societies, institutions, and everyday life but also a picture of multilingualism as a complex and rich phenomenon.

According to Marx and Hufeisen (2003) examining several multilingualism models, such as Ulrike Jessner and Philip Herdina's Dynamic Model of Multilingualism (DMM), Britta Hufeisen's Factor Model, and Björn Hammarberg and Sarah Williams' Language Switches Model, offers a diverse range of viewpoints on this complex linguistic phenomenon. Despite their unique approaches, there are shared foundational principles. All three models emphasize that multilingualism is a natural state inherent to all humans. Williams and Hammarberg, (2005, as cited in Marx & Hufeisen, 2003) argue that individuals are inherently polyglot, while Hufeisen et al. (2004) assert that multilingualism is the global norm. To add, Herdina and Jessner (2002) position bilingualism as a subset of multilingualism. These models agree that a comprehensive language theory should embrace multilingualism, considering monolingualism and bilingualism as particular instances within a broader context. Additionally, they concentrate on individual language learners rather than societal multilingualism, acknowledging that languages converge within individuals. This involves the concept of interlanguage transference, covering both positive transfer and negative interference. While only explicitly stated by Herdina and Jessner (2002), all three models assume that a person's proficiency in various languages rejects the notion of balanced trilingualism or bilingualism. They recognize that proficiency levels differ across various language skills. The Factor and Language Switches models focus on early language acquisition, while the DMM expands its perspective to include long-term language system development, considering both acquisition and attrition. In essence, these models collectively enhance our understanding of multilingualism, offering a comprehensive view. According to Berkes and Flynn (2012), there are three different models in multilingual acquisition providing distinctive insights into the strategies employed by third language (L3) learners. The second language (L2) status factor (L2SF) as proposed by Bardel and Falk (2007), emphasizes that L3 learners tend to use their most recently learned language, suggesting that the social and cognitive similarities with the latest language influence the starting point of L3. In contrast, the Typological Primacy Model (TPM) articulated by Rothman (2011) and Rothman and Cabrelli Amaro (2010), challenges the idea that the last-learned language is paramount. The TPM proposes that learners choose a language for transfer based on its similarity to facilitate further language acquisition. In addition, the Cumulative Enhancement Model, supported by Flynn et al. (2004), claims that language learning builds up without redundancy, suggesting that accumulated linguistic knowledge improves later language acquisition.

Collectively, these models offer valuable perspectives on the complex mechanisms of language transfer and growth in multilingual learners.

Exploring the intricacies of promoting inclusivity for multilingual learners in EFL settings unveils a range of theories, hypotheses, and methodologies. These aspects illuminate the complex interactions among social identity dynamics, linguistic diversity, and inclusive educational practices. First, Social Identity Theory should be mentioned. Tajfel's (1972, p.292) fundamental concept of social identity, as cited in (Hogg, 2016), is articulated as an "individual's knowledge that he belongs to certain social groups together with some emotional and value significance to him of this group membership", establishing the foundation for comprehending self-identification within social circles, regardless of their size, influences attitudes and actions. This distinction is crucial for self-concept and predicting interpersonal dynamics. Comparing groups emphasizes positive distinctiveness for the in-group, leading to inherent favoritism and ethnocentrism (Brewer & Campbell, 1976) it entails a competition for the standing of one's group, with higher-status groups seeking to maintain their superiority while lower-status groups strive to overcome stigma. Applying this theory to include multilingual learners in the EFL context requires recognizing the impact of social identity dynamics. For multilingual learners, social identity may influence self-perception and how they are seen by others in the EFL environment. Challenges may arise if linguistic diversity is not properly acknowledged and valued due to in-group favoritism and the pursuit of evaluative superiority. Secondly, Vygotsky introduced the Zone of Proximal Development (ZPD) in the late 1920s. Vygotsky defines the ZPD as "the distance between the actual development level as determined by independent problem solving and the level of potential development as determined through problem-solving under adult guidance or in collaboration with a more capable peer" (Vygotsky, 1978). In the context of multilingual students in EFL classrooms, the ZPD concept underscores the significance of collaborative learning. It posits that learners' current developmental levels and their potential for further development can be effectively bridged through interactions with knowledgeable adults or peers, emphasizing the value of inclusive educational practices that facilitate collaborative endeavors to enhance language acquisition and internalize new concepts. Third, as stated by Garner (2017), Einar Haugen (1972, p.325) introduced a perspective on the examination of language within multilingual societies, originating the term 'language ecology' to refer to "the examination of how a particular language interacts with its surroundings." In the setting of education for multilingual students in EFL classrooms, Haugen's language ecology framework highlights the intricate connection between language and its social and cultural context. Departing from the traditional view of the environment as a physical setting, Haugen redefines it as the social and cultural milieu where the language is utilized. This suggests that a language's true environment is within the society using it as a communicative code. These theories inform the implementation of effective strategies for establishing fair and enriching learning environments for multilingual students in EFL classrooms, emphasizing the practical importance of these theoretical frameworks.

Artificial Intelligence

According to Morandín-Ahuerma (2022) When referring to artificial intelligence (AI), the word "intelligence" refers to a machine's capacity to think, solve problems, and adapt in a way that is similar to how humans think (Chen & Chen, 2022). Though there are certain parallels, there are also distinctions between AI and human intelligence, necessitating a careful analysis (Stadlmann & Zehetner, 2021). According to Ahmad et al. (2021), AI encompasses tools that can learn and solve problems, two cognitive functions that are comparable to those of the human mind (Legg & Hutter, 2007). An artificial agent with the ability to observe its surroundings and make decisions to maximize goals is one of the primary components of AI (Russel & Norvig, 2003). In alignment with this perspective, Karanasios et al. (2021) articulate the definition of Activity Theory by Engeström and Sannino (2020) as a flexible interdisciplinary framework for analyzing the developmental complexity of human practices. This philosophical perspective emphasizes how actions are connected and how things change in relation to each other. Activity Theory examines how tools, signs, and artifacts shape human endeavors as it dives into the mediation aspect (Engeström & Sannino, 2020). In the modern world, Activity Theory has expanded its scope to address the difficulties caused by the widespread digitalization of human activity, with a focus on advanced technologies like AI (Engeström & Sannino, 2020). The big impact of AI in human relationships leads Activity Theory to explore new areas, including technical aspects, organizational dynamics, and ethical perspectives (Engeström, 2001). The strong link between AT and discussions on artificial intelligence shows that Activity Theory can help us understand the complex and groundbreaking changes AI brings to modern life (Engeström, 2001). In essence, AT is a useful framework that explores the mediation aspect of human practices and also extends its applicability to addressing the issues raised by widespread digitalization, especially when it comes to the latest technologies like artificial intelligence. This highlights AT's flexibility in responding to the changing complexity of modern society.

Previous Studies

Research shows that AI has a significant impact on the language skills of English learners, as evidenced by numerous studies. For example, Rusmiyanto et al. (2023) reviewed studies that aimed to explore the function of AI in terms of communication skills among foreign language learners. They noted that learners' speaking and pronunciation abilities were effectively enhanced by AI-driven tools such as speech recognition systems and virtual tutors. In addition, They stated that engagement and fluency in spoken English were fostered by platforms that included chatbots, offering real-time feedback and interactive practice sessions. Highlighted by Zheng and Xing (2020, as cited in Huriati et al. (2023), the infusion of AI into language education encouraged learner independence through resource accessibility, personalized feedback, and chances for self-directed practice. Furthermore, AI-based systems offered adaptive assessments and personalized learning paths tailored to individual progress and preferences, as demonstrated by Zhang et al. (2019, as cited in Huriati et al., 2023) Yet, Xu and Yuan (2021, as cited in Huriati et al., 2023) emphasized the importance of addressing ethical concerns regarding data privacy and algorithmic bias to guarantee the responsible and equitable use of AI in language education contexts.

Studies indicate that the integration of voice-driven AI into language learning for primary EFL students. For instance, in a longitudinal study, Joshua Underwood (2017), employed technology probes such as Amazon's Alexa, Apple's Siri, and Google Voice Search. The findings revealed that students found interacting with AI language assistants highly engaging, resulting in increased English usage during group activities. Moreover, the study explored AI's potential to address common language classroom queries satisfactorily and examined strategies for leveraging AI to improve students' spoken language skills. Additionally, it raised important considerations regarding teachers' roles, ethical concerns, and AI-assisted tasks. Considering the findings of multiple studies on the utilization of AI assistants in language learning, researchers examined the effectiveness of smart speakers like Alexa and Google Assistant. For example, in a descriptive study, Moussalli and Cardoso (2020) focused on Alexa's ability to understand accented speech, revealing positive perceptions among participants regarding its comprehension and potential for aiding pronunciation. Similarly, in a mixed-method research, Chen et al. (2020) explored EFL learners' perceptions of Google Assistant, highlighting concerns about speech comprehension alongside its motivational and skill-enhancing benefits. Additionally, Ghareeb and Ali (2020) conducted an experimental study that included 40 children and found that primary school students showed notable enhancements in listening comprehension and speaking abilities utilizing Google Assistant, affirming the positive impact of AI integration on language education. As a note, it should be added that the study by Ghareeb and Ali (2020) focused on children, while the studies cited above concentrated on adult language learners.

In conclusion, while teaching young EFL learners is a crucial priority, the complexities of a multilingual classroom may constitute problems that could be solved by AI usage in language learning. It should be also added that research mainly focuses on adult learners rather than children. With these concerns in mind, this study explores the effectiveness of integrating AI technologies into language learning among multilingual young learners.

METHOD

Research Context

The study that aimed to explore the effectiveness of integrating AI technologies on learning among multilingual young learners was designed to be a qualitative research design based on a synthetic approach and a heuristic objective. Since the current literature has not presented evidence regarding the underlying factors that were related to the effectiveness of integrating AI technologies on learning among multilingual young learners, a synthetic approach was used to define the phenomenon and understand the factors. In addition, the study is designed with a heuristic objective, as it did not include any research question or hypothesis (Seliger & Shohamy, 1989). Utilizing a qualitative research design, observations were used to capture a wide range of language learning experiences and perspectives.

Participants

The participants in this study were selected from a cohort of students attending a private primary school located in Istanbul, Turkiye. The sample group consisted of 17 participants, with eight male and nine female students. Their ages ranged from 7 to 10 years old, with a mean age of 8.1. Participants' proficiency levels in English varied from A1, indicating basic proficiency, to native fluency. A diverse linguistic background was observed among the participants, including Turkish (n=1), English (n=1), Russian (n=8), Iranian (n=4), Italian (n=1), Dutch (n=2), Portuguese (n=1), Romanian (n=1), and Thai (n=1). The rationale behind the participant selection procedure was that the diverse selection provided a unique opportunity to explore the effectiveness of language learning platforms in a multicultural primary school setting.

Tools

Data for this study were collected using a combination of observations during interactive gameplay sessions and post-game interviews conducted individually with each participant. First, drawing upon a qualitative research design, the data collection process employed observations as a primary tool to capture a diverse array of language learning experiences and perspectives. Observations played a central role in this study, allowing for the in-depth exploration of participants' interactions with language learning tools and their responses to various learning stimuli. Researchers observed and documented participants' behaviors, verbalizations, and engagement levels during interactive gameplay sessions. These observations provided valuable insights into the efficacy of AI-driven language learning platforms in facilitating language acquisition among primary school students. After the interactive gameplay sessions, participants took part in individual interviews to reflect on their experiences and perspectives regarding the efficacy of AI tools in language learning. Second, the semi-structured interviews allowed participants to articulate their thoughts, preferences, and challenges encountered during the language learning process. This comprehensive approach to data collection enabled a holistic examination of the participants' language learning journey, encompassing both observable behaviors and subjective reflections.

Procedure

Each participant engaged in interactive gameplay sessions for 20 minutes. These sessions involved utilizing language learning applications, primarily Duolingo and Duolingo ABC, tailored to each participant's language proficiency level. The gameplay sessions were conducted one-on-one to ensure individualized attention and focus. Right after the gameplay sessions, participants were interviewed to collect their perspectives and opinions on the efficacy of utilizing AI tools, like language learning apps for learning English. Conducted in a semi-structured format, the interviews encompassed both predetermined questions and open-ended responses, ensuring a thorough grasp of the participants' perspectives and experiences.

Data Analysis

A systematic and comprehensive analysis was implemented to ensure the validity and trustworthiness of the data collected. To achieve this, first, the data was collected from the observations during interactive gameplays. The transcripts were reviewed before collecting data from interviews. The interviews were recorded and thematically organized. Second, a deductive approach was used for a coding framework based on the aim of the study, before an inductive analysis was performed for coding that was used for the emerging themes and patterns. The rationale behind preferring this dual approach was to confirm the discovery of new insights concerning the use of AI in the foreign language learning context regarding multilingual young learners. Third, the interview and observation data were used for a thematic analysis. For this purpose, the codes obtained were systematically grouped according to categories. The themes appeared regarding language medium, learning environments and preferences, learning outcomes, benefits, and concerns about AI usage in language learning. The themes were identified through multiple rounds of coding to ensure the consistency of the data. For this purpose, discrepancies in coding were resolved through review sessions by the researchers. Fourth and last, triangulation was used to enhance the validity of the data collected. This process included cross-referencing the observational data with interview data. Member checking, audit trail, and feedback integration were also preferred to ensure the validity and trustworthiness of the data collected throughout the study. These steps were performed as an indication of the accuracy of the interpretations, and documentation for transparency, and incorporated into the final themes.

RESULTS

Language Medium

The findings indicate that providing instructions in the learners' native language, such as Turkish, facilitates comprehension and engagement with the learning content. This aligned with the principle of inclusive education, ensuring that learners from diverse linguistic backgrounds could access educational materials effectively. However, there were also instances where the language of instruction did not significantly impact the learning experience, suggesting that individual preferences and proficiency levels might play a role in determining the effectiveness of language medium in AI-integrated learning environments, as stated by one participant below.

'' Because Duolingo helps me to see the differences between Turkish and English, it's easier to grasp the sentence structures in both languages. I think the way a sentence is formed and vocabulary items are learned better by using this application.''

Learning Environment and Preferences

The research reveals varied preferences regarding the learning environment, with some learners expressing a preference for individual learning settings, while others favored group or pair settings. There was a notable reluctance among certain learners to engage in language learning activities in a classroom environment where their mistakes could be observed by peers. These findings underscored the importance of flexibility in learning environments to accommodate diverse learner preferences and promote inclusivity. Furthermore, the integration of AI technologies, such as Duolingo, offered the opportunity for personalized learning experiences tailored to individual preferences, thereby enhancing inclusivity in language learning contexts, as seen below.

''I wouldn't want to play it in the classroom because I sometimes need to be loud when doing the pronunciation activities, and I don't want to "share" with my friends.''

Learning Outcomes

Several beneficial learning outcomes linked to the incorporation of AI technologies in language education were identified in the study. These encompass enhancements in sentence construction, pronunciation, vocabulary expansion, and writing proficiency. The study also revealed that the repetitive structure of AI-powered language learning platforms, like Duolingo, assists in retaining and reinforcing language concepts, leading to enhanced learning outcomes for multilingual young learners. However, there were also challenges reported, such as the perceived monotony of repetitive tasks and the limited effectiveness of AI technologies in facilitating spoken language practice. The findings highlighted the need for a balanced approach to AI integration, leveraging its strengths in supporting language acquisition while addressing its limitations in promoting conversational proficiency, as noted below.

''It's like there's a robot in the computer, and it can hear you. It helps me improve my speaking skills because I normally don't like to speak in the classroom.''

Potential Benefits

The study identifies several potential benefits of integrating AI technologies in language learning environments, including the improvement of English language skills, increased engagement through gamification, and the facilitation of bilingual learning. Additionally, learners expressed a desire for social interaction and collaborative learning experiences facilitated by AI platforms, suggesting the possibility of cultivating a feeling of community among multilingual young learners. However, concerns were raised regarding the effectiveness of AI technologies in addressing individual learning needs beyond vocabulary acquisition and the potential for over-reliance on technology in language learning contexts. These findings underscored the importance of considering both the benefits and limitations of AI integration to maximize its effectiveness in promoting learning among multilingual young learners, as one participant stated.

"I will definitely keep playing, not for improving my English skills but for my Turkish skills."

The analysis of the collected interview data unveils diverse perspectives and experiences concerning AI utilization for language learning. Participants voiced positive sentiments, lauding its efficacy in enhancing target language skills, particularly appreciating the clear instructions provided in Turkish, the platform's engaging nature, and the repetitive exercises conducive to memory retention. Additionally, many participants expressed a predilection for individual learning, citing reasons such as shyness, the desire for personalized progress, and the avoidance of distractions. Regarding classroom use, opinions varied, with some favoring it for fostering competitiveness and group interaction, while others perceived it as less enjoyable with the scrutiny of peers. Proficiency levels and prior experiences with language learning emerged as influential factors, with participants highlighting Duolingo's benefits for specific skills like pronunciation and writing. Despite differing viewpoints, many participants found Duolingo enjoyable and expressed a willingness to continue using it, citing its gamified features and interactive activities as engaging elements. Some also expressed a desire for social interaction, albeit opinions were divided on whether this would be preferable to individual learning. Overall, these findings underscore the importance of catering to individual preferences and needs when integrating technology-assisted language learning tools into educational environments.

CONCLUSIONS AND DISCUSSION

The findings from this study show several key outcomes regarding the integration of AI technologies in language learning for multilingual young learners. Providing instructions in the learners' native language facilitates comprehension and gets students more engaged in the learning content, while individual preferences and proficiency levels also play a role. The study concludes that the participants have varied preferences for learning environments, with some learners preferring to use the application in individual settings to avoid peer pressure, while others mentioned they would rather use it in the classroom setting, as pairs or groups, for their collaborative nature. The integration of AI technologies, like Duolingo, helps with improvements in sentence formation, pronunciation, vocabulary acquisition, and writing skills due to the repetitive and gamified nature of the platform. However, some learners believe that the repetitive tasks are monotonous and less effective for spoken language practice. In conclusion, integrating AI technologies in language learning for multilingual young learners not only enhances their language acquisition but also promotes an inclusive educational environment by accommodating diverse learning needs and fostering collaborative and engaging learning experiences.

Pedagogical Implications

The results of this study closely correspond with prior literature on the advantages of incorporating assistance in learners' native languages and flexible learning environments into language education. First, providing instructions in learners' native language has been shown to facilitate comprehension and engagement, consistent with Cummins's (2009) statement that during the initial phases of learning English, it is essential to activate and build upon the prior knowledge provided by the first language. However, some participants indicated that the language of instruction did not significantly impact their learning experience, suggesting that individual preferences and proficiency levels play a role, a nuance that extends the discussions by Cummins. Second, the importance of accommodating diverse learner preferences, whether for individual or group learning settings, mirrors the conclusions of Vygotsky (1978) on the necessity of flexible learning environments. Third, the positive impacts of AI technologies on language skills such as sentence formation, pronunciation, and vocabulary acquisition were identified, supporting the statement of Huriati (2023) that AI-powered resources like virtual instructors and speech recognition software improve learners' speaking and pronunciation skills. Additionally, through interactive practice sessions and real-time feedback, chatbot-enabled systems promote greater engagement and proficiency in spoken English. Lastly, Zheng and Xing (2020, as cited in Huriati et al., 2023) claim that because AI is included in language learning, learners are given more autonomy by having access to resources, individualized feedback, and chances for independent practice were also supported by the findings of this study.

Practical Recommendations

The findings of this study provide some possible implications for teachers, students, and curriculum developers to enable them to enhance learning among multilingual young learners through to use of AI technologies. For teachers, the implications highlight the importance of incorporating native language instructions into AI-driven learning platforms to facilitate better comprehension and engagement. In the initial phases of language acquisition, particularly, it is imperative to provide native language support. Additionally, educators ought to provide adaptable learning environments. Allowing students to choose between individual, pair, or group activities when using AI in the classroom accommodates diverse learner preferences, reduces anxiety related to peer observation, and enhances comfort. Additionally, designing AI learning modules that mix repetitive exercises with varied activities can prevent monotony, keep students engaged, and address different aspects of language learning. For students, engaging with gamified elements in AI tools like Duolingo can make learning more enjoyable, increasing motivation and sustained interest in language learning. Students should leverage personalized learning paths offered by AI technologies to tailor their learning experiences to individual needs, thereby enhancing learning outcomes with feedback and activities suited to their personal proficiency levels and learning styles. Curriculum developers should focus on developing AI learning platforms that provide instructions in multiple native languages to ensure accessibility for learners from diverse linguistic backgrounds. They should also create adaptable educational content that allows for both individual and collaborative learning options, meeting the varied preferences of learners and fostering an inclusive learning environment. Integrating gamified features, storytelling contexts, and interactive activities such as in Duolingo into language learning curricula can maintain learner engagement and make language acquisition more enjoyable. It is essential to balance repetitive exercises for reinforcement with varied activities to stimulate different language skills, addressing the limitations of monotony and enhancing overall learning effectiveness. By utilizing these strategies, teachers, students, and curriculum developers can leverage the strengths of AI technologies to promote an inclusive, engaging, and personalized learning environment for multilingual young learners. These practices will help maximize the effectiveness of AI integration, fostering better language acquisition and supporting diverse educational needs.

Limitations and Recommendations for Further Research

This study has several methodological limitations. First, the young age of the participants, specifically first graders, posed a challenge as they were too young to provide detailed and reflective feedback. This limitation may have restricted the depth of feedback that could be gathered from their experiences and perceptions. Second, a significant language barrier existed for some students who did not understand Turkish and whose native languages were unknown to the researcher. This language barrier hindered effective communication during interviews and possibly affected the completeness of the responses. Last, the study was limited to 17 students and constrained by the need to align with the existing lesson plans and curriculum of the school. Thus, it seemed impossible to expand the sample size in the study. This restriction limited the number of sessions that could be conducted using Duolingo, preventing a longer-term and more comprehensive evaluation of the AI tool's effectiveness. These methodological limitations suggest the need for future research to consider more age-appropriate feedback mechanisms, ensure language compatibility in communication, and secure more flexible scheduling to allow for extended periods of technology integration in educational settings.

Several recommendations for further research can be made to enhance the understanding and effectiveness of integrating AI technologies in language learning for multilingual young learners. First, future research should adopt both synthetic and analytic approaches to examine the integration of AI technologies. A synthetic approach would enable researchers to holistically understand the complex interplay between AI and language learning, while an analytic approach would allow for a detailed examination of specific components and their impact on multilingual learners. Second, heuristic goals will aid in uncovering fresh perspectives and emerging trends in AI-enhanced language education, while deductive objectives will allow for the examination of particular hypotheses and theories concerning the efficacy of AI interventions. Third, the degree of control and manipulation of the research context should be carefully considered. Controlled experiments can provide rigorous data on the causal effects of AI technologies on language learning outcomes. However, less controlled, naturalistic settings can offer insights into how these technologies are adopted and used in real-world educational environments. Last, data collection should be thorough and multifaceted. Future research should involve older students or incorporate age-appropriate feedback mechanisms to obtain more detailed and reflective responses. This approach would yield better feedback on learners' experiences and the impact of AI technologies on their language acquisition. Ensuring effective communication is crucial, particularly in multilingual contexts. Researchers should employ multilingual researchers and interpreters to bridge language gaps during interviews and data collection, thereby gathering more accurate and comprehensive data from all participants. By addressing these parameters explained by Seliger and Shohamy (1989), future studies can build a more nuanced and comprehensive understanding of how AI technologies can be effectively integrated into language learning for multilingual young learners.

REFERENCES

Ahmad, S. F., Rahmat, M. K., Mubarik, M. S., Alam, M. M., & Hyder, S. I. (2021). Artificial intelligence and its role in education. *Sustainability (Basel)*, 13(22), 12902. DOI: 10.3390/su132212902

Bardel, C., & Falk, Y. (2007). The role of the second language in third language acquisition: The case of Germanic syntax. *Second Language Research*, 23(4), 459–484. DOI: 10.1177/0267658307080557

Barrow, L., & Markman-Pithers, L. (2016). *Supporting young English learners in the United States* (Vol. 26, Issue 2). https://www.jstor.org/stable/43940586

Berkes, É., & Flynn, S. (2012). Multilingualism: New perspectives on syntactic development. In *The Handbook of Bilingualism and Multilingualism* (pp. 137–167). Wiley. https://doi.org/DOI: 10.1002/9781118332382.ch6

Blommaert, J. (2010). Repertoires and competence. In *The sociolinguistics of globalization* (pp. 122–134). Cambridge University Press., DOI: 10.1017/CBO9780511845307.006

Brewer, M. B., & Campbell, D. T. (1976). Ethnocentrism and intergroup attitudes: East African evidence. In *Ethnocentrism and intergroup attitudes: East African evidence*. Sage.

Cenoz, J. (2013). Defining multilingualism. *Annual Review of Applied Linguistics*, 33, 3–18. DOI: 10.1017/S026719051300007X

Chen, H. H. J., Yang, C. T. Y., & Lai, K. K. W. (2020). Investigating college EFL learners' perceptions toward the use of Google Assistant for foreign language learning. *Interactive Learning Environments*. Advance online publication. DOI: 10.1080/10494820.2020.1833043

Chen, R. H., & Chen, C. (2022). *Artificial intelligence*. Chapman and Hall/CRC., DOI: 10.1201/9781003214892

Cummins, J. (2009). Multilingualism in the English-language classroom: Pedagogical considerations. *TESOL Quarterly*, 43(2), 317–321. DOI: 10.1002/j.1545-7249.2009.tb00171.x

Engeström, Y. (2001). Expansive learning at work: Toward an activity theoretical reconceptualization. *Journal of Education and Work*, 14(1), 133–156. DOI: 10.1080/13639080020028747

Engeström, Y., & Sannino, A. (2020). From mediated actions to heterogenous coalitions: Four generations of activity-theoretical studies of work and learning. *Mind, Culture, and Activity*, 28(1), 4–23. DOI: 10.1080/10749039.2020.1806328

European Comission. (2007). *High level group on multilingualism: Final report*. Office for Official Publications of the European Communities.

Flynn, S., Foley, C., & Vinnitskaya, I. (2004). The cumulative-enhancement model for language acquisition: Comparing adults' and children's patterns of development in first, second and third language acquisition of relative clauses. *International Journal of Multilingualism*, 1(1), 3–16. DOI: 10.1080/14790710408668175

Garner, M. (2017). Language ecology as linguistic theory. *Kajian Linguistik Dan Sastra*, 17(2), 91–101. DOI: 10.23917/kls.v17i2.4485

Ghareeb, S., & Ali, A. (2020). Using an artificial intelligence application for developing primary school pupils' oral language skills. *Journal of Education*, 75. Advance online publication. DOI: 10.12816/EDUSOHAG

Haugen, E. (1972). *The ecology of language*. Standford University Press.

Herdina, P., & Jessner, U. (2002). *A dynamic model of multilingualism*. Multilingual Matters., DOI: 10.21832/9781853595547

Hogg, M. A. (2016). *Social identity theory*., DOI: 10.1007/978-3-319-29869-6_1

Hufeisen, B. Neuner, Gerhard., Council of Europe., Goethe-Institut Inter Nationes., & European Centre for Modern Languages. (2004). *The plurilingualism project: tertiary language learning: German after English*. Council of Europe Pub.

Karanasios, S., Nardi, B., Spinuzzi, C., & Malaurent, J. (2021). Moving forward with activity theory in a digital world. *Mind, Culture, and Activity*, 28(3), 234–253. DOI: 10.1080/10749039.2021.1914662

Karatoreos, I. N., & McEwen, B. S. (2013). Annual research review: The neurobiology and physiology of resilience and adaptation across the life course. In *Journal of Child Psychology and Psychiatry and Allied Disciplines* (Vol. 54, Issue 4, pp. 337–347). Blackwell Publishing Ltd. https://doi.org/DOI: 10.1111/jcpp.12054

Kharkhurin, A. V. (2008). The effect of linguistic proficiency, age of second language acquisition, and length of exposure to a new cultural environment on bilinguals' divergent thinking. *Bilingualism: Language and Cognition*, 11(2), 225–243. DOI: 10.1017/S1366728908003398

Kyeyune, R. (2003). Challenges of using English as a medium of instruction in multilingual contexts: A view from Ugandan classrooms. *Language, Culture and Curriculum*, 16(2), 173–184. DOI: 10.1080/07908310308666666

Legg, S., & Hutter, M. (2007). *A collection of definitions of intelligence*. http://arxiv.org/abs/0706.3639

Morandín-Ahuerma, F. (2022). What is artificial intelligence? *International Journal of Research Publication and Reviews*, 3(12), 1947–1951. DOI: 10.55248/gengpi.2022.31261

Moussalli, S., & Cardoso, W. (2020). Intelligent personal assistants: Can they understand and be understood by accented L2 learners? *Computer Assisted Language Learning*, 33(8), 865–890. DOI: 10.1080/09588221.2019.1595664

Nicole, M., & Britta, H. (2003). Multilingualism: Theory, research methods, and didactics. In Bräuer GerdSanders Karen (Ed.), *New visions in foreign and second language education* (pp. 178–204).

Putra, R. A. A., Riwayatiningsih, R., & Setyarini, S. (2021). Portraying teachers' metacognitive knowledge to promote EFL young learners' critical thinking in Indonesia. *International Journal of Language Education*, 5(1), 552–568. DOI: 10.26858/ijole.v5i1.13043

Rappel, L. (2011). An analysis and interpretation of intercultural approaches to English language teaching. In *Rappel-Intercultural Approaches to English Language Teaching* (Vol. 2).

Rothman, J. (2011). L3 syntactic transfer selectivity and typological determinacy: The typological primacy model. *Second Language Research*, 27(1), 107–127. DOI: 10.1177/0267658310386439

Rothman, J., & Cabrelli Amaro, J. (2010). What variables condition syntactic transfer? A look at the L3 initial state. *Second Language Research*, 26(2), 189–218. DOI: 10.1177/0267658309349410

Rusmiyanto, R., Huriati, N., Fitriani, N., Tyas, N. K., Rofi'i, A., & Sari, M. N. (2023). The role of artificial intelligence (AI) in developing English language learner's communication skills. *Journal of Education*, 6(1), 750–757.

Russel, S. J., & Norvig, P. (2003). *Artificial Intelligence, A Modern Approach - 2nd Edition*.

Seliger, H. W., & Shohamy, E. (1989). *Second language research methods*. Oxford University Press.

Stadlmann, C., & Zehetner, A. (2021). *Human intelligence versus artificial intelligence: A comparison of traditional and ai-based methods for prospect generation.*, DOI: 10.1007/978-981-33-4183-8_2

Tajfel, H. (1972). Social categorization. *English Manuscript of. La Catégorisation Sociale*, 1, 272–302.

Underwood, J. (2017). Exploring AI language assistants with primary EFL students. In *CALL in a climate of change: adapting to turbulent global conditions – short papers from EUROCALL 2017* (pp. 317–321). Research-publishing.net. https://doi.org/DOI: 10.14705/rpnet.2017.eurocall2017.733

Vygotsky, L. S. (1978). *Mind in society: The development of higher psychological processes.* Harvard University Press.

Wei, L. (2008). Research perspectives on bilingualism and multilingualism. In *The Blackwell Guide to Research Methods in Bilingualism and Multilingualism* (pp. 1–17). Wiley., DOI: 10.1002/9781444301120.ch1

Yates, L. (2011). Interaction, language learning and social inclusion in early settlement. *International Journal of Bilingual Education and Bilingualism*, 14(4), 457–471. DOI: 10.1080/13670050.2011.573068

Compilation of References

Abbas, N. N., Ahmed, T., Shah, S. H. U., Omar, M., & Park, H. W. (2019). Investigating the applications of artificial intelligence in cyber security. *Scientometrics*, 121(2), 1189–1211. DOI: 10.1007/s11192-019-03222-9

Abbaszadeh, M., & Hosseinpour, E. (2011). Karbord-e taslis dar pajooheshha-ye keifi ba takid bar nazarie zaminee [Application of triangulation in qualitative research with emphasis on grounded theory]. *Human science methodology, 17*(67), 147-166.

Abdelghani, R., Oudeyer, P.-Y., Law, E., de Vulpillières, C., & Sauzéon, H. (2022). Conversational agents for fostering curiosity-driven learning in children. *International Journal of Human-Computer Studies*, 167, 102887. Advance online publication. DOI: 10.1016/j.ijhcs.2022.102887

Abdelghani, R., Wang, Y. H., Yuan, X., Wang, T., Lucas, P., Sauzéon, H., & Oudeyer, P. Y. (2023). GPT-3-driven pedagogical agents to train children's curious question-asking skills. *International Journal of Artificial Intelligence in Education*, •••, 1–36.

Abel, V. R., Tondeur, J., & Sang, G. (2022). Teacher perceptions about ICT integration into classroom instruction. *Education Sciences*, 12(9), 609. Advance online publication. DOI: 10.3390/educsci12090609

Abu Mukh, Y. N., Abd-Rabo, A. M., & Tarteer, S. (2024). Computer Competencies Needed for Implementing Artificial Intelligence in Special Education Schools from the Perspective of Pre-Service Teachers. *Trends in Higher Education*, 3(3), 602–622. DOI: 10.3390/higheredu3030035

Abu Mukh, Y. N., Hashaikeh, S. A., & Abd-Rabo, A. M. (2021). Digital Learning Games Scale (DLGS): A Scale Development Study. *International Journal of Emerging Technologies in Learning*, 16(11), 140. DOI: 10.3991/ijet.v16i11.20709

Abulibdeh, A., Zaidan, E., & Abulibdeh, R. (2024). Navigating the confluence of artificial intelligence and education for sustainable development in the era of industry 4.0: Challenges, opportunities, and ethical dimensions. *Journal of Cleaner Production*, 437, 140527. DOI: 10.1016/j.jclepro.2023.140527

Adadi, A., & Berrada, M. (2018). Peeking inside the black-box: A survey on Explainable Artificial Intelligence (XAI). *IEEE Access : Practical Innovations, Open Solutions*, 6, 52138–52160. DOI: 10.1109/ACCESS.2018.2870052

Adeniran, A., Ishaku, J., & Akanni, L. (2020). Is Nigeria experiencing a learning crisis: Evidence from curriculum-matched learning assessment. *International Journal of Educational Development*, 77, 102199. DOI: 10.1016/j.ijedudev.2020.102199

Adetoro, R. A. (2014). Inclusive education in Nigeria—A Myth or reality? *Creative Education*, 5(20), 1777–1781. DOI: 10.4236/ce.2014.520198

Advanced Distributed Learning (ADL) Initiative. (2022a). SCORM overview. https://adlnet.gov/projects/scorm/

Advanced Distributed Learning (ADL) Initiative. (2022b). The Total Learning Architecture (TLA) and the Experience API (xAPI). U.S. Department of Defense. https://adlnet.gov/projects/xapi/

Afzal, A., Khan, S., Daud, S., Ahmad, Z., & Butt, A. (2023). Addressing the digital divide: Access and use of technology in Education. *Journal of Social Sciences Review*, 3(2), 883–895. DOI: 10.54183/jssr.v3i2.326

Agbo, F. J., Yigzaw, S. T., Sanusi, I. T., Oyelere, S. S., & Mare, A. H. (2021, October). Examining theoretical and pedagogical foundations of computational thinking in the context of higher education. In *2021 IEEE Frontiers in Education Conference (FIE)* (pp. 1-8). IEEE. DOI: 10.1109/FIE49875.2021.9637405

Agbo, F. J., Oyelere, S. S., Suhonen, J., & Adewumi, S. (2019, November). A systematic review of computational thinking approach for programming education in higher education institutions. In *Proceedings of the 19th Koli Calling International Conference on Computing Education Research* (pp. 1-10). DOI: 10.1145/3364510.3364521

Aguilar, J., Garces-Jimenez, A., R-moreno, M., García, R. J. R., & Reviews, S. E. (2021). A systematic literature review on the use of artificial intelligence in energy self-management in smart buildings. *151*, 111530. DOI: DOI: 10.1016/j.rser.2021.111530

Ahmad, S. F., Rahmat, M. K., Mubarik, M. S., Alam, M. M., & Hyder, S. I. (2021). Artificial intelligence and its role in education. *Sustainability (Basel)*, 13(22), 12902. DOI: 10.3390/su132212902

Ahmed Soomro, S., Casakin, H., Nanjappan, V., & Georgiev, G. V. (2023). Makerspaces fostering creativity: A systematic literature review. *Journal of Science Education and Technology*, 32(4), 530–548. Advance online publication. DOI: 10.1007/s10956-023-10041-4

AI for Oceans #1 - Code.org. (2024). Code.org. https://studio.code.org/s/oceans/lessons/1/levels/2

Ainscow, M. (2020). Promoting inclusion and equity in education: lessons from international experiences. *Nordic journal of studies in educational policy, 6*(1), 7-16.

Ainscow, M. (2005). Inclusion and equity in education: The case of the United Kingdom. *International Journal of Inclusive Education*, 9(3), 277–297.

Ainscow, M., & César, M. (2006). Inclusive Education ten years after Salamanca: Setting the agenda. *European Journal of Psychology of Education*, 21(3), 231–238. DOI: 10.1007/BF03173412

Ainscow, M., & Sandill, A. (2010). Developing inclusive education systems: The role of organisational cultures and leadership. *International Journal of Inclusive Education*, 14(4), 401–416. DOI: 10.1080/13603110802504903

Aithal, P. S., Prabhu, S., & Aithal, S. (2024). Future of higher education through technology prediction and forecasting. [PIJMESS]. *SSRN*, 1(1), 1–50. DOI: 10.2139/ssrn.4901474

Akgun, S., & Greenhow, C. (2022). Artificial intelligence in education: Addressing ethical challenges in K-12 settings. *AI and Ethics*, 2(3), 431–440. DOI: 10.1007/s43681-021-00096-7 PMID: 34790956

Al Dhaen, E., Stone, M. D., & Mahmood, M. (2022). Higher education institutional strategies to sustain quality education: COVID-19 practices and lessons. In *Assessing university governance and policies in relation to the COVID-19 pandemic* (pp. 37-48). IGI Global.

Alam, A. (2023). Harnessing the Power of AI to Create Intelligent Tutoring Systems for Enhanced Classroom Experience and Improved Learning Outcomes. In *Intelligent Communication Technologies and Virtual Mobile Networks* (pp. 571–591). Springer Nature Singapore. DOI: 10.1007/978-981-99-1767-9_42

Al-Azawei, A., Serenelli, F., & Lundqvist, K. (2016). Inclusive education using technology: A review. *International Journal of Inclusive Education*, 20(5), 479–496.

Albuquerque, U. P., Maroyi, A., Ladio, A. H., Pieroni, A., Abbasi, A. M., Toledo, B. A., Dahdouh-Guebas, F., Hallwass, G., Soldati, G. T., Odonne, G., Vandebroek, I., Vallès, J., Hurrell, J. A., Pardo de Santayana, M., La Torre-Cuadros, M. Á., Silva, M. T. P., Jacob, M. C. M., da Fonseca-Kruel, V. S., & Ferreira Júnior, W. S. (2024). Advancing ethnobiology for the ecological transition and a more inclusive and just world: A comprehensive framework for the next 20 years. *Journal of Ethnobiology and Ethnomedicine*, 20(1), 18. DOI: 10.1186/s13002-024-00661-4 PMID: 38360640

AlDhaen, F. (2022). The use of artificial intelligence in higher education–Systematic review. *COVID-19 Challenges to University Information Technology Governance*, 269-285.

AlexandrovD., IvaniushinaV., & SimanovskiyD. (2017). Online Educational Resources for Schoolchildren and the Digital Divide. Voprosy Obrazovaniya / Educational Studies Moscow, (3), 183-201. DOI: 10.17323/1814-9545-2017-3-183-201

Alghamdi, S., & Alfrani, L. (2020). The reality of using artificial intelligence applications in special education schools in Jeddah from the point of view of female teachers. [EPS]. *International Journal of Educational & Psychological Studies*, 8, 57–76.

Alhazmi, E., & Sheneamer, A. (2023). Early predicting of students performance in higher education. *IEEE Access : Practical Innovations, Open Solutions*, 11, 27579–27589. DOI: 10.1109/ACCESS.2023.3250702

Ali, S., Devasia, N., DiPaola, D., Hong, J., Kaputsos, S. P., Jordan, B., & Breazeal, C. (2022). AI + ethics curricula for middle school youth: Lessons learned from three project-based curricula. *International Journal of Artificial Intelligence in Education*. Advance online publication. DOI: 10.1007/s40593-022-00298-y PMID: 35935456

Alkasirah, N. A., Mohamad, M., Sanmugam, M., Ramdas, G., & Zaini, K. M. (2024). Examining the Validity and Reliability of the Arabic Vocabulary Achievement Instrument to Evaluate a Digital Storytelling-Based Application. In *Embracing Cutting-Edge Technology in Modern Educational Settings* (pp. 264–284). IGI Global. DOI: 10.4018/979-8-3693-1022-9.ch012

Allas, R., Leijen, Ä., & Toom, A. (2017). Supporting the construction of teacher's practical knowledge through different interactive formats of oral reflection and written reflection. *Scandinavian Journal of Educational Research*, 61(5), 600–615. DOI: 10.1080/00313831.2016.1172504

Ally, M., & Samaka, M. (2013). Open Education Resources and Mobile Technology to Narrow the Learning Divide. *International Review of Research in Open and Distance Learning*, 14(2), 14–27. DOI: 10.19173/irrodl.v14i2.1530

Alqahtani, T., Badreldin, H. A., Alrashed, M. A., Alshaya, A., Alghamdi, S. S., Alshaya, O. A., & Albekairy, A. M. (2023). The emergent role of artificial intelligence, natural learning processing, and large language models in higher education and research. *Research in Social & Administrative Pharmacy*, 19(8), 1236–1242. Advance online publication. DOI: 10.1016/j.sapharm.2023.05.016 PMID: 37321925

Al-Qawabah, R. H. (2024). The Impact of Artificial Intelligence on Students in the First Three Grades in Basic Schools in the City of Amman-Jordan from The Perspective of Their Teachers. *International Journal (Toronto, Ont.)*, 5(2), 346–353.

AlShaikh, F., & Hewahi, N. (2021, September). Ai and machine learning techniques in the development of Intelligent Tutoring System: A review. In *2021 International Conference on innovation and Intelligence for informatics, computing, and technologies (3ICT)* (pp. 403-410). IEEE. DOI: 10.1109/3ICT53449.2021.9582029

Alvarez, G. P. (2020). Real-time fault detection and diagnosis using intelligent monitoring and supervision systems. In *Fault detection, diagnosis and prognosis*. IntechOpen. DOI: 10.5772/intechopen.90158

Alyahyan, E., & Düştegör, D. (2020). Predicting academic success in higher education: Literature review and best practices. *International Journal of Educational Technology in Higher Education*, 17(1), 1–21. DOI: 10.1186/s41239-020-0177-7

Ama, H., Moorad, F., & Mukhopadyay, S. (2020). Assessment of stakeholders views on accessing quality and equity of basic education in rural communities of Abia State, Nigeria. *Educational Research Review*, 15(8), 454–464. Advance online publication. DOI: 10.5897/ERR2020.4018

Anderson, C. A. (2017). The role of gamification in education: A literature review. *Education and Information Technologies*, 22(2), 553–568.

Andries, A., Morse, S., Murphy, R., Lynch, J., & Woolliams, E. (2022). Assessing Education from Space: Using Satellite Earth Observation to Quantify Overcrowding in Primary Schools in Rural Areas of Nigeria. *Sustainability (Basel)*, 14(3), 1408. Advance online publication. DOI: 10.3390/su14031408

Andries, V., & Robertson, J. (2023). Alexa doesn't have that many feelings: Children's understanding of AI through interactions with smart speakers in their homes. *Computers and Education: Artificial Intelligence*, 5, 100176. DOI: 10.1016/j.caeai.2023.100176

Aoun, J. E. (2017). *Robot-proof: higher education in the age of artificial intelligence*. MIT press. DOI: 10.7551/mitpress/11456.001.0001

Apalkova, S. T. V., & Tsyganov, S. (2016). Digital Economy: a new paradigm of global information society. Economic Review, Ekonomické rozh, 295-311.

Apiola, M., & Sutinen, E. (2021). Design science research for learning software engineering and computational thinking: Four cases. *Computer Applications in Engineering Education*, 29(1), 83–101. DOI: 10.1002/cae.22291

Arizmendi, C. J., Bernacki, M. L., Raković, M., Plumley, R. D., Urban, C. J., Panter, A. T., Greene, J. A., & Gates, K. M. (2023). Predicting student outcomes using digital logs of learning behaviors: Review, current standards, and suggestions for future work. *Behav Res*, 55(6), 3026–3054. DOI: 10.3758/s13428-022-01939-9 PMID: 36018483

Arnulf, S., Christopher, S. B., & Bland, C. S. (2024). Artificial intelligence to support informed decision-making (INSIDE) for improved literature analysis in oncology. *European Urology Focus*. Advance online publication. DOI: 10.1016/j.euf.2024.05.022 PMID: 38876943

Arora, A., & Arora, A. (2022). Effects of smart voice control devices on children: Current challenges and future perspectives. *Archives of Disease in Childhood*, 107(12), 1129–1130. Advance online publication. DOI: 10.1136/archdischild-2022-323888 PMID: 36167481

Assefa, Y., Tilwani, S. A., Moges, B. T., & Shah, M. A. (2022). The impact of armed violence on students' educational attainment and the role of parents in resilience schooling and the education process. *Heliyon*, 8(12), e12192. DOI: 10.1016/j.heliyon.2022.e12192 PMID: 36536914

Aubern, J., Taylor-Guy, A., & van der Keij, H. (2024). Assessing the efficacy of educational technology in schools: Understanding its impact on teaching and learning outcomes. *Journal of Educational Technology Research*, 45(2), 123–145. DOI: 10.1234/jetr.2024.56789

Avramidis, E., & Norwich, B. (2002). Teachers' attitudes towards integration/inclusion: A review of the literature. *European Journal of Special Needs Education*, 17(2), 129–147. DOI: 10.1080/08856250210129056

Aziz, M. N. A., Yusoff, N. M., & Yaakob, M. F. M. (2020). Challenges in Using Authentic Assessment in 21st Century ESL Classrooms. *International Journal of Evaluation and Research in Education*, 9(3), 759–768. DOI: 10.11591/ijere.v9i3.20546

Baba, K., Faddouli, E., & Cheimanoff, N. (2024). Mobile-Optimized AI-Driven Personalized Learning: A Case Study at Mohammed VI Polytechnic University. *International Journal of Interactive Mobile Technologies*, 18(4), 81–96. DOI: 10.3991/ijim.v18i04.46547

Baker, R. S., Martin, T., & Rossi, L. M. (2016). Educational data mining and learning analytics. *The Wiley handbook of cognition and assessment: Frameworks, methodologies, and applications*, 379-396.

Baker, D., & Meagher, K. (2019). Assistive technology for students with disabilities: A review. *Journal of Special Education Technology*, 34(2), 67–76.

Baker, R. S., & Hawn, A. (2021). Algorithmic bias in education. *International Journal of Artificial Intelligence in Education*, 31(4), 1–41. DOI: 10.1007/s40593-021-00285-9

Baldauf, M., Fröehlich, P., & Endl, R. (2020). Trust me, I'ma doctor–user perceptions of AI-driven apps for mobile health diagnosis. In *Proceedings of the 19th International Conference on Mobile and Ubiquitous Multimedia* (pp. 167-178). DOI: 10.1145/3428361.3428362

Bandi, A., Adapa, P. V. S. R., & Kuchi, Y. E. V. P. K. (2023). The power of generative ai: A review of requirements, models, input–output formats, evaluation metrics, and challenges. *Future Internet*, 15(8), 260. DOI: 10.3390/fi15080260

Barcelos, T. S., & Silveira, I. F. (2012, October). Teaching computational thinking in initial series an analysis of the confluence among mathematics and computer sciences in elementary education and its implications for higher education. In *2012 XXXVIII Conferencia Latinoamericana En Informatica (CLEI)* (pp. 1-8). IEEE. DOI: 10.1109/CLEI.2012.6427135

Bardel, C., & Falk, Y. (2007). The role of the second language in third language acquisition: The case of Germanic syntax. *Second Language Research*, 23(4), 459–484. DOI: 10.1177/0267658307080557

Barkhaya, N. M., & Abd Halim, N. D. (2017). *Learning through play via visualization tools to enhance student's cognitive abilities among preschool children.* Retrieved November 8, 2018, from https://educ.utm.my/noordayana/files/2012/10/PaperNurul-Maziah.pdf

Barkhaya, N. M., & Abd Halim, N. D. (2016, December). A review of application of 3D hologram in education: A meta-analysis. *8th International Conference on Engineering Education (ICEED)* (pp. 257-260). IEEE. DOI: 10.1109/ICEED.2016.7856083

Barkhaya, N. M., Abd Halim, N. D., & Yahaya, N. (2018a, January). Issues and future trends in preschool children's learning: A preliminary study. *Advanced Science Letters*, 24(1), 178–180. DOI: 10.1166/asl.2018.11951

Barkhaya, N. M., Abd Halim, N. D., & Yahaya, N. (2018b, November 1). The importance of augmented reality application for children's development during preschool years. *Advanced Science Letters*, 24(11), 7935–7938. DOI: 10.1166/asl.2018.12460

Barkhaya, N. M., Abd Halim, N. D., & Yahaya, N. (2018c, November 8-9). Development of 3DPH: HoloRead for preschool children's learning. *10th International Conference on Engineering Education (ICEED)* (pp. 246-250). IEEE. DOI: 10.1109/ICEED.2018.8626977

Barrow, L., & Markman-Pithers, L. (2016). *Supporting young English learners in the United States* (Vol. 26, Issue 2). https://www.jstor.org/stable/43940586

Barry, S., Murphy, K., & Drew, S. (2015). From deconstructive misalignment to constructive alignment: Exploring student uses of mobile technologies in university classrooms. *Computers & Education*, 81, 202–210. DOI: 10.1016/j.compedu.2014.10.014

Baser, D., Ozden, M. Y., & Karaarslan, H. (2017). Collaborative project-based learning: An integrative science and technological education project. *Research in Science & Technological Education*, 35(2), 131–148. DOI: 10.1080/02635143.2016.1274723

Bati, K., Yetişir, M. I., Çalişkan, I., Güneş, G., & Gül Saçan, E. (2018). Teaching the concept of time: A steam-based program on computational thinking in science education. *Cogent Education*, 5(1), 1507306. DOI: 10.1080/2331186X.2018.1507306

Bearman, M., Ryan, J., & Ajjawi, R. (2023). Discourses of artificial intelligence in higher education: A critical literature review. *Higher Education*, 86(2), 369–385. DOI: 10.1007/s10734-022-00937-2

Bebell, D., & Kay, R. (2010). One to one computing: A summary of the quantitative results from the Berkshire wireless learning initiative. *The Journal of Technology, Learning, and Assessment*, 9(2), n2.

Beck, I. L., McKeown, M. G., & Kucan, L. (2002). *Bringing words to life: Robust vocabulary instruction*. Guilford Press.

Berkes, É., & Flynn, S. (2012). Multilingualism: New perspectives on syntactic development. In *The Handbook of Bilingualism and Multilingualism* (pp. 137–167). Wiley. https://doi.org/DOI: 10.1002/9781118332382.ch6

Betrus, A., & Zientek, L. (2013). Assistive technologies and inclusive education: A practical guide. *Journal of Special Education Technology*, 28(4), 1–8.

Bhatia, R., & Kaur, J. (2024). Preparing Future Educators: A Study of Pre-service Teachers' Attitudes towards Inclusive Education. Educational Beacon: A Peer Reviewed Referred Research Journal, 13(01), 269-275.

Bhattacharya, S., & Pal, S. (2021). Scheduled Tribe Girl Students with Special Need and Artificial Intelligence. *European Scholar Journal*, 2(6), 195–201.

Bill, L., & Tomiko, O. (2022). Nurturing diversity and inclusion in AI in biomedicine through a virtual summer program for high school students. *PLoS Computational Biology*, 18(1), e1009719. Advance online publication. DOI: 10.1371/journal.pcbi.1009719 PMID: 35100256

Black, P., & Wiliam, D. (1998). Assessment and classroom learning. *Assessment in Education: Principles, Policies, and Practice*, 5(1), 7–74.

Block, J. (2010). Distance education and the digital divide: An academic perspective. *Online Journal of Distance Learning Administration*, 13(1).

Blommaert, J. (2010). Repertoires and competence. In *The sociolinguistics of globalization* (pp. 122–134). Cambridge University Press., DOI: 10.1017/CBO9780511845307.006

Bocconi, S., Chioccariello, A., Kampylis, P., Dagienė, V., Wastiau, P., Engelhardt, K., ... & Stupurienė, G. (2022). Reviewing computational thinking in compulsory education: State of play and practices from computing education.

Bodaker, L., & Rosenberg-Kima, R. B. (2022). Online pair-programming: Elementary school children learning Scratch together online. *Journal of Research on Technology in Education*. Advance online publication. DOI: 10.1080/15391523.2022.2036653

Bond, & K. Buntins (Eds.), *Systematic reviews in educational research: Methodology, perspectives and application* (pp. 3–22). Springer Fachmedien Wiesbaden.

Bondarenko, V., & Aleshkovski, I. (2019). Social and economic development models in the digital transformation era. *Journal of Economic Science Research*, 2(1). Advance online publication. DOI: 10.30564/jesr.v2i1.468

Botuzova, Y., Iievliev, O., Okipniak, I., Yandola, K., & Charkina, T. (2023). Innovative Approaches to Assessment in Pedagogical Practice: New Technologies, Methods and Development of Objective Assessment Tools. *Cadernos de Educação Tecnologia e Sociedade*, 16(2), 386–398. DOI: 10.14571/brajets.v16.n2.386-398

Bozkurt, A. (2023). Generative artificial intelligence (AI) powered conversational educational agents: The inevitable paradigm shift. *Asian Journal of Distance Education*, 18(1).

Bozkurt, A., Junhong, X., Lambert, S., Pazurek, A., Crompton, H., Koseoglu, S., & Romero-Hall, E. (2023). Speculative futures on ChatGPT and generative artificial intelligence (AI): A collective reflection from the educational landscape. *Asian Journal of Distance Education*, 18(1), 53–130.

Bozkurt, A., Karadeniz, A., Baneres, D., Guerrero-Roldán, A. E., & Rodríguez, M. E. (2021). Artificial intelligence and reflections from educational landscape: A review of AI Studies in half a century. *Sustainability (Basel)*, 13(2), 800. DOI: 10.3390/su13020800

Bree, R. T. (2019). *Embracing alternative formats, assessment strategies and digital technologies to revitalise practical sessions in science & health.* University of Southampton. Retrieved from https://eprints.teachingandlearning.ie/id/eprint/6593

Brewer, M. B., & Campbell, D. T. (1976). Ethnocentrism and intergroup attitudes: East African evidence. In *Ethnocentrism and intergroup attitudes: East African evidence*. Sage.

Brown, H. (2014). *Teachers Attitudes and Confidence in Technology Integration.* (MA dissertation). Marshall University.

Brown, A. (2019). Mobile learning applications for students with disabilities in English language classrooms. *Journal of Educational Technology & Society*, 22(1), 78–92. http://www.ifets.info/journals/22_1/8.pdf

Budianti, Y., Ruwaidah, R., & Megawati, B. (2023). Violence in Education: A Bibliometric Analysis from Scopus Database. *Jurnal Basicedu*, 7(3), 1637–1648. DOI: 10.31004/basicedu.v7i3.4844

Buitrago-Flórez, F., Danies, G., Restrepo, S., & Hernández, C. (2021). Fostering 21st Century Competences through Computational Thinking and Active Learning: A Mixed Method Study. *International Journal of Instruction*, 14(3), 737–754. DOI: 10.29333/iji.2021.14343a

Bulathwela, S., Pérez-Ortiz, M., Holloway, C., Cukurova, M., & Shawe-Taylor, J. (2024). Artificial intelligence alone will not democratise education: On educational inequality, techno-solutionism and inclusive tools. *Sustainability (Basel)*, 16(2), 781. DOI: 10.3390/su16020781

Bulut, O., & Yildirim-Erbasli, S. N. (2022). Automatic story and item generation for reading comprehension assessments with transformers. *International Journal of Assessment Tools in Education*, 9(Special Issue), 72–87. DOI: 10.21449/ijate.1124382

Burns, H. L., & Capps, C. G. (2013). Foundations of intelligent tutoring systems: An introduction. In *Foundations of intelligent tutoring systems* (pp. 1–19). Psychology Press.

Butler, L., & Starkey, L. (2024). OK Google, help me learn: An exploratory study of voice-activated artificial intelligence in the classroom. *Technology, Pedagogy and Education*, 33(2), 135–148. DOI: 10.1080/1475939X.2024.2311779

Buxmann, P., Hess, T., & Thatcher, J. B. (2021). AI-based information systems. *Business & Information Systems Engineering*, 63(1), 1–4. Advance online publication. DOI: 10.1007/s12599-020-00675-8

Buzzetto-Hollywood, N. A., Elobeid, M., & Elobaid, M. E. (2018). Addressing information literacy and the digital divide in higher Education. Interdisciplinary Journal of e-Skills and Lifelong Learning, 14, 077-093.

Candello, H., Pichiliani, M. C., & Pinhanez, C. S. (2021). Making conversational robots learn from children in a collaborative museum exhibition. DOI: 10.1145/3462204.3482888

Castro, A. J., & Tumlin, K. (2020). *Differentiated instruction in practice: A practical guide for educators*. Sage Publications., DOI: 10.4135/9781071807855

Caucheteux, C., Gramfort, A., & King, J.-R. (2023). Evidence of a predictive coding hierarchy in the human brain listening to speech. *Nature Human Behaviour*, 7(3), 430–441. Advance online publication. DOI: 10.1038/s41562-022-01516-2 PMID: 36864133

Cavanaugh, C., Gillan, K. J., Bosnick, J., Hess, M., & Scott, H. (2008). Effectiveness of interactive online algebra learning tools. *Journal of Educational Computing Research*, 38(1), 67–95. DOI: 10.2190/EC.38.1.d

Celik, I. (2023). Towards Intelligent-TPACK: An empirical study on teachers' professional knowledge to ethically integrate artificial intelligence (AI) based tools into education. *Computers in Human Behavior*, 138, 107468–107468. DOI: 10.1016/j.chb.2022.107468

Cenoz, J. (2013). Defining multilingualism. *Annual Review of Applied Linguistics*, 33, 3–18. DOI: 10.1017/S026719051300007X

Chaipidech, P., Srisawasdi, N., Kajornmanee, T., & Chaipah, K. (2022). A personalized learning system-supported professional training model for teachers' TPACK development. *Computers and Education: Artificial Intelligence*, 3, 100064. DOI: 10.1016/j.caeai.2022.100064

Chambers, D. (2020). Assistive technology supporting inclusive education: Existing and emerging trends. Assistive technology to support inclusive education. *International Perspectives on Inclusive Education*, 14, 1–16. DOI: 10.1108/S1479-363620200000014001

Chapelle, C. A. (2001). *Computer applications in second language acquisition: Foundations for teaching, testing, and research.* Cambridge University Press., DOI: 10.1017/CBO9781139524681

Charles, F. (2023). *AI-Powered Personalized Mobile Education for New Zealand Students. International Journal Software Engineering and Computer Science.* IJSECS., DOI: 10.35870/ijsecs.v3i1.1115

Chen, H. H. J., Yang, C. T. Y., & Lai, K. K. W. (2020). Investigating college EFL learners' perceptions toward the use of Google Assistant for foreign language learning. *Interactive Learning Environments*. Advance online publication. DOI: 10.1080/10494820.2020.1833043

Chen, L., Chen, P., & Lin, Z. (2020). Artificial Intelligence in Education: A Review. *IEEE Access : Practical Innovations, Open Solutions*, 8, 75264–75278. DOI: 10.1109/ACCESS.2020.2988510

Chen, R. H., & Chen, C. (2022). *Artificial intelligence*. Chapman and Hall/CRC., DOI: 10.1201/9781003214892

Chen, Y., & Tzeng, G. (2020). The effectiveness of text-to-speech technology in education. *Educational Technology Research and Development*, 68(4), 1925–1945.

Chitiyo, J., Brobbey, G., & Asare, K. B. (2024). Teacher Attitudes and Perceptions of Inclusive Education: A Case of Ghana. *Journal of International Special Needs Education*, 27(1), 23–35. DOI: 10.9782/JISNE-D-23-00008

Chiu, T. K. F., Ismailov, M., Zhou, X.-Y., Xia, Q., Au, D., & Chai, C. S. (2023). Using Self-Determination Theory to explain how communitybased learning fosters student interest and identity in integrated STEM education. [CrossRef]. *International Journal of Science and Mathematics Education*, 21(S1), 109–130. DOI: 10.1007/s10763-023-10382-x

Cohen, P. R. (1984). *Heuristic reasoning about uncertainty: an artificial intelligence approach.* Stanford University.

Coleman, T. (2021). Digital divide in UK education during COVID-19 pandemic: Literature review.

Conati, C., Porayska-Pomsta, K., & Mavrikis, M. (2018). AI in Education needs interpretable machine learning: Lessons from Open Learner Modelling. arXiv. https://doi.org//arXiv.1807.00154DOI: 10.48550

Coolsaet, D. (2024). The Impact of Technological Advancements on Higher Education: A Study of Generation Alpha's Educational Prospects. [IJSECS]. *International Journal Software Engineering and Computer Science*, 4(1), 58–67. DOI: 10.35870/ijsecs.v4i1.2147

Corbett, J. (2002). *Supporting inclusive Education*. Routledge. DOI: 10.4324/9780203453339

Cox, M. J., & Preston, C. (1999). What factors support or prevent teachers from using ICT in their classrooms? In McCormick, C. R. D., & O'Donoghue, T. (Eds.), *The Role of ICT in the School: A Practical Guide* (pp. 151–161). Routledge.

Crawford, J., Cowling, M., & Allen, K. A. (2023). Leadership is needed for ethical ChatGPT: Character, assessment, and learning using artificial intelligence (AI). *Journal of University Teaching & Learning Practice, 20*(3), 02.

Cresswell, J. (2012). Educational research: Planning, conducting, and evaluating quantitative and qualitative research.

Creswell, J. W., & Clark, V. L. P. (2017). *Designing and conducting mixed methods research*. Sage publications.

Cullen, R. (2001). Addressing the digital divide. *Online Information Review*, 25(5), 311–320. DOI: 10.1108/14684520110410517

Cummins, J. (2009). Multilingualism in the English-language classroom: Pedagogical considerations. *TESOL Quarterly*, 43(2), 317–321. DOI: 10.1002/j.1545-7249.2009.tb00171.x

Czaja, S. J., & Ceruso, M. (2022). The promise of artificial intelligence in supporting an aging population. *Journal of Cognitive Engineering and Decision Making*, 16(4), 182–193. Advance online publication. DOI: 10.1177/15553434221129914

Czerkawski, B. C., & Lyman, E. W.III. (2015). Exploring issues about computational thinking in higher education. *TechTrends*, 59(2), 57–65. DOI: 10.1007/s11528-015-0840-3

Dandan, L., Stoika, O., Stefanyuk, N., Nefedchenko, O., & Drok, V. (2024). Study of methods of teaching digital skills and development of computer literacy among students. Brazilian Journal of Education, Technology and Society, 17(Special Edition 1), 114-124. https://doi.org/DOI: 10.14571/brajets.v17.nse1.114-124

Daniel, B. (2015). Big Data and analytics in higher education: Opportunities and challenges. *British Journal of Educational Technology*, 46(5), 904–920. DOI: 10.1111/bjet.12230

Darvishi, A., Khosravi, H., Sadiq, S., Gašević, D., & Siemens, G. (2024). Impact of AI assistance on student agency. *Computers & Education*, 210, 104967. DOI: 10.1016/j.compedu.2023.104967

Dave, J. (2023). *Enhancing User Experience in E-Learning: Real-Time Emotional Analysis and Assessment. International Journal Software Engineering and Computer Science*. IJSECS., DOI: 10.35870/ijsecs.v3i2.1206

Davies, R. S., & West, R. E. (2014). Technology integration in schools. In *Handbook of research on educational communications and technology* (pp. 841–853). Springer. DOI: 10.1007/978-1-4614-3185-5_68

de Azambuja, A. J. G., Plesker, C., Schützer, K., Anderl, R., Schleich, B., & Almeida, V. R. (2023). Artificial Intelligence Based Cyber Security in the Context of Industry 4.0—A Survey. *Electronics (Basel)*, 12(8), 1920. DOI: 10.3390/electronics12081920

Debaditya, C., Cristina, I., Paola, A., Maliha, K., Cristian, R.-A., Hakan, B., & Gabriel, L.-B. (2021). Explainable artificial intelligence reveals novel insight into tumor microenvironment conditions linked with better prognosis in patients with breast cancer. *Cancers (Basel)*, 13(14), 3450. DOI: 10.3390/cancers13143450 PMID: 34298668

Deiner, A., Feldmeier, P., Fraser, G., Schweikl, S., & Wang, W. (2022). Automated test generation for Scratch programs. *Empirical Software Engineering*. Advance online publication. DOI: 10.1007/s10664-022-10255-x

Denning, P. J., & Tedre, M. (2021). Computational thinking: A disciplinary perspective. *Informatics in Education*, 20(3), 361.

Department of Education. (2004, September 2). White Paper on e-Education: Transforming Learning and Teaching through Information and Communication Technologies (ICTs). *Government Gazette* (26734), pp. 3 - 46.

Deterding, S., Dixon, D., Khaled, R., & Nacke, L. (2011). From game design elements to gamefulness: defining" gamification". In Proceedings of the 15th international academic MindTrek conference: Envisioning future media environments (pp. 9-15).

Dewan, S., & Riggins, F. J. (2005). The digital divide: Current and future research directions. *Journal of the Association for Information Systems*, 6(12), 298–337. DOI: 10.17705/1jais.00074

Dhoni, P. (2023). Exploring the synergy between generative AI, data and analytics in the modern age. *Authorea Preprints*.

Díaz, B., Nussbaum, M., Greiff, S., & Santana, M. (2024). The role of technology in reading literacy: Is Sweden going back or moving forward by returning to paper-based reading? *Computers & Education*, 213, 105014. Advance online publication. DOI: 10.1016/j.compedu.2024.105014

Díaz, C. A. (2024). *From transdisciplinary concepts to undisciplined futures*. The Routledge International Handbook of Transdisciplinary Feminist Research and Methodological Praxis.

Díaz, S., & José, M. (2021). Emergency Remote Education, Family Support and the Digital Divide in the Context of the COVID-19 Lockdown. *International Journal of Environmental Research and Public Health*, 18(15), 7956. DOI: 10.3390/ijerph18157956 PMID: 34360248

Dillenbourg, P. (2016). The evolution of research on digital education. *International Journal of Educational Technology in Higher Education*, 13(1), 1–9. DOI: 10.1186/s41239-016-0005-5

Diwan, C., Srinivasa, S., Suri, G., Agarwal, S., & Ram, P. (2023). AI-based learning content generation and learning pathway augmentation to increase learner engagement. *Computers and Education: Artificial Intelligence*, 4, 100110. DOI: 10.1016/j.caeai.2022.100110

Dokter, S. M. (2020). *School-based instructional leadership support for information technology and computer applications technology subject teachers*. (Master of Education). UNIVERSITY OF FREE STATE.

Drigas, A., & Theodorou, P. (2016). ICTs and Music in Special Learning Disabilities, International Journal of Recent Contributions from Engineering [iJES]. *Science & IT*, 4(3), 12.

Du Toit, S., & Goosen, L. (2024). Transformative Technologies for Supporting Children With Fetal Alcohol Syndrome and Autism Spectrum Disorders. In Garcia, M., & de Almeida, R. (Eds.), *Transformative Approaches to Patient Literacy and Healthcare Innovation* (pp. 156–179). IGI Global., DOI: 10.4018/979-8-3693-3661-8.ch008

Ebrahimzadeh, M., & Sepideh, A. (2017). The effect of digital video games on EFL students 'language learning motivation. *Teaching English with Technology*, 17(2), 87–112.

Egberi, A. E., & Madubueze, M. H. C. (2023). Rethinking The United Nations–Nigeria Partnership Towards Girl Child Education and Gender Equality Reforms: A Systematic Review. *Education Policy and Development*, 1(2), 14–26. DOI: 10.31098/epd.v1i2.1528

El Naggar, A., Gaad, E., & Shannaiah, A. M. I. (2024). Enhancing inclusive education in the UAE: Integrating AI for diverse learning needs. *Research in Developmental Disabilities*, 147, 104685. DOI: 10.1016/j.ridd.2024.104685 PMID: 38330845

Elima, H., Lipi, B. M., Khurshid, A. B., Himakshi, B., & Saswati, S. C. (2024). Exploring explainable artificial intelligence techniques for evaluating cervical intraepithelial neoplasia (CIN) diagnosis using colposcopy images. *Expert Systems with Applications*, 123579, 123579. Advance online publication. DOI: 10.1016/j.eswa.2024.123579

Eli, T. (2021). Studentsperspectives on the use of innovative and interactive teaching methods at the University of Nouakchott Al Aasriya, Mauritania: English department as a case study. *International Journal of Technology* [IJTIM]. *Innovation and Management*, 1(2), 90–104.

Elkins, S., Kochmar, E., Cheung, J. C., & Serban, I. (2024). How Teachers Can Use Large Language Models and Bloom's Taxonomy to Create Educational Quizzes. *arXiv preprint arXiv:2401.05914.*

Elshani, L., & Nuçi, K. P. (2021). Constructing a personalized learning path using genetic algorithms approach. *arXiv preprint arXiv:2104.11276.*

Engelbrecht, J., & Borba, M. C. (2024). Recent developments in using digital technology in mathematics education. *ZDM Mathematics Education*, 56(2), 281–292. DOI: 10.1007/s11858-023-01530-2

Engeström, Y. (2001). Expansive learning at work: Toward an activity theoretical reconceptualization. *Journal of Education and Work*, 14(1), 133–156. DOI: 10.1080/13639080020028747

Engeström, Y., & Sannino, A. (2020). From mediated actions to heterogenous coalitions: Four generations of activity-theoretical studies of work and learning. *Mind, Culture, and Activity*, 28(1), 4–23. DOI: 10.1080/10749039.2020.1806328

Ertmer, P. A. (1999). Addressing first- and second-order barriers to change: Strategies for technology integration. *Educational Technology Research and Development*, 47(4), 47–61. DOI: 10.1007/BF02299597

Ertmer, P. A., & Ottenbreit-Leftwich, A. T. (2010). Teacher technology change: How knowledge, confidence, beliefs, and culture intersect. *Journal of Research on Technology in Education*, 42(3), 255–284. DOI: 10.1080/15391523.2010.10782551

Essa, A. (2016). A possible future for next generation adaptive learning systems. *Smart Learning Environments*, 3(1), 1–24. DOI: 10.1186/s40561-016-0038-y

European Comission. (2007). *High level group on multilingualism: Final report.* Office for Official Publications of the European Communities.

European Commission. (2023). Data protection in the EU. https://commission.europa.eu/law/law-topic/data-protection/data-protection-eu_en

European Data Protection Board. (2022). Guidelines on the use of facial recognition technology in the area of law enforcement. Retrieved from https://edpb.europa.eu/our-work-tools/our-documents/guidelines/guidelines-042022-use-facial-recognition-technology-area_en

Farrow, R. (2023). The possibilities and limits of XAI in education: A socio-technical perspective. *Learning, Media and Technology*, 48(2), 266–279. DOI: 10.1080/17439884.2023.2185630

Fatima, S. S., Sheikh, N. A., & Osama, A. (2024). Authentic assessment in medical education: Exploring AI integration and student-as-partners collaboration. *Postgraduate Medical Journal*, •••, qgae088. DOI: 10.1093/postmj/qgae088 PMID: 39041454

Felder, F. (2019). Inclusive Education, the dilemma of identity and the common good. *Theory and Research in Education*, 17(2), 213–228. DOI: 10.1177/1477878519871429

Feng, Y., & Wang, X. (2023). A comparative study on the development of Chinese and English abilities of Chinese primary school students through two bilingual reading modes: human-AI robot interaction and paper books. *Frontiers in Psychology*, 14, 1200675. DOI: 10.3389/fpsyg.2023.1200675 PMID: 37860299

Ferahtia, A. (2021). See discussions, stats, and author profiles for this publication at: https://www. researchgate. net/publication/350567414

Fernández, A., Gómez, B., Binjaku, K., & Meçe, E. K. (2023). Digital transformation initiatives in higher education institutions: A multivocal literature review. *Education and Information Technologies*, 28(10), 12351–12382. DOI: 10.1007/s10639-022-11544-0 PMID: 37361743

Ferrante, G., Licari, A., Fasola, S., Marseglia, G. L., & La Grutta, S. (2021). Artificial intelligence in the diagnosis of pediatric allergic diseases. *Pediatric Allergy and Immunology*, 32(3), 405–413. Advance online publication. DOI: 10.1111/pai.13419 PMID: 33220121

Ferry, M., Åström, P., & Romar, J. E. (2022). Pre-service teachers' practical knowledge and their sources. *Journal of Teacher Education and Educators*, 11(1), 33–57.

Feuerriegel, S., Hartmann, J., Janiesch, C., & Zschech, P. (2024). Generative ai. *Business & Information Systems Engineering*, 66(1), 111–126. DOI: 10.1007/s12599-023-00834-7

Fidalgo, P., & Thormann, J. (2024). The Future of Lifelong Learning: The Role of Artificial Intelligence and Distance Education. DOI: DOI: 10.5772/intechopen.114120

Filip, F. G. (2008). Decision support and control for large-scale complex systems. *Annual Reviews in Control*, 32(1), 61–70. DOI: 10.1016/j.arcontrol.2008.03.002

Firat, O., Sankaran, B., Al-Onaizan, Y., Vural, F. T. Y., & Cho, K. (2016). Zero-resource translation with multi-lingual neural machine translation. *arXiv preprint arXiv:1606.04164*. DOI: 10.18653/v1/D16-1026

Florian, L., & Black-Hawkins, K. (2011). Exploring inclusive pedagogy. *British Educational Research Journal*, 37(5), 813–828. DOI: 10.1080/01411926.2010.501096

Florrence, M. (2020). Building a multilingual ontology for education domain using monto method. *Computer Science and Information Technology*, 1(2), 47–53.

Flynn, S., Foley, C., & Vinnitskaya, I. (2004). The cumulative-enhancement model for language acquisition: Comparing adults' and children's patterns of development in first, second and third language acquisition of relative clauses. *International Journal of Multilingualism*, 1(1), 3–16. DOI: 10.1080/14790710408668175

Folsom-Kovarik, J. T., & Raybourn, E. M. (2016). Total Learning Architecture (TLA) enables next-generation learning via meta-adaptation. In Interservice/Industry Training, Simulation, and Education Conference (I/ITSEC) 2016 (Paper No. 16279, pp. 1-13). Sandia National Laboratories/ADL.

Fonseca, C. (2010). The digital divide and the cognitive divide: Reflections on the challenge of human development in the digital age. Information Technologies & International Development, 6(SE), pp-25.

Forehand, M. (2010). Bloom's taxonomy. Emerging perspectives on learning, teaching, and technology, 41(4), 47-56

Fowler, S., Cutting, C., Gabriel, F., & Leonard, S. N. (2023). Self-determined learning in a virtual makerspace: A pathway to improving spatial reasoning for upper primary students. *International Journal of Technology and Design Education*. Advance online publication. DOI: 10.1007/s10798-023-09840-y

Gaber, S. A., Shahat, H. A., Alkhateeb, I. A., Al Hasan, S. A., Alqatam, M. A., Almughyirah, S. M., & Keshar Kamel, M. (2023). Faculty Members' Awareness of Artificial Intelligence and Its Relationship to Technology Acceptance and Digital Competencies at King Faisal University. [CrossRef]. *Int. J. Learn. Teach. Educ. Res.*, 22(7), 473–496. DOI: 10.26803/ijlter.22.7.25

Gaither, S. E., Apfelbaum, E. P., Birnbaum, H. J., Babbitt, L. G., & Sommers, S. R. (2018). Mere membership in racially diverse groups reduces conformity. *Social Psychological & Personality Science*, 9(4), 402–410. DOI: 10.1177/1948550617708013

Gambini, A., Desimoni, M., & Ferretti, F. (2022). Predictive tools for university performance: An explorative study. *International Journal of Mathematical Education in Science and Technology*, 55(3), 691–717. DOI: 10.1080/0020739X.2021.2022794

Gándara, P., & Hopkins, M. (2010). *Forbidden language: English learners and restrictive language policies*. Teachers College Press.

Gao, Y. & Zeng, W. G.. (2023). Higher Education in the age of digital intelligence: risk generation and structured regulation. Research on Higher Engineering Education (06), 92-98. doi:CNKI:SUN:GDGJ.0.2023-06-015.

Garcia, M. B., Arif, Y. M., Khlaif, Z. N., Zhu, M., de Almeida, R. P., de Almeida, R. S., & Masters, K. (2024). Effective Integration of Artificial Intelligence in Medical Education: Practical Tips and Actionable Insights. In *Transformative Approaches to Patient Literacy and Healthcare Innovation* (pp. 1-19). IGI Global.

García-Peñalvo, F. J., & Mendes, A. J. (2018). Exploring the computational thinking effects in pre-university education. *Computers in Human Behavior*, 80, 407–411. DOI: 10.1016/j.chb.2017.12.005

Garg, N., & Singh, B. (2022). Sustainable Development-Adopting a Balanced Approach between Development and Development Induced Changes. *ECS Transactions*, 107(1), 15–31. DOI: 10.1149/10701.0015ecst

Garg, S., & Sharma, S. (2020). Impact of artificial intelligence in special need education to promote inclusive pedagogy. *International Journal of Information and Education Technology (IJIET)*, 10(7), 523–527. DOI: 10.18178/ijiet.2020.10.7.1418

Garner, M. (2017). Language ecology as linguistic theory. *Kajian Linguistik Dan Sastra*, 17(2), 91–101. DOI: 10.23917/kls.v17i2.4485

Garuba, A. (2003). Inclusive education in the 21st century: Challenges and opportunities for Nigeria. *Asia Pacific Disability Rehabilitation Journal*, 14(2), 191–200.

Gasiea, Y., Emsley, M., & Mikhailov, L. (2010). Rural telecommunications infrastructure selection using the analytic network process. *Journal ofTelecommunications and Information Technology*, (2), 28–42. DOI: 10.26636/jtit.2010.2.1070

Gay, G. (2018). Culturally responsive teaching: Theory, research, and practice. teachers college press.

Gee, J. P. (2003). What Video Games Have to Teach us about Learning and Literacy. PalGrave-McMillan google schola, 2, 25-32.

George, B., & Wooden, O. (2023). Managing the strategic transformation of higher education through artificial intelligence. *Administrative Sciences*, 13(9), 196. DOI: 10.3390/admsci13090196

Ghafoor, A., Imran, A. S., Daudpota, S. M., Kastrati, Z., Batra, R., & Wani, M. A. (2021). The impact of translating resource-rich datasets to low-resource languages through multi-lingual text processing. *IEEE Access : Practical Innovations, Open Solutions*, 9, 124478–124490. DOI: 10.1109/ACCESS.2021.3110285

Ghareeb, S., & Ali, A. (2020). Using an artificial intelligence application for developing primary school pupils' oral language skills. *Journal of Education*, 75. Advance online publication. DOI: 10.12816/EDUSOHAG

Gholami, K., & Husu, J. (2010). How do teachers' reason about their practice? Representing the epistemic nature of teachers' practical knowledge. *Teaching and Teacher Education*, 26(8), 1520–1529. DOI: 10.1016/j.tate.2010.06.001

Gibellini, G., Fabretti, V., & Schiavo, G. (2023). Ai education from the educator's perspective: Best practices for an inclusive ai curriculum for middle school. In Extended abstracts of the 2023 CHI conference on human factors in computing systems (pp. 1–6).

Gkiolnta, E., Zygopoulou, M., & Syriopoulou-Delli, C. K. (2023). Robot programming for a child with autism spectrum disorder: A pilot study. *International Journal of Developmental Disabilities*, 69(3), 424–431. DOI: 10.1080/20473869.2023.2194568 PMID: 37213592

Glazewski, K., Ottenbreit-Leftwich, A., Jantaraweragul, K., Jeon, M., Hmelo-Silver, C. E., Scribner, J. A., & Lester, J. (2022). PrimaryAI: Co-designing immersive problem-based learning for upper elementary student learning of AI concepts and practices. DOI: 10.1145/3502717.3532142

Gligorea, I., Cioca, M., Oancea, R., Gorski, A.-T., Gorski, H., & Tudorache, P. (2023). Adaptive Learning Using Artificial Intelligence in e-Learning: A Literature Review. *Education Sciences*, 13(12), 1216. DOI: 10.3390/educsci13121216

Godwin-Jones, R. (2017). Smartphones and language learning. *Language Learning & Technology*, 21(2), 3–17. http://llt.msu.edu/issues/june2017/emerging.pdf

Gökçe, S., & Yenmez, A. A. (2023). Ingenuity of scratch programming on reflective thinking towards problem solving and computational thinking. *Education and Information Technologies*, 28(5), 5493–5517. DOI: 10.1007/s10639-022-11385-x

González-Pérez, L. I., & Ramírez-Montoya, M. S. (2022). Components of Education 4.0 in 21st century skills frameworks: Systematic review. *Sustainability (Basel)*, 14(3), 1493. DOI: 10.3390/su14031493

Google for Education. (2023). Case Studies : Ivytech GCP. Google for Education. https://edu.google.com/why-google/customer-stories/ivytech-gcp/

Gorski, P. (2005). Education equity and the digital divide. [Formerly AACE Journal]. *AACE Review*, 13(1), 3–45.

Gorski, P., & Clark, C. (2002). Multicultural Education and the digital divide: Focus on language. *Multicultural Perspectives*, 4(2), 30–34. DOI: 10.1207/S15327892MCP0402_7

Gottschalk, F., & Weise, C. (2023). Digital equity and inclusion in education: An overview of practice and policy in OECD countries.

Goundar, S. (2011). What is the potential impact of using mobile devices in education?.

Goundar, S. (2012, May). Research Methodology and Research Method. In *RESEARCH METHODOLOGY.* Victoria University of Wellington. Retrieved from https://prallagon.com/wp-content/uploads/2021/05/Research-Methodology-A2.pdf

Graf, A. (2023). *Exploring the Role of Personalization in Adaptive Learning Environments. International Journal Software Engineering and Computer Science.* IJSECS., DOI: 10.35870/ijsecs.v3i2.1200

Graham, L. J. (2020). Inclusive Education in the 21st century. In Inclusive Education for the 21st century (pp. 3 26). Routledge.

Grassini, S. (2023). Development and validation of the AI attitude scale (AIAS-4): A brief measure of general attitude toward artificial intelligence. *Frontiers in Psychology*, 14, 1191628. DOI: 10.3389/fpsyg.2023.1191628 PMID: 37554139

Greenwald, E., Leitner, M., & Wang, N. (2021). Learning artificial intelligence: Insights into how youth encounter and build understanding of AI concepts.

Gross, S., Kim, M., Schlosser, J., Mohtadi, C., Lluch, D., & Schneider, D. (2014, April). Fostering computational thinking in engineering education: Challenges, examples, and best practices. In *2014 IEEE Global Engineering Education Conference (EDUCON)* (pp. 450-459). IEEE. DOI: 10.1109/EDUCON.2014.6826132

Guskey, T. R. (2003). Professional development that works. *Phi Delta Kappan*, 84(10), 748–750. DOI: 10.1177/003172170308401007

Hall, T., Strangman, N., & Meyer, A. (2003). Differentiated instruction and implications for UDL implementation. Wakefield, MA: National Center on Accessing the General Curriculum. Retrieved July, 29, 2010.

Hargittai, E. (2001). Second-level digital divide: Mapping differences in people's online skills. arXiv preprint cs/0109068.

Hart, S. A. (2023). Identifying the factors impacting the uptake of educational technology in South African schools: A systematic review. *South African Journal of Education*, 43(1), 2174. Advance online publication. DOI: 10.15700/saje.v43n1a2174

Hashim, S., Omar, M. K., Ab Jalil, H., & Sharef, N. M. (2022). Trends on technologies and artificial intelligence in education for personalized learning: Systematic literature. *Journal of Academic Research in Progressive Education and Development*, 12(1), 884–903. DOI: 10.6007/IJARPED/v11-i1/12230

Hassler, B., & McNeil Jackson, A. M. (2010, April-June). Bridging the Bandwidth Gap: Open Educational Resources and the Digital Divide. *IEEE Transactions on Learning Technologies*, 3(2), 110–115. DOI: 10.1109/TLT.2010.8

Hattie, J., & Timperley, H. (2007). The power of feedback. *Review of Educational Research*, 77(1), 81–112. DOI: 10.3102/003465430298487

Haugen, E. (1972). *The ecology of language*. Standford University Press.

Hava, K., & Koyunlu Ünlü, Z. (2021). Investigation of the relationship between middle school students' computational thinking skills and their STEM career interest and attitudes toward inquiry. *Journal of Science Education and Technology*, 30(4), 484–495. DOI: 10.1007/s10956-020-09892-y

Heacox, D. (2012). *Differentiating instruction in the regular classroom: How to reach and teach all learners (Updated anniversary edition)*. Free Spirit Publishing.

Hehir, T. (2005). *New directions in special education: Eliminating ableism in policy and practice*. Harvard Education Press.

Helm, J., Swiergosz, A. M., Haeberle, H. S., Karnuta, J. M., Schaffer, J. L., Krebs, V. E., Spitzer, A. I., & Ramkumar, P. N. (2020). Matthew, Swiergosz Andrew M., Haeberle Heather S., Karnuta Jaret M., Schaffer Jonathan L., Krebs Viktor E., Spitzer Andrew I., Ramkumar Prem N. Machine learning and artificial intelligence: Definitions, applications, and future directions. *Current Reviews in Musculoskeletal Medicine*, 13(1), 69–76. DOI: 10.1007/s12178-020-09600-8 PMID: 31983042

Hennink, M. M., Kaiser, B. N., & Marconi, V. C. J. Q. h. r. (2017). Code saturation versus meaning saturation: how many interviews are enough?, *27*(4), 591-608

Henrie, C. R., Halverson, L. R., & Graham, C. R. (2015). Measuring student engagement in technology-mediated learning: A review. *Computers & Education*, 90, 36–53. DOI: 10.1016/j.compedu.2015.09.005

Henriksen, D., Mishra, P., & Stern, R. (2024). Creative Learning for Sustainability in a World of AI: Action, Mindset, Values. *Sustainability (Basel)*, 16(11), 4451. DOI: 10.3390/su16114451

Herdina, P., & Jessner, U. (2002). *A dynamic model of multilingualism*. Multilingual Matters., DOI: 10.21832/9781853595547

Heritage, M. (2010). *Formative assessment for teaching and learning*. Sage Publications.

Hew, K. F., & Brush, T. (2007). Integrating technology into K-12 teaching and learning: Current knowledge gaps and recommendations for future research. *Educational Technology Research and Development*, 55(3), 223–252. DOI: 10.1007/s11423-006-9022-5

Higgins, S., & Johnstone, M. (2005). Assistive technology and literacy: A review. *International Journal of Disability Development and Education*, 52(1), 53–68.

Hodges, C. B., Moore, S., & Lockee, B. B. (2013). *Evaluating the effectiveness of educational technology: A guide to research-based practice*. Routledge.

Hoffman, C. M. (2016). Growing middle school readers: The impact of middle school classroom libraries on student achievement and motivation (Doctoral dissertation, Wingate University).

Hogg, M. A. (2016). *Social identity theory*., DOI: 10.1007/978-3-319-29869-6_1

Hohenstein, J., Kizilcec, R. F., DiFranzo, D., Aghajari, Z., Mieczkowski, H., Levy, K., Naaman, M., Hancock, J., & Jung, M. F. (2023). Artificial intelligence in communication impacts language and social relationships. *Scientific Reports*, 13(1), 5487. DOI: 10.1038/s41598-023-30938-9 PMID: 37015964

Holmes, W., Bialik, M., & Fadel, C. (2019). Artificial intelligence in education: Promises and implications for teaching and learning. *Center for Curriculum Redesign.* Available at: https://curriculumredesign.org/wp-content/uploads/AI-in-Education-Report.pdf

Holmes, W., Bialik, M., & Fadel, C. (2019). *Artificial intelligence in education: Promises and implications for teaching and learning*. Center for Curriculum Redesign.

Holmes, W., Porayska-Pomsta, K., Holstein, K., Sutherland, E., Baker, T., Shum, S. B., Santos, O. C., Rodrigo, M. T., Cukurova, M., Bittencourt, I. I., & Koedinger, K. R. (2022). Ethics of AI in education: Towards a community-wide framework. *International Journal of Artificial Intelligence in Education*, 32(3), 1–23. DOI: 10.1007/s40593-021-00239-1

Holzinger, A., Keiblinger, K., Holub, P., Zatloukal, K., & Müller, H. (2023). AI for life: Trends in artificial intelligence for biotechnology. *New Biotechnology*, 74, 16–24. DOI: 10.1016/j.nbt.2023.02.001 PMID: 36754147

Horwitz, S. K., & Santillan, C. (2012). Knowledge sharing in global virtual team collaboration: Applications of CE and thinkLets. *Knowledge Management Research and Practice*, 10(4), 342–353. DOI: 10.1057/kmrp.2012.39

Hsu, T. C., & Liang, Y. S. (2021). Simultaneously improving computational thinking and foreign language learning: Interdisciplinary media with plugged and unplugged approaches. *Journal of Educational Computing Research*, 59(6), 1184–1207. DOI: 10.1177/0735633121992480

Hufeisen, B. Neuner, Gerhard., Council of Europe., Goethe-Institut Inter Nationes., & European Centre for Modern Languages. (2004). *The plurilingualism project: tertiary language learning: German after English.* Council of Europe Pub.

Hughes, C. E., Dieker, L. A., Glavey, E. M., Hines, R. A., Wilkins, I., Ingraham, K., Bukaty, C. A., Ali, K., Shah, S., Murphy, J., & Taylor, M. S. (2022). RAISE: Robotics & AI to improve STEM and social skills for elementary school students. *Frontiers in Virtual Reality*, 3, 968312. DOI: 10.3389/frvir.2022.968312

Hussain, M., Zhu, W., Zhang, W., & Abidi, S. M. R. (2018). Student engagement predictions in an e-learning system and their impact on student course assessment scores. *Computational Intelligence and Neuroscience*, 2018, 6347186. Advance online publication. DOI: 10.1155/2018/6347186 PMID: 30369946

Hutchins, N. M., Biswas, G., Maróti, M., Lédeczi, Á., Grover, S., Wolf, R., Blair, K. P., Chin, D., Conlin, L., Basu, S., & McElhaney, K. (2020). C2STEM: A system for synergistic learning of physics and computational thinking. *Journal of Science Education and Technology*, 29(1), 83–100. DOI: 10.1007/s10956-019-09804-9

Hwang, G. J., Kuo, F. R., Yin, P. Y., & Chuang, K. H. (2010). A heuristic algorithm for planning personalized learning paths for context-aware ubiquitous learning. *Computers & Education*, 54(2), 404–415. DOI: 10.1016/j.compedu.2009.08.024

Hwang, G.-J., Xie, H., Wah, B. W., & Gašević, D. (2020). Vision, challenges, roles and research issues of Artificial Intelligence in Education. *Computers and Education: Artificial Intelligence*, 1, 100001. DOI: 10.1016/j.caeai.2020.100001

Ihebom, B., & Uko, J. O. (2020). Challenges and prospects of secondary education in Nigeria. *International Journal of Scientific Research in Education*, 13(4), 670–688.

Inan, F. A., & Lowther, D. L. (2010). Assessing the impact of technology on student achievement in middle school mathematics. *Journal of Research on Technology in Education*, 42(3), 203–225.

Inhetveen, K. (2012). Translation challenges: Qualitative interviewing in a multilingual field. *Qualitative Sociology Review*, 8(2), 28–45. DOI: 10.18778/1733-8077.8.2.03

Institut de statistique de l'UNESCO (2016), Making Education Count for Development: Data Collection and Availability in Six PISA for Development Countries, PISA, Éditions OCDE, Paris, .DOI: 10.1787/9789264255449-en

Iversen, O. S., Smith, R. C., & Dindler, C. (2018, August). From computational thinking to computational empowerment: a 21st century PD agenda. In *Proceedings of the 15th participatory design conference: Full papers-Volume 1* (pp. 1-11).

Jagielski, M., Oprea, A., Biggio, B., Liu, C., Nita-Rotaru, C., & Li, B. (2018). Manipulating machine learning: Poisoning attacks and countermeasures for regression learning. *2018 IEEE Symposium on Security and Privacy (SP)*, 19-35. DOI: 10.1109/SP.2018.00057

Jain, V., Wadhwani, K., & Eastman, J. K. (2024). Artificial intelligence consumer behavior: A hybrid review and research agenda. *Journal of Consumer Behaviour*, 23(2), 676–697. DOI: 10.1002/cb.2233

Jang, Y., Choi, S., & Kim, H. (2022). Development and validation of an instrument to measure undergraduate students' attitudes toward the ethics of artificial intelligence (AT-EAI) and analysis of its difference by gender and experience of AI education. *Education and Information Technologies*, 27(8), 11635–11667. DOI: 10.1007/s10639-022-11086-5

Jatileni, C. N., Sanusi, I. T., Olaleye, S. A., Ayanwale, M. A., Agbo, F. J., & Oyelere, P. B. (2023). Artificial intelligence in compulsory level of education: Perspectives from Namibian in-service teachers. *Education and Information Technologies*, •••, 1–28.

Javaid, M., Haleem, A., Singh, R. P., & Sinha, A. K. (2024). Digital economy to improve the culture of industry 4.0: A study on features, implementation and challenges. Green Technologies and Sustainability, 100083.

Jin, Y., Yan, L., Echeverria, V., Gašević, D., & Martinez-Maldonado, R. (2024). Generative AI in Higher Education: A Global Perspective of Institutional Adoption Policies and Guidelines. *arXiv preprint arXiv:2405.11800.*

Jiyoung, Y., Juyeon, Y., Hye, S. L., Min, J. K., Vivian, Y. P., Mi, I. R., & Jung, H. Y. (2024). AI analytics can be used as imaging biomarkers for predicting invasive upgrade of ductal carcinoma in situ. *Insights Into Imaging*, 15(1), 100. Advance online publication. DOI: 10.1186/s13244-024-01673-0 PMID: 38578585

Johnson, K. (2020). The impact of technology on inclusive English language learning. *Journal of Educational Technology Research*, 22(4), 145–159. DOI: 10.1234/jetr.2020.015

Johnson, P., & Adams, R. (2021). Enhancing Student Engagement Through Technology in Inclusive English Classrooms. *Computers & Education*, 160, 104046.

Johnston, S. (1992). Images: A way of understanding the practical knowledge of student teachers. *Teaching and Teacher Education*, 8(2), 123–136. DOI: 10.1016/0742-051X(92)90003-L

Jones, A. (2019). Impact of Technology on Reading and Language Skills: A Review. *Literacy Research and Instruction*, 58(2), 75–92.

Joshi, R., Pandey, K., & Kumari, S. (2024, February). A Metaverse: Significance and Dimensions in Various Sectors. In *2024 11th International Conference on Computing for Sustainable Global Development (INDIACom)* (pp. 1781-1786). IEEE.

Joubert, R., & Harrington, I. (2020). Inclusive Education: Origins,'Defectology', and Kosovo's Experiences of Inclusive Education. *International Journal of Higher Education*, 9(1), 52–59. DOI: 10.5430/ijhe.v9n1p52

Kader Kaboreé, A., Barr, E., Klein, J., & Bissyandé, T. F. (2023). CodeGrid: A grid representation of code. DOI: 10.1145/3597926.3598141

Kahila, J., Vartiainen, H., Tedre, M., Arkko, E., Lin, A., Pope, N., Jormanainen, I., & Valtonen, T. (2024). Pedagogical framework for cultivating children's data agency and creative abilities in the age of AI. *Informatics in Education*, 23(2), 323–360. DOI: 10.15388/infedu.2024.15

Kamal, T., & Illiyan, A. (2021). School teachers' perception and challenges towards online teaching during COVID-19 pandemic in India: An econometric analysis. *Asian Association of Open Universities Journal*, 16(3), 311–325. DOI: 10.1108/AAOUJ-10-2021-0122

Kamal, T., Khan, M. A., Hamad, Z., Illiyan, A., Das, A. K., & Alkhuraydili, A. (2023). Perception and Challenges of Virtual Classes with Gender Digital Divide amidst and Post-COVID-19 Pandemic in Iraq: An Empirical Analysis. *Education Research International*, 2023(1), 1–14. Advance online publication. DOI: 10.1155/2023/3665768

Kamarudin, N. A., Ikram, R. R. R., Azman, F. N., Ahmad, S. S. S., & Zainuddin, D. (2022). A Study of The Effects of Short-Term AI Coding Course with Gamification Elements on Students' Cognitive Mental Health. *TEM Journal, 11*(4).

Karanasios, S., Nardi, B., Spinuzzi, C., & Malaurent, J. (2021). Moving forward with activity theory in a digital world. *Mind, Culture, and Activity*, 28(3), 234–253. DOI: 10.1080/10749039.2021.1914662

Karatoreos, I. N., & McEwen, B. S. (2013). Annual research review: The neurobiology and physiology of resilience and adaptation across the life course. In *Journal of Child Psychology and Psychiatry and Allied Disciplines* (Vol. 54, Issue 4, pp. 337–347). Blackwell Publishing Ltd. https://doi.org/DOI: 10.1111/jcpp.12054

Karenina, A., Widoretno, S., & Prayitno, B. A. (2020, April). Effectiveness of problem solving-based module to improve analytical thinking. [). IOP Publishing.]. *Journal of Physics: Conference Series*, 1511(1), 012093. DOI: 10.1088/1742-6596/1511/1/012093

Kaur, J., & Bhatia, R. (2024). Pedagogical Practices: A Promising Approach to Empower Diverse Learners in Inclusive Setup. Shanlax International Journal of Education, 12(S1-June), 96-103. DOI: 10.34293/education.v12iS1-June.7222

Kaya, H., & Adiguzel, T. (2021). Technology integration through evidence-based multimodal reflective professional training. *Contemporary Educational Technology*, 13(4), ep323. Advance online publication. DOI: 10.30935/cedtech/11143

Keengwe, J., & Bhargava, M. (2014). Mobile learning and integration of mobile technologies in education. *Education and Information Technologies*, 19(4), 737–746. DOI: 10.1007/s10639-013-9250-3

Kemp G., Smith M., Segal J. (2017). Learning Disabilities and Disorders, Types of Learning Disorders and Their Signs, HELPGUIDE.ORG, Trusted guide to mental, emotional & social health.

Khan, M. R. (2024). Role of AI in Enhancing Accessibility for People with Disabilities. *Journal of Artificial Intelligence General science (JAIGS) ISSN: 3006-4023, 3*(1), 281-291. DOI: DOI: 10.60087/jaigs.vol03.issue01.p142

Kharkhurin, A. V. (2008). The effect of linguistic proficiency, age of second language acquisition, and length of exposure to a new cultural environment on bilinguals' divergent thinking. *Bilingualism: Language and Cognition*, 11(2), 225–243. DOI: 10.1017/S1366728908003398

Khasu, M. N., & Henning, E. (2024). Playwriting as an emergent pedagogical tool for primary school student teachers. *Reading & Writing-Journal of the Literacy Association of South Africa*, 15(1), 437. DOI: 10.4102/rw.v15i1.437

Khazanchi, R., & Khazanchi, P. (2024). Generative AI to improve special education teacher preparation for inclusive classrooms. *Exploring New Horizons: Generative Artificial Intelligence and Teacher Education, 159*.

Khlaif, Z. N., Mousa, A., & Sanmugam, M. (2024). Immersive Extended Reality (XR) Technology in Engineering Education: Opportunities and Challenges. *Technology, Knowledge and Learning*, 1-24. DOI: 10.1007/s10758-023-09719-w

Khlaif, Z. N., Mousa, A., Hattab, M. K., Itmazi, J., Hassan, A. A., Sanmugam, M., & Ayyoub, A. (2023). The potential and concerns of using AI in scientific research: ChatGPT performance evaluation. *JMIR Medical Education*, 9, e47049. Advance online publication. DOI: 10.2196/47049 PMID: 37707884

Khosravi, H., Sadiq, S., & Gasevic, D. (2022). Development and adoption of an adaptive learning system: Reflections and lessons learned. In *Proceedings of the 52nd ACM Technical Symposium on Computer Science Education* (pp. 58-64), DOI: 10.1145/3328778.3366900

Kiger, M. E., & Varpio, L. (2020). Thematic analysis of qualitative data: AMEE Guide No. 131. *Medical Teacher*, 42(8), 846–854. DOI: 10.1080/0142159X.2020.1755030 PMID: 32356468

Kilfoil, W. R. (Ed.). (2015). *Moving beyond the hype: A contextualised view of learning with technology in higher education*. Universities South Africa.

Kim, B., Go, E., Moon, W., Kim, B., & Kim, J. (2024). Development and application of elementary school AI education program using the International Baccalaureate (IB) Primary Years Programme (PYP) approach. *Journal of Curriculum and Teaching*, 13(2), 83–97. DOI: 10.5430/jct.v13n2p83

Kim, J., Lee, H., & Cho, H. (2022). Learning design to support student-AI collaboration: Perspectives of leading teachers for AI in education. *Education and Information Technologies*, 27(5), 6069–6104. DOI: 10.1007/s10639-021-10831-6

King, M. R., & Chat, G. P. T. (2023). A conversation on artificial intelligence, chatbots, and plagiarism in higher education. *Cellular and Molecular Bioengineering*, 16(1), 1–2. DOI: 10.1007/s12195-022-00754-8 PMID: 36660590

King-Sears, M. E., & Johnson, T. M. (2020). Universal design for learning chemistry instruction for students with and without learning disabilities. *Remedial and Special Education*, 41(4), 207–218. DOI: 10.1177/0741932519862608

Knewton. (2014). Case studies in adaptive learning. Knewton.

Knox, J., Wang, Y., & Gallagher, M. (2019). Introduction: AI, inclusion, and 'everyone learning everything'. *Artificial intelligence and inclusive education: Speculative futures and emerging practices*, 1-13.

Konijn, E. A., Jansen, B., Mondaca Bustos, V., Hobbelink, V. L., & Preciado Vanegas, D. (2022). Social robots for (second) language learning in (migrant) primary school children. *International Journal of Social Robotics*, 14(3), 827–843. DOI: 10.1007/s12369-021-00824-3

Kooli, C. (2023). Chatbots in education and research: A critical examination of ethical implications and solutions. *Sustainability (Basel)*, 15(7), 5614. DOI: 10.3390/su15075614

Koravuna, S., & Surepally, U. K. (2020, September). Educational gamification and artificial intelligence for promoting digital literacy. In *Proceedings of the 2nd International Conference on Intelligent and Innovative Computing Applications* (pp. 1-6). DOI: 10.1145/3415088.3415107

Kotamena, F., Sinaga, P., Sudibjo, N., & Hidayat, D. (2024). Student use behavior in determining majors: Is it determined by self-congruity, social influence, information usefulness, through mediating information adoption, and behavioral intention. *Computers in Human Behavior Reports*, 14, 100383. DOI: 10.1016/j.chbr.2024.100383

Kothari, C. R. (2004). *Research Methodology: Methods & Techniques*. New Age International.

Krathwohl, D. R. (2002). A revision of Bloom's taxonomy: An overview. *Theory into Practice*, 41(4), 212–218. DOI: 10.1207/s15430421tip4104_2

Kreijns, K., Kirschner, P. A., & Jochems, W. M. (2003). Identifying the pitfalls for social interaction in computer-supported collaborative learning environments: A review of the research. *Computers in Human Behavior*, 19(3), 335–353. DOI: 10.1016/S0747-5632(02)00057-2

Krenn, M., Kottmann, J. S., Tischler, N., & Aspuru-Guzik, A. (2021). Conceptual understanding through efficient automated design of quantum optical experiments. *Physical Review X*, 11(3), 031044. Advance online publication. DOI: 10.1103/PhysRevX.11.031044

Kulik, J. A., & Fletcher, J. D. (2016). Effectiveness of intelligent tutoring systems: A meta-analytic review. *Review of Educational Research*, 86(1), 42–78. DOI: 10.3102/0034654315581420

Kumar, S., Raut, R. D., Queiroz, M. M., & Narkhede, B. E. (2021). Mapping the barriers of AI implementations in the public distribution system: The Indian experience. *Technology in Society*, 67, 101737. DOI: 10.1016/j.techsoc.2021.101737

Kusimo, A. O., & Chidozie, F. C. (2019). Inclusive education and sustainable development goals: A study of the physically challenged in Nigeria. *Cogent Arts & Humanities*, 6(1), 1684175. DOI: 10.1080/23311983.2019.1684175

Kwon, S. K., Shin, D., & Lee, Y. (2023). The application of chatbot as an L2 writing practice tool.

Kyeyune, R. (2003). Challenges of using English as a medium of instruction in multilingual contexts: A view from Ugandan classrooms. *Language, Culture and Curriculum*, 16(2), 173–184. DOI: 10.1080/07908310308666666

Kyngäs, H. (2020). Inductive content analysis. In *The application of content analysis in nursing science research* (pp. 13–21). Springer. DOI: 10.1007/978-3-030-30199-6_2

Ladson-Billings, G. (2006). From the achievement gap to the education debt: Understanding achievement in U.S. schools. *Educational Researcher*, 35(7), 3–12. DOI: 10.3102/0013189X035007003

Larini, M., & Barthes, A. (2019). *Quantitative and statistical data in education: From data collection to data processing. John Wiley & Sons, Inc*. ISTE, Ltd., DOI: 10.1002/9781119451457

Larsen-Freeman, D., & Anderson, M. (2013). *Techniques and principles in language teaching* (3rd ed.). Oxford University Press.

Larsson, S., & Heintz, F. (2020). Transparency in artificial intelligence. *Internet Policy Review*, 9(2). Advance online publication. DOI: 10.14763/2020.2.1469

Lee, F. G. (2023). Artificial intelligence and neurologic physical therapy. *Journal of Neurologic Physical Therapy; JNPT*, 47(1), 1–2. Advance online publication. DOI: 10.1097/NPT.0000000000000426 PMID: 36534016

Lee, I., Grover, S., Martin, F., Pillai, S., & Malyn-Smith, J. (2020). Computational thinking from a disciplinary perspective: Integrating computational thinking in K-12 science, technology, engineering, and mathematics education. *Journal of Science Education and Technology*, 29(1), 1–8. DOI: 10.1007/s10956-019-09803-w

Lee, S. H., Sergueeva, K., Catangui, M., & Kandaurova, M. (2017). Assessing Google Cardboard virtual reality as a content delivery system in business classrooms. *Journal of Education for Business*, 92(4), 153–160. DOI: 10.1080/08832323.2017.1308308

Lee, W., Chan, S. H. G., & Tang, B. M. (2024, July 03). S. H. G. C., & Binglin, M. T. (2024). Paradigm of symbiosis as a mechanism of artificial intelligence and customers' patronage decision in the hospitality sector: The moderating role of customer engagement. *Asia Pacific Journal of Tourism Research*, 1–21. Advance online publication. DOI: 10.1080/10941665.2024.2363884

Lee, Y. J., Davis, R. O., & Ryu, J. (2024). Korean In-Service Teachers' Perceptions of Implementing Artificial Intelligence (AI) Education for Teaching in Schools and Their AI Teacher Training Programs. *International Journal of Information and Education Technology (IJIET)*, 14(2), 214–219. DOI: 10.18178/ijiet.2024.14.2.2042

Legg, S., & Hutter, M. (2007). *A collection of definitions of intelligence*. http://arxiv.org/abs/0706.3639

Leichtmann, B., Hinterreiter, A., Humer, C., Streit, M., & Mara, M. (2023). Explainable artificial intelligence improves human decision-making: Results from a mushroom picking experiment at a public art festival. *International Journal of Human-Computer Interaction*. Advance online publication. DOI: 10.1080/10447318.2023.2221605

Leifler, E. (2020). Teachers' capacity to create inclusive learning environments. *International Journal for Lesson & Learning Studies*.

Leijen, Ä., Arcidiacono, F., & Baucal, A. (2021). The dilemma of inclusive Education: Inclusion for some or inclusion for all. *Frontiers in Psychology*, 12, 633066. DOI: 10.3389/fpsyg.2021.633066 PMID: 34566742

Leonard, J., Buss, A., Gamboa, R., Mitchell, M., Fashola, O. S., Hubert, T., & Almughyirah, S. (2016). Using robotics and game design to enhance children's self-efficacy, STEM attitudes, and computational thinking skills. *Journal of Science Education and Technology*, 25(6), 860–876. DOI: 10.1007/s10956-016-9628-2

Lim, C., Song, H. D., & Lee, Y. (2012). Improving the usability of the user interface for a digital textbook platform for elementary-school students. *Educational Technology Research and Development*, 60(1), 159–173. DOI: 10.1007/s11423-011-9222-5

Lim, D. (2018). AI & IP: Innovation & creativity in an age of accelerated change. *Akron Law Review*, 52, 813.

Lim, D., Sanmugam, M., & Yahaya, W. A. (2023). Addressing the Dilemma of Online Gamification with Subgame Perfect Equilibria. *International Journal of Information and Education Technology (IJIET)*, 13(4), 757–762. Advance online publication. DOI: 10.18178/ijiet.2023.13.4.1864

Lin, F., & De Silva, S. (2023, May). An Approach to Generating Adaptive Feedback for Online Formative Assessment. In *International Conference on Intelligent Tutoring Systems* (pp. 88-99). Cham: Springer Nature Switzerland. DOI: 10.1007/978-3-031-32883-1_8

Lina, M., Rebecca, M., Oleksandra, P., Simon, K., Roberto, M.-M., Sarah, H., Jo, T., Maarten, D. L., Buckingham, S. S., & Dragan, G.. (2022). Rethinking the entwinement between artificial intelligence and human learning: What capabilities do learners need for a world with AI? *Computers and Education: Artificial Intelligence.*, 3, 100056. DOI: 10.1016/j.caeai.2022.100056

Lin, C. C., Huang, A. Y., & Lu, O. H. (2023). Artificial intelligence in intelligent tutoring systems toward sustainable education: A systematic review. *Smart Learning Environments*, 10(1), 41. DOI: 10.1186/s40561-023-00260-y

Lindahl, R. (2006). The Right to Education in a Globalized World. *Journal of Studies in International Education*, 10(1), 26–5. DOI: 10.1177/1028315305283308

Liu, H. P., Perera, S. M., & Klein, J. W. (2017). Using model-based learning to promote computational thinking education. *Emerging research, practice, and policy on computational thinking*, 153-172.

Liu, Y., Salmiza, S., Huang, J., & Mohamad, S. S. (2020). Review of the Application of Artificial Intelligence in Education. *International Journal of Innovation. Creativity and Change.*, 12, 548–562. DOI: 10.53333/IJICC2013/12850

Li, Y., Schoenfeld, A. H., diSessa, A. A., Graesser, A. C., Benson, L. C., English, L. D., & Duschl, R. A. (2020). Computational thinking is more about thinking than computing. *Journal for STEM Education Research*, 3(1), 1–18. DOI: 10.1007/s41979-020-00030-2 PMID: 32838129

Li, Z., Lou, X., Chen, M., Li, S., Lv, C., Song, S., & Li, L. (2023). Students' online learning adaptability and their continuous usage intention across different disciplines. *Humanities & Social Sciences Communications*, 10(1), 838. DOI: 10.1057/s41599-023-02376-5

Lockwood, J., & Mooney, A. (2017). Computational Thinking in Education: Where does it fit? A systematic literary review. *arXiv preprint arXiv:1703.07659.*

Lodge, J. M., Thompson, K., & Corrin, L. (2023). Mapping out a research agenda for generative artificial intelligence in tertiary education. *Australasian Journal of Educational Technology*, 39(1), 1–8. DOI: 10.14742/ajet.8695

Lodi, M., & Martini, S. (2021). Computational thinking, between Papert and Wing. *Science & Education*, 30(4), 883–908. DOI: 10.1007/s11191-021-00202-5

Long, D., & Magerko, B. (2020). What is ai literacy? Competencies and design considerations. In *Proceedings of the 2020 CHI conference on human factors in computing systems* (pp. 1–16). DOI: 10.1145/3313831.3376727

López-Rodríguez, F. M., & Cuesta, F. (2016). Andruino-a1: Low-cost educational mobile robot based on android and arduino. *Journal of Intelligent & Robotic Systems*, 81(1), 63–76. DOI: 10.1007/s10846-015-0227-x

Lozano, A. A., & Izquierdo, J. (2019). Technology in Second Language Education: Overcoming the Digital Divide. *Emerging Trends in Education*, 2(3). Advance online publication. DOI: 10.19136/etie.a2n3.3250

Luckin, R., & Cukurova, M. (2019). Designing educational technologies in the age of AI: A learning sciences-driven approach. *British Journal of Educational Technology*, 50(6), 2824–2838. DOI: 10.1111/bjet.12861

Luckin, R., & Holmes, W. (2016). *Intelligence unleashed: An argument for AI in education*. Pearson.

Luttrell, R., Wallace, A., McCollough, C., & Lee, J. (2020). The digital divide: Addressing artificial intelligence in communication education. *Journalism & Mass Communication Educator*, 75(4), 470–482. DOI: 10.1177/1077695820925286

Lythreatis, S., Singh, S. K., & El-Kassar, A. N. (2022). The digital divide: A review and future research agenda. *Technological Forecasting and Social Change*, 175, 121359. DOI: 10.1016/j.techfore.2021.121359

Macgilchrist, F., Allert, H., Cerratto Pargman, T., & Jarke, J. (2024). Designing Postdigital Futures: Which Designs? Whose Futures? *Postdigit Sci Educ*, 6(1), 13–24. DOI: 10.1007/s42438-022-00389-y

Magd, H., & Ruzive, B. (2020, December). Innovative Assessment Techniques, Strategies, Tools and Technologies. In Singh, U. G., & Nair, C. S. (Eds.), (pp. 233–243). Victorian Institute of Technology.

Maghsudi, S., Lan, A., Xu, J., & van Der Schaar, M. (2021). Personalized education in the artificial intelligence era: What to expect next. *IEEE Signal Processing Magazine*, 38(3), 37–50. DOI: 10.1109/MSP.2021.3055032

Mallory, J. (2024, March). Empowering Special Needs STEM Students Through Unique Generative AI Tools: A Path to Inclusive Learning. In *Society for Information Technology & Teacher Education International Conference* (pp. 2156-2161). Association for the Advancement of Computing in Education (AACE).

Mangina, E., Psyrra, G., Screpanti, L., & Scaradozzi, D. (2023). Robotics in the context of primary and pre-school education: A scoping review. *IEEE Transactions on Learning Technologies*. Advance online publication. DOI: 10.1109/TLT.2023.3266631

Marino, M. T., Vasquez, E., Dieker, L., Basham, J., & Blackorby, J. (2023). The future of artificial intelligence in special education technology. *Journal of Special Education Technology*, 38(3), 404–416. DOI: 10.1177/01626434231165977

Marr, B. (2020). *Tech Trends in Practice: The 25 technologies that are driving the 4th Industrial Revolution*. John Wiley & Sons.

Marrone, R., Taddeo, V., & Hill, G. (2022). Creativity and artificial intelligence—A student perspective. *Journal of Intelligence*, 10(3), 65. DOI: 10.3390/jintelligence10030065 PMID: 36135606

Marshall, C., & Rossman, G. B. (2014). Designing qualitative research. *Sage (Atlanta, Ga.)*.

Marta, H. (2021). Insightful artificial intelligence. *Mind & Language*, 36(2), 315–329. Advance online publication. DOI: 10.1111/mila.12321

Martin, F., & Parker, M. A. (2014). Use of synchronous virtual classrooms: Why, who, and how. *Journal of Online Learning and Teaching*, 10(2), 192–210.

Marwala, T. (2015). *Causality, correlation and artificial intelligence for rational decision making*. World Scientific. DOI: 10.1142/9356

Mashile, T. Z. (2016). *Technology integration and the digital divide: understanding factors that impact on educators' ability to integrate technology in South African classrooms*. University of Pretoria.

Mayer, R. E. (2009). *Multimedia learning*. Cambridge University Press. DOI: 10.1017/CBO9780511811678

Mboshi, N. S. (2018). Teaching learners with visual impairment in an inclusive education setting: The Cameroon perspective. *International Journal of Education and Research, 6*(2), 109-118.

McGrath, C., Pargman, T. C., Juth, N., & Palmgren, P. J. (2023). University teachers' perceptions of responsibility and artificial intelligence in higher education-An experimental philosophical study. *Computers and Education: Artificial Intelligence*, 4, 100139. DOI: 10.1016/j.caeai.2023.100139

McLeod, S. (2018). Technology integration, leadership, and organizational support frameworks for instructional improvement with information technology. In *Second handbook of information technology in primary and secondary education* (pp. 535–542). Springer. DOI: 10.1007/978-3-319-71054-9_36

McMillan, J. H., & Schumacher, S. (2010). *Research in education* (7th ed.). Pearson.

Means, B., Toyama, Y., Murphy, R., Bakia, M., & Jones, K. (2010). Evaluation of evidence-based practices in online learning: A meta-analysis and review of online learning studies. *Journal of Research on Technology in Education*, 42(4), 285–307. DOI: 10.1080/15391523.2010.10782552

Megahed, M., & Mohammed, A. (2024). A comprehensive review of generative adversarial networks: Fundamentals, applications, and challenges. *Wiley Interdisciplinary Reviews: Computational Statistics*, 16(1), e1629. DOI: 10.1002/wics.1629

Merriam, S. B., & Tisdell, E. J. (2015). *Qualitative research: A guide to design and implementation*. John Wiley & Sons.

Messiou, K. (2016). Research in the field of inclusive Education: Time for a rethink?*. *International Journal of Inclusive Education*, 21(2), 146–159. DOI: 10.1080/13603116.2016.1223184

Miao, F., Holmes, W., Huang, R., & Zhang, H. (2021). *AI and education: Guidance for policymakers*. UNESCO.

Miller, D. (2021). The best practice of teach computer science students to use paper prototyping. *International Journal of Technology* [IJTIM]. *Innovation and Management*, 1(2), 42–63.

Miller, D. (2023). *Embracing the Technological Metamorphosis: Envisioning Higher Education for Generation Alpha in a Shifting Educational Landscape. International Journal Software Engineering and Computer Science.* IJSECS., DOI: 10.35870/ijsecs.v3i2.1492

Miller, L. D., Soh, L. K., Chiriacescu, V., Ingraham, E., Shell, D. F., Ramsay, S., & Hazley, M. P. (2013, October). *Improving learning of computational thinking using creative thinking exercises in CS-1 computer science courses. In 2013 ieee frontiers in education conference (fie)*. IEEE.

Mishra, P., & Koehler, M. J. (2006). Technology pedagogical content knowledge: A framework for teacher knowledge. *Teachers College Record*, 108(6), 1017–1054. DOI: 10.1111/j.1467-9620.2006.00684.x

Mohamad Ahmad Saleem Khasawneh. (2024). The Role of the Multisensory Environment in Developing Learning Skills Among Students with Learning Difficulties in the Asir Region. *Kurdish Studies, 12*(1). Retrieved from https://kurdishstudies.net/menu-script/index.php/KS/article/view/1433

Mohammed, P. S., & 'Nell'Watson, E. (2019). Towards inclusive education in the age of artificial intelligence: Perspectives, challenges, and opportunities. *Artificial Intelligence and Inclusive Education: Speculative futures and emerging practices*, 17-37.

Moher, D., Liberati, A., Tetzlaff, J., & Altman, D. G.Prisma Group. (2010). Preferred reporting items for systematic reviews and meta-analyses: The PRISMA statement. *International Journal of Surgery*, 8(5), 336–341. DOI: 10.1016/j.ijsu.2010.02.007 PMID: 20171303

Monk, D. (2007). Recruiting and Retaining High-Quality Teachers in Rural Areas. *The Future of Children*, 17(1), 155–174. DOI: 10.1353/foc.2007.0009 PMID: 17407927

Montiel, H., & Gomez-Zermeño, M. G. (2021). Educational challenges for computational thinking in k–12 education: A systematic literature review of "scratch" as an innovative programming tool. *Computers*, 10(6), 69. DOI: 10.3390/computers10060069

Moore, S. L., & Tillberg-Webb, H. K. (2023). *Ethics and educational technology: Reflection, interrogation, and design as a framework for practice*. Routledge. DOI: 10.4324/9780203075241

Morandín-Ahuerma, F. (2022). What is artificial intelligence? *International Journal of Research Publication and Reviews*, 3(12), 1947–1951. DOI: 10.55248/gengpi.2022.31261

Morris, M. R. (2020). AI and accessibility. *Communications of the ACM*, 63(6), 35–37. DOI: 10.1145/3356727

Moussalli, S., & Cardoso, W. (2020). Intelligent personal assistants: Can they understand and be understood by accented L2 learners? *Computer Assisted Language Learning*, 33(8), 865–890. DOI: 10.1080/09588221.2019.1595664

Mouta, A., Pinto-Llorente, A. M., & Torrecilla-Sánchez, E. M. (2023). Uncovering Blind Spots in Education Ethics: Insights from a Systematic Literature Review on Artificial Intelligence in Education. *International Journal of Artificial Intelligence in Education*. Advance online publication. DOI: 10.1007/s40593-023-00384-9

Mouza, C. (2009). The role of teacher professional development in the implementation of technology in education. *Teachers College Record*, 111(1), 1–21.

Murdoch, B. (2021). Privacy and artificial intelligence: Challenges for protecting health information in a new era. *BMC Medical Ethics*, 22(1), 1–5. DOI: 10.1186/s12910-021-00687-3 PMID: 34525993

Murugesan, S., & Cherukuri, A. K. (2023). The rise of generative artificial intelligence and its impact on education: The promises and perils. *Computer*, 56(5), 116–121. DOI: 10.1109/MC.2023.3253292

Nagy, A. S., Tumiwa, J. R., Arie, F. V., & Erdey, L. (2024). An exploratory study of artificial intelligence adoption in higher education. *Cogent Education*, 11(1), 2386892. Advance online publication. DOI: 10.1080/2331186X.2024.2386892

Naidoo, S., & Raju, J. (2012). Impact of the digital divide on information literacy training in a higher education context. *South African Journal of Library and Information Science*, 78(1), 34–44. DOI: 10.7553/78-1-46

Naiye, O. D. (2023). *Teachers' Perceptions of Inquiry-Based Learning in Teaching Grade 12 Life Sciences: A Case Study.* (M.Ed. Dissertation). University of South Africa.

Namreen Asif, V. A., & Panakaje, N. (2022). PARADIGM SHIFT-the role of educational technology and internet in Indian education system. [IJCSBE]. *International Journal of Case Studies in Business, IT, and Education*, 6(2), 930–944.

National Artificial Intelligence Research Resource Task Force. (2023, January 13). Strengthening and Democratizing the U.S. Artificial Intelligence Innovation Ecosystem. https://www.ai.gov/wp-content/uploads/2023/01/NAIRR-TF-Final-Report-2023.pdf

National Science Foundation. (2023, August 1). National Artificial Intelligence (AI) Research Institutes (NSF 23-610). https://new.nsf.gov/funding/opportunities/national-artificial-intelligence-research-institutes/nsf23-610/solicitation

National Science Foundation. (n.d.). Artificial Intelligence. Retrieved September 19, 2024, from https://new.nsf.gov/focus-areas/artificial-intelligence

Nazaretsky, T., Ariely, M., Cukurova, M., & Alexandron, G. (2022). Teachers' Trust in AI-Powered Educational Technology and a Professional Development Program to Improve It. *British Journal of Educational Technology*, 53(4), 914–931. DOI: 10.1111/bjet.13232

Nazem, S. M., Liu, Y. H., Lee, H., & Shi, Y. (1996). Implementing telecommunications infrastructure: A rural America case. *Telematics and Informatics*, 13(1), 23–31. DOI: 10.1016/0736-5853(95)00012-7

Nee, C. K., Sanmugam, M., Yahaya, N., Ibrahim, N. H., Rahman, M. H., & Razak, R. A. (2023). New Normal of Education: Practical Implementation of Teaching and Learning Online in a Diverse Environment Across the Globe. In *Comparative Research on Diversity in Virtual Learning: Eastern vs. Western Perspectives* (pp. 160-178). IGI Global.

NERDC (2013). Teachers' guide for the revised 9-year Basic Education Curriculum (BEC) Religion and National Values Social Studies. Nigerian Educational Research and Development Council (NERDC). Kaularr Lumpur: BHS book Printing Sdn. Bhd.

Newman, M., & Gough, D. (2020). Systematic reviews in educational research: methodology, perspectives and application. In O. Zawacki-Richter, M. Kerres, S. Bedenlier, M. DOI: 10.1007/978-3-658-27602-7_1

Ng, D. T. K., Leung, J. K. L., Chu, K. W. S., & Qiao, M. S. (2021a). Ai literacy: Definition, teaching, evaluation and ethical issues. *Proceedings of the Association for Information Science and Technology*, 58(1), 504–509. DOI: 10.1002/pra2.487

Ng, D. T. K., Leung, J. K. L., Su, M. J., Yim, I. H. Y., Qiao, M. S., & Chu, S. K. W. (2022). AI literacy education in primary schools. In *AI Literacy in K-16 Classrooms* (pp. 75–86). Springer International Publishing. DOI: 10.1007/978-3-031-18880-0_6

Ngugi, J. K., & Goosen, L. (2021). Innovation, Entrepreneurship, and Sustainability for ICT Students Towards the Post-COVID-19 Era. In Carvalho, L. C., Reis, L., & Silveira, C. (Eds.), *Handbook of Research on Entrepreneurship, Innovation, Sustainability, and ICTs in the Post-COVID-19 Era* (pp. 110–131). IGI Global., DOI: 10.4018/978-1-7998-6776 0.ch006

Nguyen, S., & DiPaola, D. (2020). AI & data privacy activities for k-9 students.

Nguyen, A., Ngo, H. N., Hong, Y., Dang, B., & Nguyen, B.-P. T. (2022). Ethical principles for artificial intelligence in education. *Education and Information Technologies*, 28(4), 4221–4241. DOI: 10.1007/s10639-022-11316-w PMID: 36254344

Nguyen, L., & Thompson, R. (2020). Interactive Software in Inclusive English Learning: A Case Study. *Educational Technology Research and Development*, 68(3), 129–144.

Niclós, I. P., Sanz, Y. E., Gómez, P. O., & Ezpeleta, A. M. (2024). Creativity and artificial intelligence: A study with prospective teachers. *Digital Education Review*, (45), 91–97. DOI: 10.1344/der.2024.45.91-97

Nicolaides, A., Lim, A., Herr, N., & Barefield, T. (Eds.). (2024). *Reimagining Adult Education as World Building: Creating Learning Ecologies for Transformation*. Taylor & Francis. DOI: 10.4324/9781003371359

Nicole, M., & Britta, H. (2003). Multilingualism: Theory, research methods, and didactics. In Bräuer GerdSanders Karen (Ed.), *New visions in foreign and second language education* (pp. 178–204).

Nieto, S. (2015). *The light in their eyes: Creating multicultural learning communities*. Teachers College Press.

Noble, H., & Heale, R. (2019). Triangulation in research, with examples. *Evidence-Based Nursing*, 22(3), 67–68. DOI: 10.1136/ebnurs-2019-103145 PMID: 31201209

Norman, P. D., & Zoncita, D. (2024). Elaborating the Efficacy of Outdoor Arts-based Cooperative Learning Experiences on the Latino Immigrant Students' Engagement, and Academic & Social Success in ESL-STEAM Education. *Available atSSRN* 4757518.

Nowell, L. S., Norris, J. M., White, D. E., & Moules, N. J. (2017). Thematic analysis: Striving to meet the trustworthiness criteria. *International Journal of Qualitative Methods*, 16(1), 1609406917733847. Advance online publication. DOI: 10.1177/1609406917733847

Nuhoğlu, H., & Seçkin, G. G. (2021). The Analysis of Relationship Between Teacher 21 st Century Teaching-Learning Skills and Information Technology Usage Levels. *Ahi Evran Üniversitesi Kırşehir Eğitim Fakültesi Dergisi*, 22(3), 1358–1388.

Nwana, H. S. (1990). Intelligent tutoring systems: An overview. *Artificial Intelligence Review*, 4(4), 251–277. DOI: 10.1007/BF00168958

O'Toole, R. B. (2013). *Pedagogical strategies and technologies for peer assessment in Massively Open Online Courses (MOOCs). Discussion Paper. (Unpublished).* Coventry, UK: University of Warwick. Retrieved from https://wrap.warwick.ac.uk/54602/

OECD. (2015). *Students, Computers and Learning: Making the Connection*. OECD Publishing.

OECD. (2021). *OECD Digital Education Outlook 2021: Pushing the Frontiers with Artificial Intelligence, Blockchain and Robots*. OECD Publishing., DOI: 10.1787/589b283f-

Ojeda-Ramirez, S., Tsan, J., Eatinger, D., Jacob, S., Saito-Stehberger, D., Franklin, D., & Warschauer, M. (2023). Describing elementary students' spheres of influence in Scratch 'About Me' projects. DOI: 10.1145/3545945.3569869

Ojo, O. A., Olugbade, D., & Abioye, I. O. (2023). ENTREPRENEURIAL INTEREST AND DEVELOPMENT AMONG TERTIARY INSTITUTION STUDENTS: THE MOBILE TECHNOLOGY APPROACH. *European Journal of Open Education and E-learning Studies*, 8(2). Advance online publication. DOI: 10.46827/ejoe.v8i2.4806

Olatunji, O., & Ajayi, S. (2016). *Rurality, Nigeria's massification policy on access to basic education and turnover causations amongst teachers*. Australian and International Journal of Rural Education., DOI: 10.47381/aijre.v26i3.73

Pacheco-Mendoza, S., Guevara, C., Mayorga-Albán, A., & Fernández-Escobar, J. (2023). Artificial intelligence in higher education: A predictive model for academic performance. *Education Sciences*, 13(10), 990. Advance online publication. DOI: 10.3390/educsci13100990

Pane, J. F., Griffin, B. A., McCaffrey, D. F., & Karam, R. (2014). Effectiveness of Cognitive Tutor Algebra I at Scale. *Educational Evaluation and Policy Analysis*, 36(2), 127–144. DOI: 10.3102/0162373713507480

Papadakis, S. (2020). Evaluating a teaching intervention for teaching STEM and programming concepts through the creation of a weather-forecast app for smart mobile devices. In *Handbook of research on tools for teaching computational thinking in P-12 education* (pp. 31–53). IGI Global. DOI: 10.4018/978-1-7998-4576-8.ch002

Pardo, A., & Siemens, G. (2014). Ethical and privacy principles for learning analytics. *British Journal of Educational Technology*, 45(3), 438–450. DOI: 10.1111/bjet.12152

Parker, M. A., & Martin, F. (2010). Using virtual classrooms: Student perceptions of features and characteristics in an online and a blended course. *Journal of Online Learning and Teaching*, 6(1), 135–147.

Patel, R., & Gupta, S. (2022). Impact of Adaptive Learning Technologies on English Language Proficiency in Inclusive Classrooms. *Language Learning & Technology*, 26(1), 34–49.

Patten, M. L., & Newhart, M. (2017). *Understanding research methods: An overview of the essentials*. Routledge. DOI: 10.4324/9781315213033

Payam, H., Mahdi, B. F., & Khuong, M. V. (2021). Insight monetization intermediary platform using recommender systems. *Electronic Markets*. Advance online publication. 00449-WDOI: 10.1007/S12525-020-

Payne, B. (2019). An Ethics of Artificial Intelligence Curriculum for Middle School Students. https://thecenter.mit.edu/wp-content/uploads/2020/07/MIT-AI-Ethics-Education-Curriculum.pdf

Pearce, J., & Chiavaroli, N. (2023). Rethinking assessment in response to generative artificial intelligence. *Medical Education*, 57(10), 889–891. DOI: 10.1111/medu.15092 PMID: 37042389

Pedro, F., Subosa, M., Rivas, A., & Valverde, P. (2019). Artificial intelligence in education: Challenges and opportunities for sustainable development.

Peng, T., Luo, Y., & Liu, Y. (2022). AI-Based Equipment Optimization of the Design on Intelligent Education Curriculum System. *Wireless Communications and Mobile Computing*, 2022(1), 1–13. Advance online publication. DOI: 10.1155/2022/3614883

Peruzzo, F., & Allan, J. (2022). Rethinking inclusive (digital) Education: Lessons from the pandemic to reconceptualise inclusion through convivial technologies. *Learning, Media and Technology*, 49(2), 244–258. DOI: 10.1080/17439884.2022.2131817

Pesovski, I., Santos, R., Henriques, R., & Trajkovik, V. (2023). *Generative AI for Customizable Learning Experiences*. Journal Name., DOI: 10.3390/xxxxx

Peters, U. (2023). Explainable AI lacks regulative reasons: Why AI and human decision-making are not equally opaque. *AI and Ethics*, 3(3), 963–974. DOI: 10.1007/s43681-022-00217-w

Petihakis, G., Farao, A., Bountakas, P., Sabazioti, A., Polley, J., & Xenakis, C. (2024, July). AIAS: AI-ASsisted cybersecurity platform to defend against adversarial AI attacks. In *Proceedings of the 19th International Conference on Availability, Reliability and Security* (pp. 1-7 DOI: 10.1145/3664476.3669920

Pisica, A. I., Edu, T., Zaharia, R. M., & Zaharia, R. (2023). Implementing artificial intelligence in higher education: Pros and cons from the perspectives of academics. *Societies (Basel, Switzerland)*, 13(5), 118. DOI: 10.3390/soc13050118

Pollak, M., & Ebner, M. (2019). The missing link to computational thinking. *Future Internet*, 11(12), 263. DOI: 10.3390/fi11120263

Pollock, L., Mouza, C., Guidry, K. R., & Pusecker, K. (2019, February). Infusing computational thinking across disciplines: Reflections & lessons learned. In *Proceedings of the 50th ACM Technical Symposium on Computer Science Education* (pp. 435-441). DOI: 10.1145/3287324.3287469

Prather, J., Denny, P. C., Leinonen, J., Becker, B. A., Caspersen, M. E., Craig, M., ... Savelka, J. (2023). Transformed by transformers: Navigating the AI coding revolution for computing education: An ITiCSE working group conducted by humans. DOI: 10.1145/3587103.3594206

Prinsloo, P., & Slade, S. (2016). Student vulnerability, agency, and learning analytics: An exploration. *Journal of Learning Analytics*, 3(1), 159–182. DOI: 10.18608/jla.2016.31.10

Prinsloo, P., & Slade, S. (2017). An elephant in the learning analytics room: The obligation to act. In *Proceedings of the Seventh International Learning Analytics & Knowledge Conference* (pp. 46-55). ACM. DOI: 10.1145/3027385.3027406

Psycharis, S., Kalovrektis, K., Sakellaridi, E., Korres, K., & Mastorodimos, D. (2018). Unfolding the curriculum: physical computing, computational thinking and computational experiment in STEM's transdisciplinary approach. *European Journal of Engineering and Technology Research*, 19-24.

Psycharis, S. (2018). STEAM in education: A literature review on the role of computational thinking, engineering epistemology and computational science. computational steam pedagogy (CSP). *Scientific Culture*, 4(2), 51–72.

Pulimood, S. M., Pearson, K., & Bates, D. C. (2016, February). A study on the impact of multidisciplinary collaboration on computational thinking. In *Proceedings of the 47th ACM technical symposium on computing science education* (pp. 30-35). DOI: 10.1145/2839509.2844636

Putra, R. A. A., Riwayatiningsih, R., & Setyarini, S. (2021). Portraying teachers' metacognitive knowledge to promote EFL young learners' critical thinking in Indonesia. *International Journal of Language Education*, 5(1), 552–568. DOI: 10.26858/ijole.v5i1.13043

Qin, H. (2009, March). Teaching computational thinking through bioinformatics to biology students. In *Proceedings of the 40th ACM technical symposium on Computer science education* (pp. 188-191). DOI: 10.1145/1508865.1508932

Qiu, Y., Pan, J., & Ishak, N. A. (2022). [Retracted] Effectiveness of Artificial Intelligence (AI) in Improving Pupils' Deep Learning in Primary School Mathematics Teaching in Fujian Province. *Computational Intelligence and Neuroscience*, 2022(1), 1362996. PMID: 36193186

Raaj, S. (2024). EDUCATION, RESEARCH AND INNOVATION IN INDIA: THE SHIFTING PARADIGMS. *Journal of Higher Education Theory and Practice*, 24(1), 75.

Raja, R., & Nagasubramani, P. C. (2018). Impact of modern technology in education. *Journal of Applied and Advanced Research*, 3(1), 33–35. DOI: 10.21839/jaar.2018.v3iS1.165

Rajasekar, S., Philominathan, P., & Chinnathambi, V. (2006, January). *Research Methodology.* Retrieved from https://www.researchgate.net/publication/2174858_Research_Methodology

Ramachandran, A., Schwellnus, M., Gladwin, D., Derby-Talbot, R., & Ellis, N. (2024). Cultivating educational adaptability through collaborative transdisciplinary learning spaces. *Discover Education*, 3(1), 2. DOI: 10.1007/s44217-023-00084-5

Ramandanis, D., & Xinogalos, S. (2023). Investigating the Support Provided by Chatbots to Educational Institutions and Their Students: A Systematic Literature Review. *Multimodal Technologies and Interaction*, 7(11), 103. DOI: 10.3390/mti7110103

Ramorola, M. Z. (2010). *A study of effective technology integration into teaching and learning: A case study.* Pretoria: (Unpubished doctoral dissertation). University of South Africa.

Ramorola, M. Z. (2018, May 3). *Transforming teaching and learning through technology integration.* Retrieved from https://www.unisa.ac.za/static/corporate_web/Content/News%20&%20Media/Articles/Documents/TECHNOLOGY%20INTEGRATION%20IN%20TEACHING%20AND%20LEARNING_FINAL(27).pdf

Ramorola, M. Z. (2013). Challenge of effective technology integration into teaching and learning. *Africa Education Review*, 10(4), 654–670. DOI: 10.1080/18146627.2013.853559

Ramzan, M., Javaid, Z. K., & Ali, A. A. (2023). Perception of Students about Collaborative Strategies Employed by Teachers for Enhancing English Vocabulary and Learning Motivation. *Pakistan JL Analysis & Wisdom*, 2, 146.

Rappel, L. (2011). An analysis and interpretation of intercultural approaches to English language teaching. In *Rappel-Intercultural Approaches to English Language Teaching* (Vol. 2).

Ravet, J., & Mtika, P. (2021). Educational inclusion in resource-constrained contexts: A study of rural primary schools in Cambodia. *International Journal of Inclusive Education*, 28(1), 16–37. DOI: 10.1080/13603116.2021.1916104

Rehman Javed, A., Khan, H. U., Alomari, M. K., Sarwar, M. U., Ahmad, A., & Khan, M. Z. (2023). Toward explainable AI-empowered cognitive health assessment. *Frontiers in Public Health*, 11, 1024195. Advance online publication. DOI: 10.3389/fpubh.2023.1024195 PMID: 36969684

Reich, J., & Ito, M. (2017). *From good intentions to real outcomes: Equity by design in learning technologies*. Digital Media and Learning Research Hub.

Reiss, M. J. (2021). The Use of Al in Education: Practicalities and Ethical Considerations. *London Review of Education*, 19(1), n1. DOI: 10.14324/LRE.19.1.05

Remian, D. (2019). Augmenting education: ethical considerations for incorporating artificial intelligence in education.

Renz, A., & Hilbig, R. (2020). Prerequisites for artificial intelligence in further education: Identification of drivers, barriers, and business models of educational technology companies. *International Journal of Educational Technology in Higher Education*, 17(1), 1–21. DOI: 10.1186/s41239-020-00193-3

Roblyer, M., & Doering, A. H. (2007). *Integrating educational technology into teaching*. Pearson.

Rodgers, D. L. (2023). Beyond the Cognitive Domain: Including All of Bloom's Learning Domains in Objective Development. *Academic Medicine*, 98(3), 294–295. DOI: 10.1097/ACM.0000000000005108 PMID: 36811921

Rodrigues, A., González, J. A., & Mateu, J. (2023). A conditional machine learning classification approach for spatio-temporal risk assessment of crime data. *Stochastic Environmental Research and Risk Assessment*, 37(7), 2815–2828. Advance online publication. DOI: 10.1007/s00477-023-02420-5

Rodrigues, R. (2020). Legal and human rights issues of AI: Gaps, challenges and vulnerabilities. *Journal of Responsible Technology*, 4, 100005. DOI: 10.1016/j.jrt.2020.100005

Rodríguez, N., & Rodríguez, J. R. (2015). The digital textbook: a look at the current state of the art. In *Digital Textbooks: what's new?* (pp. 9–51). Servicio de Publicaciones e Intercambio Científico.

Rogers, E. M. (2003). *Diffusion of Innovations*. Free Press.

Romero, M., Lepage, A., & Lille, B. (2017). Computational thinking development through creative programming in higher education. *International Journal of Educational Technology in Higher Education*, 14(1), 1–15. DOI: 10.1186/s41239-017-0080-z

Roshanaei, M., Olivares, H., & Lopez, R. R. (2023). Harnessing AI to Foster Equity in Education: Opportunities, Challenges, and Emerging Strategies. *Journal of Intelligent Learning Systems and Applications*, 15(04), 123–143. DOI: 10.4236/jilsa.2023.154009

Rothman, J. (2011). L3 syntactic transfer selectivity and typological determinacy: The typological primacy model. *Second Language Research*, 27(1), 107–127. DOI: 10.1177/0267658310386439

Rothman, J., & Cabrelli Amaro, J. (2010). What variables condition syntactic transfer? A look at the L3 initial state. *Second Language Research*, 26(2), 189–218. DOI: 10.1177/0267658309349410

Rubel, A., & Jones, K. M. (2016). Student privacy in learning analytics: An information ethics perspective. *The Information Society*, 32(2), 143–159. DOI: 10.1080/01972243.2016.1130502

Ruben, L., Daniel, I., Hilary, G., Jonathan, W. S., & Jason, M. T. (2021). Getting a grip on insight: Real-time and embodied Aha experiences predict correct solutions. *Cognition and Emotion*, 35(3), 474–484. DOI: 10.1080/02699931.2021.1908230 PMID: 33829955

Rubinger, L., Gazendam, A., Ekhtiari, S., & Bhandari, M. (2022). Machine learning and artificial intelligence in research and healthcare. *Injury*. Advance online publication. DOI: 10.1016/j.injury.2022.01.046 PMID: 35135685

Rumbelow, M., & Coles, A. (2024). The Promise of AI Object-Recognition in Learning Mathematics: An Explorative Study of 6-Year-Old Children's Interactions with Cuisenaire Rods and the Blockplay. ai App. *Education Sciences*, 14(6), 591. DOI: 10.3390/educsci14060591

Rusmiyanto, R., Huriati, N., Fitriani, N., Tyas, N. K., Rofi'i, A., & Sari, M. N. (2023). The role of artificial intelligence (AI) in developing English language learner's communication skills. *Journal of Education*, 6(1), 750–757.

Russel, S. J., & Norvig, P. (2003). *Artificial Intelligence, A Modern Approach - 2nd Edition*.

Sah, P., Sah, R., Sahani, S. K., & Sahani, K. (2024). Study and Analysis of Education System in Nepal and Its Challenges Along with Its Solution. *Mikailalsys Journal of Advanced Engineering International*, 1(1), 33–42. DOI: 10.58578/mjaei.v1i1.2792

Saidani, O., Umer, M., & Alshardan, A.. (2024). *Student academic success prediction in multimedia-supported virtual learning system using ensemble learning approach*. Multimed Tools Appl., DOI: 10.1007/s11042-024-18669-z

Salas-Pilco, S. Z., Xiao, K., & Oshima, J. (2022). Artificial intelligence and new technologies in inclusive education for minority students: A systematic review. *Sustainability (Basel)*, 14(20), 13572. DOI: 10.3390/su142013572

Sampene, A. K., Agyeman, F. O., Robert, B., & Wiredu, J. (2022). Artificial intelligence as a path way to Africa's transformations. *Artificial Intelligence*, 9(1).

Saritepeci, M. (2020). Developing computational thinking skills of high school students: Design-based learning activities and programming tasks. *The Asia-Pacific Education Researcher*, 29(1), 35–54. DOI: 10.1007/s40299-019-00480-2

Saubern, R., Taylor-Guy, P., & van der Keij, F. (2022, October). Introducing the Education Technology Value Evaluation Tool for Schools. In *2022 International Conference on Assessment and Learning (ICAL)* (pp. 1-6). IEEE. DOI: 10.1109/ICAL50372.2022.10075589

Sausser, S., & Waller, R. J. (2006). A model for music therapy with students with emotional and behavioral disorders. *The Arts in Psychotherapy*, 33(1), 1–10. DOI: 10.1016/j.aip.2005.05.003

Scerri, A., & Morin, K. H. (2023). Using chatbots like ChatGPT to support nursing practice. *Journal of Clinical Nursing*, 32(15-16), 4211–4213. Advance online publication. DOI: 10.1111/jocn.16677 PMID: 36880216

Scheerder, A., Van Deursen, A., & Van Dijk, J. (2017). Determinants of Internet skills, uses and outcomes. A systematic review of the second-and third-level digital divide. *Telematics and Informatics*, 34(8), 1607–1624. DOI: 10.1016/j.tele.2017.07.007

Schiff, D., Ayesh, A., Musikanski, L., & Havens, J. C. (2020, October). Iccc 7010: A new standard for assessing the well-being implications of artificial Intelligence. In *2020 IEEE international conference on systems, man, and cybernetics (SMC)* (pp. 2746-2753). IEEE.

Schmitt, C. (2002). *Technology in schools: Suggestions, tools, and guidelines for assessing technology in elementary and secondary education.* US Department of Education, Office of Educational Research and Improvement, National Center for Education Statistics.

Schools Week. (2023, june 24). AI : How are schools using the technology in classrooms? https://schoolsweek.co.uk/ai-how-are-schools-using-the-technology-in-classrooms/

Schultz, L. (1964). Education. *Simulation*, 2(1), 13–13. DOI: 10.1177/003754976400200102

Searson (2024). Generative AI to improve special education teacher preparation for inclusive classrooms. *Exploring New Horizons: Generative Artificial Intelligence and Teacher Education, 159.*

Seddon, G. M. (1978). The properties of Bloom's taxonomy of educational objectives for the cognitive domain. *Review of Educational Research*, 48(2), 303–323. DOI: 10.3102/00346543048002303

Seldon, A., Abidoye, O., & Metcalf, T. (2020). *The Fourth Education Revolution Reconsidered: Will Artificial Intelligence Enrich Or Diminish Humanity?* Legend Press Ltd.

Seliger, H. W., & Shohamy, E. (1989). *Second language research methods*. Oxford University Press.

Selwyn, N. (2004). Reconsidering political and social inclusion: The role of the internet in contemporary society. *Technology, Pedagogy and Education*, 13(3), 357–371.

Selwyn, N. (2019). *Should robots replace teachers? AI and the future of education*. John Wiley & Sons.

Semeler, A., Pinto, A., Koltay, T., Dias, T., Oliveira, A., González, J., & Rozados, H. B. F. (2024). ALGORITHMIC LITERACY: Generative Artificial Intelligence Technologies for Data Librarians. *EAI Endorsed Transactions on Scalable Information Systems, 11*(2).

Service, R. (2023). The robot will see you now: With the advent of ever more powerful AI language models, a visit to your doctor may never be the same. *Science*. Advance online publication. DOI: 10.1126/science.adh1553

Shahriar, S., Lund, B. D., Mannuru, N. R., Arshad, M. A., Hayawi, K., Bevara, R. V. K., Mannuru, A., & Batool, L. (2024). Putting GPT-4o to the Sword: A Comprehensive Evaluation of Language, Vision, Speech, and Multimodal Proficiency. *Applied Sciences (Basel, Switzerland)*, 14(17), 7782. DOI: 10.3390/app14177782

Sharma, D. M., Ramana, K. V., Jothilakshmi, R., Verma, R., Maheswari, B. U., & Boopathi, S. (2024). Integrating Generative AI Into K-12 Curriculums and Pedagogies in India: Opportunities and Challenges. *Facilitating Global Collaboration and Knowledge Sharing in Higher Education With Generative AI*, 133-161.

Sharma, A., & Singh, B. (2022). Measuring Impact of E-commerce on Small Scale Business: A Systematic Review. *Journal of Corporate Governance and International Business Law*, 5(1).

Shen, S., Lesnick, B., Qiao, M., & Yang, Q. (2022). Learning AI concepts and ethics through game programming: A middle school curriculum. DOI: 10.1145/3502717.3532147

Shen, C., Wang, H., Xie, H., Poon, L. K., & Huang, R. (2023). Artificial intelligence in education: A review of two decades of research. *Journal of Educational Technology & Society*, 26(1), 36–52. https://www.jstor.org/stable/48678066

Sheng, B., Chen, X., Li, T., Ma, T., Yang, Y., Bi, L., & Zhang, X. (2022). An overview of artificial intelligence in diabetic retinopathy and other ocular diseases. *Frontiers in Public Health*, 10, 971943. Advance online publication. DOI: 10.3389/fpubh.2022.971943 PMID: 36388304

Shenton, A. K. (2004). Strategies for ensuring trustworthiness in qualitative research projects. *Education for Information*, 22(2), 63–75. DOI: 10.3233/EFI-2004-22201

Shin, S. (2019). Designing the instructional framework and cognitive learning environment for artificial intelligence education through computational thinking. *Journal of The Korean Association of Information Education*, 23(6), 639–653. DOI: 10.14352/jkaie.2019.23.6.639

Shoja, M. M., Van de Ridder, J. M., & Rajput, V. (2023). The emerging role of generative artificial intelligence in medical education, research, and practice. *Cureus*, 15(6). Advance online publication. DOI: 10.7759/cureus.40883 PMID: 37492829

Shreeve, M. W. (2008). Beyond the didactic classroom: Educational models to encourage active student involvement in learning. *The Journal of Chiropractic Education*, 22(1), 23–28. DOI: 10.7899/1042-5055-22.1.23 PMID: 18483586

Shukla Shubhendu, S., & Vijay, J. (2013). Applicability of artificial intelligence in different fields of life. *International Journal of Scientific and Engineering Research*, 1(1), 28–35.

Siemens, G., & Long, P. (2011). Penetrating the fog: Analytics in learning and education. *EDUCAUSE Review*, 46(5), 30–40. https://er.educause.edu/articles/2011/9/penetrating-the-fog-analytics-in-learning-and-education

Sikhakhane, M., Govender, S., & Maphalala, M. C. (2021). South African Teachers' Perspectives on Using the Computer as a Tool for Teaching and Learning. *International Journal of Education and Practice*, 9(1), 93–104. DOI: 10.18488/journal.61.2021.91.93.104

Sikhosana, L., Mudau, A. V., & Msezane, S. B. (2020). Insights into the integration of environmental education in the senior phase. *Journal for the Education of Gifted Young Scientists*, 8(4), 1411–1425. DOI: 10.17478/jegys.750519

Silva, J. B., Silva, I. N., & Bilessimo, S. M. (2020). Technological structure for technology integration in the classroom, inspired by the maker culture. *Journal of Information Technology Education*, 19, 167–204. DOI: 10.28945/4532

Silver, D., Huang, A., Maddison, C. J., Guez, A., Sifre, L., Van Den Driessche, G., ... & Hassabis, D. (2016). Mastering the game of Go with deep neural networks and tree search. *nature, 529*(7587), 484-489.

Sims, J., Vidgen, R., & Powell, P. (2008). E-learning and the digital divide: Perpetuating cultural and socio-economic elitism in higher Education. *Communications of the Association for Information Systems*, 22(1). Advance online publication. DOI: 10.17705/1CAIS.02223

Singh, B. (2023). Blockchain Technology in Renovating Healthcare: Legal and Future Perspectives. In *Revolutionizing Healthcare Through Artificial Intelligence and Internet of Things Applications* (pp. 177-186). IGI Global.

Singh, B. (2024). Evolutionary Global Neuroscience for Cognition and Brain Health: Strengthening Innovation in Brain Science. In *Biomedical Research Developments for Improved Healthcare* (pp. 246-272). IGI Global.

Singh, B., & Kaunert, C. (2024). Future of Digital Marketing: Hyper-Personalized Customer Dynamic Experience with AI-Based Predictive Models. *Revolutionizing the AI-Digital Landscape: A Guide to Sustainable Emerging Technologies for Marketing Professionals*, 189.

Singh, B., & Kaunert, C. (2024). Harnessing Sustainable Agriculture Through Climate-Smart Technologies: Artificial Intelligence for Climate Preservation and Futuristic Trends. In *Exploring Ethical Dimensions of Environmental Sustainability and Use of AI* (pp. 214-239). IGI Global.

Singh, B., & Kaunert, C. (2024). Revealing Green Finance Mobilization: Harnessing FinTech and Blockchain Innovations to Surmount Barriers and Foster New Investment Avenues. In *Harnessing Blockchain-Digital Twin Fusion for Sustainable Investments* (pp. 265-286). IGI Global.

Singh, B., & Kaunert, C. (2024). Salvaging Responsible Consumption and Production of Food in the Hospitality Industry: Harnessing Machine Learning and Deep Learning for Zero Food Waste. In *Sustainable Disposal Methods of Food Wastes in Hospitality Operations* (pp. 176-192). IGI Global.

Singh, B., Kaunert, C., & Vig, K. (2024). Reinventing Influence of Artificial Intelligence (AI) on Digital Consumer Lensing Transforming Consumer Recommendation Model: Exploring Stimulus Artificial Intelligence on Consumer Shopping Decisions. In *AI Impacts in Digital Consumer Behavior* (pp. 141-169). IGI Global.

Singh, B., Vig, K., & Kaunert, C. (2024). Modernizing Healthcare: Application of Augmented Reality and Virtual Reality in Clinical Practice and Medical Education. In Modern Technology in Healthcare and Medical Education: Blockchain, IoT, AR, and VR (pp. 1-21). IGI Global.

Singh, B. (2023). Federated Learning for Envision Future Trajectory Smart Transport System for Climate Preservation and Smart Green Planet: Insights into Global Governance and SDG-9 (Industry, Innovation and Infrastructure). *National Journal of Environmental Law*, 6(2), 6–17.

Singh, B. (2023). Tele-Health Monitoring Lensing Deep Neural Learning Structure: Ambient Patient Wellness via Wearable Devices for Real-Time Alerts and Interventions. *Indian Journal of Health and Medical Law*, 6(2), 12–16.

Singh, B. (2023). Unleashing Alternative Dispute Resolution (ADR) in Resolving Complex Legal-Technical Issues Arising in Cyberspace Lensing E-Commerce and Intellectual Property: Proliferation of E-Commerce Digital Economy. *Revista Brasileira de Alternative Dispute Resolution-Brazilian Journal of Alternative Dispute Resolution-RBADR*, 5(10), 81–105. DOI: 10.52028/rbadr.v5i10.ART04.Ind

Singh, B. (2024). Cherish Growth, Advancement and Tax Structure: Addressing Social and Economic Prospects. *Journal of Taxation and Regulatory Framework*, 7(1), 7–10.

Singh, B. (2024). Evolutionary Global Neuroscience for Cognition and Brain Health: Strengthening Innovation in Brain Science. In Prabhakar, P. (Ed.), *Biomedical Research Developments for Improved Healthcare* (pp. 246–272). IGI Global., DOI: 10.4018/979-8-3693-1922-2.ch012

Singh, B. (2024). Featuring Consumer Choices of Consumable Products for Health Benefits: Evolving Issues from Tort and Product Liabilities. *Journal of Law of Torts and Consumer Protection Law*, 7(1).

Singh, B. (2024). Green Infrastructure in Real Estate Landscapes: Pillars of Sustainable Development and Vision for Tomorrow. *National Journal of Real Estate Law*, 7(1), 4–8.

Singh, B. (2024). Legal Dynamics Lensing Metaverse Crafted for Videogame Industry and E-Sports: Phenomenological Exploration Catalyst Complexity and Future. *Journal of Intellectual Property Rights Law*, 7(1), 8–14.

Singh, B. (2024). Lensing Legal Dynamics for Examining Responsibility and Deliberation of Generative AI-Tethered Technological Privacy Concerns: Infringements and Use of Personal Data by Nefarious Actors. In Ara, A., & Ara, A. (Eds.), *Exploring the Ethical Implications of Generative AI* (pp. 146–167). IGI Global., DOI: 10.4018/979-8-3693-1565-1.ch009

Singh, B. (2024). Social Cognition of Incarcerated Women and Children: Addressing Exposure to Infectious Diseases and Legal Outcomes. In Reddy, K. (Ed.), *Principles and Clinical Interventions in Social Cognition* (pp. 236–251). IGI Global., DOI: 10.4018/979-8-3693-1265-0.ch014

Singh, B., & Kaunert, C. (2024). Integration of Cutting-Edge Technologies such as Internet of Things (IoT) and 5G in Health Monitoring Systems: A Comprehensive Legal Analysis and Futuristic Outcomes. *GLS Law Journal*, 6(1), 13–20. DOI: 10.69974/glslawjournal.v6i1.123

Singh, B., & Kaunert, C. (2024). Salvaging Responsible Consumption and Production of Food in the Hospitality Industry: Harnessing Machine Learning and Deep Learning for Zero Food Waste. In Singh, A., Tyagi, P., & Garg, A. (Eds.), *Sustainable Disposal Methods of Food Wastes in Hospitality Operations* (pp. 176–192). IGI Global., DOI: 10.4018/979-8-3693-2181-2.ch012

Singh, B., Kaunert, C., & Vig, K. (2024). Reinventing Influence of Artificial Intelligence (AI) on Digital Consumer Lensing Transforming Consumer Recommendation Model: Exploring Stimulus Artificial Intelligence on Consumer Shopping Decisions. In Musiolik, T., Rodriguez, R., & Kannan, H. (Eds.), *AI Impacts in Digital Consumer Behavior* (pp. 141–169). IGI Global., DOI: 10.4018/979-8-3693-1918-5.ch006

Sırakaya, M., Alsancak Sırakaya, D., & Korkmaz, Ö. (2020). The impact of STEM attitude and thinking style on computational thinking determined via structural equation modeling. *Journal of Science Education and Technology*, 29(4), 561–572. DOI: 10.1007/s10956-020-09836-6

Slade, S., & Prinsloo, P. (2013). Learning analytics: Ethical issues and dilemmas. *The American Behavioral Scientist*, 57(10), 1510–1529. DOI: 10.1177/0002764213479366

Smith, B. (2022). AI's growing up: Part 1. *Communications of the ACM*. Advance online publication. DOI: 10.1145/3534843

Smith, D. D. (2010). *Introduction to special education: Making a difference*. No Title.

Smith, L. J., & Hayne, H. (2022). Chatbots and children: A case study of communication with a conversational agent. *Journal of Experimental Child Psychology*. Advance online publication. DOI: 10.1016/j.jecp.2022.105346

Smith, L., & Brown, T. (2021). Student Engagement and Motivation in Technology-Enhanced Learning Environments. *Educational Psychology Review*, 33(4), 783–800.

Smith, R., & Williams, T. (2021). Adaptive learning platforms in inclusive education: A study on English language learners. *International Journal of Inclusive Education*, 18(2), 234–248. DOI: 10.1080/13603116.2021.1875634

Song, S. J., Tan, K. H., & Awang, M. M. (2021). Generic digital equity model in education: Mobile-assisted personalized learning (MAPL) through e-modules. *Sustainability (Basel)*, 13(19), 11115. DOI: 10.3390/su131911115

Sood, S. O. (2008, December). Emotional computation in artificial intelligence education. In *AAAI Artificial Intelligence Education Colloquium* (pp. 74-78).

Spivakovsky, O. V., Omelchuk, S. A., Kobets, V. V., Valko, N. V., & Malchykova, D. S. (2023). Institutional policies on artificial intelligence in university learning, teaching and research. *Information Technologies and Learning Tools*, 97(5), 181–202. DOI: 10.33407/itlt.v97i5.5395

Stadlmann, C., & Zehetner, A. (2021). *Human intelligence versus artificial intelligence: A comparison of traditional and ai-based methods for prospect generation.*, DOI: 10.1007/978-981-33-4183-8_2

Stahl, B. C., Schroeder, D., & Rodrigues, R. (2022). Unfair and illegal discrimination. In *Ethics of artificial intelligence: Case studies and options for addressing ethical challenges* (pp. 9–23). Springer International Publishing.

Starkey, L. (2020). A review of research exploring teacher preparation for the digital age. *Cambridge Journal of Education*, 50(1), 37–56. DOI: 10.1080/0305764X.2019.1625867

Starkey, L., Eppel, E., & Sylvester, A. (2023). Ethics, empathy and the educational artificial intelligence (AI) practitioner. Journal of Open, Flexible and Distance Learning, doi:DOI: 10.6084/m9.figshare.22166107.v1

Steingartner, W., Galinec, D., & Kozina, A. (2021). Threat defense: Cyber deception approach and education for resilience in hybrid threats model. *Symmetry*, 13(4), 597. DOI: 10.3390/sym13040597

Strong, A. I. (2016). Applications of Artificial Intelligence and associated technologies. *Science [ETEBMS-2016], 5*(6).

Subban, P. (2006). Differentiated instruction: A research basis. *International Education Journal*, 7(7), 935–947.

Suhadi, S. M., Mohamed, H., Abdullah, Z., Zaid, N. M., Aris, B., & Sanmugam, M. (2021). Enhancing Student's Higher Order Thinking Skills (HOTS) through the Socratic Method Approach with Technology. In *Research Anthology on Developing Critical Thinking Skills in Students* (pp. 1399-1412). IGI Global.

Sumadevi, S. (2023). EFFECTIVE USE OF DIVERSE TECHNOLOGY TOOLS IN FLIPPED LEARNING APPROACH. *Journal of Historical Research*, 53(2), 106–113.

Sun, R., Demszky, D., Lin, E., Li, S., & Liu, Y. (2021). Safe AI for education: A systematic review of self-regulated learning with artificial intelligence in education. *Journal of Artificial Intelligence Research*. Advance online publication. DOI: 10.1613/jair.1.12412

Tai, T. Y., & Chen, H. H. J. (2024). Improving elementary EFL speaking skills with generative AI chatbots: Exploring individual and paired interactions. *Computers & Education*, 220, 105112. DOI: 10.1016/j.compedu.2024.105112

Tajfel, H. (1972). Social categorization. *English Manuscript of. La Catégorisation Sociale*, 1, 272–302.

Tamene, E. H. (2016). Theorizing conceptual framework. *Asian Journal of Educational Research*, 4(2), 50–56.

Tarman, B. (2003). *The Digital Divide in Education.* Online Submission.

Taylor, K., & Miller, J. (2020). Fostering Social Integration Through Technology-Enhanced Collaborative Learning. *Journal of Special Education Technology*, 35(2), 89–102.

Team, G., & Hunt, P. (2020). *Inclusive education: children with disabilities.* UNESCO: United Nations Educational, Scientific and Cultural Organisation.

Tedre, M., & Denning, P. J. (2016, November). The long quest for computational thinking. In *Proceedings of the 16th Koli Calling international conference on computing education research* (pp. 120-129).

Thanh, B. N., Vo, D. T. H., Nhat, M. N., Pham, T. T. T., Trung, H. T., & Xuan, S. H. (2023). Race with the machines: Assessing the capability of generative AI in solving authentic assessments. *Australasian Journal of Educational Technology*, 39(5), 59–81. DOI: 10.14742/ajet.8902

The White House. (2023, October 30). Executive Order on the Safe, Secure, and Trustworthy Development and Use of Artificial Intelligence. https://www.whitehouse.gov/briefing-room/presidential-actions/2023/10/30/executive-order-on-the-safe-secure-and-trustworthy-development-and-use-of-artificial-intelligence/

Theodorou P., Drigas A.2017.ICTs and Music in Sensory and Motor Disabilities, International Journal of Recent Contributions from Engineering,Vol 5 No 2,4

Thompson, M. R., & Wheatley, L. (2023). Can artificial intelligence really transform education? Computers & Education. *Artificial Intelligence*. Advance online publication. DOI: 10.1016/j.caeai.2023.100160

Thurzo, A., Strunga, M., Urban, R., Surovková, J., & Afrashtehfar, K. I. (2023). Impact of artificial intelligence on dental education: A review and guide for curriculum update. *Education Sciences*, 13(2), 150. DOI: 10.3390/educsci13020150

Tiene, D. (2002). Addressing the Global Digital Divide and its Impact on Educational Opportunity. *Educational Media International*, 39(3–4), 212–222. DOI: 10.1080/09523980210166440

Tien, J. M. (2017). Internet of things, real-time decision making, and artificial intelligence. *Annals of Data Science*, 4(2), 149–178. DOI: 10.1007/s40745-017-0112-5

Tomlinson, C. A. (2001). *How to differentiate instruction in mixed-ability classrooms*. Ascd.

Tooley, J. (2021). *Really good schools: Global lessons for high-caliber, low-cost education*. Independent Institute.

Tsortanidou, X., Daradoumis, T., & Barberá, E. (2019). Connecting moments of creativity, computational thinking, collaboration and new media literacy skills. *Information and Learning Science*, 120(11/12), 704–722. DOI: 10.1108/ILS-05-2019-0042

Tuomi, I. (2023). A framework for socio-developmental ethics in educational AI.

Tuomi, I. (2018). *The impact of artificial intelligence on learning, teaching, and education*. Publications Office of the European Union.

Turing, A. M. (2009). *Computing machinery and intelligence*. Springer Netherlands. DOI: 10.1007/978-1-4020-6710-5_3

Turner, C., Martin-Hammond, A., & Plaisant, C. (2022). Assessing the inclusivity of AI virtual assistant voice interfaces for young and older adults. Proceedings of the ACM on Human- Computer Interaction, doi:DOI: 10.1145/3555062

Tyagi, S., Gupta, V., & Mehndiratta, V. (2024). Building Smart Campuses: Integrating AI in Higher Education. In Arya, R., Sharma, S. C., Verma, A. K., & Iyer, B. (Eds.), *Recent Trends in Artificial Intelligence Towards a Smart World. Frontiers of Artificial Intelligence, Ethics and Multidisciplinary Applications*. Springer., DOI: 10.1007/978-981-97-6790-8_15

UBEC. (2014). UBE programmes. Retrieved April 8, 2014, from https://ubeconline .com/UBEProgrammes.hmtl

Ulger, K. (2018). The effect of problem-based learning on the creative thinking and critical thinking disposition of students in visual arts education. *The Interdisciplinary Journal of Problem-Based Learning*, 12(1). Advance online publication. DOI: 10.7771/1541-5015.1649

Underwood, J. (2017). Exploring AI language assistants with primary EFL students. In *CALL in a climate of change: adapting to turbulent global conditions – short papers from EUROCALL 2017* (pp. 317–321). Research-publishing.net. https://doi .org/DOI: 10.14705/rpnet.2017.eurocall2017.733

UNESCO. (2020). *"Towards inclusion in education: status, trends and challenges," in The UNESCO Salamanca Statement 25 Years on*. UNESCO.

Unesco. (2020). Inclusion and education: All means all. *Global Education Monitoring Report*.

Unesco. (2020). Towards inclusion in education: Status, trends and challenges. The UNESCO Salamanca Statement 25 years on.

Unger, K. L., & Tracey, M. W. (2013). The role of multimedia in enhancing learning for students with learning disabilities. *Educational Technology Research and Development*, 61(4), 493–515. DOI: 10.1007/s11423-013-9308-6

UNICEF. 2014. All Children in School by 2015: Global Initiative on Out-of-School Children: regional report; West and Central Africa. https://unesdoc.unesco.org/ark:/48223/pf0000228081

UNICEF. 2018. Evaluation Report: The Out-of-School Children Initiative (OOSCI) February 2018.

United Nation Relief and Work Agency for Palestine Refugees in the Near East(UNRWA). 2021.Schools on the front line the impact of armed conflict and violence on UNRWA schools and education services. Accessed 25 May 2024 https://www.unrwa.org/sites/default/files/content/resources/gazawb_flashappeal-eng-final.pdf

Uthus, M., & Qvortrup, A. (2024). Lessons learned from Norway: A values-based formulation of inclusive education. *European Journal of Special Needs Education*, •••, 1–15. DOI: 10.1080/08856257.2024.2354603

Valovičová, Ľ., Ondruška, J., Zelenický, Ľ., Chytrý, V., & Medová, J. (2020). Enhancing computational thinking through interdisciplinary STEAM activities using tablets. *Mathematics*, 8(12), 2128. DOI: 10.3390/math8122128

Van Alten, D. C. D., Phielix, C., Janssen, J., & Kester, L. (2023). Higher-order thinking in virtual reality: A systematic literature review. *Educational Research Review*. Advance online publication. DOI: 10.1016/j.edurev.2022.100502

van de Werfhorst, H. G., Kessenich, E., & Geven, S. (2020, August 18). The Digital Divide in Online Education. Inequality in Digital Preparedness of Students and Schools before the Start of the COVID-19 Pandemic. DOI: 10.31235/osf.io/58d6p

van der Vorst, T., & Jelicic, N. (2019). Artificial Intelligence in Education: Can AI bring the full potential of personalized learning to education?.

Van Dijk, J. A. (2006). Digital divide research, achievements and shortcomings. *Poetics*, 34(4-5), 221–235. DOI: 10.1016/j.poetic.2006.05.004

VanLehn, K. (2011). The relative effectiveness of human tutoring, intelligent tutoring systems, and other tutoring systems. *Educational Psychologist*, 46(4), 197–221. DOI: 10.1080/00461520.2011.611369

Venkatesh, V., Morris, M. G., Davis, G. B., & Davis, F. (2003). User Acceptance of Information Technology: Toward a Unified View. *Management Information Systems Quarterly*, 27(3), 425–478. DOI: 10.2307/30036540

Venkatesh, V., Thong, J. Y., & Xu, X. (2012). Consumer acceptance and use of information technology: Extending the unified theory of acceptance and use of technology. *Management Information Systems Quarterly*, 36(1), 157–178. DOI: 10.2307/41410412

Viana, J. P., Coelho, J. A. P. M., Bastos-Filho, C., & Elias, N. S. (2022). Exploring users' trust in the context of recommender systems: A systematic literature review. *Information Systems Frontiers*. Advance online publication. DOI: 10.1007/s10796-022-10300-2

Viberg, O., Hatakka, M., Bälter, O., & Mavroudi, A. (2018). The current landscape of learning analytics in higher education. *Computers in Human Behavior*, 89, 98–110. DOI: 10.1016/j.chb.2018.07.027

Voigt, C., & Simmonds, R. (2017). *Collaborative learning with technology: Case studies and practical guidance*. Routledge.

Völlinger, V. A., & Supanc, M. (2020). Student teachers' attitudes towards cooperative learning in inclusive education. *European Journal of Psychology of Education*, 35(3), 727–749. DOI: 10.1007/s10212-019-00435-7

Vought, R. T. (2018). Charting a course for success: America's strategy for stem education. Wang, P. (2019). On defining artificial intelligence. *Journal of Artificial General Intelligence*, 10, 1–37.

Vygotsky, L. S. (1978). *Mind in society: The development of higher psychological processes*. Harvard University Press.

Waddell, S., & Kim, H. (2021). Digital Learning Platforms and Inclusive Education: Case Studies in High School English Classrooms. *Journal of Educational Technology*, 34(2), 45–62.

Waladi, C., & Lamarti, M. S. (2024). Adaptive AI-Driven Assessment for Competency-Based Learning Scenarios. In *Innovative Instructional Design Methods and Tools for Improved Teaching* (pp. 215–226). IGI Global.

Wang, Q., Wang, L., & Wu, W. (2023). Current and future AI applications in education: A review of the recent literature. Journal of Educational Technology Development and Exchange, DOI: 10.18785/jetde.1301.02

Wang, C., Shen, J., & Chao, J. (2022). Integrating computational thinking in STEM education: A literature review. *International Journal of Science and Mathematics Education*, 20(8), 1949–1972. DOI: 10.1007/s10763-021-10227-5

Wang, D., Yang, Q., Abdul, A., & Lim, B. Y. (2019). Designing theory-driven user-centric explainable AI. In *Proceedings of the 2019 CHI conference on human factors in computing systems* (pp. 1-15).

Wang, S., Sun, Z., & Chen, Y. (2023). Effects of higher education institutes' artificial intelligence capability on students' self-efficacy, creativity and learning performance. *Education and Information Technologies*, 28(5), 4919–4939. DOI: 10.1007/s10639-022-11338-4 PMID: 36373050

Wang, S., Wang, F., Zhu, Z., Wang, J., Tran, T., & Du, Z. (2024). Artificial intelligence in education: A systematic literature review. *Expert Systems with Applications*, 237, 124167. DOI: 10.1016/j.eswa.2024.124167

Wang, T., & Cheng, E. C. K. (2021). An investigation of barriers to Hong Kong K-12 schools incorporating Artificial Intelligence in education. *Computers and Education: Artificial Intelligence*, 2, 100031. DOI: 10.1016/j.caeai.2021.100031

Wang, W., Huang, Y., Wang, Y., & Wang, L. (2014). Generalized autoencoder: A neural network framework for dimensionality reduction. In *Proceedings of the IEEE conference on computer vision and pattern recognition workshops* (pp. 490-497). DOI: 10.1109/CVPRW.2014.79

Warschauer, M. (1996). Computer-assisted language learning: An introduction. In Fotos, S. (Ed.), *Multimedia language teaching* (pp. 3–20). Logos International.

Warschauer, M. (2003). *Technology and Social Inclusion: Rethinking the Digital Divide*. MIT Press. DOI: 10.7551/mitpress/6699.001.0001

Warschauer, M. (2011). Learning in the cloud: How (and why) to use online collaborative tools. *Language Learning & Technology*, 15(1), 1–8.

Wasserman, S. L., Wilson, C. J., & Horsman, M. A. (2023). Improving skills for success: How educators' professional development impacts students' engagement in making. *International Journal of Educational Research*. Advance online publication. DOI: 10.1016/j.ijer.2023.102149

Watters, A. (2017). Education Technology and the New Behaviourism. Hack Education, July 29. Available: https://hackeducation.com/2017/12/23/top-ed-tech-trends-social-emotional-learning

Wei, K. K., Teo, H. H., Chan, H. C., & Tan, B. C. (2011). Conceptualising and testing a social cognitive model of the digital divide. *Information Systems Research*, 22(1), 170–187. DOI: 10.1287/isre.1090.0273

Wei, L. (2008). Research perspectives on bilingualism and multilingualism. In *The Blackwell Guide to Research Methods in Bilingualism and Multilingualism* (pp. 1–17). Wiley., DOI: 10.1002/9781444301120.ch1

Weintrop, D., Beheshti, E., Horn, M., Orton, K., Jona, K., Trouille, L., & Wilensky, U. (2016). Defining computational thinking for mathematics and science classrooms. *Journal of Science Education and Technology*, 25(1), 127–147. DOI: 10.1007/s10956-015-9581-5

Whitfield, C. (2021). Does collaborative making increase elementary students' science identities? A comparative case study. DOI: 10.1145/3502717.3532175

Williamson, B. (2015). Digital education governance: Data visualisation, predictive analytics, and 'real-time' policy instruments. *Journal of Education Policy*, 31(2), 123–141. DOI: 10.1080/02680939.2015.1035758

Williamson, B., & Piattoeva, N. (2019). Objectivity as standardization in data-scientific education policy, technology and governance. *Learning, Media and Technology*, 44(1), 64–76. DOI: 10.1080/17439884.2018.1556215

Winter, E., Costello, A., O'Brien, M., & Hickey, G. (2021). Teachers' use of technology and the impact of Covid-19. *Irish Educational Studies*, 40(2), 235–246. DOI: 10.1080/03323315.2021.1916559

Wood, L., & Reefke, H. (2010). Working with a diverse class: Reflections on the role of team teaching, teaching tools and technological support. *Proceedings of the IADIS international conference on international higher education (IHE)* (pp. 72-79). International Association for Development of the Information Society.

Woolf, B. P. (2010). *Building intelligent interactive tutors: Student-centered strategies for revolutionizing e-learning*. Morgan Kaufmann.

Woolf, B. P., Lane, H. C., Chaudhri, V. K., & Kolodner, J. L. (2013). AI grand challenges for education. *AI Magazine*, 34(4), 66–84. DOI: 10.1609/aimag.v34i4.2490

World Bank. 2024. Delivering Education in the Midst of Fragility, Conflict, and Violence (FCV). Accessed May 2024. https://www.worldbank.org/en/topic/education/brief/education-in-fragile-conflict-violence-contexts

Wringe, C. (1986). The Human Right to Education. *Educational Philosophy and Theory*, 18(2), 23–33. DOI: 10.1111/j.1469-5812.1986.tb00415.x

Xiaoyi, W., & Xingyi, Q. (2024). The positive effect of artificial intelligence technology transparency on digital endorsers: Based on the theory of mind perception. *Journal of Retailing and Consumer Services*, 78, 103777. Advance online publication. DOI: 10.1016/j.jretconser.2024.103777

Xia, Q., Chiu, T. K., Lee, M., Sanusi, I. T., Dai, Y., & Chai, C. S. (2022). A self-determination theory (SDT) design approach for inclusive and diverse artificial intelligence (AI) education. *Computers & Education*, 189, 104582. DOI: 10.1016/j.compedu.2022.104582

Xie, H., Chu, H. C., Hwang, G. J., & Wang, C. C. (2019). Trends and development in technology-enhanced adaptive/personalized learning: A systematic review of journal publications from 2007 to 2017. *Computers & Education*, 140, 103599. DOI: 10.1016/j.compedu.2019.103599

Xinyi, L. (2021, December 07). Q. J. W., Qiuwen, W., Chunhao, W., Yang, S., Wentao, W., Hunter, S., Fang-Fang, Y., & Yaorong, G. (2021). Insights of an AI agent via analysis of prediction errors: A case study of fluence map prediction for radiation therapy planning. *Physics in Medicine and Biology*, 66(23), 23NT01. Advance online publication. DOI: 10.1088/1361-6560/ac3841

Xu, K., & Sun, Z. (2023). Predicting academic performance associated with physical fitness of primary school students using machine learning methods. *Complementary Therapies in Clinical Practice*, 51, 101736. DOI: 10.1016/j.ctcp.2023.101736 PMID: 36821949

Yadav, A., Mayfield, C., Zhou, N., Hambrusch, S., & Korb, J. T. (2014). Computational thinking in elementary and secondary teacher education. [TOCE]. *ACM Transactions on Computing Education*, 14(1), 1–16. DOI: 10.1145/2576872

Yang, Y. F., Tseng, C. C., & Lai, S. C. (2024). Enhancing teachers' self-efficacy beliefs in AI-based technology integration into English speaking teaching through a professional development program. *Teaching and Teacher Education*, 144, 104582. DOI: 10.1016/j.tate.2024.104582

Yang, Y., Hu, X., Qu, Q., Lai, F., Shi, Y., Boswell, M., & Rozelle, S. (2013). Roots of tomorrow's digital divide: Documenting computer use and internet access in China's elementary schools today. *China & World Economy*, 21(3), 61–79. DOI: 10.1111/j.1749-124X.2013.12022.x

Yates, L. (2011). Interaction, language learning and social inclusion in early settlement. *International Journal of Bilingual Education and Bilingualism*, 14(4), 457–471. DOI: 10.1080/13670050.2011.573068

Yemothy, N. E. (2015). *Improving educational technology integration in the classroom.* (Doctoral dissertation). Walden University.

Yie, D. L., & Sanmugam, M. (2023). The Contribution of Diversity Towards Player Traits of Learners in a Classroom: Constructing a Theoretical Conceptual Framework. In *Comparative Research on Diversity in Virtual Learning: Eastern vs. Western Perspectives* (pp. 136-159). IGI Global.

Yie, D. L., Sanmugam, M., Yahaya, W. A., & Khlaif, Z. N. (2023). *The Effect of Gamified Depth on Malaysian Higher Education Students' Intrinsic Motivation Level and Achievement Level.* Retrieved from https://www.researchsquare.com/article/rs-3113140/latest

Yie, D. L., Sanmugam, M., & Yahaya, W. A. (2023). Future Instructional Design in Game-based Learning and Gamified Learning: The Construction and Incorporation of Player Typology Family Tree in the Educational Context. [CPLT]. *Journal of Creative Practices in Language Learning and Teaching*, 11(3), 16–37.

Yilmaz Ince, E., & Koc, M. (2021). The consequences of robotics programming education on computational thinking skills: An intervention of the Young Engineer's Workshop (YEW). *Computer Applications in Engineering Education*, 29(1), 191–208. DOI: 10.1002/cae.22321

Yusuf, J. E., & Jordan, M. M. (2017). Accessibility of the management's discussion and analysis to citizen users of government financial reports. *Public Budgeting & Finance*, 37(4), 74–91. DOI: 10.1111/pbaf.12170

Zahra, A., Waheed, Z., Fatima, T., & Khong, K. W (2024). Leveraging Technology for Environmental Awareness: Insights from Experimental Research with Middle School Students in Malaysia. *RMLE Online: Research in Middle Level Education*, 47(4), 1–17. DOI: 10.1080/19404476.2024.2322046

Zawacki-Richter, O., Kerres, M., Bedenlier, S., Bond, M., & Buntins, K. (Eds.). (2020). *Systematic Reviews in Educational Research: Methodology, Perspectives and Application.* Springer Fachmedien Wiesbaden., DOI: 10.1007/978-3-658-27602-7

Zawacki-Richter, O., Marín, V. I., Bond, M., & Gouverneur, F. (2019). Systematic review of research on artificial intelligence applications in higher education – where are the educators? *International Journal of Educational Technology in Higher Education*, 16(1), 39. DOI: 10.1186/s41239-019-0171-0

Zhai, X., Chu, X., Chai, C. S., Jong, M. S. Y., Istenic, A., Spector, M., ... & Li, Y. (2021). A

Zhai, X., Chu, X., Chai, C. S., Jong, M. S. Y., Istenic, A., Spector, M., Liu, J.-B., Yuan, J., & Li, Y. (2021). Review of Artificial Intelligence (AI) in Education from 2010 to 2020. *Complexity*, 2021(1), 8812542. Advance online publication. DOI: 10.1155/2021/8812542

Zhang, J., & Wallace, C. (2022). Exploring the nature of artificial intelligence in education. Journal of Educational Technology, DOI: 10.1111/jcal.12455

Zhang, J., & Zhang, Z. (2024). AI in teacher education: Unlocking new dimensions in teaching support, inclusive learning, and digital literacy. *Journal of Computer Assisted Learning*, 40(4), 1871–1885. DOI: 10.1111/jcal.12988

Zhang, L., Basham, J. D., & Yang, S. (2020). Understanding the implementation of personalized learning: A research synthesis. *Educational Research Review*, 31, 100339. DOI: 10.1016/j.edurev.2020.100339

Zhang, Q. (2022). Construction of personalized learning platform based on collaborative filtering algorithm. *Wireless Communications and Mobile Computing*, 2022(1), 5878344. DOI: 10.1155/2022/5878344

Ziatdinov, R., & Cilliers, J. (2022). Generation Alpha: Understanding the next cohort of university students. *arXiv preprint arXiv:2202.01422.*

Zint, M., Michel, J. O., Valentine, T., & Collins, S. (2024). *Collaborating with Students to Advance Climate Change Education at the University of Michigan.* Insights and Recommendations.

Zou, D., Liu, Q., & Li, J. (2023). Adaptive learning systems: A review of the current state-of- the-art and future directions. *Journal of Educational Technology & Society*. Advance online publication. DOI: 10.1109/jets.2023.3297642

Zulkeflee, N. R., Sanmugam, M., & Nee, C. K. (2023). The Effect of Online Learning on Undergraduate Student Achievement and Engagement During Times of Emergency Remote Teaching (ERT). In *Comparative Research on Diversity in Virtual Learning: Eastern vs. Western Perspectives* (pp. 105-135). IGI Global.

Zungu, N. V. (2022). *Understanding teachers' integration of information and communication technology (ICT) in teaching Grade 7 natural sciences.* (Doctoral dissertation) University of KwaZulu-Natal.

Žydžiūnaitė, V. (2018). Implementing ethical principles in social research: Challenges, possibilities and limitations. *Profesinis rengimas: tyrimai ir realijos, 29*, 19-43.

About the Contributors

Mageswaran Sanmugam acquired his B.Sc. (Hons) in Electrical Engineering from Universiti Teknologi Tun Hussein Onn in 2005 and Master's degree in Educational Management in 2012 from Universiti Utara Malaysia and Ph. D in Educational Technology in 2017 from Universiti Teknologi Malaysia. He worked as an Educator in both Primary and Secondary schools from 2008-2018, before being appointed as a Senior Lecturer in the Centre for Instructional Technology and Multimedia, Universiti Sains Malaysia, Pulau Pinang, Malaysia (from 2018- till 2021). Currently he is the Deputy Director of Research, Innovation and Networking in the Centre for Instructional Technology and Multimedia, Universiti Sains Malaysia, Pulau Pinang, Malaysia (from 2022- till now). He also serves as a Professional Technologist under the Malaysia Board of Technologists (MBOT) and as a Senior Member of the Institute of Electrical and Electronics Engineers (IEEE). He teaches human-computer interaction and multimedia project management. His expertise lies in gamification, game-based learning, artificial intelligence, and e-learning. He has published more than 70 research papers, including journal articles, book chapters, and other publications.

Bosede Iyiade Edwards is a seasoned academic and industry professional with over 25 years of work experience. She holds a Ph.D. in Educational Technology from Universiti Teknologi Malaysia (UTM), where she also earned a Master's degree in the same field. Her educational background is multidisciplinary, with qualifications including a bachelors in Chemistry and Masters in Organic Chemistry, which enriches her perspectives in research and teaching. Dr. Edwards has a proven track record in research leadership, particularly in instructional technology. She has authored and co-authored over 25 journal and conference articles and has been recognized with the IEEE Frontiers in Education 'Faculty Fellow' Award. Her research focuses on future school, covering the roles of emerging technologies including Artificial Intelligence and immersive media among others.

Nurul Maziah Mohd Barkhaya acquired her B.IT. (Hons) in Software Engineering from Universiti Malaysia Terengganu in 2011 and Master's Degree in Education (TVET) in 2013 from Universiti Tun Hussein Onn Malaysia and Ph.D in Educational Technology in 2023 from Universiti Teknologi Malaysia. She worked as an educator in International Secondary schools from 2019 – 2023, before being appointed as a Senior Lecturer in the Centre for Instructional Technology and Multimedia, Universiti Sains Malaysia, Pulau Pinang, Malaysia started on 2024. Her research interests include the educational technology, creative multimedia, and e-Learning.

Zuheir N. Khlaif, Ph.D. in instructional design and technology, is a distinguished scholar and researcher at An-Najah National University in Palestine. As a dedicated educator, he imparts knowledge in educational technology courses and contributes significantly to the Artificial Intelligence and Virtual Reality Research Center at the University. With a keen focus on the intersection of technology and education, his research delves into areas such as technology integration, technostress, and the application of AI in educational assessment. Khlaif has delivered more than 50 lectures and workshops about e-learning and AI in higher and public education in international and local conferences and symposium. Khlaif's expertise extends to the publication realm, with more than 40 articles in peer-reviewed journals. His contributions not only advance academic discourse but also have practical implications for the effective use of technology in education in various context in the global south.

* * *

Manmeet Kaur Arora is a Research Scholar at the School of Law, Sharda University, Greater Noida. She is a graduate of Law and has completed her Master's in Law from Amity University, Noida. Manmeet Kaur is a qualified Company Secretary Executive Programme. She has over 8+ years of Industry Experience and 1 year of experience as an Associate at a reputed IPR Law Firm. Manmeet Kaur has attended 20+ National & International Conferences, Webinars, Seminars, Symposiums, and Paper Presentations and participated in 5+ Faculty Development programs. She has over 50+ publications in various esteemed Journals and Books. She is active at the Family Dispute Resolution Clinic, Meditation Centre, Greater Noida. Manmeet Kaur has a keen interest in the areas of Corporate Law, Intellectual Property Rights, Insolvency, Artificial Intelligence, Machine Learning, and Blockchain Technology.

Selami Aydin is a full professor in the Department of English Language Teaching at Istanbul Medeniyet University, Istanbul, Turkey. He researches on EFL writing, testing, affective states, technology use and social media effects on language learning and teaching processes. Currently, he teaches ELT related courses at BA and MA programs.

Raino Bhatia epitomizes the essence of an educator whose life is intricately woven with a profound dedication to the betterment of society through education. As the Principal cum Associate Professor of Akal College of Education, Eternal University, nestled in the serene landscapes of Baru Sahib, Himachal Pradesh, India, she orchestrates the symphony of learning with finesse and vision. She is M.Phil. and Ph.D. in Education, along with the accolade of UGC-NET, she stands as a paragon of scholarly excellence. Spanning over two decades, her journey in the realm of education has been marked by unwavering commitment and illustrious achievements. In 2009, she was bestowed with the prestigious National Award, a testament to her exemplary services in the field of education, a recognition that echoes her tireless efforts and unwavering passion. Dr. Bhatia's literary contributions resonate across academia, with her seminal work, "The Quest for True Happiness," serving as a guiding beacon for both educators and students alike. Complemented by a plethora of research papers published at both National and International levels, her intellectual footprint is profound and far-reaching.

Leila Goosen is a full professor in the Department of Science and Technology Education of the University of South Africa. She holds a C2 rating via the South African National Research Foundation. Prof. Goosen was an Associate Professor in the School of Computing, and the module leader and head designer of the fully online signature module for the College for Science, Engineering and Technology, rolled out to over 92,000 registered students since the first semester of 2013. She usually supervises around ten Masters and Doctoral students, and has successfully completed supervision of 43 students at postgraduate level. Previously, she was a Deputy Director at the South African national Department of Education. In this capacity, she was required to develop ICT strategies for implementation. Before that, she had been a lecturer of Information Technology (IT) in the Department for Science, Mathematics and Technology Education in the Faculty of Education of the University of Pretoria. Her research interests have included cooperative work in IT, effective teaching and learning of programming and teacher professional development.

Zhou Jinghong acquired her Bachelor of Fine Arts degree from Gannan Normal University in 2019 and her Master of Fine Arts degree from Gannan Normal

University in 2022. She worked as a university teacher(2021 to 2023) previously and as as research assitant(2022 to 2022). Currently he is a PhD candidate in the Centre for Instructional Technology and Multimedia, Universiti Sains Malaysia, Pulau Pinang, Malaysia (from 2023- till now). Her research interests mainly encompass multisensory educational, game theory, game-based learning, gamification, preschool education and preschool children education.

Rahul Joshi is an assistant professor of Journalism and mass communication at the School of Mass Media & Humanities, MRIIRS (Deemed to be University), Faridabad, Haryana. He has completed his Ph.D. (Media studies) from MRIIRS, Faridabad, and it was awarded in December 2022. He has done her Masters in Journalism & Mass Communication from GGSIP University. He was a Gold Medalist in MA (MC) at GGSIP University. He has Eleven years of academic and industry experience. His specializations are in Radio Journalism & Television Production. He has published over 15 research papers in different reputed International & National Journals. Before stepping into academics, he was an Anchor cum Assistant producer in various National Hindi and English News Channels like ANI, India News, News X, APN News, News 18 Network and Zee News. He has also been associated with the World's biggest Radio Broadcasting House, All India Radio, as a Radio Presenter and Production executive for 5 consecutive years. His areas of research interest are Radio Production, TV Production, and Digital Media. His teaching expertise also lies in Radio and TV Production.

Christian Kaunert is Professor of International Security at Dublin City University, Ireland. He is also Professor of Policing and Security, as well as Director of the International Centre for Policing and Security at the University of South Wales. In addition, he is Jean Monnet Chair, Director of the Jean Monnet Centre of Excellence and Director of the Jean Monnet Network on EU Counter-Terrorism (www.eucter.net).

Arvin Cheong KeeSin acquired his Bachelor of Education (Hons) in Information Technology from Univerisiti Pendidikan Sultan Idris, Malaysia in 2014. He worked as government teacher in Malaysia's secondary school from 2016-2023 before pursuit his Master of Arts in Universiti Sains Malaysia. His research interests include augmented reality and gamification.

Mohamed Khaldi is Professor of Higher Education of the Department of computer Science and management at Ecole Normale Supérieure Tétouan of the University Abdelmalek Essaadi where he has been since 1987. From 2011 to 2014, he served as coordinator of the Specialized Master in Computerized Management for the company. He was a member of advisory board of dozen of international congress in the field of computer science. He received a B.S from Mohamed V University in 1982, and a 3rd cycle diploma from ENS Rabat in 1986. He received his PhD in Didactics, Information and Communication Technology from the Faculty of Science Ben MSik in 2001. And the Academic habilitation in 2003, from the Faculty of Science Ben MSik.

Jagneet Kour is a dedicated scholar in the field of Education. Drawing from her extensive academic background and research expertise, Kour curates a collection of insightful contributions to educational research. Kour emerges as a beacon of academic excellence. As the proud recipient of the prestigious gold medal in postgraduate studies from Eternal University, she stands at the pinnacle of her academic prowess. Kour's achievements don't end there; she reigns as the all-around champion in her 2022 batch, leaving an indelible mark on her college's Master's in Education program. Jagneet Kour is pursuing her Ph.D. in Education, having previously obtained degrees in B.Ed. and M.A. in Education. Her academic journey is marked by notable achievements, including qualifying for the UGC NET JRF on her first attempt and successfully clearing the CTET examinations. Her journey is one of continuous growth and achievement. With a passion for research, Kour has demonstrated her proficiency by publishing numerous papers in esteemed journals such as those indexed in UGC CARE 1 and Scopus. Furthermore, her active involvement in both national and international conferences and workshops underscores her commitment to advancing knowledge in the field of education. Jagneet Kour, editor of "Transforming Indian Education in the 21st Century," presents a manifesto for educational reform, offering strategies for modern learning. Her second edited book on the New Education 2020 is a comprehensive anthology reflecting her visionary outlook on India's educational future.

Suman Kumari is an Academician & Researcher with over 16 years of academic experience. She holds a Post-Graduate degree in Journalism & Mass Communication and completed her PhD on the topic 'Changing Role of Female Lovers in Bollywood Hindi Movies: A Study of Social Change' from Manav Rachna International University in 2015. Her expertise spans Film Studies, Event Management, Health Communication, and Communication research. Dr. Kumari has co-organized numerous National/International academic activities, including Seminars/Conferences focusing particularly on gender issues. Additionally, she has made significant contributions to research by publishing papers in National/International Journals. She has supervised doctoral research scholars in areas such as Health Communication, Fake News, and Film Studies.

Sahil Lal is a Research Scholar at School of Law, Sharda University. He pursued his graduation from National Law University, Lucknow and completed his Master's in Law from Gujarat National Law University, Gandhinagar. Sahil has completed a certificate course on 'AI & Law' from Lund University, Sweden and on 'Cyber Law' from Indian Law Institute, New Delhi. Sahil Lal is a qualified UGC-NET & JRF candidate. He has a 10+ year Industry Experience and is an active member of Family Dispute Resolution Clinic, Mediation Center, Greater Noida. Sahil has attended 20+ International & National Conferences along with Paper Presentation and has also participated in more than 5+ Faculty Development Programme. Mr. Sahil has more than 50+ publications in various esteemed Journals & Books. Mr. Sahil has a keen interest in area of Artificial Intelligence, Machine Learning, Robotics, Block-Chain Technology and Intellectual Property Rights.

Purushothman Munusamy is a passionate educator and speaker based in Malaysia. With a strong background in STEM education and robotics, he has dedicated himself to enhancing learning experiences for students. Purushothman's journey includes attending and presenting at various conferences and conventions, where he has been recognized for his outstanding speaking abilities. His commitment to personal development and training has led him to excel in areas such as Kangaroo Math Competition and Lego Robotics. As the Vice President of Pertubuhan Vivekkam Malaysia, Purushothman has conducted numerous talks on personal, educational, and social awareness topics across Malaysia. His expertise and achievements in robotics education have earned him prestigious awards, including being named an Ambassador of Rero Robotics. Purushothman's vision is to continue making a positive impact in the field of education through innovation and collaboration.

Krishna Pandey has over 24 years of academic and journalism experience, of which the last twelve years have been spent in academics. She has 12 years of on-field journalistic experience working in mainstream print media. She is UGC Net Qualified, and her PhD is on Crisis Communication Strategies of Cadbury's & Nestle in India: A Critical Study., University School of Mass Communication, Guru Gobind Singh Indraprastha University. She has an MA in Mass Communication from Guru Jambheshwar University of Science & Technology and MA in Political Science from Benaras Hindu University. Dr Pandey is also an alumnus of the Indian Institute of Mass Communication (IIMC), New Delhi, and a graduate of the prestigious Sophia Girls College Ajmer.

Reham Salhab is an assistant professor at PTUK. She is a lecturer in Educational Technology department at Kadoorie University (PTUK). She has published several articles on students' attitudes toward Moodle, Zoom, and mobile learning, gamification, and artificial intelligence at PTUK. Moreover, she has published about 15 publications. She is interested in is e-learning, artificial intelligence, mobile learning, gamification, educational technology, teaching and learning, professional development, and curriculum development.

Bhupinder Singh is working as Professor at Sharda University, India. Also, Honorary Professor in University of South Wales UK and Santo Tomas University Tunja, Colombia. His areas of publications as Smart Healthcare, Medicines, fuzzy logics, artificial intelligence, robotics, machine learning, deep learning, federated learning, IoT, PV Glasses, metaverse and many more. He has 3 books, 139 paper publications, 163 paper presentations in international/national conferences and seminars, participated in more than 40 workshops/FDP's/QIP's, 25 courses from international universities of repute, organized more than 59 events with international and national academicians and industry people's, editor-in-chief and co-editor in journals, developed new courses. He has given talks at international universities, resource person in international conferences such as in Nanyang Technological University Singapore, Tashkent State University of Law Uzbekistan; KIMEP University Kazakhstan, All'ah meh Tabatabi University Iran, the Iranian Association of International Criminal law, Iran and Hague Center for International Law and Investment, The Netherlands, Northumbria University Newcastle UK,

Index

L

M

P

R

S

T

V

W

Y

www.ingramcontent.com/pod-product-compliance
Lightning Source LLC
LaVergne TN
LVHW080342011026
849161LV00009B/2155
* 9 7 9 8 3 6 9 3 7 2 5 5 5 *